FIX IT GOOD CAR

Jack Strachan

FIX IT GOOD CAR

HOW TO CARRY OUT YOUR CAR FIXES LIKE A PROFESSIONAL

TED SMART

This edition produced for
THE BOOK PEOPLE LTD
Hall Wood Avenue, Haydock
St Helens, WA11 9UL

THE IVY PRESS LIMITED
The Old Candlemakers
Lewes, East Sussex BN7 2NZ

Creative Director PETER BRIDGEWATER
Publisher SOPHIE COLLINS
Editorial Director JASON HOOK
Design Manager SIMON GOGGIN
Senior Project Editor REBECCA SARACENO
Designer GINNY ZEAL
Illustrations TONY TOWNSEND

Printed and bound in China

1 3 5 7 9 10 8 6 4 2

Contents

Introduction

Aimed fairly and squarely at the beginner, this book works on two levels. On the very basic level, it tells you how to do the minimum to look after your car and keep it running smoothly, as well as explaining what courses of action are open to you when things go wrong – from what that red light on the dashboard means to what to do when the car won't start. It covers common problems that are simple to fix, and gives temporary solutions to tide you over until you can seek professional help, as well as those occasions when you simply have to resort to an expert.

On a second level, this compact book gives a basic explanation of the functioning of the car's major components and systems, and how they all work together. This is designed not so much to enable you to carry out major repairs – that level of information is beyond the scope of this book – as to give you a basic understanding of how the car works. Armed with this knowledge, you can talk to the professionals in a more informed way.

With step-by-step illustrations and clear explanations that are accessible to the complete beginner, *Fix It Good: Car* guides you all over the car, system by system. Advice on related topics is also given, such as fitting children's car seats, the do's and don'ts of airbags, fuel economy, buying new tyres... while additional sections cover troubleshooting (what does that noise mean?), roadside emergencies (what to do when you have a puncture) and bad weather (how to drive safely in snow).

The importance of regular maintenance to keep your car roadworthy cannot be emphasized too strongly. Even in the modern car where computers monitor and adjust systems automatically, regular maintenance will help you avoid problems or at least spot them before they get out of hand or cause you to break down miles from anywhere, with just a bag of sweets and the dog to keep you company. Just follow the list of regular checks on pages 22–25 to ensure your car is in top condition.

Although there are many different makes and models of car, nearly all engines and systems follow the same basic function, with a few notable exceptions, such as the Wankel engine (a rotor instead of pistons). Within these basic parameters, there are many variations of design and layout – far too many to be covered in this, or indeed any one, book. However, your car owner's handbook should provide you with all the specific information that you need.

One of the first things that might strike you once you venture under the bonnet is just how much of a paradox the car really is. On the one hand, all its parts work together in unison, everything minutely engineered so that it fits together perfectly: one wheel drives another, which drives a belt that powers a shaft, which opens a valve... It is all so ingenious.

And yet on the other hand, in the advanced age of the computer chip and the mind-bogglingly small world of nano-technology, the car is something of a dinosaur – large chunks of metal chug away within a cumbersome steel carcass, the whole powered by fossil fuel (say no more). True, the computer does now play a large part, but the essentials have remained little changed since the early twentieth century.

This handy little book is certainly not dinosaur-sized, but don't be deceived by its small format. It is jam-packed with all the information to keep your car on the road and more besides. Pop it in the glove compartment, safe in the knowledge that its help and advice are close at hand, relax and enjoy your motoring.

BASICS

Equipment

Tools need to be well made and strong – it will pay dividends in the long run not to buy the cheapest, but building up a basic tool kit from scratch is expensive. Investigate buying tools second-hand, but make sure they are in good condition.

The following list of tools and other equipment is divided into those that you should keep in the car at all times and those that you can keep at home.

See 'Preparing for winter and summer' on pages 304–307 for additional seasonal items.

In the car

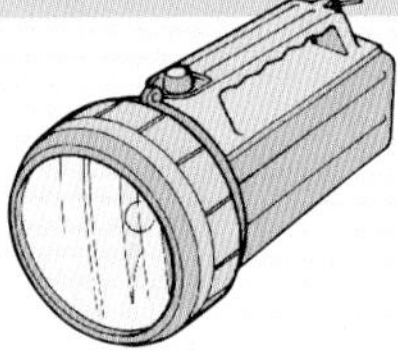

1. **torch** (a torch attached to a head band is useful, in addition to a conventional torch, as it frees both hands for working. A hands-free torch is available from outdoor pursuits shops)
2. **mirror on the end of a flexible shaft** (for inspecting inaccessible engine parts)
3. **long wheel-brace**
4. **jack**

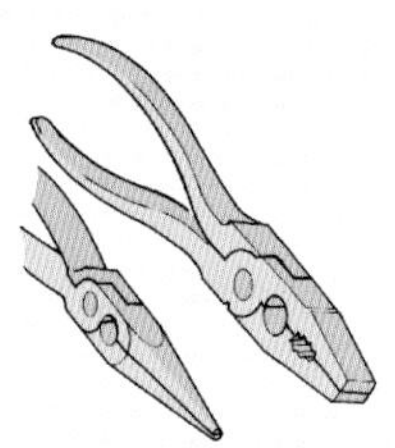

5. **pliers** (long-nosed and wide-jawed)

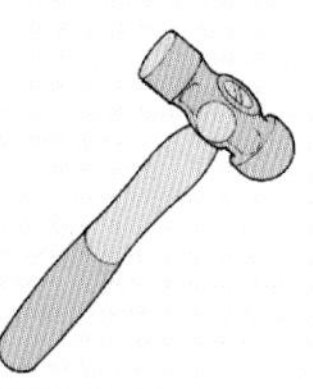

6. **small ball-pein hammer** (one rounded head, one flat)

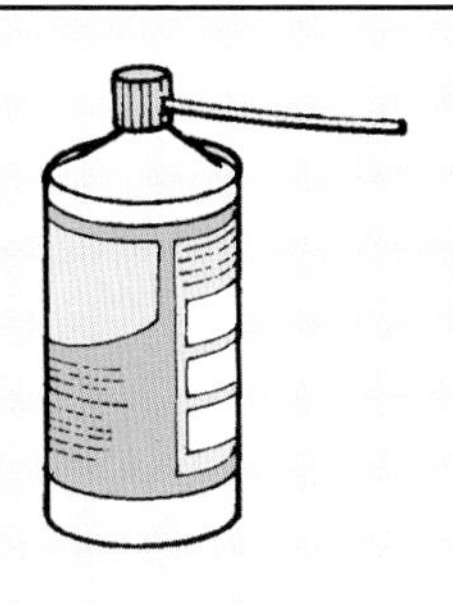

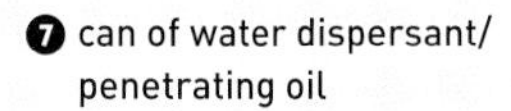

❼ **can of water dispersant/ penetrating oil**

❽ **de-icer/ice scraper**

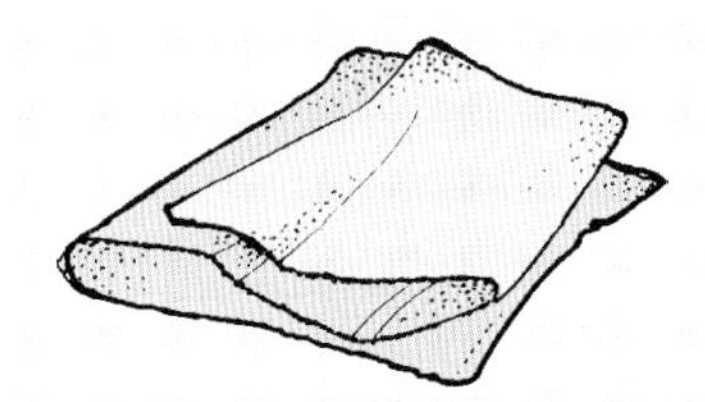

❾ **chamois leather** and a good supply of **clean cloth/rag**

❿ **glass cleaner**

⓫ **screenwash**

⓬ **elastic 'bungees'** of different sizes

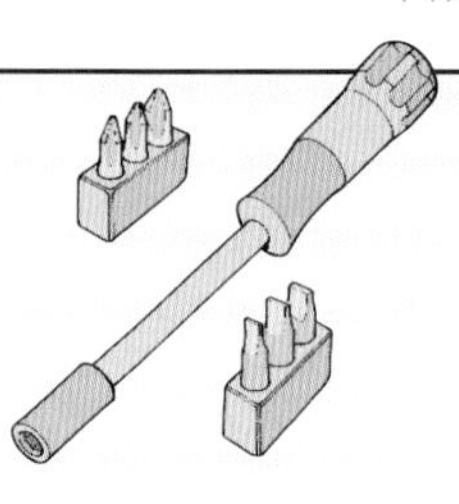

⓭ **flat-head and cross-head screwdrivers** of different sizes

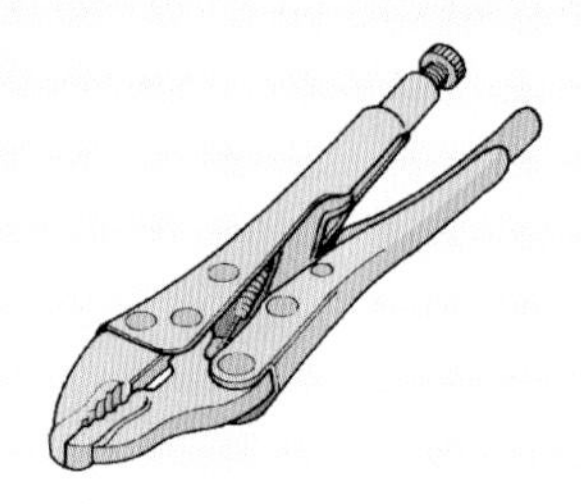

⓰ **self-locking grips**

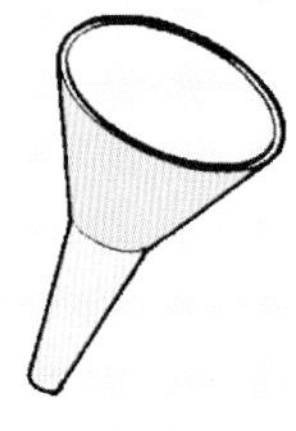

⓮ **plastic funnel**

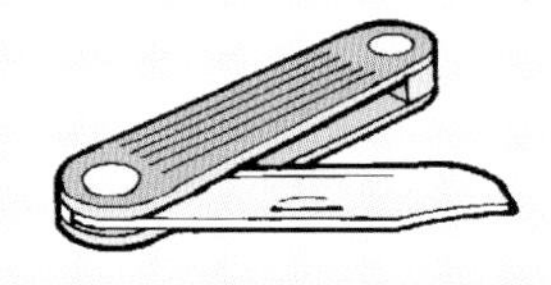

⓱ **knife** (preferably with a selection of blades and tools)

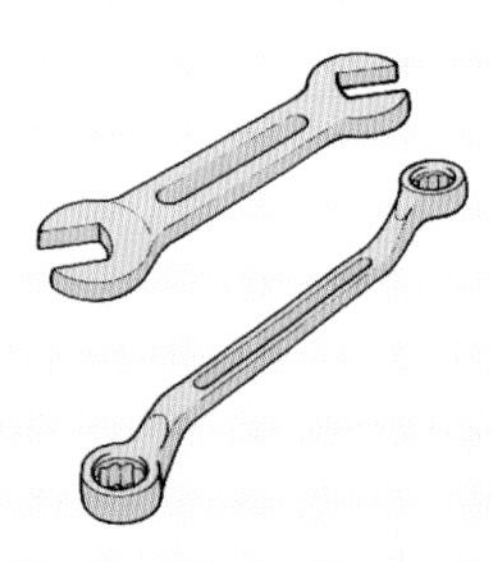

⓯ **ring and open-ended spanners** of different sizes (ring spanners grip more firmly and can access recessed bolts)

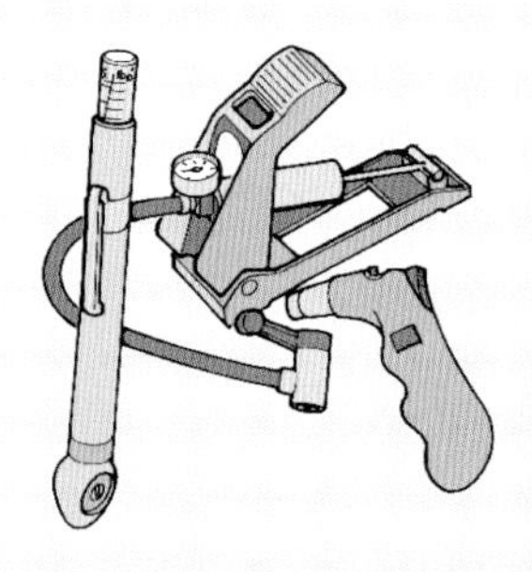

⓲ **tyre pressure gauge and tread depth gauge**

⓳ **foot pump**

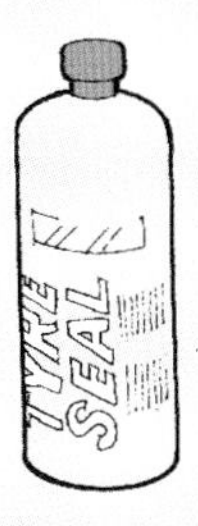

20 **tyre sealant** (but *see page 96*)

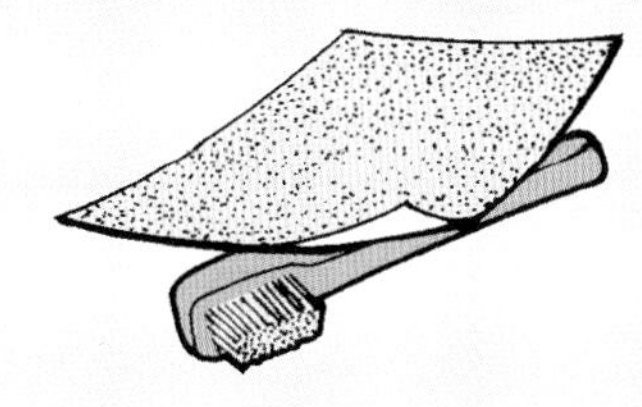

21 **fine emery paper and small wire brush**

22 **strong vinyl tape and strong string**

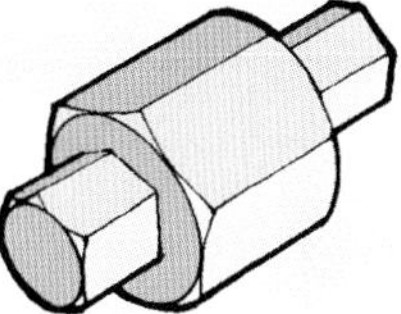

23 **security wheel nut adapter** (if you have locking wheel nuts)

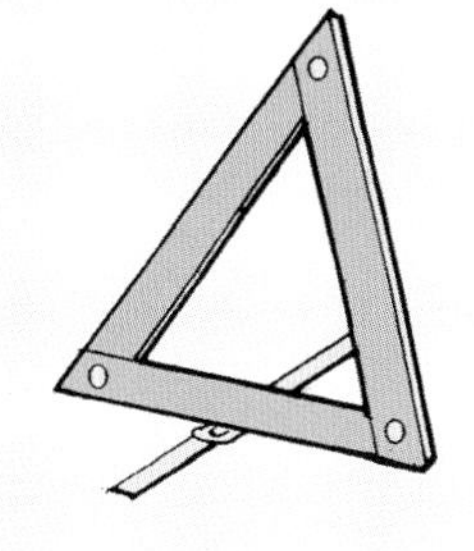

24 **red warning triangle** (compulsory in some countries)

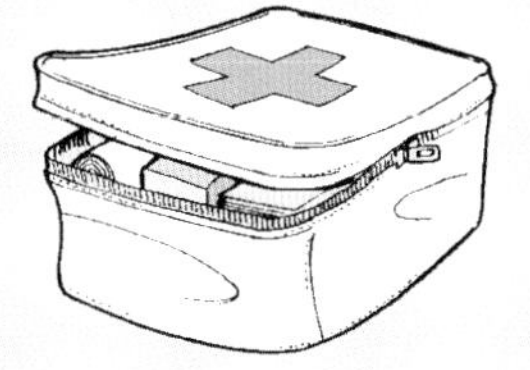

25 **first aid kit** (compulsory in some countries)

TIP

Keep a note of useful phone numbers in the glovebox or your handbook in case you are stranded (including breakdown or motoring organizations), plus a few coins and/or a telephone card for a pay phone – even if you have a mobile phone, you could find the signal weak or the battery low.

26 **fire extinguisher** (compulsory in some countries) – electrical fires require a special fire extinguisher

27 **jump leads**

28 **tow rope**

TIP

In the summer if it is hot, keep a bottle of drinking water in the car.

Spares

TIP

You may wish to carry some old clothes in case of emergency repairs.

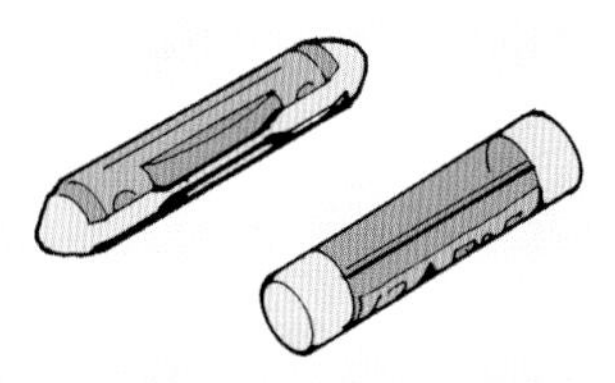

29 **spare fuses** (10, 20 and 30 amps)

30 **spare bulbs** (compulsory in some countries)

31 **engine oil for topping up**

32 **emergency fuel** in approved container or emergency fuel container

TIP

If you have spanner and screwdriver sets, you may not wish to carry all of them with you. If not, just select the ones you use most frequently.

At home

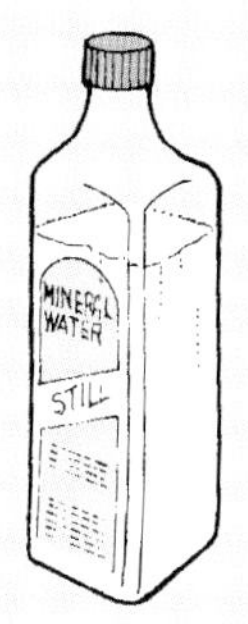

33 battery topping-up fluid

34 brake and clutch fluid

35 automatic transmission fluid

36 oil filter removal tool

37 container for draining oil

38 oil sump drain-plug tool

39 junior hacksaw

40 spark plug gapping tool and spark plug spanner

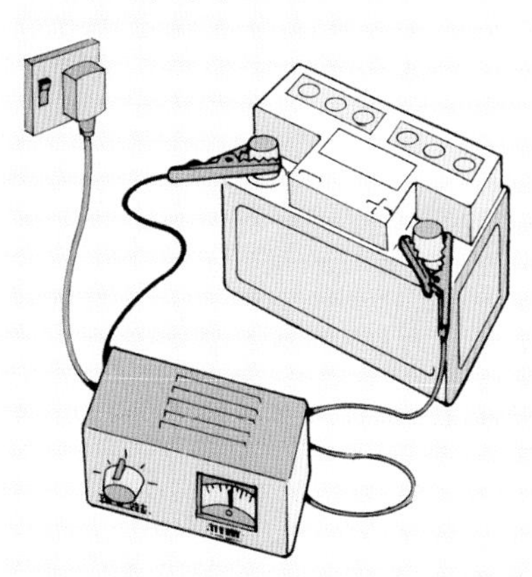

41 battery charger

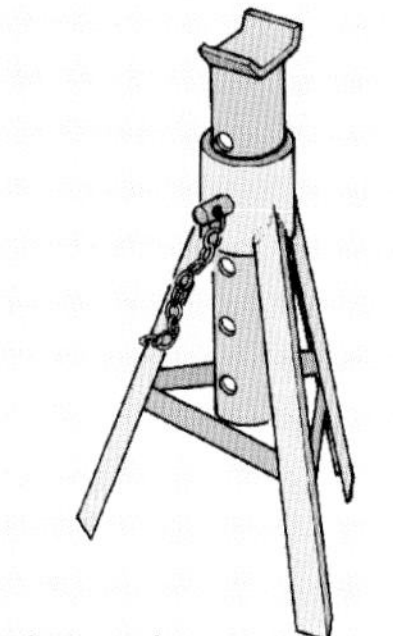

42 axle stands

43 car ramps

Safety

Remember that when working on a car you will get dirty. Don't wear your best clothes, and if you are likely to get your hands oily or greasy, have a can of degreasing hand cleaner ready. Working on the car can be dangerous, so read these safety guidelines:

Guidelines

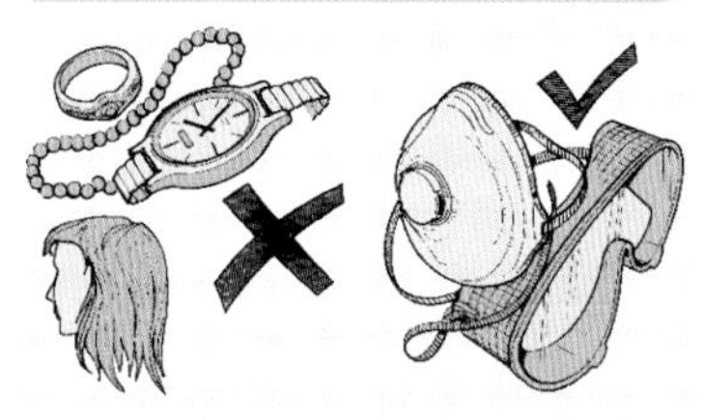

- Remove all jewellery and rings, your watch, etc. and tie back long hair.
- Ensure that the garage floor is free from oil and grease.
- If you think your skin may react to oil, rub in a barrier cream or wear thin rubber gloves.
- Don't put oily rags in your pocket or wear oil-soaked clothing.
- Wear protective clothing (but not loose-fitting; keep cuffs tight or roll sleeves above elbows) and shoes with reinforced toe caps.
- Wear a face mask if necessary, and goggles if there is a risk of foreign bodies entering your eyes.
- It is best not to work in an enclosed space with the engine running. If this is unavoidable, make sure there is adequate ventilation by opening doors and windows. Exhaust fumes are toxic and can kill.

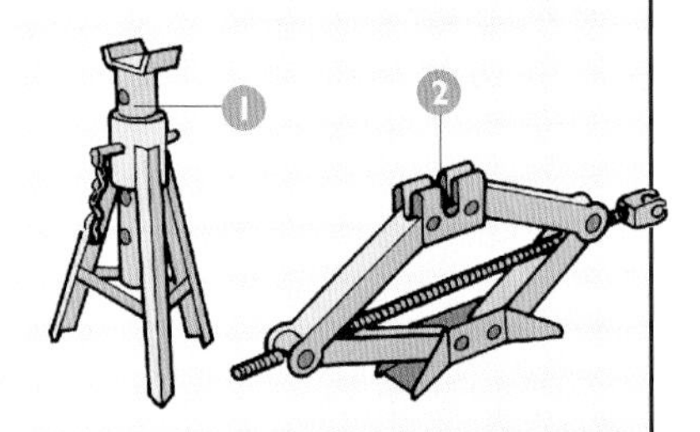

❶ Axle stand ❷ Scissor jack

- Never put any part of your body under a car that is raised on a jack in case the car slips off or the jack collapses. If you have to get under a car that is jacked up, make sure it is supported by axle stands, or if you have access to wheel ramps, use these.

- Keep toxic and corrosive substances (antifreeze, brake/clutch fluid, battery electrolyte) firmly sealed in labelled containers, and store out of reach of children. Mop up any spillages and wash off immediately any fluids that get on to the skin .
- When working on the wheels, take care not to breathe in any brake dust that has collected on them – it may contain harmful asbestos.
- Avoid electric shock – never work on the electrical system while the ignition is switched on. Check that any mains-operated equipment you use is earthed.
- If working near the cooling fan, make sure the ignition is switched off (in case it starts up suddenly).
- Keep a fire extinguisher to hand. (Remember that electrical fires require a CO_2 extinguisher.)
- Never smoke or allow a naked flame near an engine, battery or the fuel system. This could cause a fire.
- Never allow fuel to spill on to hot engine parts. It could cause a fire.
- Never open the radiator or expansion-tank pressure cap while the engine is hot or still warm.
- Remember that hot metal (such as the exhaust pipe) can burn.
- Dispose of old engine oil and batteries at authorized sites.

TIPS

When removing a car part to clean or replace it, you need to be able to reassemble it, or to fit a new part correctly. This can be easier said than done – many different kinds of fitting are used, and it is easy to forget in which order or how a part should be reassembled. Here are some tips to help you solve the problem:

- Make a careful mental note of how you remove a part.
- Make a sketch of the way something is assembled.
- Take Polaroid or digital photographs as you dismantle the assembly.
- If you are working on two or more identical parts, such as the windscreen wipers, dismantle and reassemble or fit them one at a time, so that you can use one of them as a reference.
- Place screws, nuts and bolts, and parts (in a safe place where they won't get knocked) in a line in the order in which they are removed. Work your way back down the line in reverse order when you reassemble the part. Remember that screws and bolts in particular have a habit of rolling away.

Getting into awkward places

Some screws are very difficult to access. A 90° cranked screwdriver may do the trick. It will fit flat- and cross-head screws.

A mirror on the end of a long flexible shaft is invaluable for helping you inspect parts of the car that are awkward to see.

TIP

In motoring, familiarity does not breed contempt. Familiarize yourself with the location of the bonnet release, fuse box, battery terminals, fluid reservoirs, oil dipstick, jack and wheel brace – and even change a wheel when you have some spare time. Then you will be prepared if an emergency occurs.

Motoring organizations

Consider joining a motoring organization. Despite the yearly fee, they often prove worthwhile in the long run, offering a range of different services and motoring advice, as well as peace of mind. Being towed to a garage or your home is never cheap.

Replacement parts

Buying branded replacement parts from a dealer for your make of car can be extremely expensive. Accessory shops sell a variety of small parts that will fit many different makes of car. You will need to know the make, model and year of manufacture to make sure you buy the right one. Larger parts or parts that are specific to a particular model can be bought second-hand from a car breaker's yard. Whatever the reason for the scrapping of a car, there are usually a number of parts that are still perfectly serviceable and can be bought for a fraction of the price of new parts.
You just need to find a yard that contains a car of your make and model. Sometimes, just finding a car of the same make and about the same year will do; it depends on the part you need.

Screws and bolts

Over time, screws can seize up and bolts will rust, becoming very difficult to undo. Here are some ideas for removing them:

❶ Protect your knuckles from painful scraping if your hand slips by wrapping a piece of cloth around your hand.

❷ Don't use excessive force – you will probably end up breaking something and making the situation worse.

❸ Clean off rust with a wire brush and spray the fixing with penetrating oil. Leave it to soak in for at least an hour, then try again.

❹ To loosen corrosion, tap the centre of a bolt sharply with a hammer, or insert the blade of a screwdriver in the centre of a screw and tap the end of the handle smartly several times.

❺ Try tightening a nut or screw slightly by a quarter or even half a turn, then try to undo it.

❻ If a screw slot is deformed, you may be able to cut a new one with a hacksaw.

❼ Use a centre-punch and hammer to loosen a nut – place the centre-punch on one side of the nut and tap the end of it sharply, but be careful that it doesn't slip and damage something else.

7

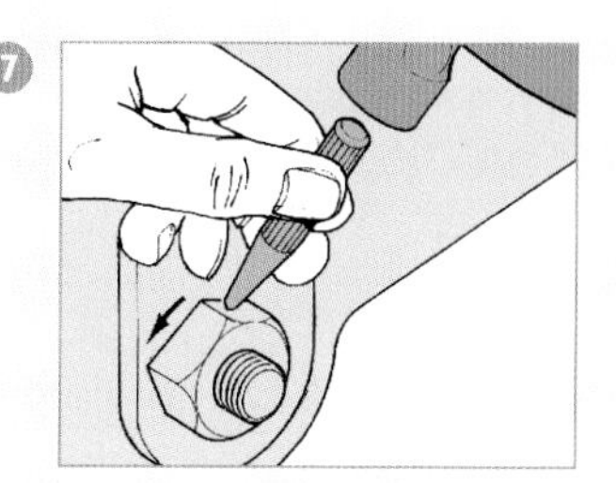

8

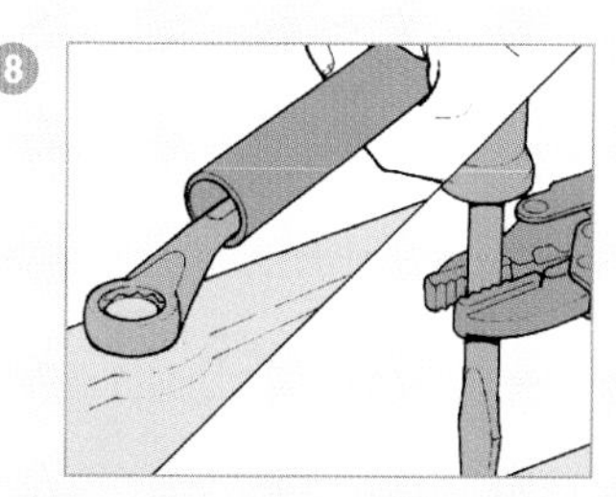

❽ Increase leverage by slipping a metal tube over the end of a spanner – but don't do this on rusted bolts or nuts, as they could sheer off. Hold the top of a screwdriver in place with one hand and grip the shaft with a pair of pliers or self-locking grips, to exert extra force.

❾ Provided there is no danger of getting it on to electrical components (battery, coil, etc.), pour boiling water over the screw or bolt, then spray with a penetrating oil/water dispersant.

❿ Alternatively, take the car to a garage where they have specialist equipment to help remove screws and bolts that are stuck fast.

Regular checks

Establishing a routine of basic checks is one of the most important things you can do to keep your car in good working order. It won't take much time and yet will go a long way towards keeping your car on the road and highlighting potential problems before they become serious.

Servicing

These checks should not replace your routine garage service. Have your car serviced at a garage at the intervals recommended in your handbook.

TIP

Consult your car handbook. Follow the intervals given in your handbook for the checks that follow, but if you cannot find this information, the intervals given here can act as a general guide.

Weekly

❶ The engine oil level with the dipstick (*see page 247*).

❷ The brake fluid level in its reservoir; it may share the same reservoir as the clutch fluid (*see pages 130–31*).

❸ The clutch fluid level in its reservoir; it may share the same reservoir as the brake fluid (*see pages 130–31*).

❹ The coolant level in the expansion tank (*see page 179*).

❺ The screenwash level in its reservoir (*see page 67*).

❻ Check all exterior lights are working (*see pages 70–79*).

❼ Check tyre pressures and general tyre condition – including the spare (*see pages 84–93*).

❽ Check the windscreen wiper blades for damage and that the screenwash jets work (*see pages 66–69*).

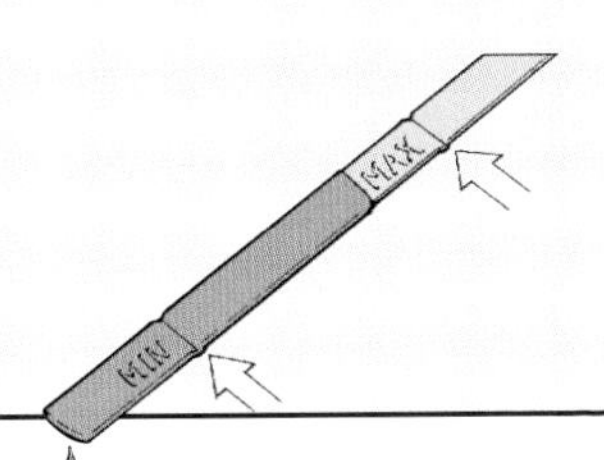

Monthly

Automatic transmission fluid in its reservoir or with its dipstick.

Power steering fluid in its reservoir (*see pages 108–109*).

A thorough inspection of tyre condition and tread depth – including the spare (*see pages 84–93*).

❶ Tool for measuring tread depth

❷ Tread pattern

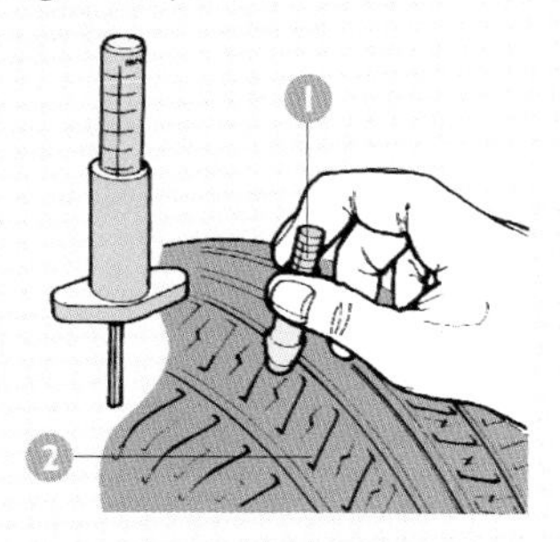

TIP

Things start getting a little complicated after three months, as the checking and replacement intervals vary so much. Keep a diary of what is done and when, to avoid confusion.

Every three months

Level of electrolyte in the battery (*see pages 196–97*) and condition of battery terminals (*see pages 194–95*).

Shock absorbers – carry out your own 'push test', as described on page 115, but also have them checked at a garage every year.

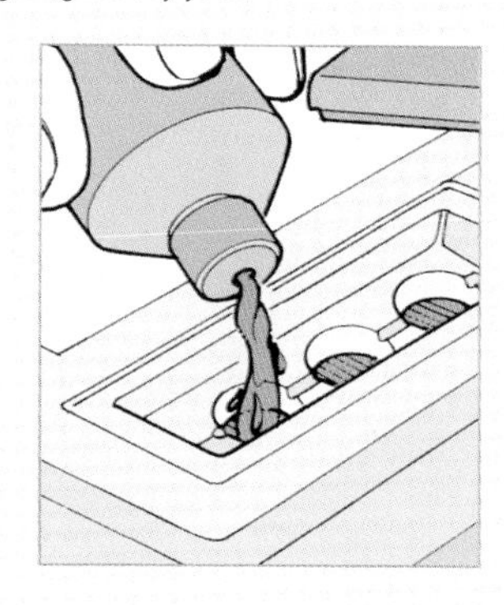

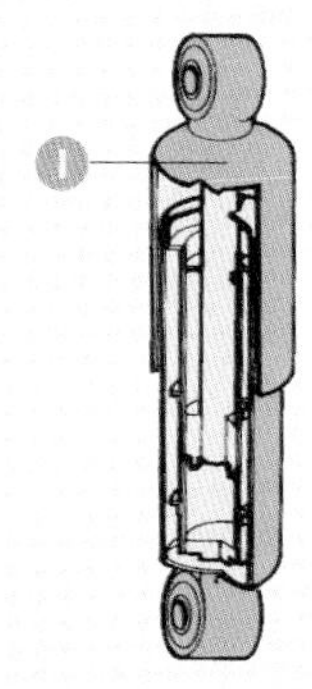

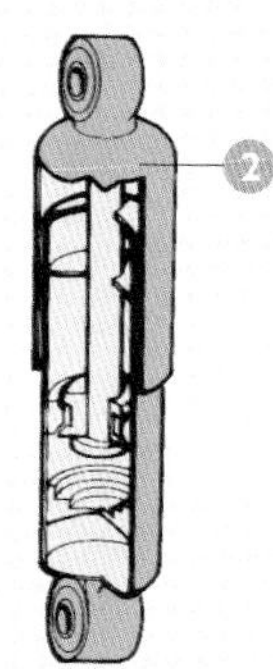

❶ Oil-filled shock absorber

❷ Gas-filled shock absorber

When to change fluids

Apart from engine oil, the following fluids and oils should be changed at a garage during servicing:

Engine oil
Every 12,000 miles if the car is used normally, or every 6,000 miles if the car makes lots of short journeys (*see page 248*).

Brake and clutch fluid
Every two years.

Coolant
Minimum every two years, but once a year before winter is a good idea.

Manual gearbox oil
Every 60,000 miles, but have its level and condition checked at a garage every 12,000 miles, or 12 months, unless it is 'lifetime' oil.

Automatic transmission fluid
Every 30,000 miles, but also have its condition checked at a garage every 6,000 miles, or 12 months, whichever is sooner.

Power steering fluid
Every 50,000 miles for conventional fluid; 'lifetime' fluid should never need replacing, although you may prefer to have it changed after 100,000 miles.

When to renew filters

Air filter
Every year or 12,000 miles, whichever is sooner (*see pages 234–35*).

Oil filter
Whenever you change the oil (*see page 248*).

Fuel filter
(At a garage.) The interval varies from car to car – check in your handbook.

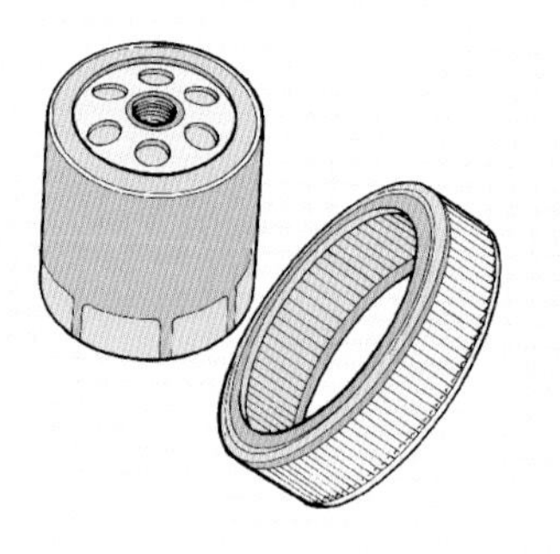

When to drain the diesel

Water should be drained from the diesel fuel filter every 6,000 miles or six months, whichever is sooner, or if the dashboard warning light comes on (*see pages 144, 236*).

Spark plugs

Check them every 6,000 miles, and replace them every 12,000 miles (*see page 216*).

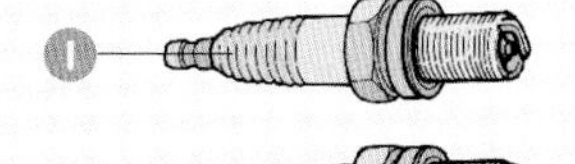

❶ New spark plug ❷ Worn spark plug

Wiper blades

Renew the windscreen wiper blades every year (*see page 68*).

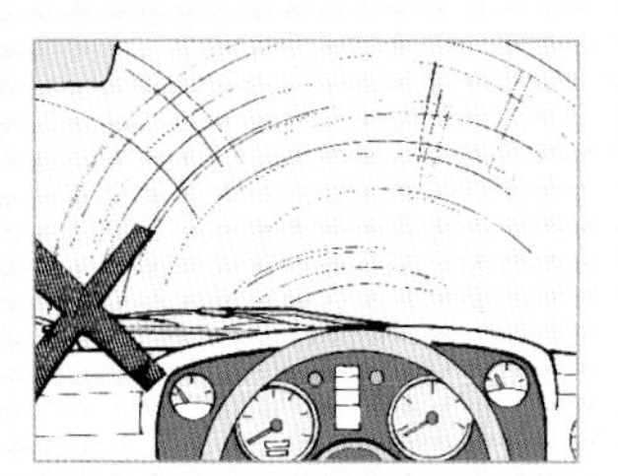

Other checks

Air conditioning refrigerant
This should be recharged at a garage around every 18,000 miles, or as recommended in your handbook.

Shock absorbers
Have them checked at a garage during your annual service.

Hoses
Have them checked for leaks and cracks at your annual service.

Seat belts
Check for tension and fraying – every three months (*see page 27*).

Brake system including handbrake
Have them checked at a garage during your annual service.

Exhaust system and emissions
Have them checked at a garage during your annual service.

Timing belt or cam belt

This may only be carried out once or twice in a car's lifetime (at a garage), but don't neglect it. If it breaks, the engine could be ruined, particularly if running at high speed.

The recommended replacement interval varies from car to car; refer to your handbook. Typically, it is around 30–40,000 miles.

Safety inside the car

Car safety is primarily concerned with protecting the occupants as much as possible. The following pages contain advice on seat belts, carrying babies and children, the importance of a correct driving position and everything you need to know about air bags.

How much protection does the car structure provide?

- The bodywork of the car is usually made of steel, which is strong, but there is an inevitable trade-off between lightness for fuel economy, strength for safety, and the cost of materials and manufacture.

- The front and rear of a car act as 'crumple zones', where the steel structure will deform and give, but absorb energy from an impact. The framework surrounding the passenger area is strengthened to prevent the roof from collapsing if the car rolls over, and the doors are reinforced with heavy-duty steel braces for protection against side impact.

- The engine and transmission are positioned to increase the likelihood of their being pushed under, rather than into, the passenger area in a severe frontal collision, while the steering column is designed to collapse or telescope.

- The degree of protection afforded by the structure and design varies from car to car. Look for comparative surveys in the press, or contact a consumer group for information concerning the safety rating of different makes and models.

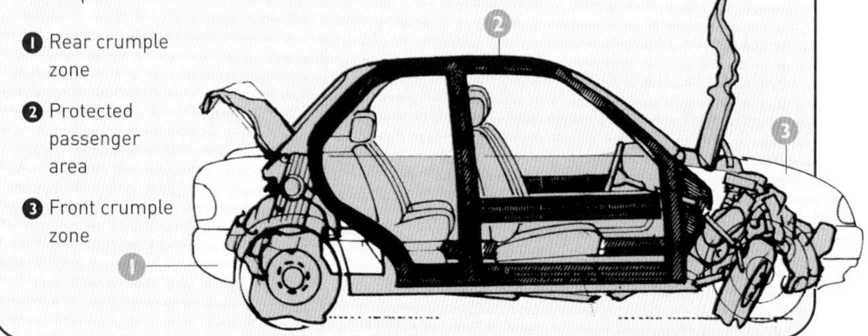

1. Rear crumple zone
2. Protected passenger area
3. Front crumple zone

Seat belts

Seat belts are designed to protect the car occupants in the event of a collision and reduce the risk of serious injury. Without a seat belt, even a minor collision at slow speed could cause injury to the chest, head or neck (whiplash), so always wear them, even for short journeys.

Seat belts must be fitted correctly to restrain the occupants and prevent them from being thrown around in a collision.

1. The diagonal belt should fit centrally over the shoulder and across the chest (not touching the neck), and the lap belt should fit as low as possible over the hips (not the waist or tummy).
2. Don't wear the belt under the arm instead of across the shoulder diagonal, as it will not be effective.
3. Seat belts should fit snugly against the body with no slack.
4. Don't try to modify a seat belt in any way, or pad it against the body, as this could affect its correct operation.
5. If you find you cannot wear the seat belt as described above for physical reasons, see page 31.

Seat belt care

Check seat belts periodically for frayed edges and ensure that they extend and retract freely. Make sure they are not twisted, or they may not perform correctly in the event of an accident.
If your car is involved in a collision, have the belts checked and replaced if necessary – a collision could damage the mechanism and reduce its efficiency.

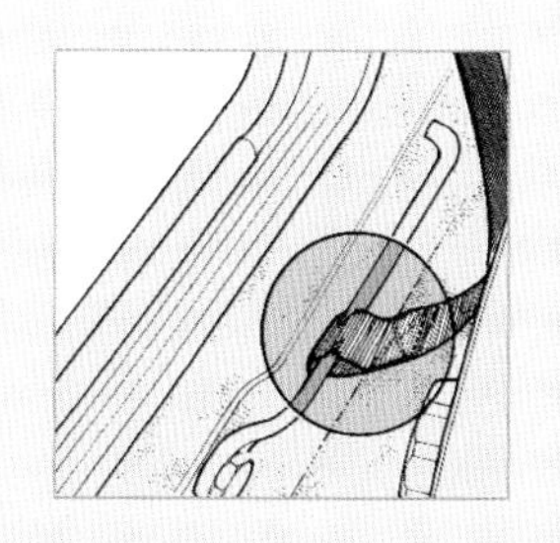

Pregnant women

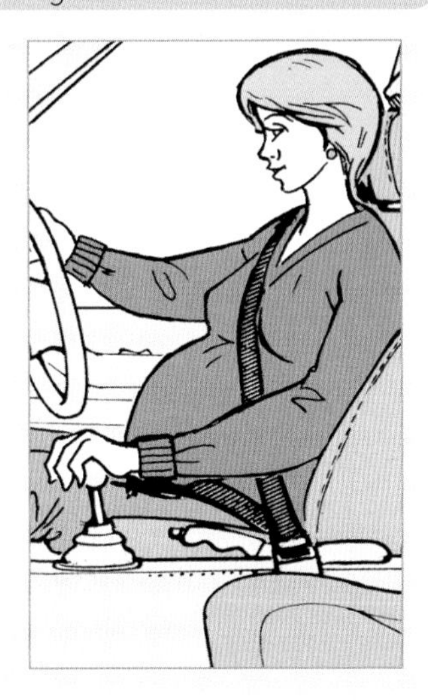

• Many women find wearing a seat belt uncomfortable during pregnancy, but it must be worn to protect both mother and child in the event of an accident.

• Ensure the lap strap is worn across the hips, not the tummy (where it would press against the baby and cause injury in a collision) and the shoulder strap rests between the breasts.

• Don't try to modify the belt in any way, or pad it against the body, as this could affect its correct operation.

• If you have to travel as a passenger in an advanced state of pregnancy, push the seat back as far as possible from the dashboard to help minimize risk of injury in the event of a collision.

• If you are heavily pregnant and have to drive, there may be little you can do to increase the space between the 'bump' and the steering wheel while still being able to work the pedals comfortably. The best advice in this situation is not to drive, although this is not always practicable.

The Law

It is a legal requirement in most countries to wear a seat belt if one is available. Passengers in the rear of the car should also wear seat belts if they are fitted. Many people are unaware that in a crash at 30 mph, someone who is unrestrained would be thrown forward and hit whatever is directly in front of them at 30–60 times their own body weight. Always wear a seat belt, unless you are exempted on medical grounds. To check when you are legally required to wear one, refer to the websites on page 310.

Types of seat belt

Seat belts can vary with the make, model and age of a car – some offer more protection than others, but any belt is better than no belt at all.

Pre-tensioned

These have a mechanism that allows the belt to be pulled out to fit the occupant. The belt then retracts and is automatically tightened firmly against the body when the ignition is switched on.

Three-point

The normal type of seat belt with one anchor point on the door pillar and one on each side of the seat.

Static

This is fixed to the three anchor points and is adjusted to fit with the buckle.

Inertia-reel

This has a mechanism that allows the belt to be pulled out to fit the occupant and then retract to take up the slack. It locks instantly to restrain the occupant if he or she is thrown forward suddenly.

Lap belt

This is often fitted to the central seat in the rear of the car. This is not as effective as a three-point seat belt, but it should still be worn if provided (over the hips).

Head restraints

Most cars have head restraints fitted. Don't be tempted to remove them for better vision to the rear; they perform an important function in helping to prevent whiplash injury in a collision. Position them so that the central rigid part of the head-rest is in line with the centre of the back of the head (at about eye level).

Correct driver position

It is dangerous to sit too close to the steering wheel, due to the risk of injury in an accident or from the activation of the air bag (*see page 33*). Adjust your seat until you are sitting in the correct position. You should be at a minimum of 25–30cm (10–12in) from the steering wheel, reclining very slightly, but sitting upright enough so that you can see the road ahead clearly and your feet can operate the pedals comfortably. You should be able to hold the steering wheel comfortably with your arms relaxed at the elbows. In many cars, the position of the steering wheel can also be adjusted. If you have trouble achieving the correct driving position for physical reasons, (*see page 31*).

1. Arms relaxed at the elbows
2. Body slightly reclined
3. Knees bent

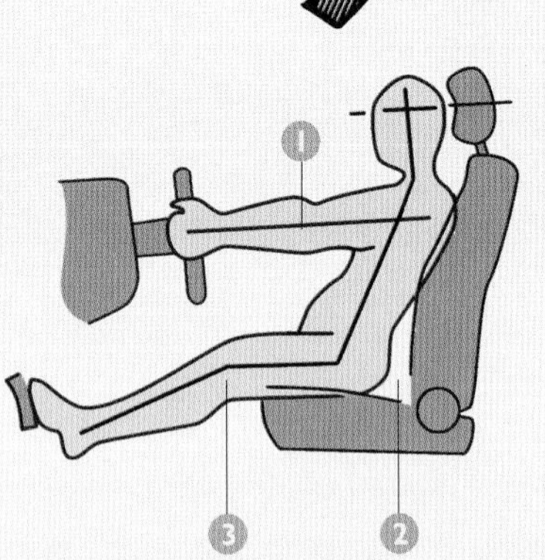

1. Arms stiff
2. Body leaning too far back
3. Legs extended and too far from the pedals

A car that fits

Car design varies a great deal, and not all cars will 'fit' you if you are slightly smaller or taller than average. Don't buy a car if you cannot achieve a safe driving position or cannot reach the pedals comfortably. Shop around for a make and model that suits you.

The tall driver

Tall drivers need to seek out car makes and models that have extra head and leg room. Steering wheel and seat position are adjustable in many cars, but unfortunately this may not be enough to make a car comfortable for a tall person to drive. If fitted, height-adjustable seat belts can help to accommodate a tall person. Contact motoring organizations for advice.

The small driver

- Drivers of 1.6m (5ft 2in) and under can find that seat belts don't fit across them correctly, and also may find themselves positioned too close to the steering wheel or have difficulty reaching the pedals. Pedal extenders can be fitted, but they must be approved structural extenders fitted at a garage that has experience of this kind of work.
- A support (such as a block of wood) can also be fixed in place on the floor under the carpet to make sure the driver's feet are in the correct positions to press on the pedals. It must be fitted in place firmly and not able to move. If you wish to fit pedal extenders or a foot support, check first with the appropriate government body (*see page 310*) to make sure this will be legal.
- If the diagonal strap of the seat belt is across your neck, you may be able to lower the height of the belt fixing on the door pillar – this can be adjusted in some cars; alternatively, it may be possible to raise the seat height.
- Avoid sitting too close to the steering wheel: there should be a minimum space of 25–30cm (10–12in). In some cars it is possible to move the steering wheel back, or try reclining the seat back.

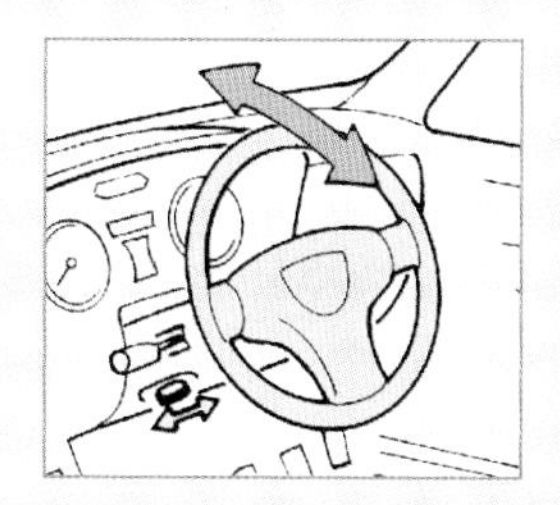

Air bags and child seats

If you are lucky, you may never see the air bags in your car; they are concealed in the steering wheel and interior panels, but they make a vital contribution to your safety in an accident. Young children, however, need the extra protection of purpose-made child seats.

Air bags

Also known as the Supplemental Restraint System (SRS), air bags are fitted as standard to the driver's side of most new cars, and may be fitted as standard or extra to the passenger side and/or car side panels, helping to protect the car occupants in a collision.

On the driver's side, the air bag is located inside the steering wheel, while on the passenger side, it is in the dashboard. The side air bags can be located in the wings of the seats or the door frames.

WARNING

On no account attempt to dismantle or tamper with an air bag system. If you do, you are likely to trigger the air bag, with potentially disastrous results. If you think the system needs work, take your car to a garage.

How do they work?

In most cars, air bags are controlled electronically and only work when the ignition is switched on. A control unit (ECU) is connected to sensors that feed back information concerning the car's speed, detecting when the car decelerates very rapidly and impact occurs. The ECU activates the air bag, which inflates with gas very rapidly. The bag deflates almost immediately to avoid smothering the passenger or hindering exit from the car. The gas is harmless but may cause slight irritation to some people.

1. Gas generator
2. Airbag
3. Cover

Avoiding injury

Be aware that, while designed to protect the car occupants, air bags inflate with such speed and force that they can cause broken ribs or wrists.

To minimize the possibility of this kind of injury, see the advice given below and also the information about 'Correct driver position' on page 30.

Air bag do's and don'ts

❶ Never put a rear-facing baby seat on the front passenger seat of a car with an air bag. If the bag inflates, it could cause severe injury to the baby.

❷ A seat belt must be worn for the air bag to work effectively.

❸ The driver should sit a minimum of 25–30cm (10–12in) from the steering wheel. If you are closer than this, see pages 30–31, and make the adjustments necessary to ensure you are in the correct driver position.

❹ If possible, frail elderly passengers should travel in the back of the car. (In some cars, the front passenger air bag may be disarmed – see your handbook.)

❺ Ensure that the air bag (set into the centre of the steering wheel – see your car handbook) is not aimed too high, at just your head and neck. It should also be aimed at your chest. Try tilting the steering wheel down slightly to achieve this, but make sure the instrument panel is still visible.

❻ Sit upright and don't hold the steering wheel by the spokes, or rest your hands on its centre. Grip the wheel rim.

❼ Don't place an object between the car occupant and an air bag.

❽ If possible, pregnant women should travel in the rear of the car. If driving, pregnant women should move the seat as far away from the steering wheel as possible, while still being able to reach the pedals comfortably.

❾ Air bags are sensitive to heat, so don't allow excessive heat close to an air bag. Also, don't knock or jolt the steering wheel with any degree of force, in case the air bag inflates.

Air bag warning light

Some cars are fitted with a dashboard warning light. It normally warns when the passenger air bag is 'armed' and comes on for several seconds when the ignition is switched on, then goes off. If the passenger air bag is disarmed, the light may remain on. If the light flashes, it may indicate that there is a fault and your dealer should be contacted. Check your car handbook for the operation of the warning light.

Replacing an air bag

If an air bag has been inflated, it must be replaced by an authorized dealer. If an air bag is never inflated, it will normally be effective for around ten years, but should be replaced by an authorized dealer at the end of this time. Refer to your car handbook for specific information on the life of the air bags in your car.

TIP

Have the air bags checked if your car is stolen, to make sure they have not been damaged.

Side air bags

These are incorporated into the sides of the seats or the door frames and offer protection from side impact. They normally operate independently of each other and are controlled by two ECUs. Sensors detect when the car's speed decelerates rapidly, and impact is about to occur, and inflate the bags. They may be connected to a dashboard warning light (see your handbook). The actual inflation of side air bags causes far less injury than front air bags. If the bags are located in the sides of the seats, don't place loose covers over the seats, as this would impede their inflation.

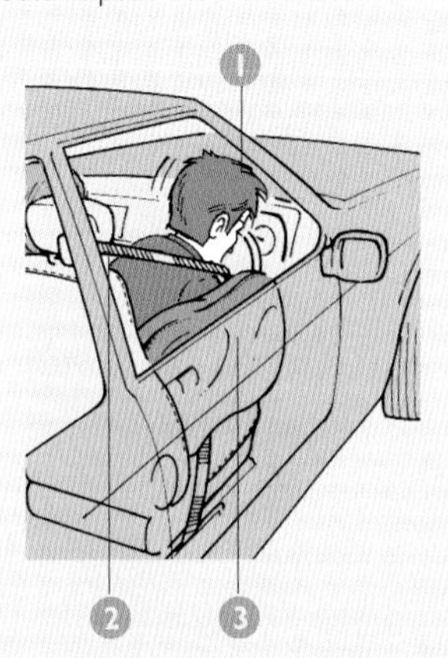

1. Driver flung forward as vehicle rapidly decelerates
2. Seat belt tightens
3. Air bag inflates

Carrying children safely

• There is a variety of child seats and restraints designed to ensure that children can travel comfortably and safely in the car until they are big enough to use adult seat belts. The amount of protection they offer does vary; nevertheless, a child is better protected in a child seat than out of one.

• In most countries, it is illegal for a child to travel without the use of an appropriate restraint if one is available. Children travelling in the front seat must make use of an appropriate restraint or seat belt, and children under the age of three in a front seat must have an appropriate child seat. For the legal requirements concerning the use of child restraints and seat belts, refer to the websites listed on page 310.

• Never travel with a child in your lap; they will be crushed or could be torn out of your arms in an accident. Never fix a seat belt around both you and a child, or around more than one child. Put children in the rear of the car whenever possible.

Safety standards

Most countries have a safety standard that seats must meet, and seats can only display an accepted quality mark when they do so. Despite this, the amount of protection each seat offers varies a great deal. Check with consumer organizations or government agencies for advice on which seats offer the most protection, and for details of the latest safety standard.

Buying a child seat

• Don't buy a second-hand child seat, as you don't know its history. It could have been in an accident and not be visibly damaged, but may have been weakened as a result. Older car seats won't meet the latest safety standards and the instructions may be missing.

• You may want to use the seat in more than one car, or other family members may transport the child at some time. Make a list of the cars in which the seat will be used.

• Ask the retailer for a list of cars that the seat you are interested in will fit. Not all seats fit all cars. Make sure the seat you choose is suitable for your make and model – check with the car or seat manufacturer if in doubt.

• Ask the retailer if you can try the seat in your car before you buy it. Ask the retailer to demonstrate how to fit it. Check that you can have a refund if it will not fit.

• Check your car seat belt is long enough to fasten around the seat and that the slots in the seat line up with the seat belt. Seat belt length varies from car to car.

ISOFIX (International Standards Organisation FIX)

Pressure has been put on car and seat manufacturers to adopt a universal fixing system so that all child seats can be used in all cars. The seat just snaps into place on special mountings installed in the car, and doesn't rely on the car seat belt to hold it in place. Not many manufacturers have taken up the system yet and progress is slow. Some ISOFIX seats are available, but designed for specific models rather than all cars, so the industry is still some way from the ideal solution.

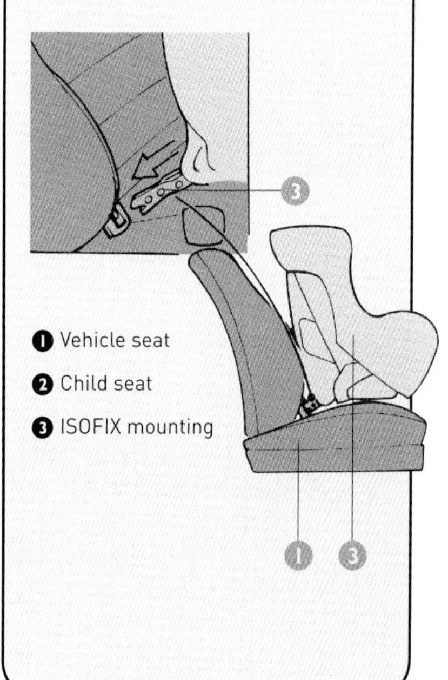

❶ Vehicle seat

❷ Child seat

❸ ISOFIX mounting

Seat sizes

Weight	Approximate age	Group	Type of seat
Birth–10kg (22lb)	Birth–9 months	0	Rearward-facing baby seat
Birth–13kg (29lb)	Birth–15 months	0+	Rearward-facing baby seat
9–18kg (20–40lb)	9 months–4 years	1	Forward-facing child seat
15–25kg (33–55lb)	4–6 years	2	Booster seat
22–36kg (48–79lb)	6–11 years	3	Booster cushion

(The numbers under the 'Group' heading refer to the stages of children's development – a grading system used by some retailers.)

The importance of weight

Weight is the determining factor in choosing a child seat; age is given as a guide only, since children grow at different rates. The exception to the rule is babies who may have reached the manufacturer's weight limit, but have not yet matured enough to move on to a forward-facing seat – they must be able to sit unaided to do so.

Front vs rear

All seats can normally be used in both the front and rear of the car. Some people like to place children where they can keep an eye on them when driving, but NEVER fit a rearward-facing baby seat to a front seat with a passenger air bag. The force with which the air bag inflates could cause serious injury to the baby. It is normally safer to put child and baby seats in the rear of the car.

Rearward-facing baby seat

WARNING

This type of seat can be used in the front passenger seat, but NEVER if there is a passenger air bag fitted that cannot be disabled. The force with which the bag inflates could seriously injure the baby.

• Suitable for children from birth to 13kg (29lb), these seats often have a handle and so can be used as a baby carrier too. Make sure the handle is safely folded away when the seat is being used to transport the baby in the car.

• It is normally safer to put the baby seat on the back seat. If the front seat is used, make sure it is pushed as far back as possible to distance it from the dashboard in the event of a collision. The seats are normally angled so that the baby is reclining, to prevent its head from flopping forwards. Some seats have a removable base that can be secured and left in the car while the carrier portion is removed.

• A rearward-facing seat offers greater protection than a forward-facing type, so keep the baby in it as long as possible – but change to a forward-facing seat when the baby exceeds the maximum weight or when the baby's head is higher than the top of the baby seat. The child should not change to a forward-facing seat until it can sit up unaided.

2 Strap

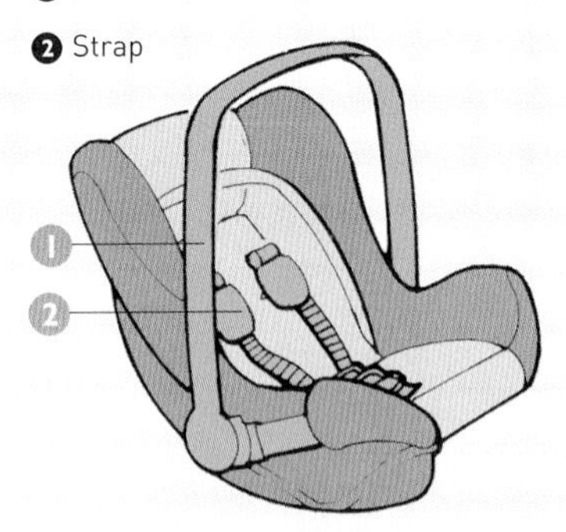

Forward-facing child seat

Suitable for babies and toddlers weighing 9–18kg (20–40lb), this seat can be placed on the front seat, although use on the back seat is preferable, particularly if a front passenger air bag is fitted. If the front car seat is used, make sure it is pushed back to be as far as possible from the dashboard in the event of a collision.

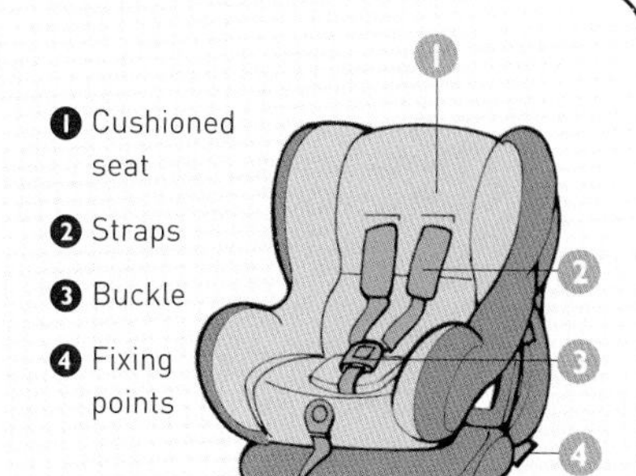

❶ Cushioned seat

❷ Straps

❸ Buckle

❹ Fixing points

WARNING

The child should move on to a booster seat when he or she exceeds the maximum weight recommended by the manufacturer, or the top of his or her head is higher than the top of the seat.

Booster seat

Suitable for children weighing 15–25kg (33–55lb), some booster seats are designed to convert to a cushion by removing the upright back section. There is normally no integral harness; the seats are designed to make use of the car seat belts safely. The lap belt should lie over the hips (not tummy), and the diagonal belt over the shoulder and chest (not neck).

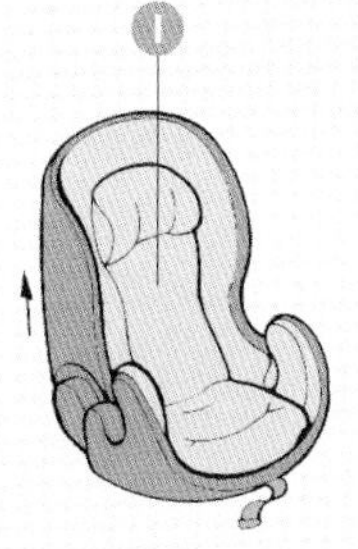

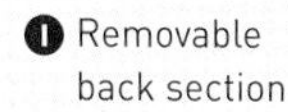

❶ Removable back section

❷ Seat belt over shoulder and hips

Booster cushion

Suitable for children weighing 22–36kg (48–79lb), these seats are designed to raise the height of the child so that he or she can make use of the car seat belts safely. There is no upright section at the back. The lap belt should lie over the hips (not tummy), and the diagonal belt over the shoulder and chest (not neck).

1 Cushioned seat raises the height of the child

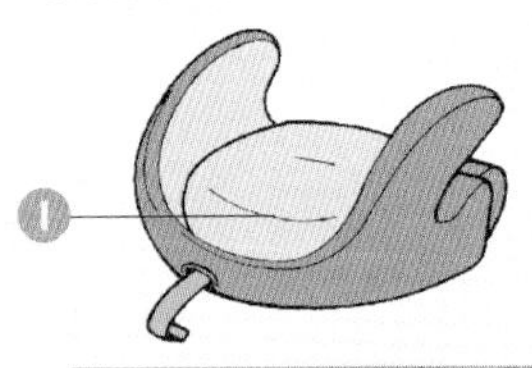

Using standard seat belts

When a child exceeds 36kg (79lb), it should be safe to use a normal seat belt. Make sure, however, that the diagonal and lap belts can be positioned correctly (*see page 27*).

Premature/low-weight babies

Always consult your doctor or hospital to check if a premature or low-weight baby may use a baby seat, since they can cause breathing problems in low-weight children. If it is safe to use one, don't keep the baby in it for longer than is necessary, and don't travel with the baby unattended. If possible, an adult should travel beside the baby.

Fitting child seats

- Child and baby seats can be tricky to fit, but it is very important that they are mounted correctly to make sure they offer maximum protection in the event of an accident. Follow the manufacturer's fitting instructions carefully. (If these are lost, contact the manufacturer for replacements.)

- Ensure that the seat is correct for the child. Don't be tempted to buy a seat that is too big and wait for the child to grow into it. If the child is too small, he or she could slip under the restraints. If the child is too big, the seat will be uncomfortable and will not offer the proper protection.

Using child seats

• Press the seat firmly against the car seat while tightening the fixing belt.

• Make sure that the seat belt is threaded through all the correct slots in the seat.

• There should be very little room for forwards or sideways movement. When the seat belt is opened, the seat should spring forward slightly.

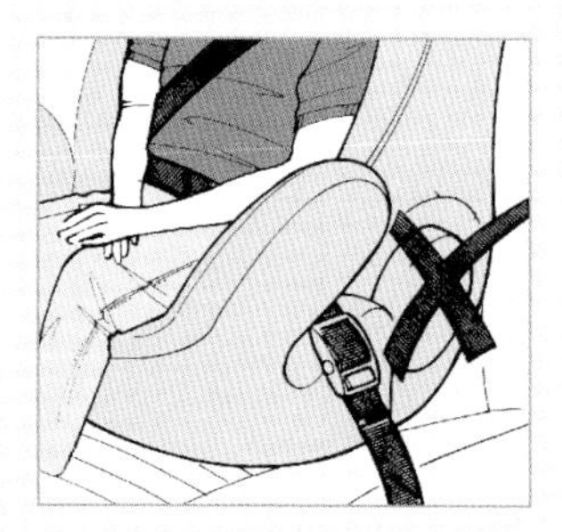

• The buckle must not rest on the frame of the child seat. This would put it under pressure when tightened, and it could spring open in a collision. Nor should the buckle lie across the child's tummy.

• Make sure the car seat belt is not twisted or frayed.

• Seat belts and harnesses should fit snugly so that there is only room to slide one or two fingers under the harness or seat belt.

• If fitting a child seat to a front car seat, push the seat right back, so that the distance from the dashboard is as great as possible. (Never fit a rearward-facing seat to a front seat where a front passenger air bag is fitted.)

• If a seat has an integral harness, raise the harness so that it fits through higher slots in the seat as the child grows. The buckle should not be across a child's tummy. Don't place the shoulder straps under the child's arms.

• Don't attempt to modify a child or baby seat or car seat belts in any way to make the seat fit. It could prevent the seat functioning correctly in an impact.

• Don't place a blanket or cover over the child and under the harness or seat belt. Buckle the child into the seat first and place the blanket over the top.

• If the child undoes the buckle, don't modify it to prevent this, as you may not be able to release the child quickly in the event of an accident.

Security

It takes most thieves just a matter of seconds to break into a car. Some makes and models are more secure than others, and there may be little you can do to stop the determined thief, but there is much you can do to deter the opportunist.

Basic security

- Lock the car in a garage if possible. (Always lock both car and garage.)
- Always lock all doors and close all windows, the boot and sunroof (but don't leave pets in a car with all the windows closed).
- Whenever possible, park in a secure or attended car park, or where your car is visible to passers-by, and in a well-lit area at night. If the area is covered by surveillance cameras, this will be an added deterrent.
- Make sure the car's security system and any security code associated with audio equipment are activated when you park.
- Don't leave money, valuables or a phone in the car; always take them with you.
- Don't leave goods visible in the car otherwise a watching thief may decide to target your car; if possible, lock them in the boot.
- Always remove the ignition key, even when parked outside your flat or home.
- If your car has a steering column lock (which engages when the ignition key is removed), use it.
- Lock the car if it is unattended when paying for fuel at a petrol station.
- Don't leave car documents in the car – a thief could use them to sell it.

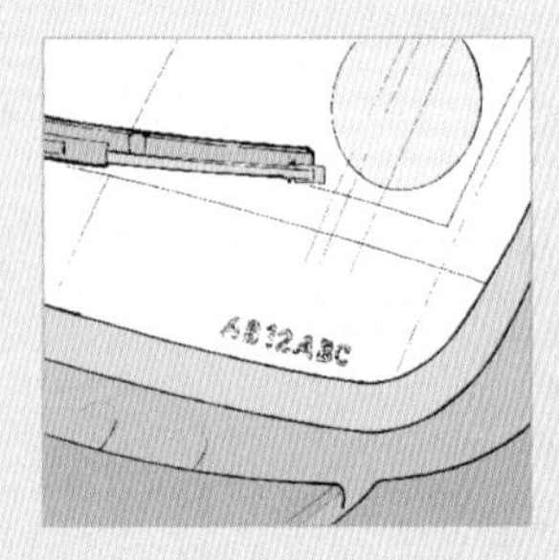

- Have your car registration number etched on all the windows.

- If you have a removable radio, mark it prominently with an indelible pen. Thieves will be less able to sell it if it is marked. Keep a note of the serial number and any security code.
- Fit locking wheel nuts to the wheels, particularly if they are alloy – a special adapter is needed to undo them.
- Keep bags and money out of sight while you are driving – an opportunist thief could open the door and snatch a bag when you are stationary in heavy traffic. Lock the doors and close the windows if you are travelling through an area where you feel unsafe.
- Remember to set the immobilizer if it is not set automatically when you remove the ignition key. Fit an immobilizer if the car doesn't already have one.
- Remember to set the alarm; fit one if the car doesn't have one.
- Fit a visible anti-theft device (such as a steel arm that locks the steering wheel or gear lever).
- When returning to your car, have your key at the ready and check the interior, including the back seat, before you enter.
- Install a tracking system – these operate via Global Positioning System (GPS) and are expensive, but effective. They track the car's movement after theft, increasing the chance of recovery.

Audio equipment

Audio equipment is protected against theft in a number of ways. Some equipment has a security code that needs to be input each time it is used. Other equipment has a detachable front panel that can easily be popped in a bag or pocket, while the circuitry and wiring remain fixed inside the dashboard – the vehicle's unique equipment is coded so that it will only work in the car to which it was fitted by the manufacturer.

If the whole unit is removable, take it out when you leave the car and hide it from view, or lock it in the boot if you cannot take it with you. As an additional precaution, mark it prominently with an indelible pen; this will make it harder for the thief to sell on the black market.

1 Removable unit

Locks and alarms

The locks on your car doors and boot lid are your first line of defence against thieves – always use them whenever you leave your car unattended. An alarm and/or immobilizer will provide even more protection, sending many a thief on his way.

Conventional locking mechanism

All doors are locked and unlocked individually with a key.

Central locking

All doors are locked and unlocked simultaneously by the key on the driver's side. This avoids leaving a door unlocked by mistake. If the central locking fails to work, try changing the fuse (*see pages 208–209*).

Deadlocking/double locking

This is a locking device operated by a key that prevents the car from being unlocked from inside (even if the window is broken) or outside without the correct key. Don't activate it if people are inside the car, though, as they will not be able to get out without the key.

Infra-red remote-control locking

All doors and the boot are locked and unlocked when a button on the remote-control unit is pressed. The remote (transmitter) has to be pointed at a certain part of the car (often the driver's door or behind the rear-view mirror) and be within a certain distance – usually around 5m (16ft). If an object is between the remote control and the receiver, the remote action locks may not work.

If the remote control no longer works, try changing the battery. Many remotes have a small light that comes on when the remote is working. If you notice that this fails to come on, then the battery probably needs replacing. If a new battery does not cure the problem, contact the manufacturer or a garage.

Child locking

This locks the rear doors so that they can only be opened from the outside, not the inside.

Alarms

Some cars have alarms already fitted, but you can also have one installed at a garage. An alarm normally provides exterior protection and is activated when a door, bonnet or boot is opened. It may include sensors that react to changes in air pressure or movement inside the car, triggering the alarm if a door is opened or a window broken. The alarm may also be triggered when the car is moved or lifted (tilt sensing).

Immobilizers

- Electronic immobilizers are now fitted as standard to all new cars. They are electronically controlled devices that interrupt the power supply to two or more of the systems required to start the engine.

- Each ignition key has an ID code registered with the manufacturer. When the ignition is switched on, the code is recognized by the system and the engine can be started. If the correct key is not used, the engine will not start. The immobilizer is normally set automatically when the key is removed. There is usually a small light that flashes on or near the instrument panel to show that the immobilizer is activated. If this light does not flash, or stays on when the correct key is inserted, consult a garage or the manufacturer.

- If a new key is required, contact the car dealer or the manufacturer; a key cut at a high street locksmith will not work as it won't incorporate the special ID code.

TIP

If the central or remote locking won't work, and changing the fuse or remote battery doesn't fix the problem, the driver's door can normally be opened manually with the key .

Carrying items

Whether it's a trip to the supermarket, a visit to the DIY store or a family holiday, our cars are regularly used to carry all manner of items. But safety is still a consideration when loading up your car; badly distributed loads can be harzardous to you and other road users.

Loads inside the car

Place heavy objects low down, whether in the boot or in the interior of the car, with lighter objects on top. Distribute heavy objects as evenly as possible to avoid damaging the car's suspension. Secure objects wherever possible or pack them so that they hold each other in position to prevent them from flying forwards if you brake suddenly. If you are carrying a very heavy load, refer to your car handbook, which may give a maximum weight that should not be exceeded.

TIP

Carry a shallow cardboard box in your boot; you can place small items in it to prevent them from rolling around. Alternatively, buy a cargo net from a car accessory store and use it to hold items to the boot floor.

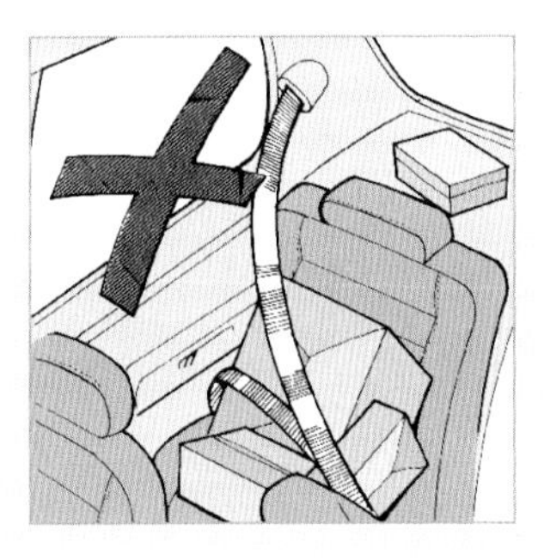

Despite its name, don't put goods on the parcel shelf, as they slide forward easily when the car brakes. Use seat belts to secure loads being carried on seats.

If you have to put goods on the back seat, make sure they don't project over the top of the seat and impede vision and, again, secure them well.

Never load the inside of the car with anything that could slide forwards and hit you or a front-seat passenger on the back of the head.

Loads on a roof rack

• Carrying loads on a roof rack creates wind resistance and therefore increases fuel consumption. If you have a particularly heavy load to carry, refer to your car handbook in case the manufacturer states a maximum load that must not be exceeded.

• Arrange the load so that smaller items are placed at the front, and heavier items are placed on the bottom; make sure that the weight is distributed as evenly as possible. Wrap all the goods in a large tarpaulin or in plastic sheeting and secure it well, particularly the corners, which are apt to flap in the wind. If something falls off the car roof it could easily cause an accident.

• Rooftop boxes that fit on to a rack are also available; using them avoids the packing problem. They have an aerodynamic shape to reduce wind resistance, but have a limited amount of space. When driving with a loaded roof rack, bear in mind that the car will be more susceptible to cross-winds.

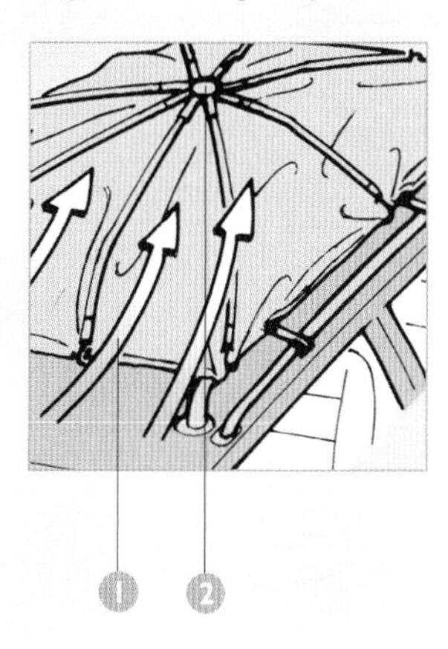

❶ Wind resistance

❷ Tarpaulin securely tied at centre

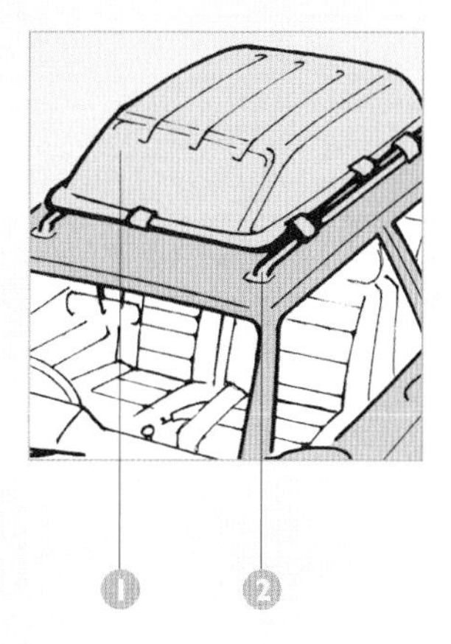

❶ Rooftop box with aerodynamic shape

❷ Roof rack

Carrying bikes

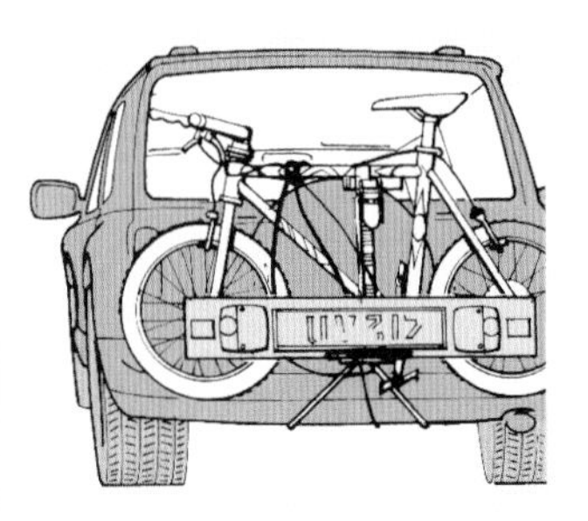

Bikes can be carried on top of the car, fixed to a special rack, but they will create wind resistance and increase petrol consumption. An alternative is to fix them to a cycle carrier at the rear of the car. Make sure that they are very well secured and stop ten minutes or so after leaving to check that they are still securely fixed. If on a long journey, stop a couple of times to check them again.

Carrier considerations

- Rear vision must be good.
- The car number plate and all rear lights must be visible. If necessary, fix a second number plate panel to the bike, with lights wired to the car's lighting system.
- If you have a hatchback, don't rest the carrier on the glass of the rear window as it can be damaging.

Carrying long objects

If possible, carry long objects on a roof rack and make sure they are tied down well. If you have a hatchback, the rear seats can be folded down and the object can protrude from the boot opening, but make sure that it does not interfere with your ability to control the car. No matter how the object is carried, it must be firmly secured and the tailgate held down if it protrudes from the boot. Be careful not to obstruct visibility through the rear window. If the object projects from the end of the car by more than 30cm (1ft), attach a red flag to it.

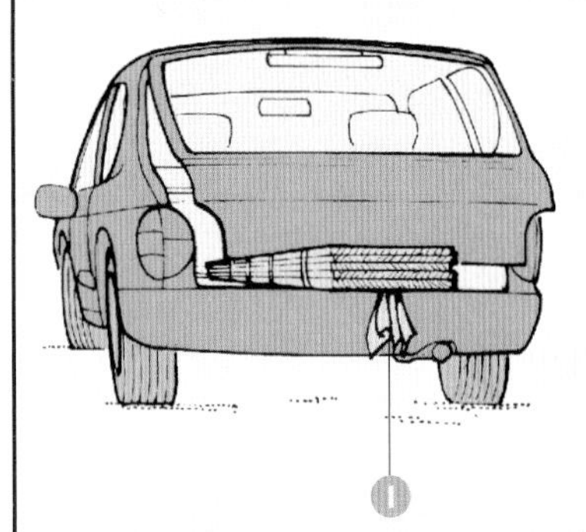

1 Flag attached to end of long object

Carrying animals

Animals must be kept under control should not be allowed to travel loose in the car; they could distract the driver and cause an accident. Don't let a dog travel with its head out of a window, as dirt and insects can get into its nose and eyes.

- Safety harnesses are available for medium-sized and large dogs. The dog is clipped into the harness, and the harness is attached to the car seat belt, which should be fastened.

- Small dogs and other small pets, such as cats, can be transported in a pet carrier. Make sure it is the right size for your pet and allows the animal enough room. Position the carrier in the car so that it cannot move about in the footwell, or secure it with a car seat belt, ensuring that it has enough ventilation.
- Never put the carrier in the boot of the car, as the animal could suffocate.
- If you put the carrier in the rear of a hatchback or estate car, make sure it is held securely.

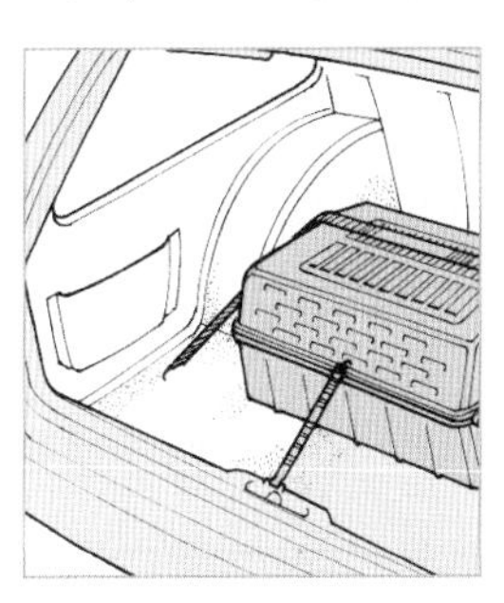

- If your car is fitted with air bags, make sure your pet will not be hit by one, should it inflate in an accident.
- Larger animals and dogs can be carried in a travel cage. Make sure it is securely anchored to the car. Dogs can also be carried in the rear of a hatchback or estate car fitted with a dog guard that keeps the animal away from the driver.

Greenhouse effect

Never under any circumstances leave an animal in a car during warm weather. Even on a cloudy day with the windows partially open, the temperature in a car can rise fatally.

EXTERIOR

Cleaning

The traditional Sunday chore of cleaning the car plays an important part in preserving its paintwork. Clean it once a week if possible. If dirt is allowed to build up, the paint eventually discolours and moisture retained by the dirt in crevices and joints helps corrosion to set in.

Shampooing

❶ Rinse the car well with cold water to get rid of dirt. If you don't do this, you risk scratching the paintwork by rubbing dirt across it. Using a stiff brush, rinse clean the wheels as well. (But if you have alloy wheels, *see page 54.*)

❷ Add car shampoo to a bucket of fresh lukewarm water, but don't use more than the recommended amount. Too many suds take a long time to rinse off.

❸ Soak a sponge well and start washing the bodywork. Begin on the roof and work your way down the bonnet, rear and sides. (Use fresh water without any shampoo in it on the windows if the shampoo you have chosen contains wax.)

TIP

Tar and squashed insects can be hard to remove with shampoo. Special cleaners are available from car accessory shops.

you will need

- → bucket
- → 2 large sponges
- → soft brush (with hose attachment if possible)
- → garden hose
- → stiff brush (for wheels)
- → chamois leather
- → car shampoo*

* don't use washing-up liquid, as this leaves smears and removes wax.

❹ Use a second sponge on very dirty areas around the bottom of the car.

❺ Using a soft brush, clean the radiator grille, bumper and front area around the number plate, and any other cracks and crevices.

❻ Clean the wheels and rims under the wheel arches using the stiff brush.

Rinsing and leathering

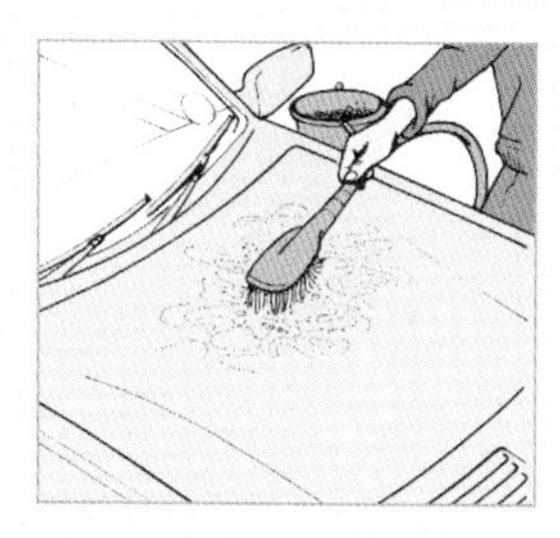

❶ Rinse the car thoroughly with a sponge and plenty of fresh water or a soft brush attached to a garden hose.

❷ If possible, clean under the wheel arches with a hose and strong jet of water to remove mud.

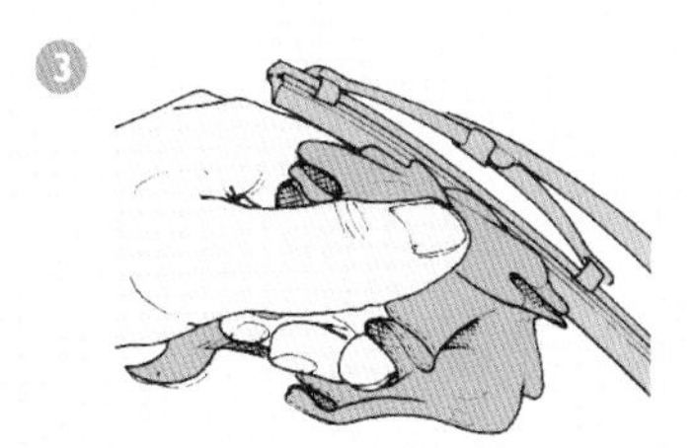

❸ Wash all the windows with the 'clean' sponge, using clean water. Pick up the wipers and wash beneath them, and wipe down the wiper blades (you may want to use a rag for the blades, as this might leave a black mark). Special glass cleaners are available from car accessory shops, or you can use household glass cleaner (not silicone-based), but washing-up liquid is not recommended, as this is apt to leave smears.

❹ Fill the bucket with fresh water, immerse the chamois leather in it and wring it out well. Wipe all the bodywork and windows to remove the water droplets. Keep rinsing out the chamois leather in the water as you go, working quickly if it is a hot day, as the water could evaporate, leaving marks.

A few golden rules

- Use plenty of fresh, clean water.
- Always rinse the car before you wash it.
- Don't clean windows with shampoo containing wax, as it will leave smears.
- Don't wash the car in direct sunlight or when the bonnet is hot, as it will leave smears.
- Don't leave the car to dry in sunlight, as it will leave marks.

TIP

Clean chrome (brightwork) with car shampoo and water in the same way that you clean the rest of the car, and wipe it down with a chamois leather. Polish it with a wax polish to give it a protective coating. If it is marked, try using a special chrome cleaner.

Alloy wheels

Alloy wheels can be cleaned with a special alloy wheel cleaner available from car accessory shops. Follow the manufacturer's instructions, but don't leave the cleaner on the wheels for longer than recommended, as it can leave marks, and be careful not to get it on the bodywork. Use a soft brush to clean inside crevices. When the wheels are clean, apply a coat of polish to help protect them. Normal car polish with wax can be used if the wheels already have a clear protective coating. If not, special alloy wheel polishes are also available.

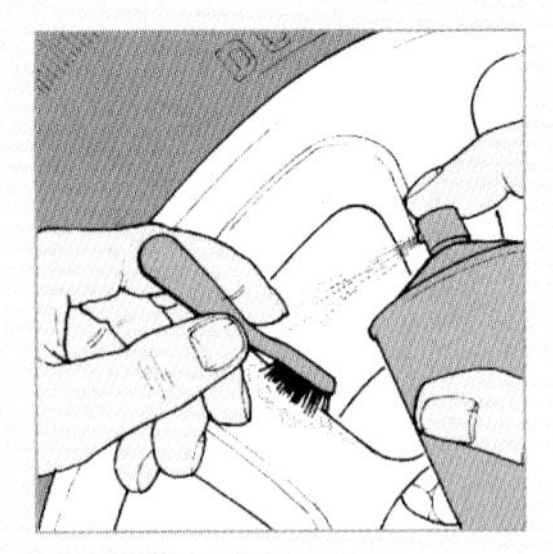

Don't use a power water jet on alloy wheels for any length of time, as this will remove any protective coating that has been applied and may cause damage to the surface of the wheel.

WARNING

When cleaning wheels, take care not to breathe in the brake dust that collects on them, as this can be very harmful to health.

Polish schedule

Another Sunday chore, and one that plays an important part in keeping bodywork in good condition. However, it does not need to be done so frequently. How often depends on the polish you use and the state of your car's paintwork, but it could be necessary from every six weeks to three or four months.

Some don'ts

- Never polish a dirty or wet car.
- Don't polish in direct sunlight, as the polish will dry too quickly and be hard to remove, causing streaking.
- Don't polish the car it if it has just been driven and is still hot.
- Don't apply polish to anything other than paintwork and brightwork, as it could cause staining.

Polish

• Water breaks up into hundreds of small droplets on a polished surface. If water lies in flat splodges and spreads out over your car's paintwork, it needs a polish.

• With age, the hard protective coating applied over the paintwork at the factory begins to wear away, leaving the surface of the car more vulnerable to water, salt, tree sap, bird droppings, etc. Polish is invaluable for protecting the bodywork against environmental damage, as it restores that important protective layer the car needs.

• If you can only bring yourself to use polish twice a year, time it before the onset of winter and summer.

• There are many different polishes available. Choose one that is suitable for your car; some are not suitable for metallic finishes. Polish normally contains wax or silicone, which creates the protective layer.

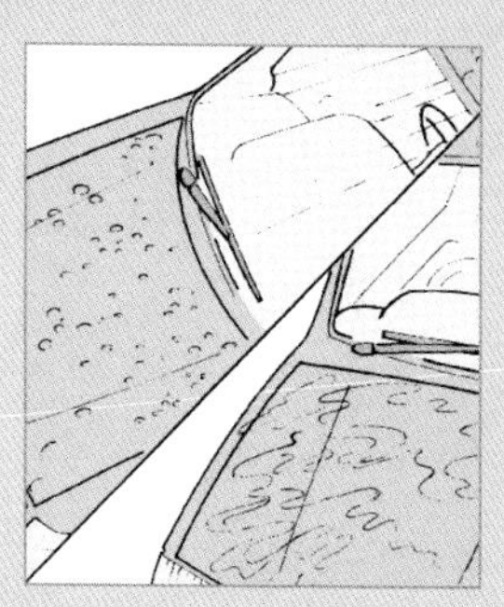

Polishing the car

1 Wash the car thoroughly and then dry it off with a chamois leather (*see pages 52–53*).

2 Apply the polish according to the manufacturer's instructions – with either a damp or clean dry cloth. Some polishes need to dry before you buff them off, and others need only dry to a haze.

3 Apply the polish with a circular motion. If you need to buff the polish before it dries, apply it to small areas at a time.

you will need

→ several soft clean cloths

→ suitable car polish

4 Buff it with a separate piece of cloth.

5 If polish gets on to the trim, wipe it off immediately, as it could stain.

Retouching bodywork

There are plenty of products available to help you make repairs to the bodywork yourself, but it is not easy to make a good (invisible) repair, so you may prefer to take the car to a specialist. However, if the damage is only minor, here are a few DIY guidelines.

Restoring paintwork

- Paintwork becomes dull over time, but it can be restored by using an abrasive polish or cutting compound. This removes a very thin layer of paint when it is applied, revealing a fresh layer underneath. Some compounds are tinted with a colour.

- Make sure you buy a restorer that is suitable for your car's paintwork, and try it out first on a small area in an inconspicuous place. Use plenty of soft cotton cloth. When applying the compound, use a fresh piece once the paint starts to build up on the cloth, and use a clean piece for buffing. Follow the manufacturer's instructions, but don't rub too hard, particularly on edges and corners, as the paint can be worn away quickly in these areas.

- Avoid getting restorer on the trim. If you do, wipe it off immediately, as it will probably stain.

Light scratches

If there are light scratches that have not broken through the paint, you can apply a cutting compound that removes a thin layer of paint as it polishes. Follow the manufacturer's instructions carefully. Take care not to remove more paint than you need. Some compounds are available in different colours.

Retouching small chips and scratches

It is best to deal with any chips or deep scratches as soon as you notice them. If left, rust could set in quickly and spread, causing the paintwork to bubble. If you cannot attend to them immediately, apply a layer of polish to the affected area to offer it some protection until you can repair the damage or have it attended to by a professional sprayer.

Touch-up paint

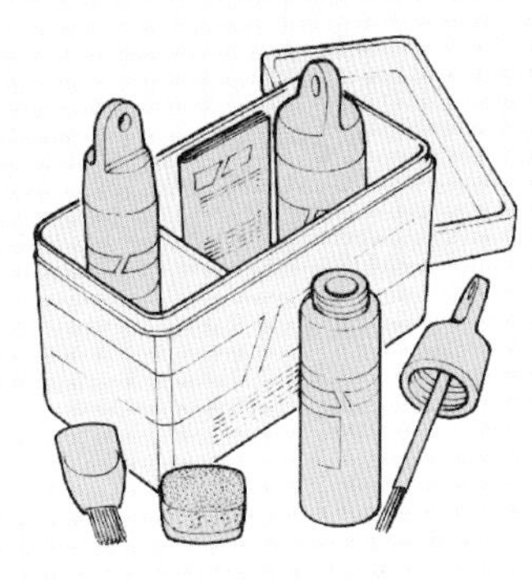

To obtain an exact match, it is best to buy touch-up paint from a dealer for your make of car. A paint code is given on the car somewhere, but it can be hard to find, so just take the car to the dealer's garage, where they can identify the correct shade. Car accessory shops also sell ranges of touch-up paint, but they may not be an exact match. You will need to know the make, model and year of manufacture before buying.

You normally need to rub down the area around the blemish to bare metal. You may wish to stick masking tape around the area on which you are going to work to protect it from accidental damage. If you do this, remove the tape as soon as you have finished. If it leaves any marks, clean them off with methylated spirit.

Wheel damage

If the clear protective coating on your alloy wheels becomes damaged, it will leave the metal beneath exposed and could result in staining or oxidization (a chemical reaction caused by exposure to the air).

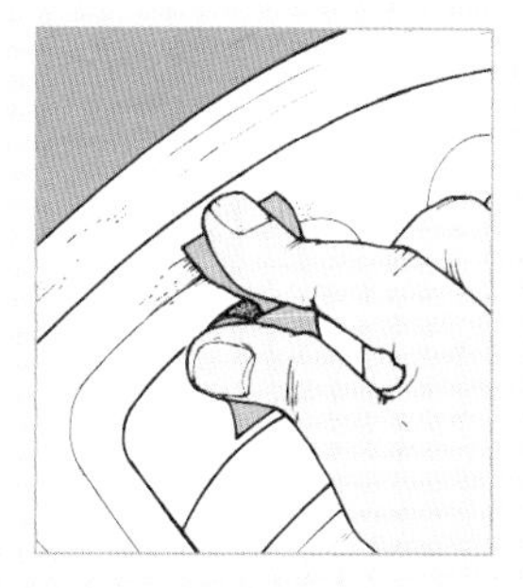

Make sure the damaged area is clean. Using a piece of very fine abrasive paper, lightly chamfer the chipped edges of the protective coating, but take care not to scratch the exposed metal. Wipe the area with a cloth and paint on a new protective coating, using clear alloy wheel lacquer. Apply several layers until the correct thickness has been achieved.

Repairing small chips

Small stones kicked up by other cars can easily chip the paintwork of your car, especially around the front and on the bonnet. With care, however, you can make effective repairs.

Using a kit

Kits are available that supply the equipment and paint you need to treat the small chips and scratches, but you may also need to buy a rust treatment.

❶ Work in warm, dry weather if possible. If you have to work inside, make sure there is good ventilation.

you will need

- → suitable touch-up kit*
- → rust preventative**
- → knife**
- → masking tape (if required)
- → soft cloth

* remember that it may not be possible to get an exact paint match from a kit

**depending upon the severity of the damage to the paintwork

2

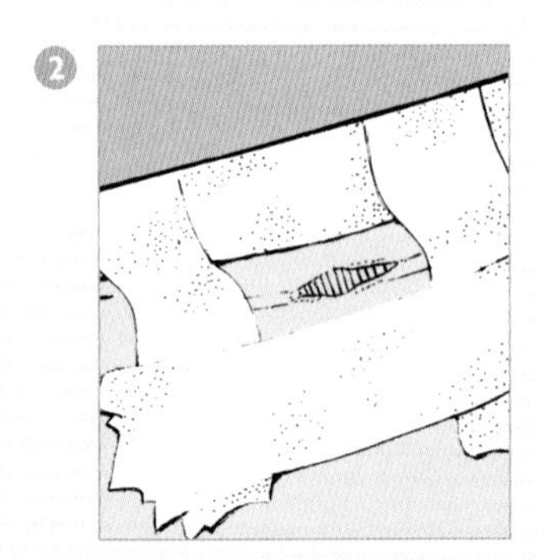

❷ Stick masking tape around the damaged area if you are worried about damaging the surrounding 'good' paintwork. Remove the tape as soon as you have finished the repair, as it can leave marks from the adhesive, although you should be able to remove these with methylated spirit.

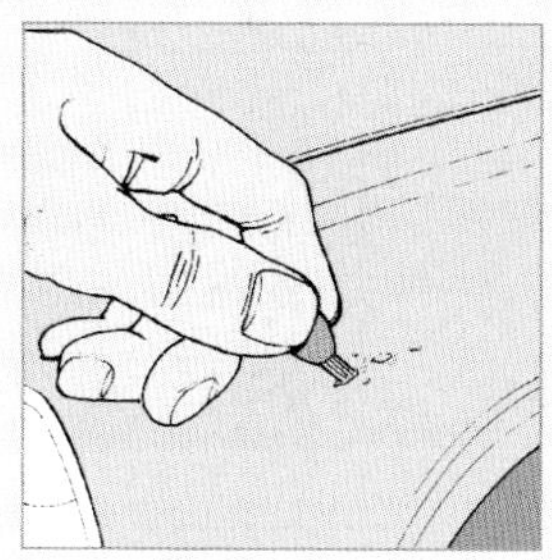

❸ Remove any flaking paint or rust with the tool supplied (or a knife).

❹ If rust is present, it will be necessary to get down to the bare metal – check the manufacturer's instructions.

❺ Wash down the area to be treated and wait for it to dry thoroughly.

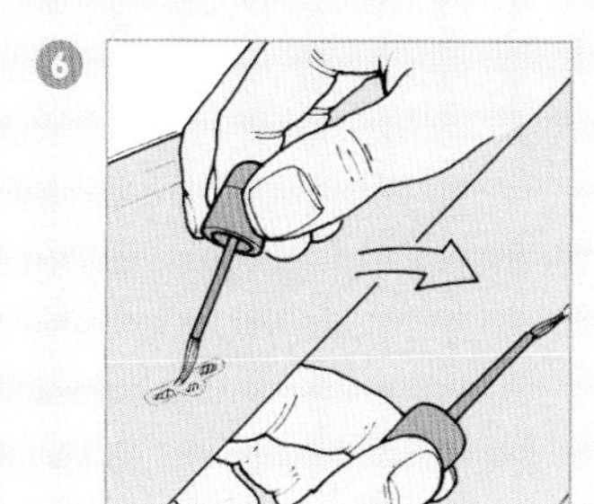

❻ Apply a suitable rust preventative.

❼ Apply the primer and leave it to dry until it is hard.

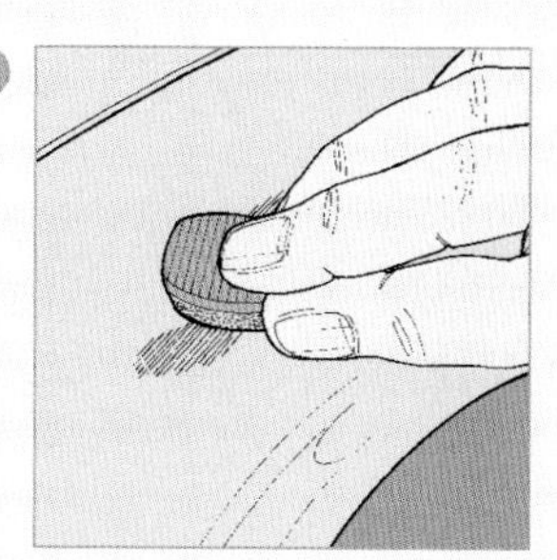

❽ With the abrasive tool provided, rub down the primed area lightly to provide a key for the top coat, and wipe it clean.

❾ Apply the top coat lightly, using several layers to build it up. Rub it down very lightly between each coat.

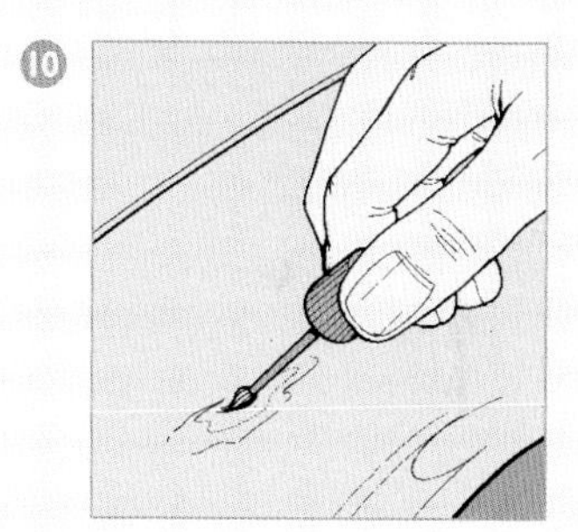

❿ For metallic finishes, wait for a minimum of 24 hours and then apply the lacquer provided following the manufacturer's instructions.

⓫ Once the lacquer is dry, buff the repair with a cloth or the tool provided.

⓬ Wait for at least a week before polishing the damaged area.

More serious damage

If rust has taken hold and caused pitting, the area needs to be rubbed down to bare metal and filler applied to the same level as the rest of the metal.

❶ Work in warm, dry weather if possible. If you have to work inside, make sure there is good ventilation.

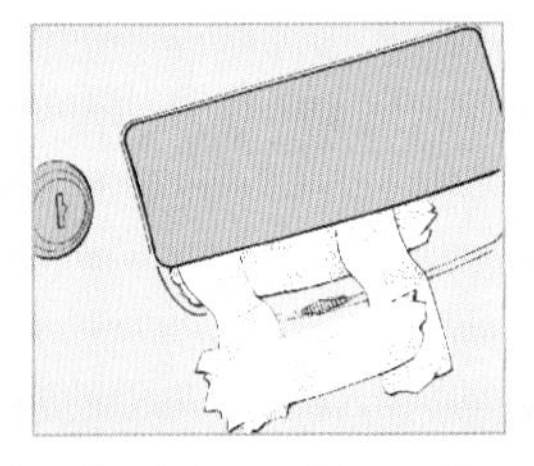

❷ Stick masking tape around the damaged area to protect the good paintwork. (If it leaves a sticky residue when you remove it, this can be cleaned off with methylated spirit.)

❸ Remove any flaking paint with a knife, being careful not to damage any of the surrounding good paintwork.

❹ Rub the entire damaged area down to bare metal with the wet or dry paper, used wet. Dry the area thoroughly afterwards with a clean cloth.

TIP

Remember that touch-up paint from accessory shops may not provide an exact match.

you will need

- → knife
- → smooth blade
- → suitable anti-rust treatment (if needed)
- → filler
- → wet or dry paper (400-grit)
- → suitable touch-up paint

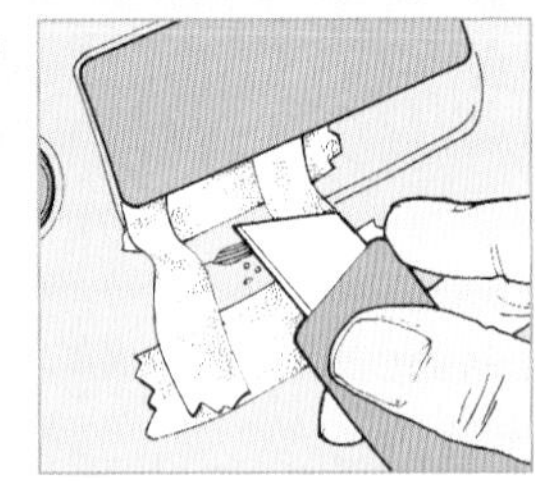

❺ Remove all trace of rust with the knife and wet or dry abrasive paper.

❻ Wash the area and dry it immediately. Then apply a coating of anti-rust treatment according to the manufacturer's instructions. Don't delay in doing this, otherwise rust may take hold again.

❼ Wait for the anti-rust treatment to dry, then smear filler over the damaged area, smoothing it with the knife blade.

❽ Once this is dry, using the wet or dry paper (wet), rub down the filled area until it is smooth and level with the rest of the metal. Dry it off.

❾

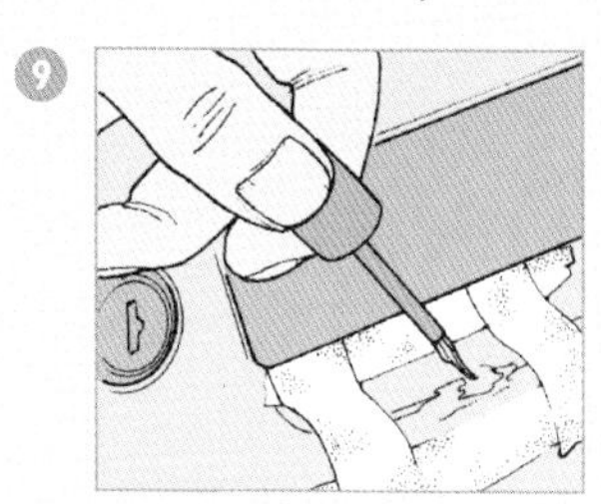

❾ Apply the touch-up paint according to the manufacturer's instructions. It is better to apply several thin coats, waiting for each to dry and lightly rubbing down to provide a key for the next coat, than to try to apply the paint too thickly.

Treating rust

There is a variety of anti-rust products on the market, ranging from touch-up kits for small areas to treatments for larger areas, which remove rust and act as a preventative as well.

If you are unsure which treatment you need for a particular job, ask the retailer's advice.

TIP

If you are concerned about rust underneath your car, ask your garage to put it on a ramp and check it for you.

Rust

Rust is caused by a chemical reaction between steel, water and air, but it is exacerbated by salt – salty air or the salt put on the roads in winter. Clean your car regularly and rust spots will be easier to find. Deal with them quickly, as rust soon spreads, causing paintwork to bubble.

Rust is liable to start in scratches and nicks in the paintwork, and cracks and joints between panels, in fact anywhere that water can collect, especially if the car is dirty, as dirt retains moisture.

Particularly vulnerable areas are the edges of the bodywork, the bottoms of the doors, boot lid and tailgate, the wheel arches, the front of the bonnet and the suspension mounting points.

Rust is not just a problem for paintwork; it also attacks the underside of the car and ultimately results in structural weakening. If a car is badly rusted underneath, it can fail a roadworthiness test. If the rusting is severe and the car is quite old, it is often not worth repairing and the car has to be scrapped.

Windows and mirrors

Manufacturers have reduced the risks posed by the close proximity of glass windows to the occupants of a car by developing toughened and laminated glass. In the event of a stone flying up and chipping the windscreen, or a collision, passengers are relatively well protected.

Windscreen

All modern windscreens are made of laminated glass, which consists of a layer of thin transparent plastic sandwiched between two thin layers of glass. If the windscreen is hit by a stone, it should not break, but should just show a chip or crack in the area where the stone has struck. As long as it is possible to see through the windscreen easily, the car can still be driven, but have the windscreen repaired or replaced by a specialist as soon as you can.

Windscreens used to be made of toughened glass, which shatters into tiny fragments when struck, to reduce the likelihood of injury to the car occupants from large shards of glass. However, this frequently meant that it was not possible to drive the car until all the glass had been knocked out, as the driver simply could not see. Side and rear windows in modern cars are still normally made of toughened glass.

The windscreen may be held in place by a special adhesive that bonds it to the window surround, or it may be secured by a rubber seal. If a window seal begins to leak, it can be repaired relatively easily using a silicone sealant available from car accessory shops.

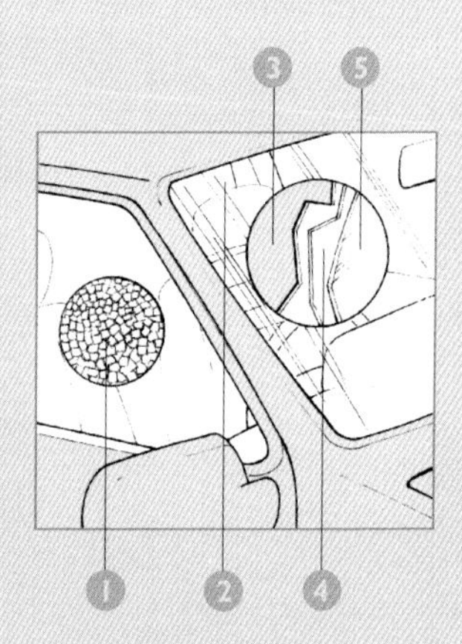

1. Toughened glass shatters into fragments when broken
2. Laminated glass
3. Inner glass
4. Plastic layer
5. Outer glass

Scratches and chips

A specialist in windows may be able to polish out chips and scratches if they are not too deep. First, the damaged area is filled with a special resin, which is allowed to harden and then is polished. The finished repair must be invisible, and a poor job may not pass a road-worthiness test.

You should have a chipped or cracked window repaired or replaced as soon as you can, as although you may be able to see out of it clearly, it could soon worsen if the car is jolted by running over a bump in the road, the doors being slammed or the simple vibration of driving – and avoid automatic car washes.

Smears and misting up

- Regular cleaning of the inside of the windscreen with a commercial glass cleaner will help prevent it getting smeary. Some kinds of plastic trim give off a vapour that leaves a greasy film on the inside of the windscreen, and the problem is exacerbated if people smoke in the car. A smeary windscreen causes particular problems at night, when oncoming lights are diffused by the smears, making visibility poor. Try putting some concentrated screenwash on a rag and wiping it across the windscreen.

- To help reduce misting up, clean the windscreen with ordinary household glass cleaner or a special car glass cleaner. Keep a chamois leather or pad in the car to wipe the windscreen down. Some cars have heated windscreens, which also help to reduce mist and condensation.

Heated rear windows

In most modern cars, the heater elements are embedded in the glass of the rear window, which protects them and keeps them intact. In some older cars, the elements are made of a thin conductive material and are applied to the inner face of the window, where they are easily damaged. However, they can be repaired with electrical conductive paint, which is available from car accessory shops. If a broken element is not the problem, check that the wiring connectors at the side of the window are making good contact (wiggle them and push them in firmly).

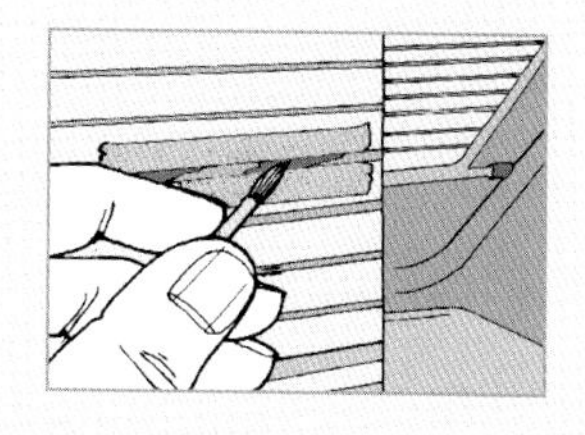

Electric (power) windows

Many cars are now fitted with electric windows. They are an advantage from the security point of view, as normally they cannot be forced open. They are operated by switches inside the car and are controlled by an ECU, which may also operate other accessories such as side mirrors and courtesy lights. The motor that drives the windows up and down is electric, so these windows normally only work when the ignition is switched on. However, in some cars, they may work for a short time after the key has been taken out of the ignition; this prevents having to insert the key again when leaving the car if you forget to raise the windows first.

Some cars have an automatic setting where, if you press the switch and release it quickly, the window goes all the way up or down. However, these can cause injury if something (such as a child's hand or a dog's paw) gets in the way, so they should have a mechanism that stops them closing and reverses the movement if they encounter an obstruction.

1 Electric window

2 Child's hand at risk of being trapped

TIP

If electric windows start moving more slowly than normal, or seem to drag, check that nothing is obstructing them, such as a torn seal. If they seem to be clear, try lubricating the runners with penetrating oil. If this does not solve the problem, the cable could have stretched or the mechanism could be damaged, and you will need to seek expert advice.

Window failure

If the windows fail to work at all, check the fuse (*see pages 208–209*). If the fuse is OK or the windows jam completely, there could be a problem with the operating mechanisms or cables, or the motors or circuitry. In this situation, you will need to seek professional advice.

Mirrors

- Mirrors play an extremely important role in safe driving, so make sure they are kept clean and are adjusted correctly. Some cars have heated side mirrors to keep them clear of ice during the winter months.
- The rear-view mirror is often stuck to the centre of the windscreen rather than being mounted more securely on the roof. Mirrors mounted on the windscreen can be knocked off or can simply fall off after a while, when the glue ages. Kits are available from car accessory shops to remount the mirror. When remounting, mark its position on the windscreen with tape.
- Clean the area on the windscreen where the mirror is to stick with methylated spirits. Follow the manufacturer's instructions. The windscreen also needs to be warm. If you have real difficulty or the mirror drops off again after a few days, try asking a windscreen specialist.

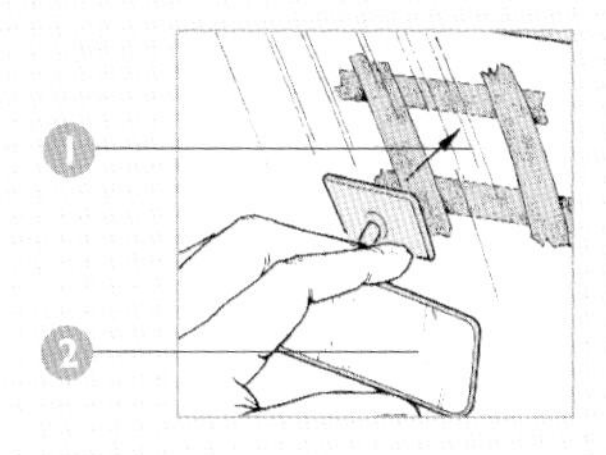

❶ Position marked with tape ❷ Rear-view mirror

Replacing a side mirror

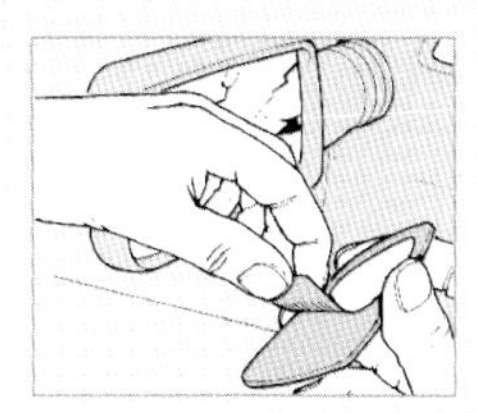

Side mirrors can easily be knocked by a passing car, particularly in urban areas where motorists are forced to drive down roads lined with parked cars. Replacing the actual mirror part is relatively easy.

Car accessory shops sell replacement mirrors, but if you cannot find one to fit your car you may have to buy one from a dealer for your model of car, which will probably be more expensive.

Be careful when extracting the remains of the old mirror: follow the instructions for fitting the new one. The mirror may simply clip into place or be held by an adhesive backing. If it is adhesive, remove all traces of the old glue with methylated spirits. If the mirror is heated, be careful not to damage the printed circuit.

Windscreen wipers

Windscreen wipers are extremely important, but often neglected, parts of the car. A damaged wiper blade can leave the windscreen smeary and difficult to see through in bad weather, but replacing the blades and wiper arms are relatively simple jobs.

Automatic wipers

The wipers are driven by an electric motor and normally operate at several speeds. Some cars have an automatic wiper function. A rain sensor located at the top of the windscreen, in the centre, feeds information about the amount of rain hitting the windscreen to an ECU, which adjusts the speed of the wipers accordingly.

TIP

If the wipers will not operate when switched on, check the fuse (*see pages 208–209*). If the fuse is OK, there is probably a fault in the motor, and you will need to seek expert help.

Legal concerns

It is illegal in most countries to travel with a windscreen that cannot be kept clean by the wipers to ensure good visibility in poor weather conditions.

Wiper blades

- The wiper blades are made of rubber. They are kept in contact with the windscreen by spring-loaded wiper arms, which are flexible enough to allow them to follow the curved shape of the glass.
- Check the wiper blades once a week. If they are damaged or torn, they will not clean the windscreen properly, but will leave smears, reducing visibility and making driving potentially dangerous. In addition, they could scratch the windscreen.
- If the windscreen is smeary, and cleaning or replacing the wiper blades does not solve the problem, take the car to a garage. The wiper angle may need adjusting.
- Don't get polish or oil-based substances on the windscreen; they will cause smearing.

Screenwash

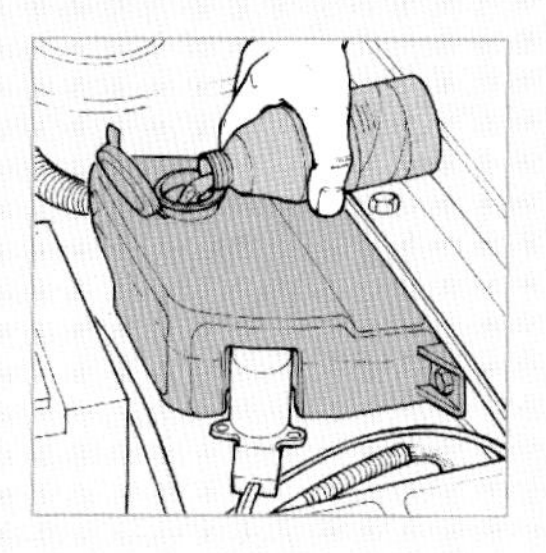

The screenwash is kept in a reservoir under the bonnet. Check in your car handbook if you are not sure of its location. Always keep this topped up, and check it is full before long journeys, particularly in winter. A small electric pump feeds screenwash through narrow tubes to jets in front of the windscreen. Some cars have a jet fitted to the rear window as well. It is a legal requirement in most countries to make sure the reservoir contains sufficient screenwash and that it can be sprayed on to the windscreen effectively when needed.

Plain water can be used for screenwash, but a concentrated screenwash additive can be bought at car accessory shops, which will help reduce smearing and prevent the water from freezing in winter. Add according to the manufacturer's instructions. Never use antifreeze in the screenwash reservoir.

Clear the jets

Keep the jets clear by gently inserting a pin in them, or clean them with an old toothbrush. If they are not aimed correctly at the windscreen, the pin can also be used to redirect the jets by pulling them around, although some are adjusted with a screw.

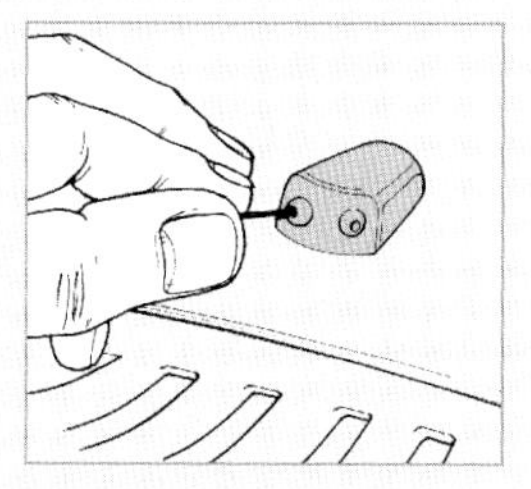

In winter, don't use the wipers to try to clear ice from the windscreen; scrape it off or spray on de-icer. If the wipers are iced up and won't move when they are switched on, don't persist. Switch them off immediately or the motor could burn out. Use a de-icing spray, but not hot water, as this could crack the windscreen.

TIP

Don't use the wipers on a dry windscreen as it could cause scratching on the glass.

Renewing wiper blades

Check the blades regularly once a week. If they are torn or damaged, they will not clean the windscreen properly, so make cleaning the blades part of your normal car wash routine. Clean them with a rag dipped in concentrated screenwash if they are very dirty.

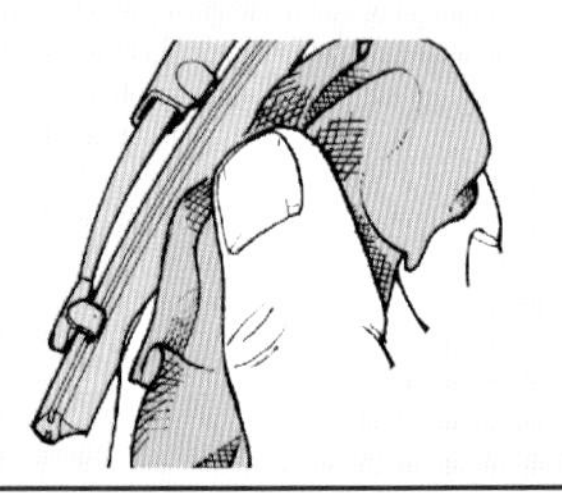

Dirt dragged across the glass by wipers could scratch it. The blades also harden with age, reducing their ability to make good contact with the glass, so replace them once a year.

When you buy new wiper blades, you need to know the year, make and model of your car. Many come with adaptors to fit a range of cars.

Always replace both blades at the same time. It is best to replace the whole blade unit, including its metal support, not just the blade itself, as the whole unit becomes worn over time.

Fitting new blades

❶ Replacing the blades one at a time will allow you to use one blade as a guide for fitting the other. Follow the manufacturer's installation instructions.

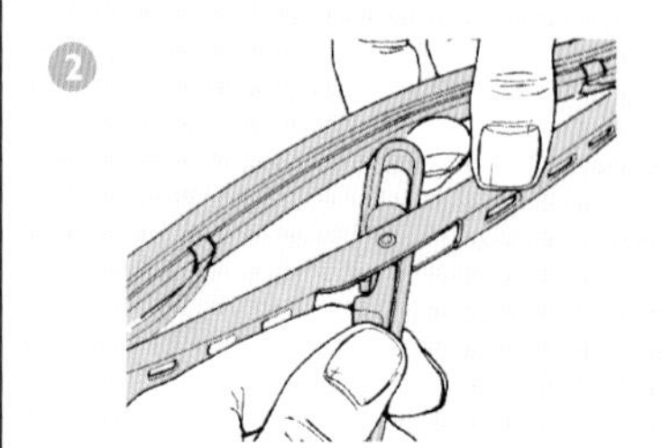

❷ Pick up the wiper arm and turn the blade back on itself.

you will need

→ wiper blades of the correct type

❸ The way the blades are attached to the arms varies from car to car [refer to your handbook]. There may be a pin, clip or hook that must be released or pushed off.

❹ Remove the old blade and fit the new one, making sure it is the right way round.

❺ Make sure it clicks firmly into place. Replace the blade in its normal position.

Renewing wiper arms

1 Switch the ignition off. Make sure the wipers are in the 'rest' position at the bottom of the windscreen.

2 Pay attention to how you remove the wiper arm so that you know how to fit the new one. Remove them one at a time, using the other as a positioning guide.

you will need

- → cloth
- → spanner
- → wiper arms of the correct type
- → coin to prise off cover

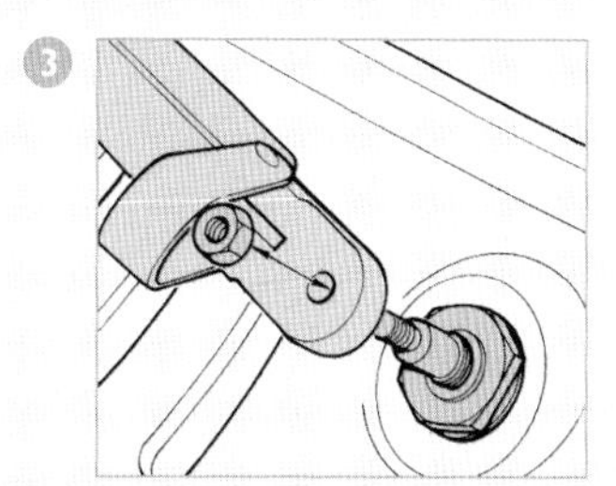

3 There are normally two types of fitting over a splined (grooved) shaft. One type has a central retaining screw concealed by a cover that flips up. Undo the screw and pull the arm from the shaft. (It may be a bit tight.)

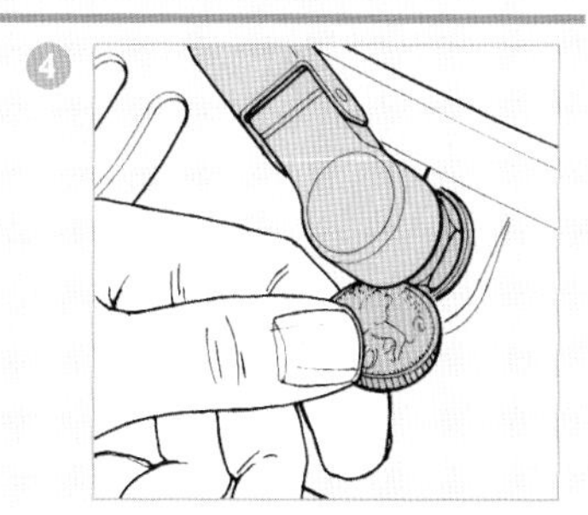

4 The other type has a push-on fitting with no screw and a flip-up cover. Prise off the arm with a coin or screwdriver. It may be stiff and need a little wiggling. If there is a nut beneath the cover, undo it with a spanner.

5 Wipe the shaft with a cloth and push the new arm on to the spindle firmly, making sure it is in the same position as the other arm. Fit the screw or nut, if there is one.

6 Squirt some water on the windscreen and switch the wipers on briefly to check that they are working.

When to replace

Wiper arms normally only need to be renewed when they are damaged or the loading springs have become weak, preventing them from working efficiently. When you buy new wiper arms, you need to know the year, make and model of your car.

Lights

It is important to see and be seen, so always make sure your lights are in good working order by checking them regularly. Keep the lens covers clean, as dirt can reduce the strength of a light considerably. Some headlights are cleaned by small electric washers and wipers.

Check lights regularly

Check all exterior lights once a week and before long journeys. It is a legal requirement to drive with all lights in working order (even in the daylight); it is potentially dangerous to drive with a failed light. You can check the head, side, direction indicator and rear lights by switching them on and walking around the car, but the brake lights only work when the brake pedal is depressed, so you'll need a friend to help you. You can check the reversing lights on your own by switching the ignition on (but not the engine), engaging reverse gear and walking around the car. To check brake lights alone, park the rear of the car close to a wall; you should be able to see the brake lights reflecting on the wall.

TIP

It's a good idea to carry spare bulbs in the car at all times; in some countries, this is compulsory.

Headlamp

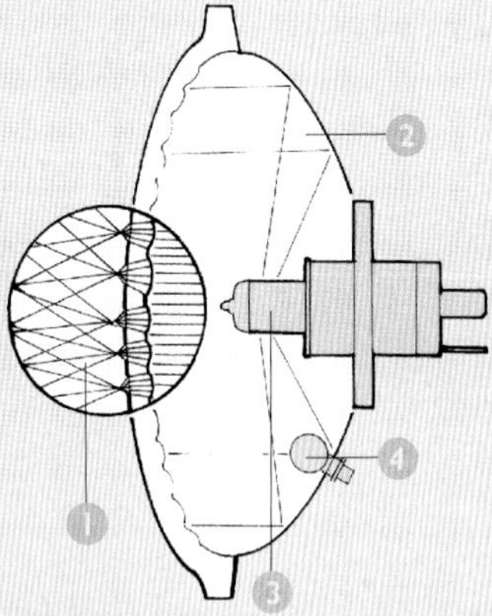

1. Light is thrown forward through prisms
2. Reflector
3. Halogen bulb
4. Sidelight

A reflective shell behind the bulb projects the light forward and through prisms cut into the lens covering the light, creating a distinct beam.

Halogen bulb

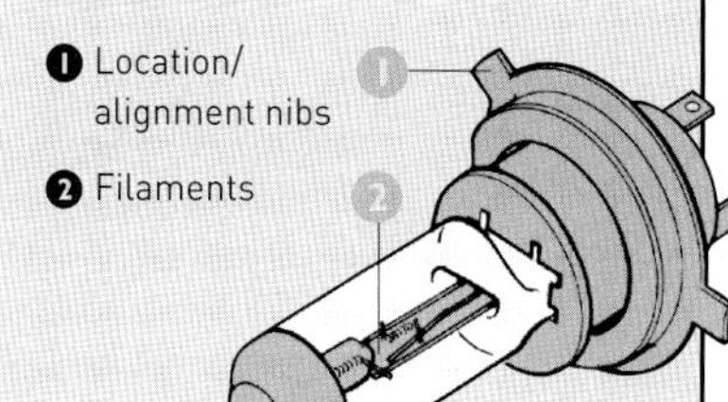

Halogen bulbs produce a brighter, more powerful light than conventional bulbs. Instead of glass, the outer envelope is made from quartz, and it is filled with halogen gas. They have a black cap on the end of the envelope.

Blue headlights

Some cars are now being fitted with blue headlights. These are normally of the H.I.D. (high-intensity discharge) sort, commonly known as xenon lights, after the xenon gas that fills the bulbs. Although they are more powerful than halogen lights, they consume less energy.

Xenon bulbs cannot be fitted to all car headlights; check with your dealer or car accessory retailer if you want to use them in your car. They will be able to tell you if this is possible. Alternatively, this may be covered in your car handbook.

Care of halogen

- All bulbs used to be made of tungsten, which has a tendency to blacken with age, causing the light to become dim. Replace a tungsten bulb before it fails, when you see it starting to blacken.
- Modern headlight bulbs are of the halogen type. They are brighter than tungsten bulbs, producing more light for the same amount of current, and they don't become dim with age, but they get hotter than tungsten bulbs.
- Always hold a halogen bulb by the base; don't touch the quartz envelope with your fingers, only with a soft cloth, otherwise the oil from your skin will cause the bulb to 'blow' when it gets hot. If you do touch the glass accidentally, clean it with a bit of cloth dipped in methylated spirit. Halogen bulbs are filled with a gas and can burst even if just scratched.
- Don't be tempted to fit a bulb with a higher wattage than recommended. The bulb could get too hot for the reflector or the wiring and melt them.
- The lens is the clear, white, red or amber-coloured plastic or glass cover that protects the light. If you break a lens, tape it up until you can have it repaired or replaced. It is important not to let water into the light unit.

Headlights

The headlights have two settings: full beam, when the maximum amount of light is thrown on to the road ahead of the car; and dipped beam, when the light is deflected downwards and to the side, away from oncoming traffic.

Some cars have two headlights on each side of the car (four in total) – one producing a full beam and the other a dipped beam. In cars with just one headlight on each side, the bulbs contain two filaments – one producing a full beam and the other a dipped beam.

Modern headlights are pre-focused – a slot cut into the metal mounting of the bulb ensures that it can only be fitted in one position so that the filaments are correctly positioned for the reflector.

Most headlight bulbs are now of the halogen type (marked on the base with the letter 'H').

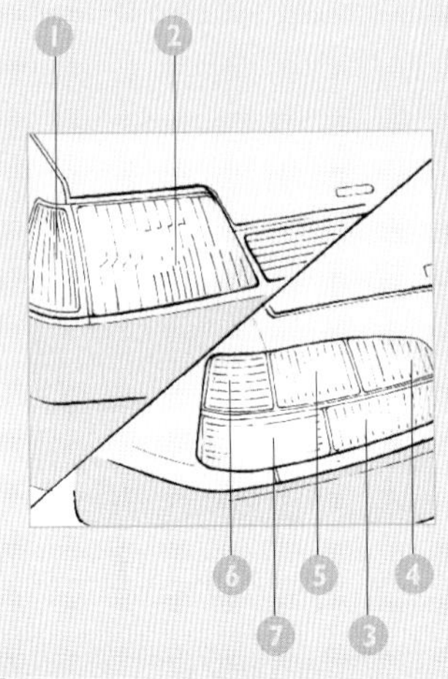

1. Direction indicator
2. Headlight and sidelight
3. Brake light
4. Reversing light
5. Reflector
6. Direction indicator
7. Rear light

Reversing lights

These come on automatically when reverse gear is selected. They are set behind clear lenses, usually incorporated in the rear lights, and allow you to see where you are going in the dark.

Sidelights

These may be separate from the headlights, but are sometimes incorporated in the same units as the headlights. Never rely on them alone in misty or foggy conditions.

Rear lights

These are often part of clusters that include the direction indicators behind amber lenses, reversing lights behind clear lenses and combined brake/rear lights behind red lenses. The brake/rear light is often a single bulb with two filaments; one for the brake light and the other for the rear light. Special pins in the base ensure that the bulb is fitted the correct way round.

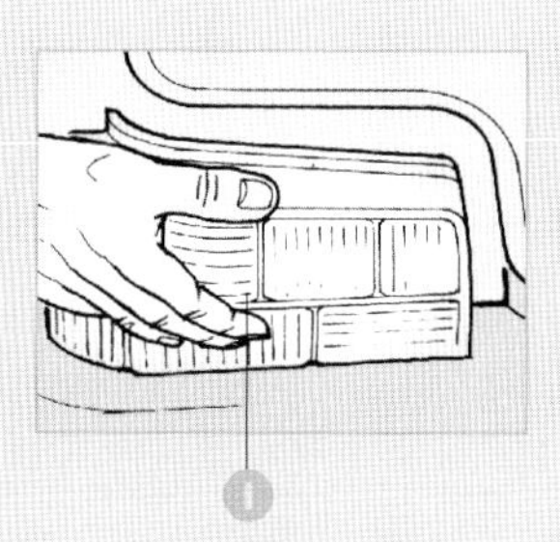

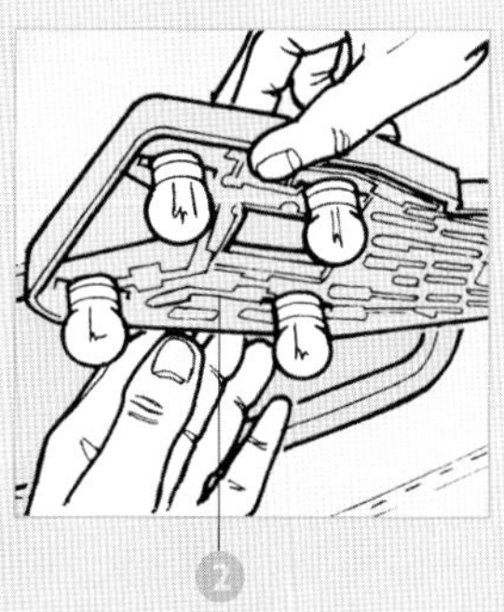

❶ Whole unit is removed

❷ Bulb holder

Number plate light

The side, rear and number plate lights (and also the instrument panel light) are operated by the same switch. They are usually connected to a separate electrical circuit from the other lights so that they can be left on when the car is parked.

Direction indicators

The direction indicators may be clear bulbs behind amber lenses, or amber bulbs behind white or clear lenses. The bulbs always have single filaments. Side repeaters have clear bulbs/amber lenses or amber bulbs/white lenses, and are fitted to the sides of the car, flashing along with the direction indicators.

The flasher unit

This is a small electrical unit that is usually situated behind or under the dashboard, sometimes in the fuse box. It controls the operation of the direction indicator lights. Many cars have a separate flasher unit for the hazard lights.

Problems with lights

Positioned on the corners of your car, the lights are vulnerable to physical damage as well as suffering from water leakage, poor electrical connections and bulb failure.

A failed light

If a light fails to work, check the bulb first and replace it if it appears to have blown. You will probably have to remove the bulb to check it. Is it blackened or has the filament broken? If so, fit a new bulb (*see pages 76–77*).

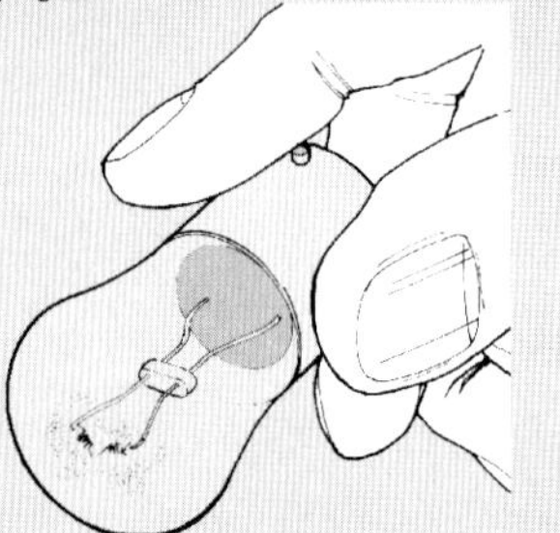

Seek expert help

If you cannot identify the problem, you will need to seek advice from a garage; there is probably a fault in the wiring or switch.

Checking lights

- If the bulb is OK, check the fuse (*see pages 208–209*). If the fuse is OK, check for a bad electrical connection. Look for a loose connection by waggling the connectors in their sockets, and check for corrosion (whitish deposits) around the connectors.
- Make sure that the bulb is making good electrical contact inside the bulb holder. Remove it and look at the base – if corrosion is present, clean it off with fine abrasive paper or a coarse cloth. If there is water inside the light unit, allow it to dry out. Condensation sometimes collects on the inside of the lens. Remove the bulb and reflector, and dry the lens.

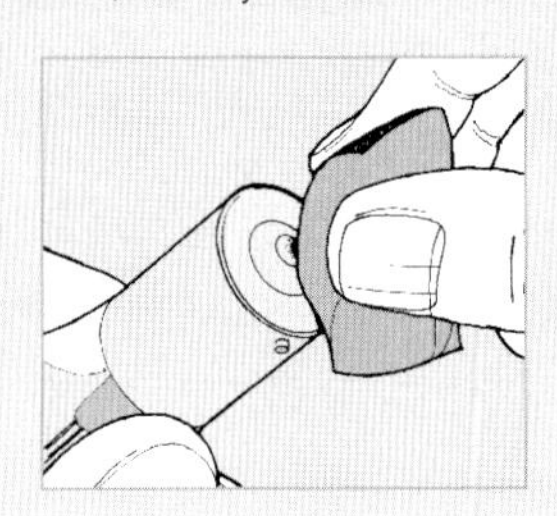

Indicators

If the direction indicator lights fail to come on, check the bulbs and then the fuse (*see pages 208–209*). If both are OK, try replacing the flasher unit (*see page 73*), but if that does not cure the problem, the fault must be in the circuitry or switch, so you will need to seek expert help.

If the direction indicator lights come on, but don't flash, try replacing the flasher unit. If that does not work, there must be a fault in the circuitry or switch and you will need to seek expert help.

If the direction indicator lights flash faster on one side than on the other, one bulb could need replacing, or the bulb wattage could be too low. Remove the bulbs and check the wattage. Replace with higher-wattage bulbs if necessary. There could be a bad earth connection (*see page 206*) or the bulb wattage could be too high. Remove the bulbs and check the wattage. Replace with bulbs of lower wattage if necessary.

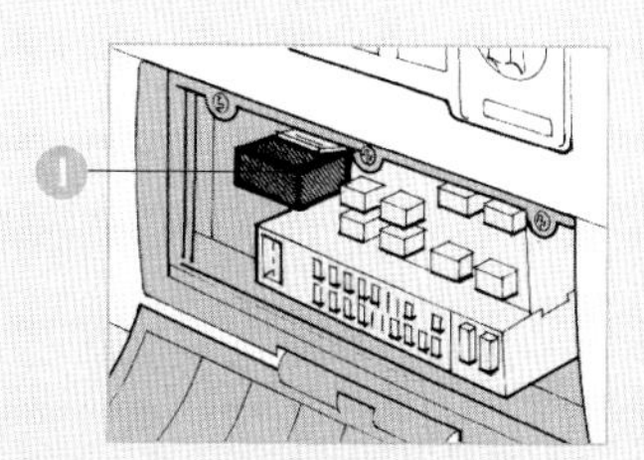

1 Flasher unit

Non-cancelling indicators

If the direction indicators don't cancel after the car has cornered and you have to cancel them manually, the indicator switch may be faulty. Seek expert advice.

Other problems

A bad earth connection can cause certain lights to come on when they should not do so. For example, the direction indicators may come on when the rear lights are switched on.

If lights are dimmer than usual, they are not receiving enough current. This could be due to a bad connection, a fault in the circuit or a low battery charge (*see* 'Recharging a battery', *pages 198–201*). You can check electrical connections by waggling the connectors in their sockets; otherwise seek expert help.

Broken lenses

If a lens breaks, it is important to stop water getting into the light unit. Tape over the break until it can be repaired. You may be able to repair the damage with glue or simply buy a new lens, but if it forms an integral part of the light assembly, you will have to buy a complete replacement unit.

Changing a headlight bulb

you will need

→ replacement bulb of the correct type
→ screwdriver (possibly)

❶ Switch off the ignition and make sure the bulb is cool to the touch. (If the headlight has just been on, wait for several minutes for it to cool down.)

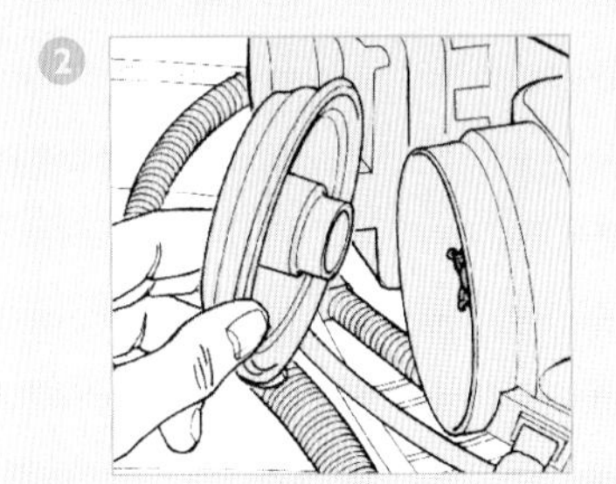

❷ Unclip or unscrew the protective cover from the rear of the headlight.

❸ Disconnect the electrical connector from the back of the light.

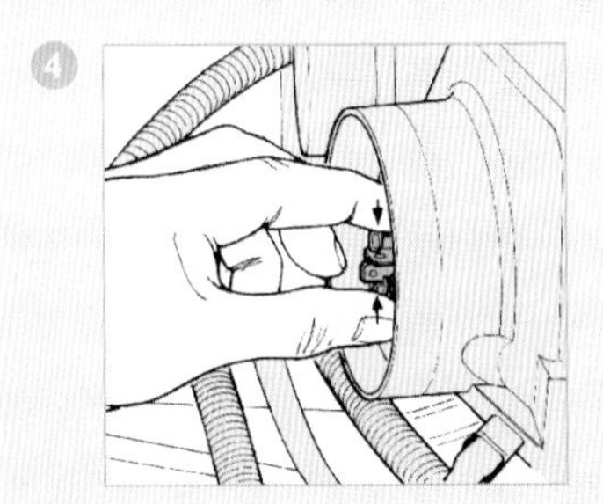

❹ There is normally a spring holding the bulb in place; press or squeeze the spring to release it and remove the bulb. The bulb may need to be rotated before it can be removed from the unit.

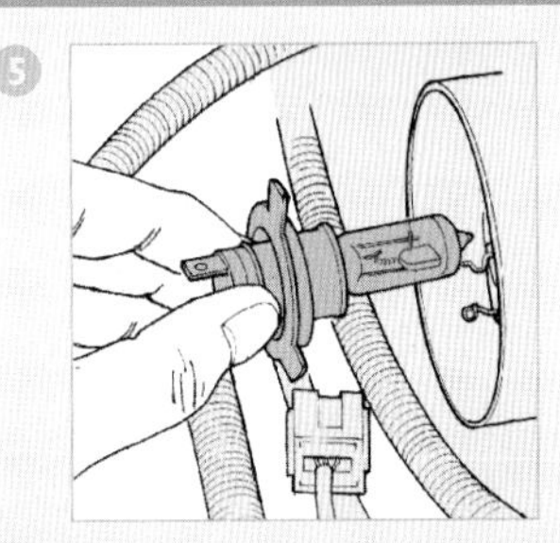

❺ Fit the new bulb (handling it by the base if it is of the halogen type). Check that any direction notches or pins are positioned correctly and that the bulb is pushed firmly in place (but be gentle).

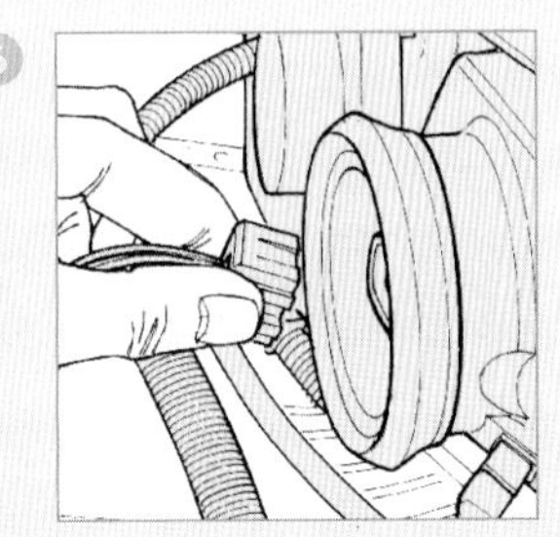

❻ Replace the spring, refit the electrical connector and put back in position the protective cover.

Use your handbook

Headlight fittings vary from car to car, so the information given here is only a guide. Refer to your car handbook for specific instructions on how to access the lights – you normally have to open the bonnet and get to the light from the rear of the unit.

Replacement bulbs

When buying a replacement bulb, make sure you know what type you need – check its wattage rating (given as 'W') and fitting (such as bayonet). The wattage is usually marked on the bulb itself or its base.

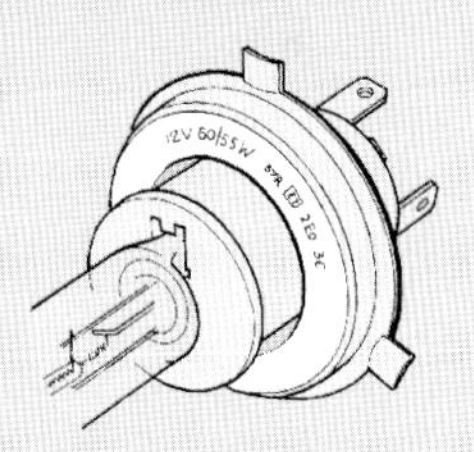

Changing other lights

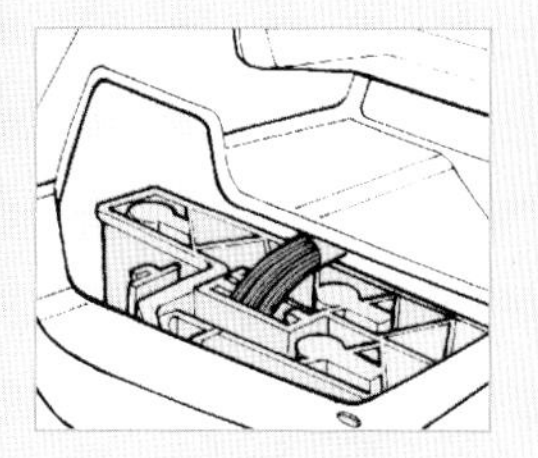

The fixings and fittings for other exterior lights vary, but the method should be similar to that used for changing the headlight bulb. Refer to your car handbook for specific instructions. The bulb may be in a bulb holder that twists out. The rear lights are normally accessed from inside the boot. Front fog lights are usually reached from the front of the light – undo the screws holding the cover in place and remove it. The bulb will probably need to be pushed in and twisted to be removed.

Sealed-beam headlights

Some old cars have sealed-beam headlights, the lens, reflector and bulb being one sealed unit. If this fails, a complete new one must be fitted. To do so, removed the chrome bezel around the unit by releasing its screw.

Then slacken the unit's retaining screws (don't confuse them with the adjustment screws) until it can be turned and pulled free. Disconnect the wiring plug. Replacement is a reversal of this procedure.

Headlight alignment

Having correctly aligned headlights is essential, not only so that you can see where you are going when driving in the dark, but also so that you do not dazzle other road users.

Essential requirement

Both headlights should be aligned at the same height horizontally. If a headlight unit is knocked or disturbed in any way, it can put the light out of alignment. Similarly, if a headlight unit is replaced (but this does not apply to just replacing the bulb), the alignment should be checked. You can use the headlight that has not been knocked or replaced as a guide, provided you are certain that its alignment is correct.

TIP

When driving a reasonable distance behind another car at night, your dipped headlights should not illuminate any part of its rear window or interior rear-view mirror. If they do, they are set too high and should be adjusted, as described opposite.

Heavy loads

A heavier than normal load in the back of the car affects headlight alignment – as the rear of the car is weighed down, the front rises and with it the headlights. Some cars have a dashboard control that allows the alignment to be adjusted to take into account different car loads, but this cannot adjust headlights individually and only alters the horizontal level of the beam.

1. Excess weight in boot forces rear of car down
2. Front rises making headlamp beam too high

Checking alignment

❶ Check that the load in the car is normal and that the tyres are inflated to their correct pressure.

❷ On level ground, position the car close to a flat wall. With the headlights off, mark the position of the centre of each light on the wall with a large cross.

❸ Reverse the car straight back until it is about 10m (32ft) from the wall.

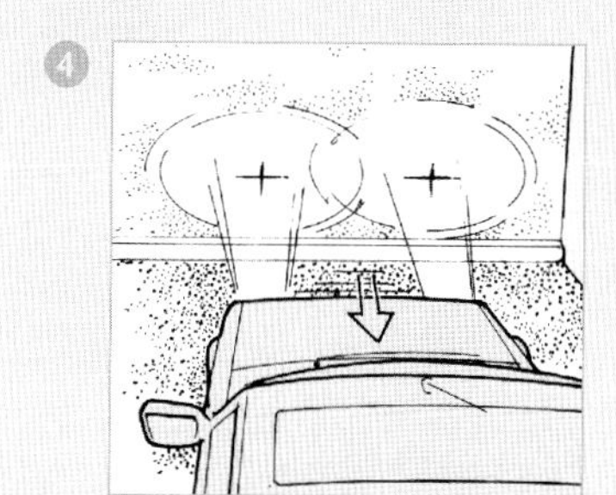

❹ Switch on the headlights at full beam. The centre of each light beam should fall slightly below the horizontal line of the cross, but it should be centred on the vertical line.

❶ Incorrect (too high)

❷ Correct

❺ If one of the lights does not align correctly, check that the light unit is correctly seated. If it is, locate the adjusting screws on the rear of the headlight fitting – the upper screw moves the beam up and down, while the side screw moves it from left to right – and adjust the light beam until it is in the correct position.

WHEELS, BRAKES AND STEERING

Wheels and tyres

The wheels of a car are fixed to the hubs by fixing bolts or nuts, sometimes concealed by a hub cap. Make sure that the bolts or nuts are securely tightened, as having a wheel come loose mid-journey would be disastrous. Also check that hub caps are securely clipped on.

Steel wheels

Steel wheels are cheap and strong, and are usually designed to look decorative, with a hub cap displaying a logo or a motif.

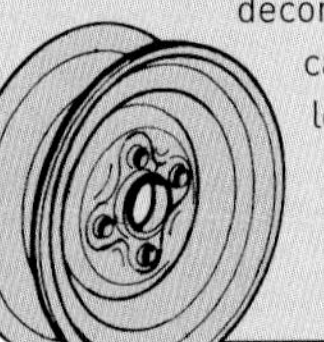

Wire-spoke wheels

There are very few cars with wire-spoke wheels on the roads these days. The spokes are positioned between the rim and the hub in an arrangement designed to take the weight of the car and distribute the forces created during acceleration and braking evenly. Rim-tape is fitted to stop the inner tube chafing on the spoke ends.

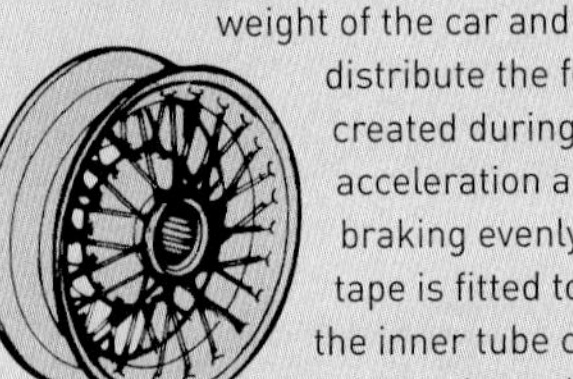

Alloy wheels

Aluminium-alloy wheels are very common now and are found on a wide variety of vehicles. They are more decorative than steel wheels, and are often fitted as replacements for steel wheels to enhance the look of a vehicle.

A disadvantage of alloy wheels is that they are more likely to be stolen, so fit wheel locking nuts if you have them, to help prevent theft. Make sure you keep the adaptor handy in case you have to change a wheel in an emergency.

WARNING

If a wheel becomes dented or damaged, often from hitting the kerb, it may cause tyre deflation or run out of balance, leading to handling problems. Seek advice from a garage.

Wheel dimensions

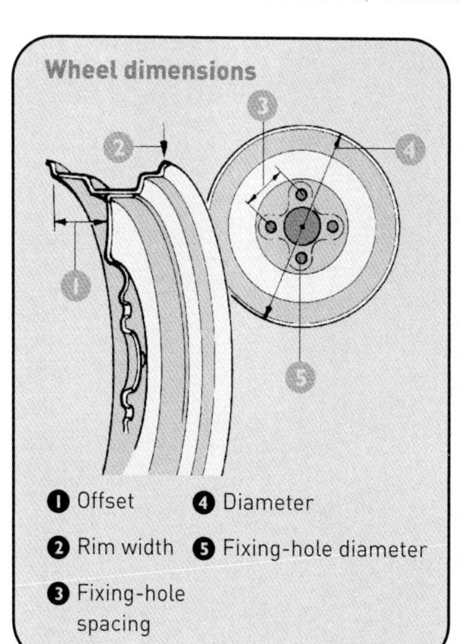

1. Offset
2. Rim width
3. Fixing-hole spacing
4. Diameter
5. Fixing-hole diameter

Fit the correct type of wheel

As wheels are a very visible part of the car, people often like to change them to improve the look of the car or to make it a little more individual. Many different sizes and styles of wheel are available. However, you should only fit wheels that are designed for your car, otherwise the safety of the vehicle could be compromised. If you are thinking of fitting different wheels to your car, consult an expert supplier or your dealer first.

Wheel dimensions

The following aspects of a wheel are important and need taking into account if a new wheel is to be fitted:

Diameter: the measurement across the wheel, which corresponds to the diameter of tyre that can be fitted to the wheel.

Width: the measurement across the rim of the wheel, which indicates what width of tyre is suitable.

Offset: refers to the distance between the back face of the wheel centre and the back edge of the wheel rim. This is critical both to prevent the tyre or wheel from fouling the suspension or structure of the vehicle, and to ensure that excessive stress is not placed on the suspension components.

Fixing-hole diameter: refers to the size of the holes for the wheel studs or bolts. If these are too small, the wheel cannot be fitted, and if they are too large, the wheel may work loose and fall off.

Fixing-hole spacing: the distance between the fixing holes, which must match studs or bolts on the vehicle.

Tyre construction

The principal component of a tyre is rubber, but beneath the exterior lies the casing, formed by layers of nylon and rayon, with steel wire forming a ring around the centre of the tyre where it fits on to the wheel.

Typical tyre markings

165 SR 14

165 – inflated width of the tyre in mm.

14 – wheel diameter in inches.

S – speed rating code letter; refers to the safe running speed of the tyre.

R – radial-ply construction.

185/65 R14T

185 – inflated width of the tyre in mm.

65 – aspect ratio; refers to the inflated height of the tyre on the wheel rim compared to its inflated width.The aspect ratio of a conventional radial tyre is 85, meaning the inflated height is 85% of the inflated width. Anything less than this is referred to as a low-profile tyre.

R – radial-ply construction.

The 'S' rating is for normal-use tyres; only very high-performance vehicles need tyres with a higher rating.

Tyre size and speed rating

Tyres are available in various sizes, and must be suited to both the car and the wheel to which they are fitted. They are marked with their size and speed rating.

Tyre speed rating	km/h	mph
N	140	87
P	150	93
Q	160	99
R	170	106
S	180	112
T	190	118
U	200	124
V	240	149
H	210	130
V	Over 210	Over 130
Z	Over 240	Over 149

The maximum speed of a tyre fitted should be equal to, or greater than, the car's maximum speed, as the speed rating takes into account the acceleration and braking capabilities of the vehicle.

Tubed or tubeless

Most tyres today are of the tubeless, radial-ply type. Tubeless means that they do not have a separate inner tube to contain the air, as was the case with older types of tyre. Instead, the inside of the tyre casing is specially treated to make it airtight.

Run-flat tyres

New technology has enabled manufacturers to produce a tyre that can be driven for up to 80km (50 miles) at 50 mph when completely flat. This allows the car to be driven to a garage or place where the wheel can be changed safely.

Radial-ply tyres

Radial-ply refers to how the tyre is made. This type of tyre has almost totally eclipsed the old type of cross-ply tyre, as it gives much better roadholding, longer life, and a more controlled and comfortable ride.

Although the situation is unlikely to arise, it must be remembered that to mix radial and cross-ply tyres is unsafe and must never be done, even as a temporary measure, as both types handle differently, and the car would be unstable and unsafe to drive. It would also be illegal.

1. Radial-ply tyre
2. Casing layers parallel to each other

3. Cross-ply tyre
4. Casing layers at 30° to each other

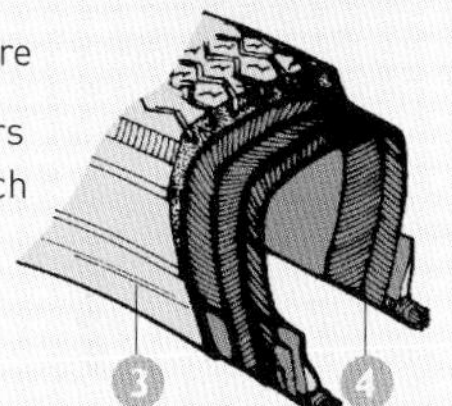

Buying new tyres

It is false economy to buy second-hand tyres and could be dangerous as their true condition is unknown.

Tyre prices vary, but generally speaking, the more expensive the tyre, the better it will perform and the longer it will last.

TIP

When fitting new tyres, it is always advisable to fit them in axle pairs (both front or both back), and to ensure that they are of the same size, specification and tread pattern. This will ensure that the car remains in balance and safe to drive.

TIP

Tyres can deteriorate with age or if they are not stored correctly (discolouring, cracking in the sidewall). The week and year of manufacture are marked on the side of the tyre – 2104 indicates that they were made in the 21st week of 2004. Ideally, don't buy any tyres that are older than nine months.

Remoulds and retreads

While remould and retread tyres are available, it must be remembered that these are old tyres that have been remanufactured with new external rubber – the casings have probably done many thousands of miles!

It is always advisable to buy quality brand-new tyres that will give long and reliable service. This cannot be guaranteed with remoulds and retreads. It is also unwise to mix brand-new and remould or retread tyres, as they do not give the same level of roadholding and performance, and could prove dangerous.

Tyre valves

This is the rubber device that protrudes from the wheel rim and through which the tyre is inflated. Inside the rubber tube is a one-way valve that allows air into the tyre, but will only let air out if the centre of the valve is depressed or the valve is faulty. A faulty valve can be unscrewed from its tube with a special tool and replaced with a new one.

A valve cap should always be fitted to keep dirt from entering the valve and possibly causing leakage.

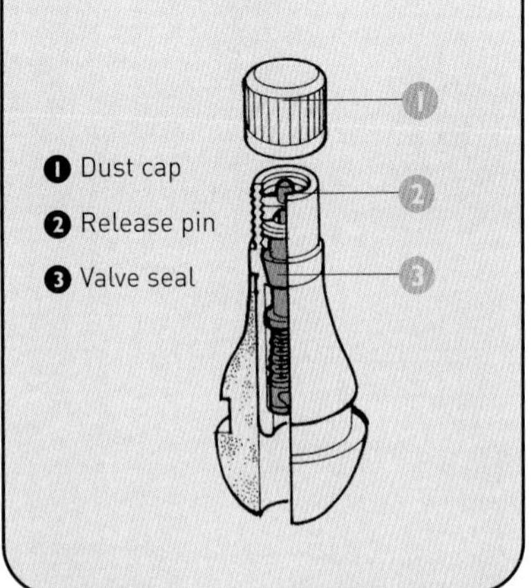

1. Dust cap
2. Release pin
3. Valve seal

Wide wheels and tyres

Some people fit extra-wide wheels and tyres or larger-diameter wheels with ultra-low-profile tyres to their cars. If you are considering doing this, take advice from a specialist supplier first. Large wheels and tyres could foul the bodywork or suspension, and even cause the latter to fail.

Tyre pressure

Refer to your car handbook to find the recommended pressures for the tyres on your car. Higher pressures are normally quoted for increased loads (the number of occupants of the car and the weight of goods carried) and high speeds. Select the right pressures for your use of the vehicle.

WARNING

- Incorrectly inflated tyres can make the car difficult and dangerous to handle, particularly affecting steering and braking. If tyre pressures are too low, they can also cause tyres to overheat, possibly resulting in a blow-out, which is extremely dangerous.
- If tyre pressures are too low, your car will use more fuel due to the extra frictional resistance of the tyres on the road – more power is needed to drive the car, so the engine uses more fuel.
- The tyres will last longer when kept at the correct pressure – over-inflated tyres will wear abnormally in the centre of the tread; under-inflated tyres will wear along the edges of the tread.

Checking tyres

Tyre pressures should always be checked and, if necessary, adjusted when the tyres are cold. Never check and adjust pressures when the car has travelled several miles, as the tyres will be hot, the air inside will have expanded and the pressures will have increased. If the pressures are then adjusted to manufacturer's recommendations, they will be low when the tyres are cold. This could cause severe handling problems and serious damage to the tyres.

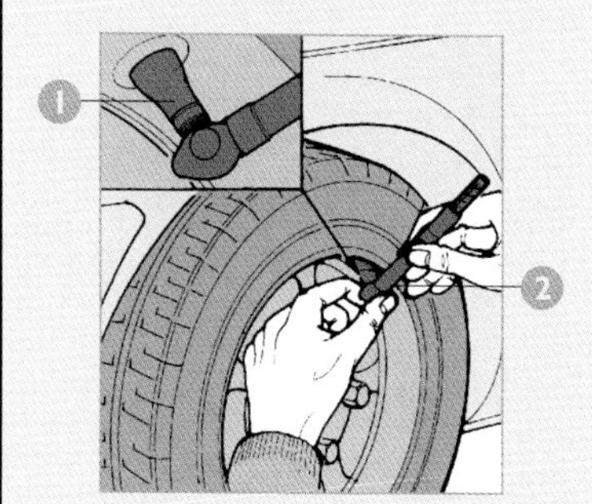

❶ Valve ❷ Pressure gauge

It is best to check and adjust tyre pressures at a garage or petrol station, where the pressure gauge will read accurately and there is a ready supply of compressed air. Checking and adjusting pressures at home involves using a foot pump and pressure gauge that may not be so accurate.

Tyre inflators

Garage tyre inflators normally have an operating lever and a dial to show the air pressure. Some will remove air as well.

1. Pressure gauge
2. Depress half-way to deflate
3. Depress fully to inflate

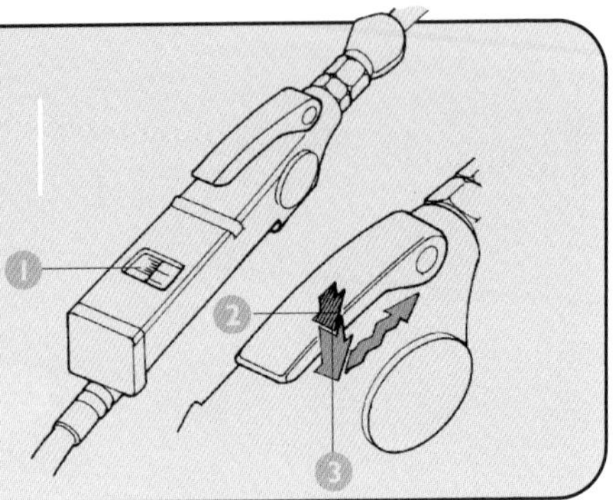

Using an air-line

1. Park the vehicle close to the air-line, with the handbrake on and the engine off.

2. Remove the valve cap and connect the air-line to the valve by pushing the connector carefully but firmly on to the end of the valve.

3. Some air-lines have a means of pre-setting the required pressure; if this is the case, set the pressure on the machine and press the start button. The machine will stop automatically when the correct pressure has been achieved in the tyre.

4. If the air-line is not of the pre-set pressure type, the control handle will have a lever to let air into or out of the tyre, together with a pressure gauge showing the exact pressure in the tyre. To let air into the tyre, press the lever down fully. To let air out of the tyre, press the lever half-way down. Keep releasing the lever to check the pressure, as the gauge will not work when air is being let in or out of the tyre.

5. When the correct pressure has been set, disconnect the air-line from the tyre valve and replace the valve cap.

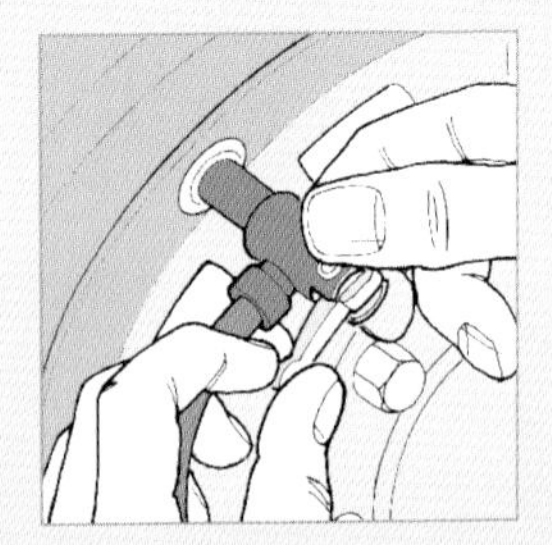

Repeat the procedure for each road wheel – and the spare!

Using a foot pump and pressure gauge

❶ Park the vehicle with handbrake on and engine off.

❷ **If the foot pump has a pressure gauge:** remove the valve cap and connect the foot pump hose to the valve, placing the connector carefully over the valve and pressing down firmly – there should be a small lever on the top of the connector that should be pushed down to lock it on to the valve. If it has been correctly fitted, you should not be able to hear any air escaping, other than a short, sharp hiss when you fit the connector. The tyre pressure will now be shown and air can be pumped in as necessary.

❸ **If the foot pump has no pressure gauge:** use a tyre pressure gauge to check the pressure in the tyre. Position the nozzle of the gauge squarely over the valve and press down firmly to get a reading. You should not be able to hear air escaping, just a short, sharp hiss as you fit the gauge. If air is required, connect the foot pump to the valve to increase the pressure.

❹ If too much pressure is in the tyre, disconnect the foot pump and push in the centre of the valve to release air (*see diagram page 86*).

❺ Recheck the pressure and readjust it until correct.

Using an electric-type pump

Follow the instructions above, but at (2), plug the pump into the cigar lighter socket. In some cars, the ignition key must be turned to the auxiliary position before any power becomes available. Switch the pump on to add air to the tyre and switch it off when the correct pressure is reached.

Looking after tyres

A little time spent checking your tyres regularly will pay off – tyres that are well looked after will give many thousands of miles of trouble-free motoring. Check their condition on a monthly basis and always before setting off on a long journey.

Condition matters

Tyres in good condition and inflated to the correct pressures will help to ensure that the vehicle handles, steers and brakes safely.

Badly worn or incorrectly inflated tyres will make the vehicle difficult and dangerous to drive.

Tyre rotation

It used to be recommended that tyres, including the spare, be moved around the vehicle periodically. This was intended to even out wear so that all the tyres could be replaced together.

This is no longer recommended. Indeed, it was never really necessary and usually only meant that you ended up buying four or five new tyres at the same time. By leaving them in one position, you will probably only end up buying two at a time.

Space-saver tyres

These are often used for spare wheels where storage space is limited. They are much narrower than the standard tyre and take up less storage room. However, they can only be used for limited distances in an emergency and not exceeding certain speeds. Check in your car handbook for the limitations of use and do not exceed them, as it could be dangerous and illegal. The limitations may also be marked on the space-saver tyre. They are often inflated at a different pressure to the other tyres on the vehicle (refer to your car handbook).

Checking tread depth

The depth of the tread pattern on the tyre will affect the tyre's ability both to grip the road surface and to remove surface water from its contact patch – the part of the tyre that actually touches the road surface. The driven wheels normally wear the most quickly.

Most tyre tread patterns are about 10mm (3/8in) deep when new and are safe to use until they wear down to about 2mm (1/8in) deep, although the legal minimum in some countries is slightly lower than this. The depth of tread can be measured with a special tool.

Some tyres are fitted with built-in wear indicators at regular intervals around the tyre. The tyres must be changed when they become visible.

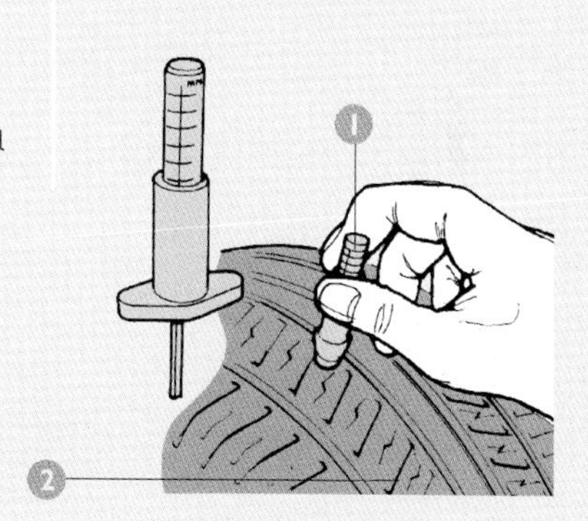

1. Tool for measuring tread depth
2. Tread pattern

Spare wheels

It is always advisable to carry a spare wheel, jack and wheel-brace (see page 96 for location). It is also essential that the spare wheel and tyre are in a safe and serviceable condition. Always check the pressure of the spare tyre whenever you check the other tyres on the vehicle.

TIP

If your spare tyre is carried beneath the boot floor, position it so that the valve points upwards and is nearest the back of the car, so that you can reach it easily for checking the tyre pressure. If the spare is mounted beneath the car, make sure the valve points down and to the back of the car for the same reason.

Checking wear

The tyres of your car provide the vital link with the road surface, so making sure they are always in tip-top condition is essential to ensure your comfort and safety when driving.

Inspecting tyres

Check for evenness of wear over the width of tread, and for any signs of nails or other sharp items having penetrated the tyre casing.

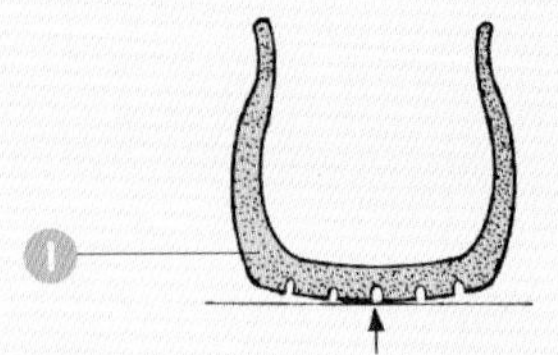

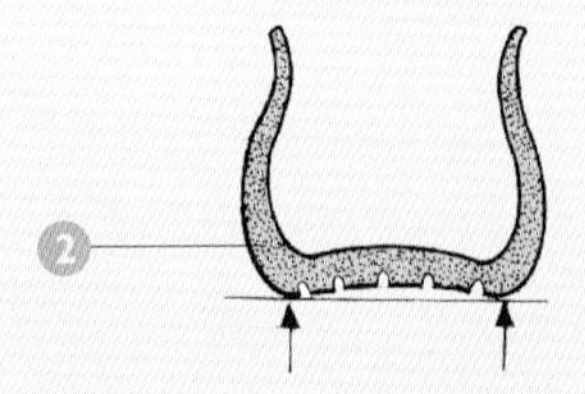

❶ Over-inflated

❷ Under-inflated

The more a tyre is inflated, the narrower will be the part of it that is in contact with the road surface.

If a tyre is over-inflated, it wears more at the centre. If it is under-inflated, it wears more at the sides.

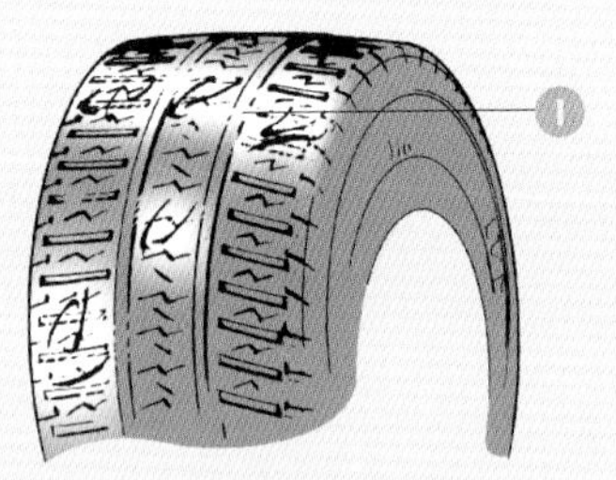

❶ Uneven/patchy wear

If the wear is uneven, such as on one side only, it could be due to incorrectly aligned steering or suspension. If the wear is in patches, it could be due to an unbalanced wheel.

If the pattern of wear is uneven in any way, always seek advice at your garage.

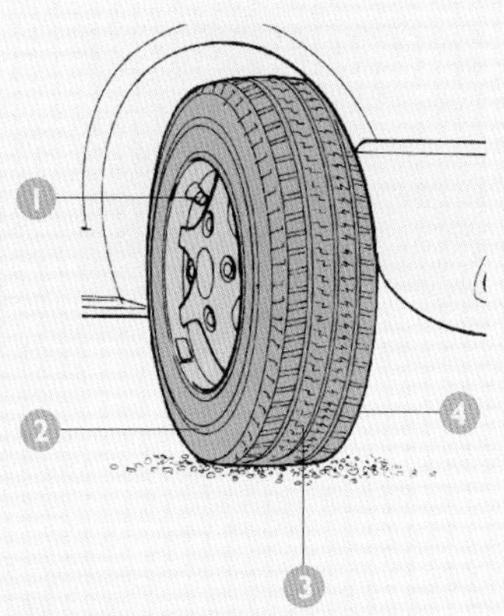

❶ Valve

❷ Side wall

❸ Tread

❹ Back of tyre

Examine the tyre walls for damage caused by hitting kerbs, potholes, etc., not forgetting the back of the tyre, and make sure the valve cap is secure. If there is any sign of damage or undue wear (cracks, nicks, bulges, etc.), take the car to a garage for advice.

Remove any stones from between the tread blocks. If you find a nail in the tyre, fit the spare and take the wheel to a tyre specialist to find out whether it can be repaired or needs replacing.

If you are in any doubt about the condition or serviceability of a tyre, seek advice from your garage.

If handling deteriorates suddenly, it may be due to one or more of the steering or suspension angles (camber, castor, toe-in, toe-out) having been altered due to hitting a kerb or pothole. This will show up as undue wear on one or more tyres.

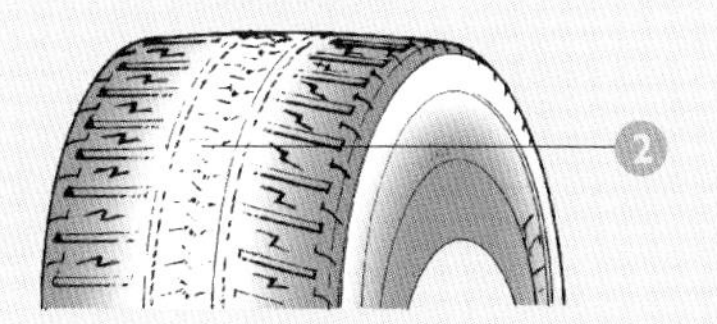

❶ Shoulder wear

❷ Centre wear

Remember the spare

When you check the condition and pressure of your car's tyres, **don't forget the spare.**

Finding that your spare tyre is unfit for use when you really need it could be disastrous.

Problems with wheels and tyres

Wheels and tyres may be slightly unbalanced as a result of the manufacturing process. Being slightly heavier in one area than another will cause the wheels to wobble at a certain speed when the car is driven. This can be cured by having the wheels balanced at a garage.

Wheel wobble

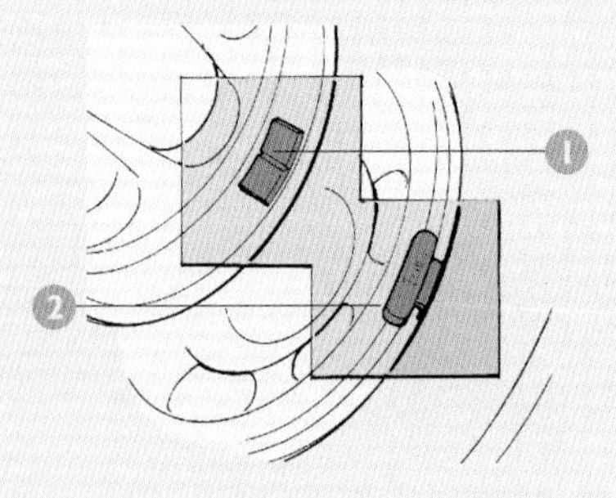

1. Stick-on weights
2. Clip-on weights

• Wheel wobble is noticeable as vibration at the steering wheel. To counterbalance any heavy areas, lead weights are fitted to the wheel rim with clips. If you think that your wheels may be unbalanced, have them checked at a garage.

• Tyre and wheel assemblies are balanced on a special machine that takes into account what are known as 'static' and 'dynamic' imbalance forces. 'Static' is when there is one heavy spot, and 'dynamic' when there are two diagonally opposite each other. Both need to be corrected, as leaving them out of balance could cause severe handling problems and excessive wear to tyres, steering and suspension components. Tyre and wheel assemblies should always be balanced when new tyres are fitted.

• Self-adhesive weights that don't require metal clips are used to balance aluminium-alloy wheels to prevent electrolytic corrosion, which is caused by dampness in the atmosphere producing a small electric current between the steel of the clip and the aluminium of the wheel. This eats away the surface of the aluminium-alloy, causing pitting.

TIP

When having alloy wheels balanced, make sure they are clean; self-adhesive weights will not stick well otherwise.

The effects of ice and water on tyres

The weather is unlikely to adversely affect the tyres themselves. Modern tyres are made to perform in the hottest and coldest temperatures normally expected. However, constant exposure to extreme temperature may reduce the tyre's life expectancy, while correct tread depth is crucial in snow and ice.

Aquaplaning

While the weather may not affect the tyres, it may well affect the way in which they perform.

Tyres rely on grip between their tread and the surface of the road. If the road is wet or icy, the amount of grip will be reduced. Provided the tyres are in good condition, with plenty of tread pattern, a wet road surface will have little effect on their performance, as the tread pattern is designed to channel water away from the grip area. If there is standing water on the road surface, however, the tyres may not be able to clear it and the car will glide over the surface of the water. This effect is known as 'aquaplaning' and is the cause of many accidents, as the car spins out of control.

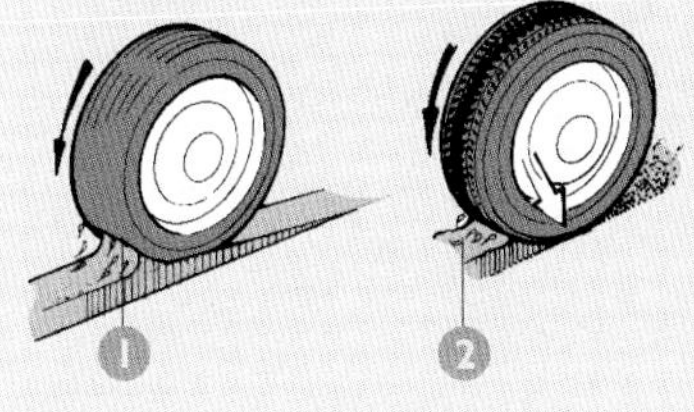

❶ Wedge of water builds up in front of tyre

❷ Tyre loses grip and glides over water

Snow and ice

When there is ice on the road, the tyres cannot generate any grip and the vehicle becomes uncontrollable. Snow is a combination of ice and water, and can be very unpredictable for driving. The best test for whether it is safe to drive on ice or snow is if you can stand up and walk on it safely and easily, you can assume that the vehicle can be driven – albeit slowly and with care.

Never be tempted to reduce the pressure in the tyres to improve grip in snow and ice. This can cause serious damage to the structure of the tyres and make the vehicle even less controllable.

Equipment for wheels

The locations of the spare wheel, wheel-brace and jack vary from car to car. They should be shown in your car handbook. The equipment itself also varies. You may prefer to buy a different wheel-brace than the one supplied with the car if it will not provide enough leverage.

Tyre sealants

Several types of sealant are available in accessory shops. Most sealants are supplied in an aerosol can. It is important to follow the manufacturer's instructions carefully and to note the limitations for subsequent use of the damaged tyre.

Tyre sealants should only be regarded as a temporary measure. After putting sealant in a tyre, speed must be restricted. Take the wheel to a specialist for advice as soon as possible. Remember to tell the specialist that sealant has been used, as it may affect the way in which the tyre is subsequently repaired.

TIP

Keep a small piece of old carpet in the car to kneel on when changing a tyre. This will prove invaluable in wet or muddy conditions.

Locating the equipment

In most cars, this is stored in the boot. It should be explained in your handbook. The jack and wheel-brace are normally stowed to one side of the boot, secured by a fixing of some kind that will have to be undone before they can be removed. The spare wheel is normally set into a recess in the floor of the boot, under the boot floor covering.

In some cars, the spare wheel is under the car beneath the boot, held in place by a wire frame.

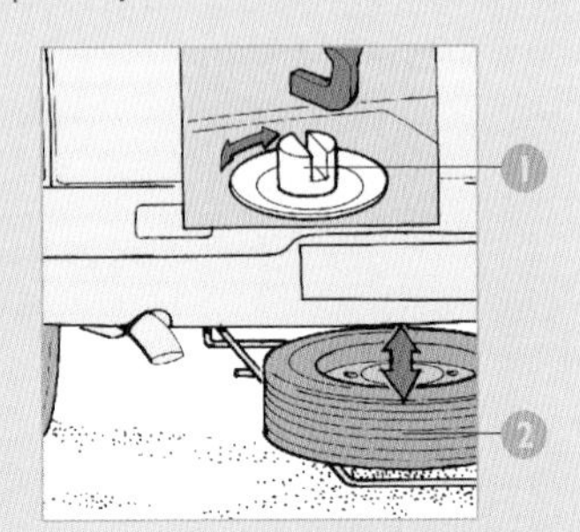

1. Spare wheel securing bolt
2. Spare tyre in frame under boot

Using the equipment

If the nuts or bolts holding the wheel on to the wheel hub have been put on at a garage, you may have a lot of trouble undoing them. To give yourself the best chance of loosening tight bolts, buy a wheel-brace with a long handle. This will ensure you apply the maximum amount of leverage to the fixing.

A wheel-brace can be extended with a length of pipe, provided you can find something that will fit. Make sure you always carry it in the car.

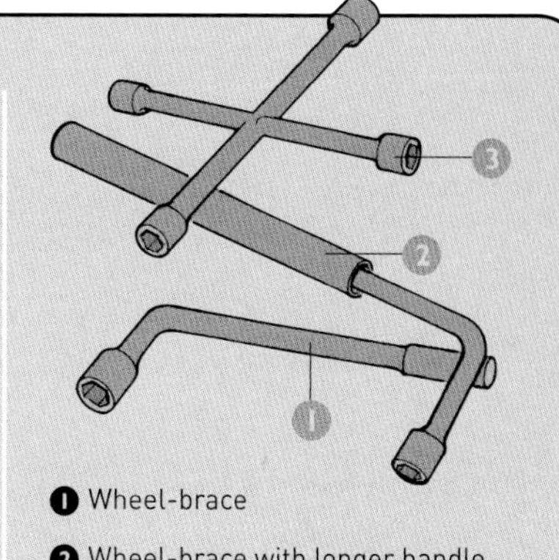

1. Wheel-brace
2. Wheel-brace with longer handle
3. Spider brace

The jack

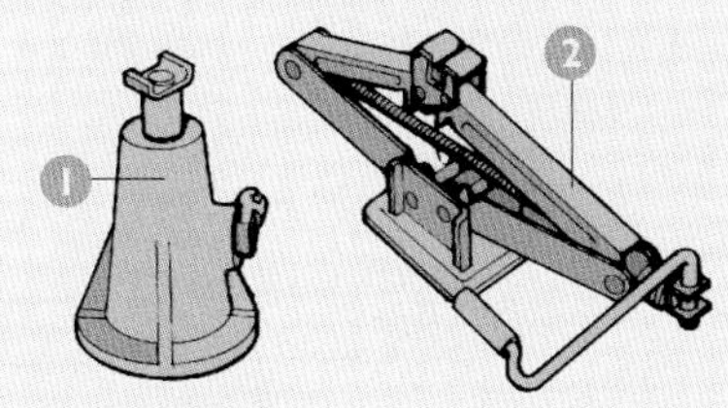

1. Hydraulic bottle jack
2. Diamond-shaped jack

The jacking points of your car should be shown in the handbook. If you don't have this, look for flat, reinforced areas just behind both front wheels and in front of both back wheels. These may have a small dimple or hole for locating the jack. It is vital to ensure that the jack is secure and on firm ground.

NEVER reach under the car with any part of your body or crawl under it, as jacks cannot be relied upon.

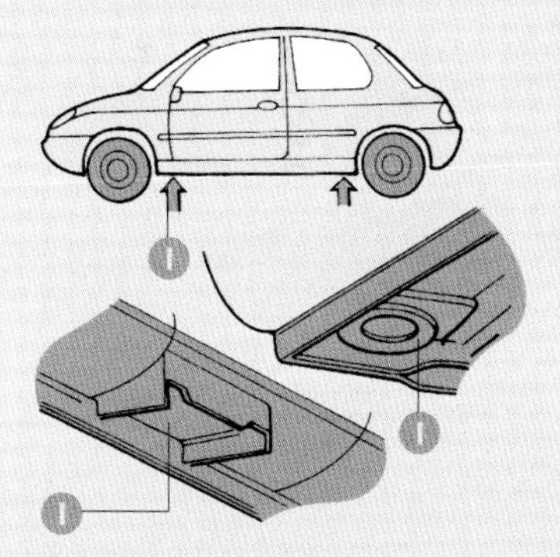

1. Look for a slot or hole in which to locate the jack

Changing a wheel

Forewarned is forearmed. When you have a spare moment, check out where your spare wheel, jack and wheel-brace are stored and how to remove them. It will be one less thing to worry about if you are ever unlucky enough to have a flat tyre at the roadside.

How to do it

❶ Check that the handbrake is on and the engine off. As an extra precaution, if the car is on a slope, put large stones behind the wheels not being jacked up, to prevent the car from rolling.

SAFETY

When changing a wheel on the road, make sure you can work safely without risk of being struck by passing cars. If necessary, drive the car to a side road or nearby parking area. Although this may ruin the punctured tyre, it is a price worth paying to avoid injury, or worse.

you will need

→ spare wheel
→ jack
→ wheel-brace*
→ rag for cleaning hands
→ adaptor for unlocking wheel nuts
→ red warning triangle (if available)

*one with a long handle is preferable (*see page 97*)

❷ Get everyone, including animals, out of the vehicle and to a safe location away from the road. People and animals moving about in the car may cause it to fall off the jack completely, with potentially disastrous results.

❸ If you carry a red warning triangle, position it 10–15m (30–45ft) behind the car to warn oncoming traffic – and switch the hazard warning lights on. Get the spare wheel, jack and wheel-brace out of the car.

❹ Put the jack under the nearest jacking point to the flat tyre, making sure it stands firmly on the road surface (*see page 97*).

❺ Slide the spare wheel half-way under the car (but without reaching under or crawling under it). If the car falls off the jack when you remove the punctured tyre, it should still be clear of the road and enable you to refit the jack. Make sure the wheel is positioned so that it does not interfere with the operation of the jack or removal of the damaged tyre.

WARNING

NEVER crawl under the car, or put any part of your body under it, when it is supported by a jack. They cannot be relied upon completely and could collapse without warning, or the car could slip off the jack.

See also pages 96–97 for further advice on equipment and jacking.

❻ Raise the jack until it just starts to take the weight of the vehicle, then stop (the wheel should still be in contact with the ground so that you can undo the bolts or nuts without it rotating).

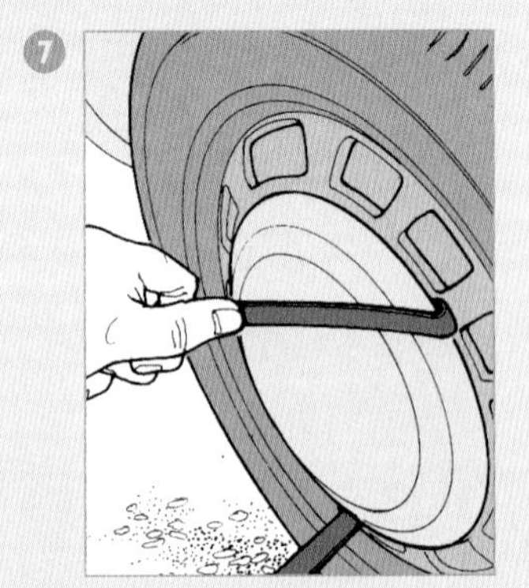

❼ If a hub cap is fitted to the wheel, remove it, either by levering it off or, if it has a central fixing screw, undoing the screw and lifting it off.

❽ Using the wheel-brace, loosen the wheel nuts (or bolts) half a turn by unscrewing them anti-clockwise. If they are really tight, and you cannot gain extra leverage with a length of pipe, you may have to resort to standing on the wheel-brace to increase leverage. This should only be done in an emergency as it could bend the wheel studs or cause injury if your foot slips off. If you have to do this, take great care and have the studs checked later by a garage.

❾ Raise the jack fully to lift the flat tyre well clear of the road.

❿ Undo and remove the wheel nuts or bolts and lift off the wheel. Take care to keep wheel nuts or bolts safe and clean. (Put them in the hub cap if there is one.) If a bolt rolls under the car, hook it back with a twig; don't reach under the vehicle.

11 Remove the spare wheel from under the car and push the damaged tyre half-way under the car (but without reaching or crawling under it).

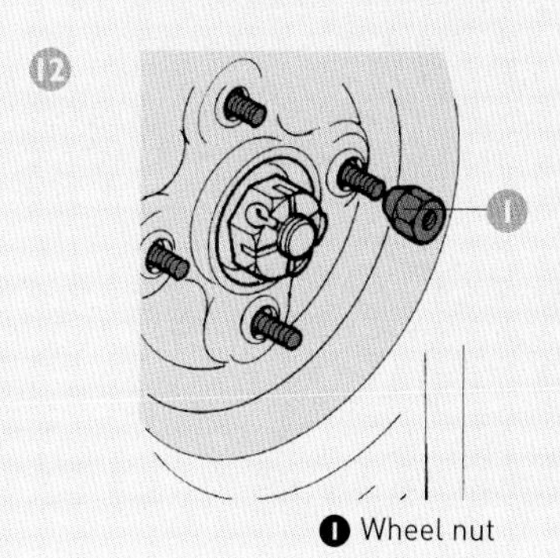

1 Wheel nut

12 Carefully lift the spare wheel into position and fit the wheel nuts (or bolts). Make sure you put them on with the tapered ends inwards, or the nuts (or bolts) could work loose and fall off. Do them up finger-tight, then tighten them

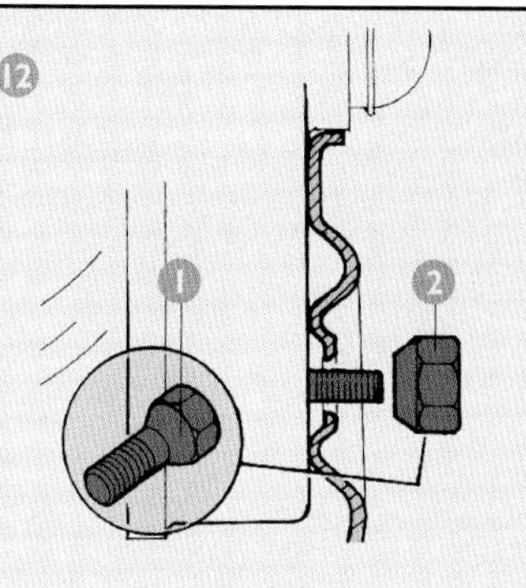

1 Wheel bolt 2 Tapered end inwards

further with the wheel-brace – do not try to tighten them fully at this stage, as you may jerk the vehicle off the jack.

13 Lower the jack until the tyre is resting on the road surface, then fully tighten the wheel nuts or bolts with the brace. Don't stand on the wheel-brace to tighten them, as it could bend the studs and cause them to break at a later stage.

14 Lower the jack fully and remove it. Then replace the hub cap (if fitted). Return the jack, wheel-brace, wheel and warning triangle to their correct storage positions, switch off the hazard warning lights and resume your journey.

15 Remember to have the flat tyre repaired as soon as possible and either replaced on the vehicle or in the spare wheel storage position. If you have fitted a space-saver wheel, see page 90.

The steering

The steering system transfers the driver's movement of the steering wheel to the front wheels to steer the car in the required direction. The design of the system has to take into account the car's weight, which affects the amount of effort needed to turn the steering wheel.

The steering column

In the early days of car design, the steering wheel was connected to the steering box by a single straight shaft. Due to safety requirements and space constraints, steering columns in modern cars always consist of several shafts at different angles and connected by universal joints. The shafts are misaligned so that they will collapse in the event of a head-on collision, or are arranged so that they telescope into each other to help minimise the possibility of injury to the driver.

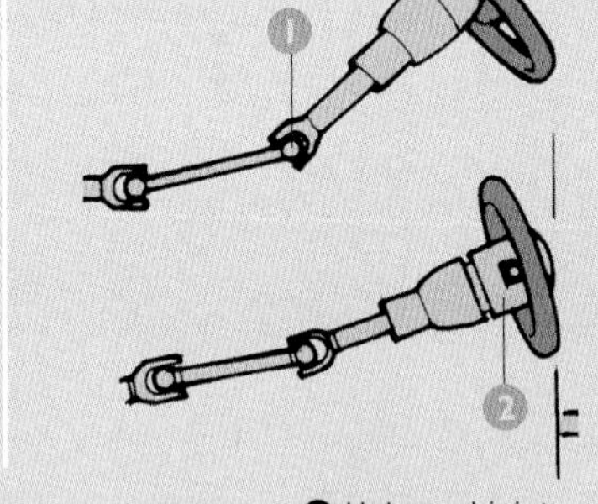

1. Universal joint
2. Collapsible hub
3. Collapsible column
4. Telescopic column

Steering linkage

The steering wheel is connected to the road wheels by the steering column and a series of gears, rods and levers. The rods and levers are joined together by ball joints or universal joints, which allow movement in all directions. The rods, levers and joints are known collectively as the steering linkage.

How it works

• In cars with front-mounted engines, about half the total weight of the car is borne by the front wheels. This weight, coupled with the tyres' grip on the road surface, makes it very difficult to turn the steering wheel without any assistance. The steering system is therefore designed to reduce the amount of effort needed to turn the wheels when steering the car. This is achieved by incorporating gears and levers into the system so that the steering wheel is not linked directly to the road wheels. As a result, it can take several full turns of the steering wheel to turn the steering to a certain angle. An average-sized car takes three or four turns of the steering wheel to turn the road wheels from a full right-hand to full left-hand lock. Generally, the bigger and heavier the car, the more turns of the steering wheel are necessary.

• In addition to assisting driver effort, the gearing mechanism enables the driver to make very small adjustments to the steering direction, which would not be possible if the road wheels were connected directly to the steering wheel.

• The steering system also needs to be sensitive enough to provide the driver with feedback from the road surface, without causing the car to swing out of control when driving over potholes.

• Many cars are fitted with power-assisted steering, which reduces the effort required by the driver considerably (*see pages 106–107*).

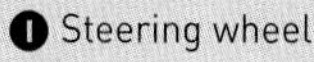

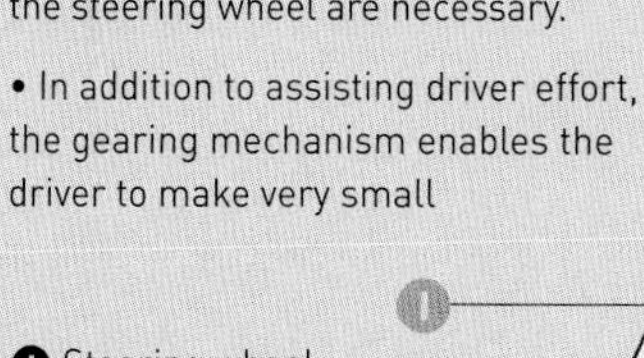

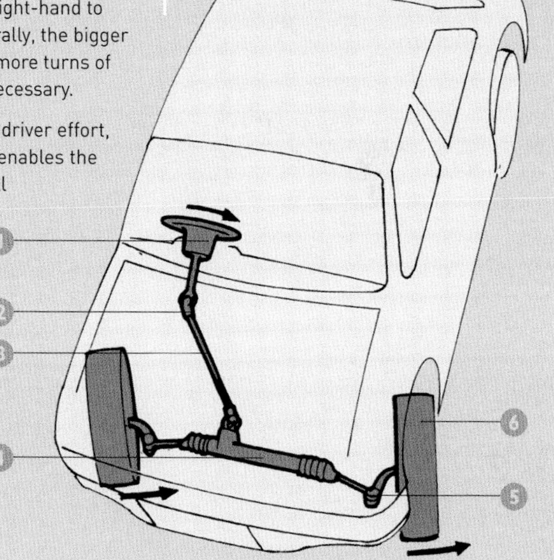

1 Steering wheel

2 Universal joint

3 Steering column

4 Steering rack

5 Rubber boot

6 Road wheel

Rack-and-pinion steering

This is the most common steering system layout, as it is compact and gives the driver good control of the road wheels. The steering wheel shaft connects the steering wheel to the rack through a pinion gear on the end of the steering shaft. As the steering wheel is turned, the pinion gear rotates against gear teeth cut into the rack, moving it to the left or right. The rack is connected at both ends to the wheel hubs by track rods. The joints connecting the track rods to the rack are encased in rubber gaiters. The rack contains oil, and if any leaks out and the joints inside become dry, they will soon wear and be damaged.

1. Rubber gaiter concealing ball-and-socket joints
2. Universal joint
3. Collapsible section
4. Rack
5. Track rod
6. Steering arm
7. Pinion gear
8. Rack

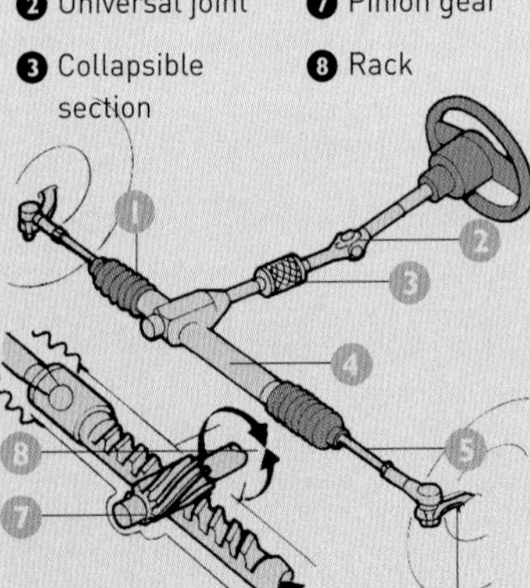

Steering box

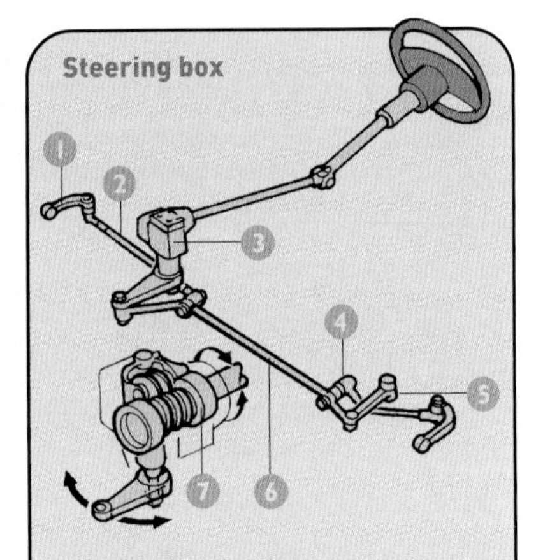

1. Steering arm
2. Track rod
3. Steering box
4. Ball joint
5. Idler arm
6. Drag link
7. Worm gear at end of steering column

The steering box system is fitted to some older cars. It has a small gear mechanism that is contained in a box. The end of the steering column has a thread called a worm gear cut into it, which fits inside a metal block called a nut. The interior of the nut is threaded so that the steering column can turn inside it. When the steering column turns, the nut moves up or down the column and rotates a steering lever, which moves a series of metal arms and rods, pushing or pulling the road wheels in the required direction. The joints are ball-and-socket joints that rotate as they move and are usually covered by rubber gaiters.

Steering problems

The most common problems encountered are the car veering to one side when being driven and 'play' in the steering. 'Play' occurs when parts of the steering mechanism become worn, permitting increased movement in components that should be fixed or have more restricted movement. It causes the car to 'wander', requiring repeated correction of the steering. It can be difficult to tell if a car is pulling to one side due to a fault in the steering or another system (such as the suspension or brakes), but excessive play in the steering wheel is normally due to wear. There should be no play in the steering wheel of a new car, and in an older car only a small amount of play is accepted in roadworthiness tests. Test for play by attempting to rock the steering wheel gently from side to side when the car is stationary and feel for movement. It should not be possible to move the steering wheel more than about 30–40mm (1¼–1½in), before making the road wheels move.

Faults in the steering system are dangerous because they can cause the driver to lose control. They can also cause extra strain on components, accelerating wear.

Oversteer/understeer

These terms apply when the steering does not appear to obey the driver's actions. In oversteer, the rear wheels slip sideways; in understeer, the car tends to run straight ahead rather than turning. It usually occurs when the car is cornering at high speed, and can be due to the way a car is loaded, how it is driven, or whether it has front- or rear-wheel drive, rather than a steering problem.

Gaiters

Have the rubber gaiters of the steering system checked every 10,000 miles, or annually, whichever is sooner. Normally, a garage will do this when the car is serviced, at the same time as inspecting the various joints of the system. They will also be examined during a roadworthiness inspection. Split gaiters could allow dirt and grit to enter the joints of the steering system.

Power steering

Power steering supplements driver effort by supplying extra power to help turn the wheels, making the car lighter and easier to steer. It also helps minimize jolts to the steering caused by badly cratered road surfaces. It is fitted to an increasing number of cars as standard.

The power steering system

In a power steering system, movement of the steering wheel is augmented by a hydraulic pump and a piston incorporated in the steering rack or box.

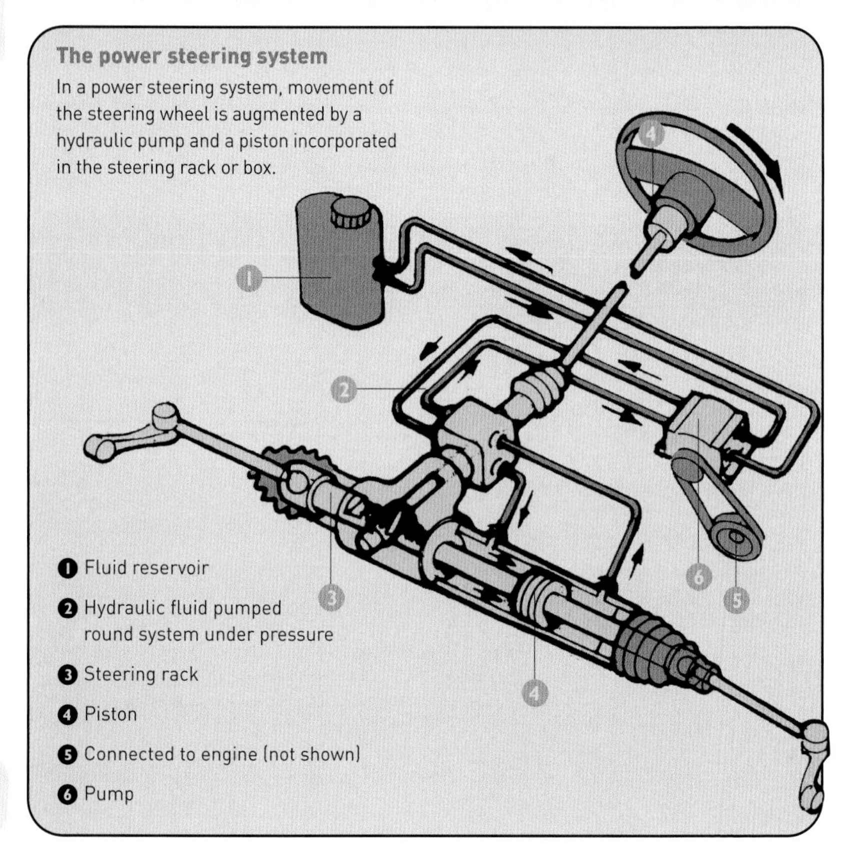

1. Fluid reservoir
2. Hydraulic fluid pumped round system under pressure
3. Steering rack
4. Piston
5. Connected to engine (not shown)
6. Pump

How it works

• Although the gearing mechanism in a manual steering system assists the driver considerably, the steering wheel can still be difficult to turn, particularly in a big heavy car with a front-mounted engine. Power steering assists the driver by making the car feel lighter and therefore easier to steer.

• All power steering systems are hydraulic. A pump, driven by the engine via a belt and pulley, feeds hydraulic fluid under pressure to the steering rack. When the steering wheel is turned, it opens a valve that allows the fluid through, forcing a piston to the left or right. This extra pressure from the piston boosts the steering movement as the driver turns the steering wheel.

• Power steering also helps to reduce the amount of 'kickback' (jolt) the driver feels when driving over a large hole or when a tyre bursts. However, it also tends to desensitize the steering, i.e. reduce the amount of feedback that the driver receives from the road via the steering wheel. Power steering is a back-up system, so if it fails, the driver is still able to steer the car, although it feels a lot heavier and requires more effort. It will also have more free play.

Power steering problems

Common power steering problems are caused by air getting into the hydraulic system (causing the car to tend to veer off course), a low hydraulic fluid level (causing loss of power steering efficiency), and a worn or incorrectly adjusted pump drive belt (causing a screeching noise).

Fluid level

The power steering fluid level should be checked regularly once a month (*see pages 108–109*), and always before a long journey. If it becomes harder than usual to turn the steering wheel, the fluid level could be low due to a leak in the system. Hissing or squealing sounds as the steering wheel is turned could also indicate a low fluid level. You will still be able to drive the car, but the steering will feel much heavier than usual with more free play.

Checking the power steering fluid

Keeping an eye on the power steering fluid level is quite simple to do, while maintaining the level is essential to ensure that the system performs efficiently.

Checking fluid level

you will need

- → power steering fluid of the correct type
- → a funnel (possibly)
- → clean cloth (lint-free)

There are a number of different types of fluid, and it is important to use the right type for your car – using the wrong one could damage the system (refer to your car handbook). Some systems use automatic transmission fluid. Conventional fluid should be replaced around every 50,000 miles, but some manufacturers supply fluid that lasts the car's lifetime and does not need changing. However, changing this 'long life' fluid at around 100,000 miles could be beneficial.

1. Park the car on the level, put the handbrake on and switch off the engine.

The power steering fluid reservoir is normally near the top of the engine. Refer to your handbook if you cannot locate it.

2

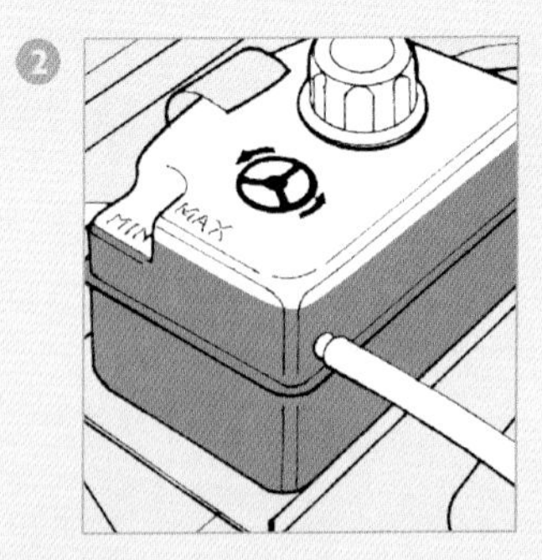

2. If the reservoir is translucent, you may be able to check the level without unscrewing the cap. It should be between the maximum and minimum marks.

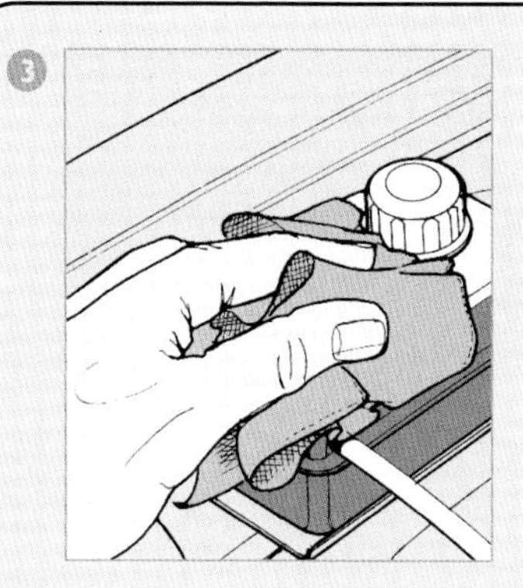

❸ If you cannot check the level from the outside, wipe the top of the reservoir clean and unscrew the cap. Be careful not to allow dirt or anything else (such as water) that could contaminate the fluid entering the reservoir.

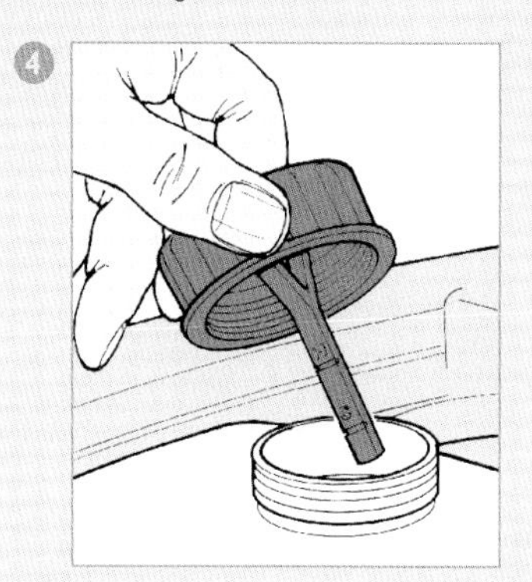

❹ A dipstick may be fitted to the inside of the cap. If so, wipe it and screw the cap back on so that the dipstick is fully reinserted. Don't allow any threads from the cloth to enter the reservoir.

Unscrew the cap again and check the level on the dipstick. It should be between the maximum and minimum marks. If the dipstick is marked with 'hot' and 'cold' levels, check that the fluid is up to the 'hot' mark if the engine has been running, or to the 'cold' mark if the engine is cold.

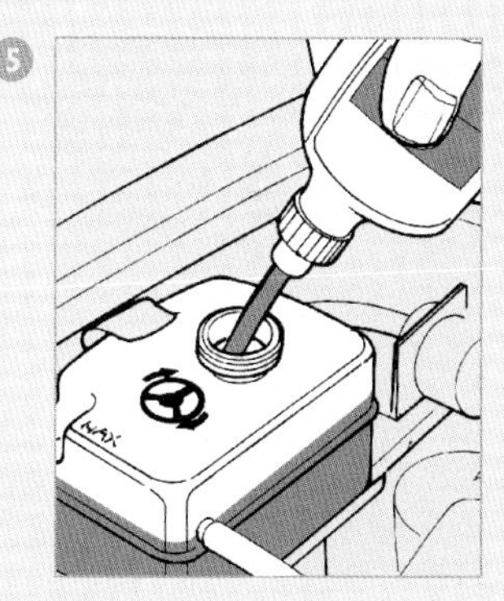

❺ If the level is low, top up the fluid, using the correct type, to the appropriate mark on the dipstick or reservoir. Be careful not to overfill the reservoir.

❻ Screw the cap back on firmly and wipe the top of the reservoir with a cloth.

Suspension

The suspension is designed to ensure passengers have a smooth ride by absorbing the jolts and shocks caused by unevenness in the road and to allow the wheels to move up and down while maintaining contact with the road, but keeping the body of the car reasonably level.

How it works

Most cars have independent suspension on both front and back wheels, so that each wheel can move up and down independently of the others. This gives better handling of the vehicle and more comfort for the passengers. Some older cars have independent front suspension only, with beam-axle rear suspension. In some beam-axle systems, movement of one wheel affects the other.

Suspension systems are designed to take into account the car's weight and handling needs and consist of springs, shock absorbers, links and pivots.

Rubber bushes help cushion the shocks and noise of the suspension as it works. The suspension must not have a detrimental effect on the car's handling by allowing too much roll or bouncing.

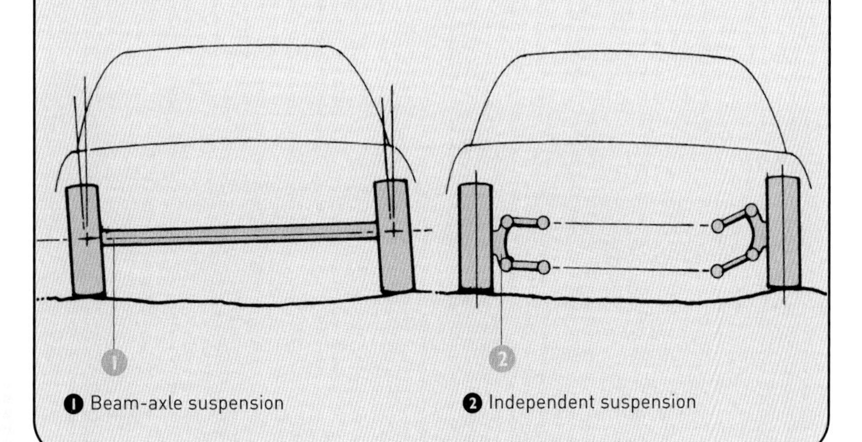

❶ Beam-axle suspension

❷ Independent suspension

Stiff vs soft

Ideally, to give better handling of the car, the suspension should be stiff so that the car does not roll and tend to lose adhesion on the road surface, particularly when cornering at speed, but stiff suspension gives the passengers an uncomfortable ride. Soft suspensions are generally used on everyday cars to give a good degree of comfort to the occupants, while stiff suspensions are used on sports cars where roadholding is more important than passenger comfort.

Anti-roll bar

This connects the suspension of the two front wheels. When a car corners, the body tends to roll, putting more of the car's weight on to the outside wheel. The anti-roll bar counteracts this effect, transferring some of the force thrown on to the outside wheel to the inside wheel, helping to keep both wheels on the ground and the body level. Some cars have rear anti-roll bars as well.

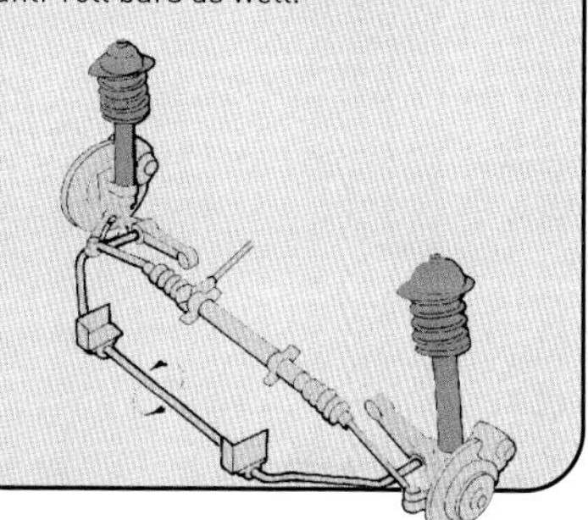

Front suspension

Each road wheel is independently connected to the structure of the vehicle by its own suspension linkage and road spring. The suspension on each side of the vehicle is joined by an anti-roll bar. As the front wheels are used to steer the vehicle, it is essential that suspension movement does not affect the steering of the vehicle; this is ensured by the design of the suspension, allowing it to maintain the distance between the front wheels as it deflects over bumps and potholes.

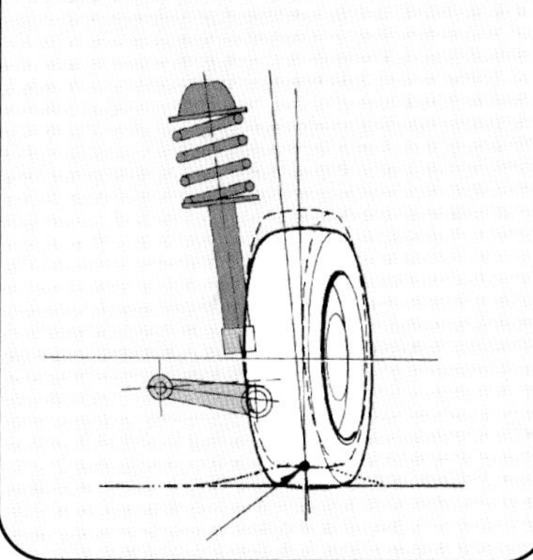

Rear suspension

This is usually independent using trailing arms, although some vehicles are fitted with a semi-independent beam-axle system.

Types of suspension

There are several different types of suspension, designed to fit the different needs of the front and rear wheels – the MacPherson strut and double-wishbone systems are commonly fitted to the front wheels and the trailing arms to the rear wheels.

MacPherson strut

This is a type of independent suspension commonly fitted to front wheels. It combines the spring and shock absorber in one unit, known as the 'strut'. The spring compresses as the car hits a bump on the road, and extends as the car passes over it, bouncing up and then returning to its normal rest position. The shock absorber limits the bouncing of the road spring.

1. MacPherson strut
2. Anti-roll bar
3. Cross-member
4. Track-control arm
5. Shock absorber
6. Coil spring

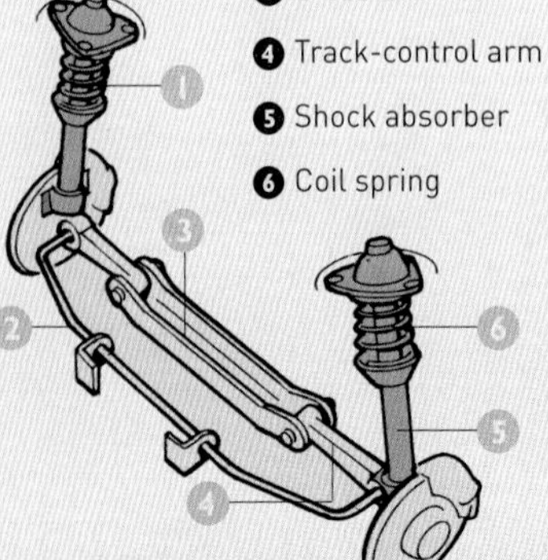

Double-wishbone suspension

Here, each wheel hub pivots between two triangular frames known as wishbones. A coil spring and shock absorber may be mounted between the upper or lower wishbone and the car body. Alternatively, a torsion bar may be fitted between a wishbone and the body to provide springing. As the suspension compresses and extends, the wishbones hold the wheel hub and wheel at a fixed angle to the road for good handling.

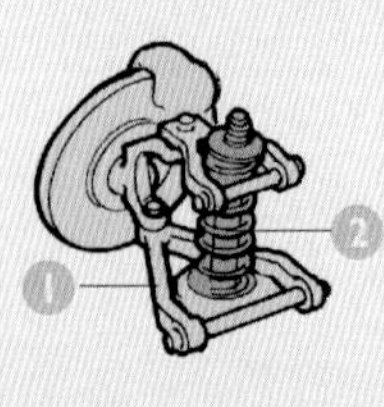

1. Lower wishbone
2. Coil spring
3. Shock absorber
4. Upper wishbone

Trailing arms

This is the most common type of independent suspension fitted to the rear wheels. It consists of a triangulated suspension arm on each side of the vehicle, pivoted on rubber bushes where it attaches to the vehicle structure. This system can be used on both driven and non-driven wheels.

1. Shock absorber
2. Final drive
3. Coil spring
4. Drive shaft
5. Trailing arm

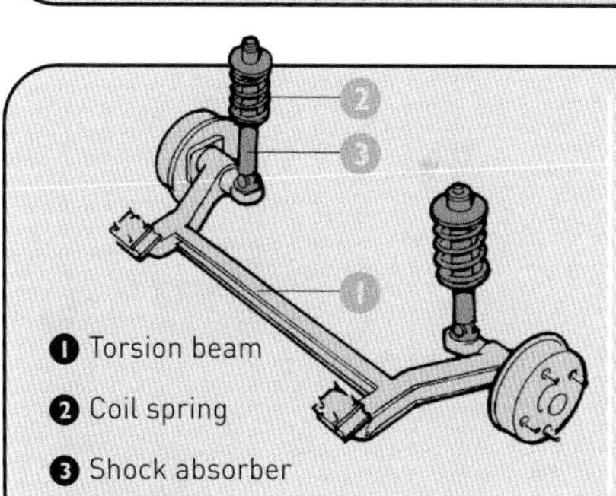

1. Torsion beam
2. Coil spring
3. Shock absorber

Beam axle

Beam axles, made of pressed steel and rubber-mounted to the vehicle structure, are a cheaper alternative to trailing arms and are often found on the rear of front-wheel-drive vehicles. These systems give a semi-independent operation, the pressed-steel beam allowing some flexibility between the two wheels.

Springs

Together with the shock absorbers, correctly called dampers, the spring plays a major role in the suspension system of modern cars.

Most cars use coil or torsion-bar springs. Some cars have pneumatic or hydraulic springs, although these are exceptions to the norm. Leaf springs are still found on some vans and heavy vehicles.

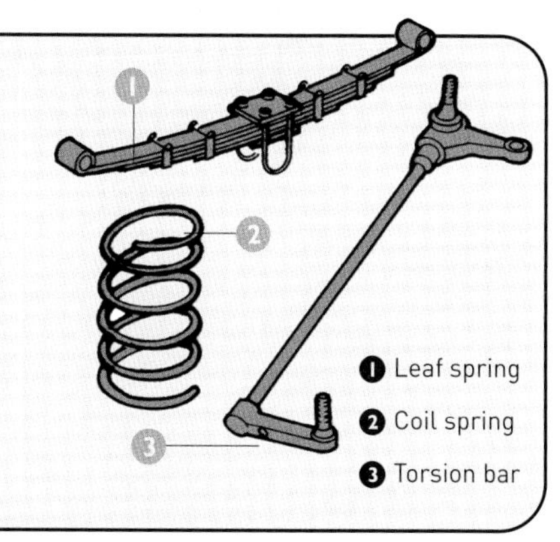

1. Leaf spring
2. Coil spring
3. Torsion bar

Shock absorbers

The shock absorbers are vital parts of your car's suspension system, preventing the springs from bouncing uncontrollably, which could lead to handling problems and an uncomfortable ride.

Purpose

Shock absorbers (or dampers) absorb the movement energy of the road springs if travelling over uneven ground. Each wheel is fitted with a shock absorber so that movements of the suspension are controlled independently at all four car corners. The shock absorbers are either filled with oil or with oil and gas. They are attached at one end to the structure of the car and at the other to a major part of the suspension linkage.

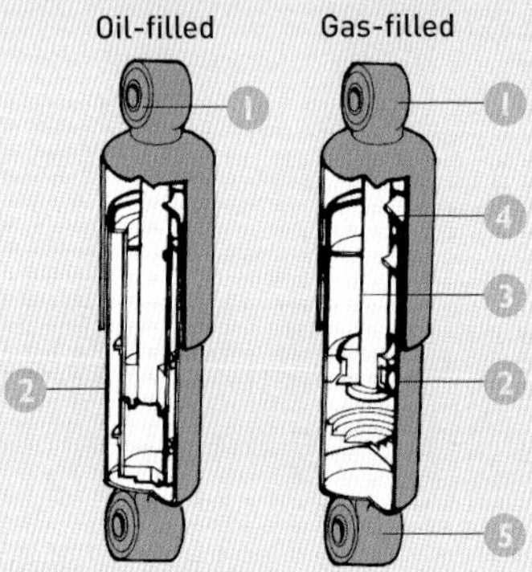

Oil-filled   Gas-filled

Oil-filled

1. Piston
2. Oil

Gas-filled

1. Fixing eye attached to body
2. Piston
3. Oil
4. Gas
5. Fixing eye attached to suspension

How to tell when the suspension is worn

If the suspension is worn, it affects how the car handles, both under normal driving conditions and braking. It can also cause increased wear on tyres. There may be a rattling or knocking sound as the car is driven over uneven ground. If you think there is something wrong with the suspension, have it checked at a garage as soon as possible. It could be dangerous to drive the car, as the handling and braking could be affected, and may cause the driver to lose control. See 'Checking shock absorbers' opposite.

How they work

• Inside each shock absorber is a piston contained within a cylinder filled with hydraulic fluid (oil).

• When a road wheel rises over a bump in the road, the road spring deflects and the shock absorber is compressed; the oil in the shock absorber flows from one side of the piston to the other through valves. When the road spring returns to its normal position, the valves restrict the return flow of the oil in the shock absorber, absorbing movement energy from the road spring and 'damping' its return. In this way, the shock absorber prevents the continual bouncing of the suspension.

• Without shock absorbers, the road springs would continue to bounce and rebound until all their energy had been dissipated, like a ball bouncing ever lower until eventually it stops. If a car's suspension were allowed to behave in this manner, the car would become uncontrollable and very uncomfortable for the passengers.

Checking shock absorbers

• Check the shock absorbers by pressing down heavily on each corner of the car and then releasing it. The car body should regain its normal position after one-and-a-half 'bounces' – the corner of the car should rise up past its normal position then settle back into its rest position. If it moves more than this or if you hear any strange noises (knocking or hissing) coming from the suspension, then there is a problem.

• If you suspect the shock absorbers are faulty or worn, have them checked at a garage. (The car will bounce more than normal when being driven, which may cause difficulty in handling and could potentially be dangerous.) In most cars, the shock absorbers should last for around 100,000 miles, although in heavy cars or four-wheel-drive vehicles used off-road, they may wear more quickly.

• Shock absorbers always need to be replaced in axle pairs (both front or both back) to ensure the car is well balanced side-to-side when driven.

Wheel alignment

You may be surprised to learn that the wheels on your car are not set dead upright or straight. They are very slightly misaligned, for a variety of reasons. If you have any concerns about wheel alignment, take the car to a garage for checking.

Camber

When viewed from the front, the front wheels on some cars lean slightly outwards at the top. This is known as 'positive camber' and is designed to make the steering of the vehicle lighter. On most sports and high-performance vehicles, the tops of the front wheels lean slightly inwards. This is known as 'negative camber', which improves roadholding at high speed. As a rule, camber is not adjustable, but if the car pulls to one side or there is abnormal tyre wear, it could be that the camber angle has been upset. In this case, take the car to a garage.

❶ Positive camber ❷ Negative camber

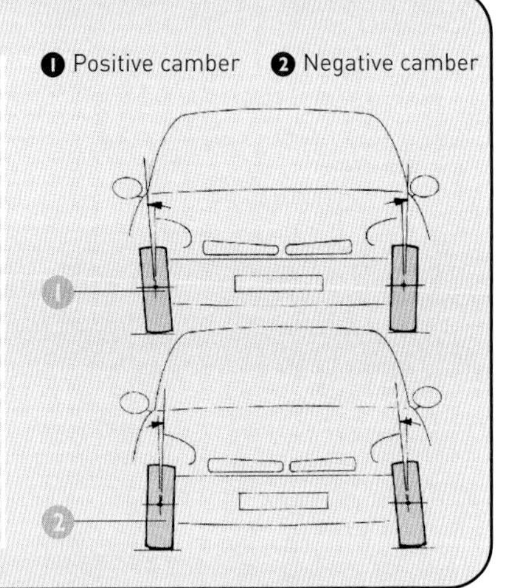

Castor

This is designed into the steering to make the car run straight, and to ensure that the steering returns to the straight-ahead position after cornering. Basically, the pivot that allows each front wheel to turn from side to side is tilted so that if its centre-line were projected, it would meet the road in front of the tyre contact patch. This causes the wheel to act like a furniture castor, automatically aligning with the direction of travel. If the car wanders when being driven straight or there is abnormal tyre wear, the castor angle may have been upset – perhaps by hitting a kerb. In this case, take the car to a garage.

Toe-in, toe-out

In addition to camber and castor, wheels are also angled inwards or outwards at their front edge. They are said to toe-in if they are pointing slightly inwards, and toe-out if they point slightly outwards. This is to ensure that the wheels run parallel to each other when the vehicle is moving forwards and is necessary because all steering/suspension systems have a small amount of 'give' in them as a result of the various joints and bushes used, many of which are rubber. If the front wheels were set parallel at rest on a rear-wheel-drive car, forward movement would tend to push their front edges apart, so they are set to toe-in slightly at rest. On a front-wheel-drive car, the turning force applied to the wheels by the engine tends to push the front edges closer together, so as a rule these are set to toe-out slightly.

The toe-in/toe-out angle is adjustable, but this should only ever be done by a garage, which will have the correct equipment for measuring the angle.

WARNING SIGNS

Signs of badly aligned front wheels are excess wear of the tyre tread on the inner or outer edges, or the vehicle tending to pull to one side or not cornering very smoothly.

On cars with independent rear suspension, the signs of incorrect rear wheel alignment are excess wear of the tyre edges and a tendency to wander, particularly when cornering.

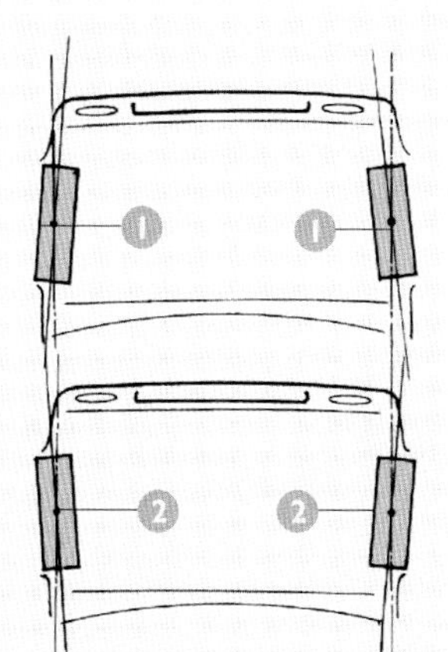

❶ Toe-in

❷ Toe-out

Brakes

The brakes on a car work through friction. When the driver presses down on the brake pedal, it forces metal pads coated with friction material against the braking surfaces, slowing down or stopping the car due to the friction generated by the two surfaces rubbing together.

Types of brake

There are two types of car brake, drum and disc. In most cars, disc brakes are fitted to the front wheels and drum brakes to the rear. Both types of brake are hydraulically operated. When the driver presses the brake pedal, the brakes operate on all four wheels simultaneously. Many cars are also fitted with ABS (anti-lock braking system), which helps prevent the car from skidding when braking (*see pages 134–35*). The handbrake (or parking brake) is operated mechanically by a cable and, in most cases, works on the rear wheels only.

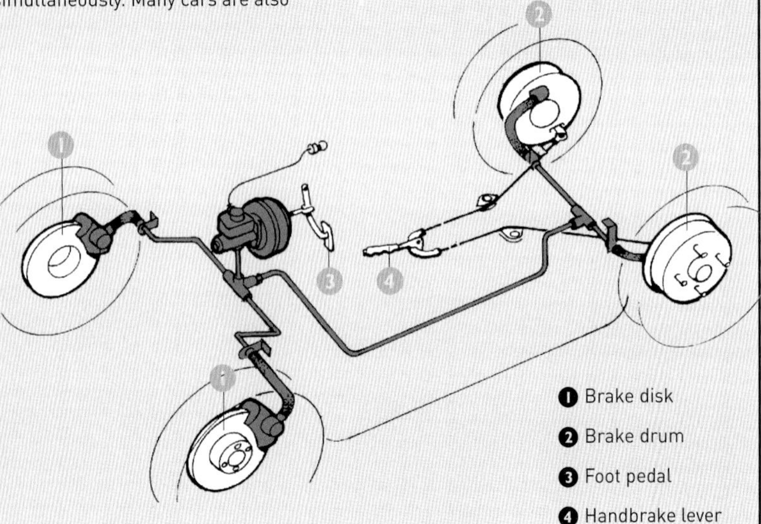

❶ Brake disk

❷ Brake drum

❸ Foot pedal

❹ Handbrake lever

Problems with brakes

Brake pad warning light

Some cars have a dashboard warning light that comes on when the layer of friction material on the brake pads is getting low (*see pages 124–125*). Sensors trigger the warning light when the pads are worn to a certain level.

Overheating and brake fade

The friction action of braking generates a great deal of heat, so the friction material in the brakes has to be able to withstand high temperatures. Air flowing over the brakes cools them, but overheating can occur when they are applied continuously for a length of time, such as when descending a long, steep hill, or when braking hard at high speed.

When brakes overheat, they lose some of their efficiency, resulting in 'brake fade', where the driver has to press harder on the brake pedal to make them work. However, when the brakes cool down again, they should regain their efficiency. Overheating can also damage rubber components in the hydraulic system, or even distort metal components. Overheating affects drum brakes, but rarely disc brakes.

TIP

To help prevent brakes overheating when descending a steep hill, engage a low gear and make use of the engine's own braking capacity, applying the brakes intermittently.

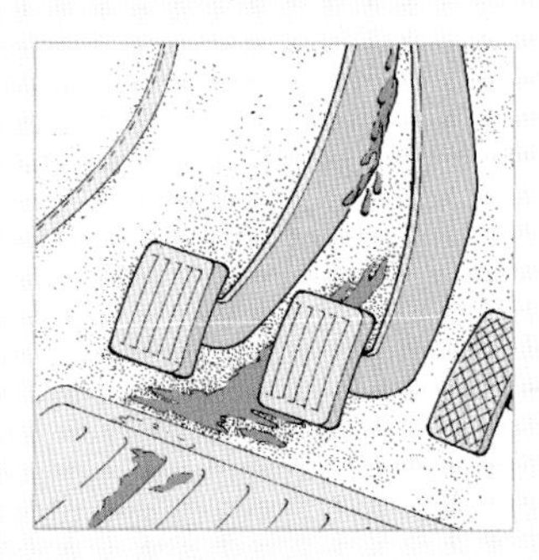

Leaking brake fluid

If you can press the brake pedal right down to the floor, the brake fluid level must be low. This can indicate a leak, so check for any brake fluid under the brake pedal.

The fluid may be coming from the brake master cylinder, in which case the cylinder itself will probably need replacing. However, the fluid may leak from other parts of the system. A warning sign is a low fluid level in the brake fluid reservoir, especially if you are topping it up frequently.

The hydraulic system

The hydraulic system makes use of the fact that fluid cannot be compressed when pressure is applied. Imagine a hollow pipe filled with fluid and sealed. If pressure is applied to the fluid at one end of the pipe, it is simply forced farther along the pipe, breaking the seal. The fluid does not reduce in volume.

1. Brake pedal at rest
2. Brakes released
3. Brake pedal pressed
4. Pressure in system applies brakes

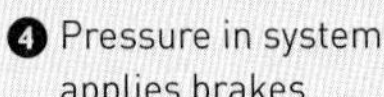

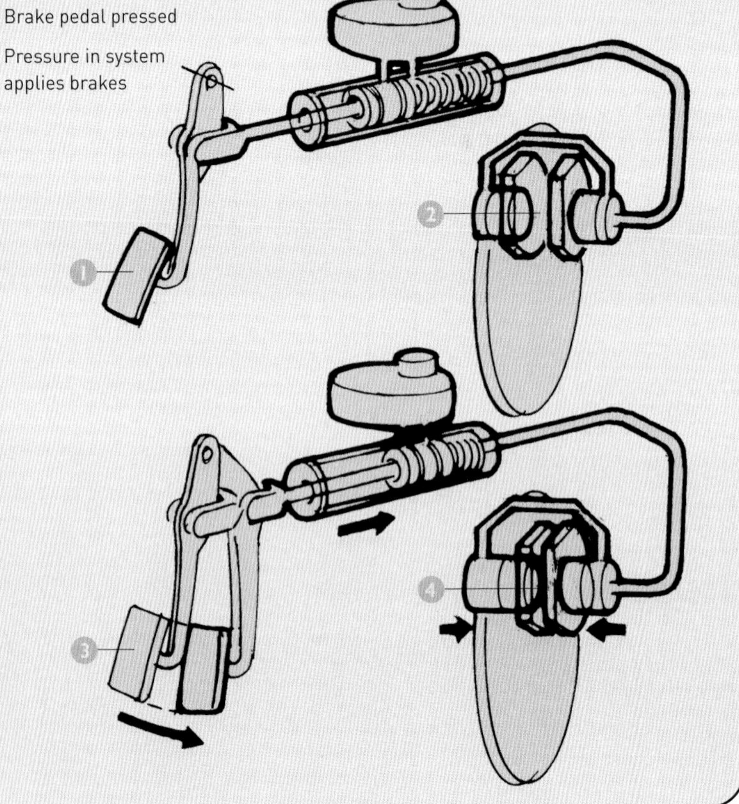

Hydraulic brakes

The hydraulic braking system consists of a fluid reservoir, a master cylinder and four or more small cylinders (called wheel or slave cylinders) at each wheel, connected by metal pipes and flexible hoses. The master cylinder is fed by the reservoir, which keeps the system full of fluid. In a dual-circuit system (*see page 122*), the master cylinder contains a double piston, which allows the brake system to be split into two separate circuits for safety. When pressure is applied by the brake pedal to the master cylinder, it forces fluid through the pipes, moving the pistons in the wheel cylinders. The pistons force the brake pads or shoes against the brake discs or brake drums to slow the car.

When the brake pedal is removed, the pressure on the fluid is released and the pistons return to their normal position. The hydraulic system ensures that equal force is applied simultaneously to all four wheels.

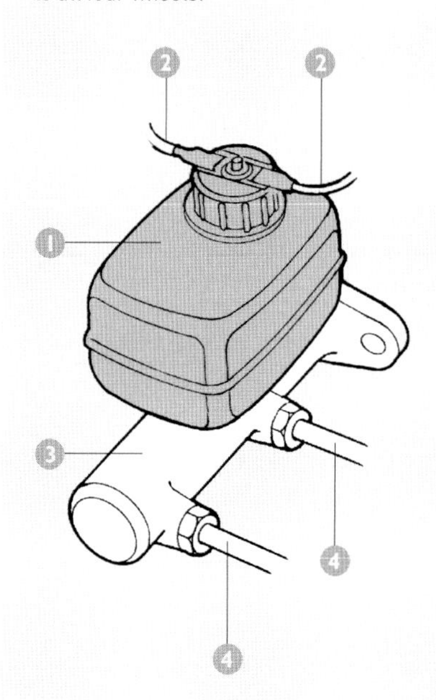

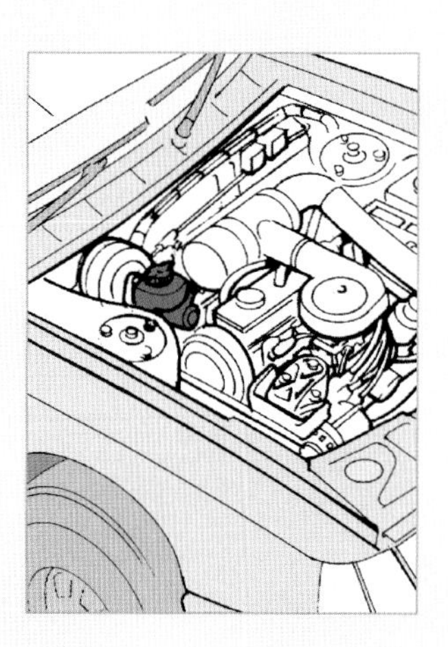

1. Hydraulic fluid reservoir
2. Fluid level sensor connections
3. Brake master cylinder
4. Pipes to dual-circuit brakes

Dual-circuit brakes

The hydraulic system is normally dual-circuit, consisting of two separate hydraulic circuits. This is a safety measure so that if one circuit fails, the other should still work and enable the car to be braked safely. The separate circuits normally pair diagonally opposed wheels, that is a front-wheel brake and a rear-wheel brake. This ensures that the car stops in a straight line. The circuits are sometimes divided differently, into both front and both rear brakes, although this arrangement can result in skidding on wet surfaces.

1. Brake master cylinder
2. Front/rear dual-circuit
3. Diagonal/diagonal dual-circuit

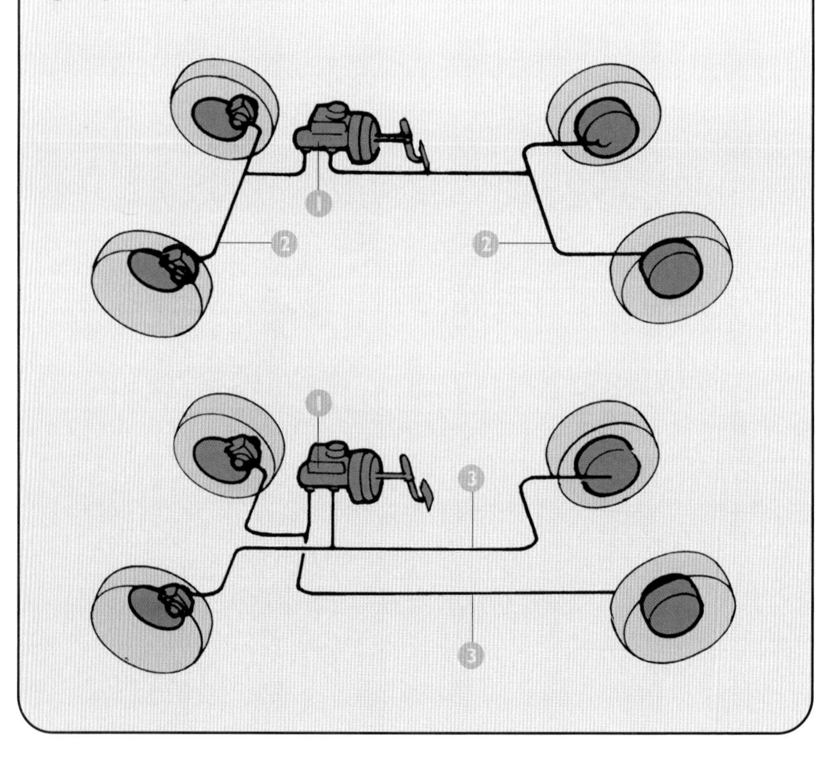

Servo-assisted brakes

Most cars are fitted with this system, which assists the driver's braking effort, reducing the amount of effort needed to depress the brake pedal by about half. The servo assembly is connected to the brake master cylinder. It operates by making use of a vacuum produced by the engine at the inlet manifold, so only operates when the engine is running. When the driver depresses the brake pedal, the servo increases the pressure that is being applied to the brake fluid. The more the brake pedal is depressed, the more additional pressure is exerted by the servo system. If the servo system becomes faulty or fails, the brakes will still work, but the driver needs to press down harder on the pedal in order to achieve the same amount of braking force.

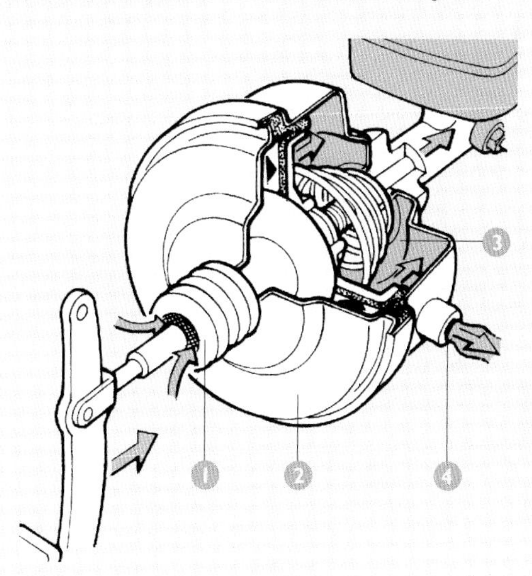

In diesel engines, the vacuum in the inlet manifold is usually not sufficient to operate a brake servo. An engine-driven vacuum pump is usually fitted instead.

1. Air inlet valve
2. Air cylinder
3. Vacuum cylinder
4. Vacuum pipe

Disc brakes

Of the two types of brake unit that are found on modern cars – disc and drum – disc brakes are by far the most efficient. Their high level of braking efficiency makes them standard equipment on all four wheels of high-performance and sports cars, while even the most mundane of family cars will have them on the front wheels at least. One disadvantage of disc brakes is that, unlike enclosed drum brakes, they tend to throw brake dust on to their wheels, which can mar the appearance of alloy wheels.

Front brakes

In a front-engined car, the front-wheel brakes need to be more powerful than those at the rear, because when the car brakes, about two-thirds of its weight is thrown forward on to the front wheels. The front brakes supply about 70 per cent of the car's total braking force. The front brakes in most cars are of the disc type, as these are more efficient than drum brakes. Some cars with more powerful engines also have rear disc brakes.

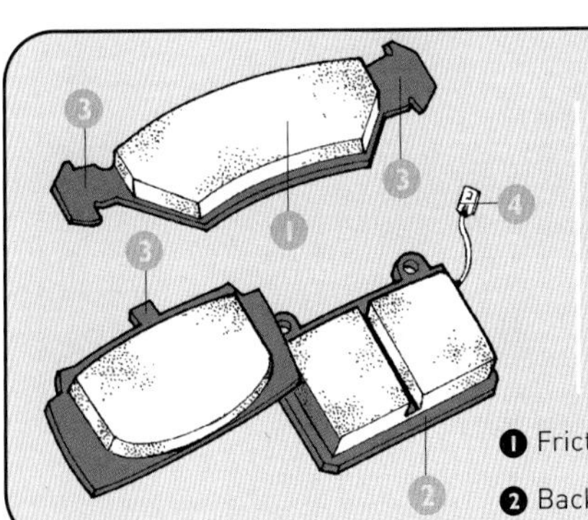

How they work

The disc brake assembly incorporates a brake caliper holding two brake pads lined with friction material. One or two hydraulic pistons are situated in the caliper behind the pads. A brake disc, attached to the road wheel, rotates between the pads. A backplate protects the disc from splashing water.

1. Friction material
2. Backing plate
3. Locating lugs
4. Wear indicator connection

Each caliper has one or two cylinders, each containing a piston, and fits over the brake disc. The single-piston sliding caliper is the type most commonly used. When the brake pedal is pressed down, the piston or pistons squeeze the pads against each side of the revolving brake disc, slowing it down through friction. The brake pads are metal plates lined with a layer of friction material, which gradually wears away.

Disc brakes are normally self-adjusting, the pistons moving inwards slightly to accommodate wear on the brake pads. They are less susceptible to overheating than drum brakes, as air can flow over them and carry away heat, assisted by vents in the disc in some cars.

❶ Caliper

❷ Piston

❸ Piston forces pads against disc

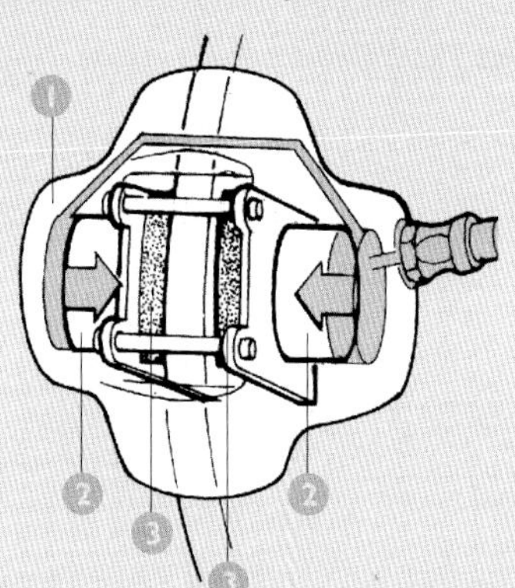

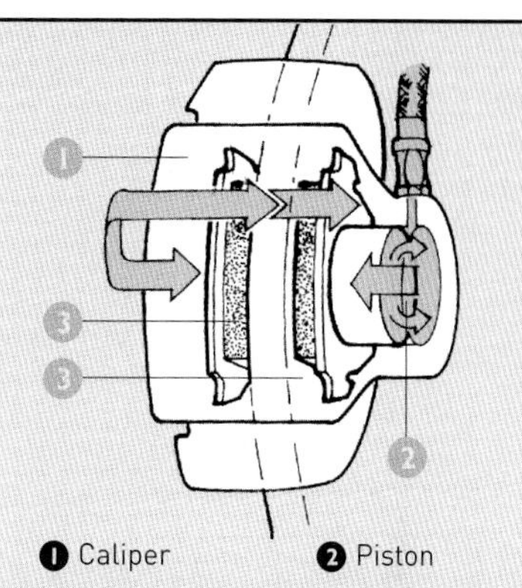

❶ Caliper ❷ Piston

❸ Piston forces pad against disc and causes caliper to slide and bring other pad against disc

Caliper types

Sliding – the caliper contains a single piston and can slide from side to side to centre itself. When the brake is applied, the piston forces the inner pad against the disc, while the caliper moves in the opposite direction, pulling the outer pad against the disc.

Fixed – the caliper cannot move; there are normally two pistons, one on each side of the disc, which force the brake pads against the disc simultaneously.

Brake pads need to be replaced regularly, on average around every 18,000–28,000 miles, but it is important to have them checked annually at a garage in case they wear more quickly than usual. Both brake pads must be renewed at the same time, otherwise braking could be uneven, causing the car to pull to one side.

Drum brakes

Drum brakes have been fitted to cars since the very early days of motoring, and their design has changed very little in that time, although originally they were operated by rods or cables rather than hydraulics, as today. They are more complex than disc brakes, so there are more components to wear or break, but their design makes it easy for the manufacturer to incorporate an efficient handbrake – one of the reasons why they are commonly still used for rear brakes.

Rear brakes

Drum brakes are normally fitted to the rear wheels, although they used to be fitted to the front wheels of older cars. Since the front disc brakes are more powerful and do most of the work, rear-mounted drum brakes only need to supply around 30 per cent of the car's total braking force.

The handbrake usually operates on the rear brakes, but mechanically by a system of rods and cables, not hydraulically (*see pages 132–33*).

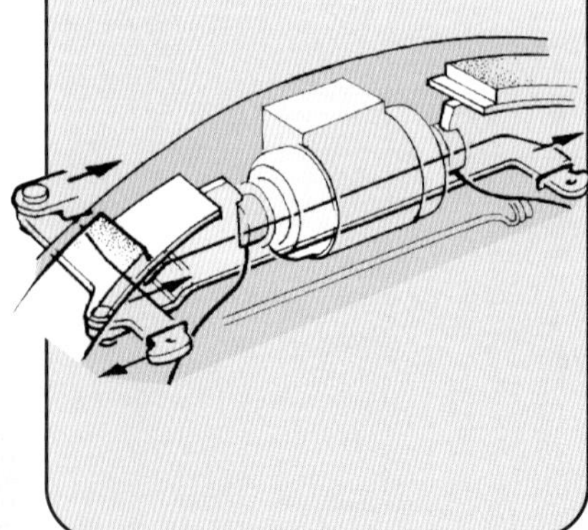

How they work

The drum brake assembly consists of a cast-iron drum attached to the wheel hub, two curved metal brake shoes, lined with friction material, one or two wheel cylinders containing pistons, and a backplate that protects the drum from splashing water.

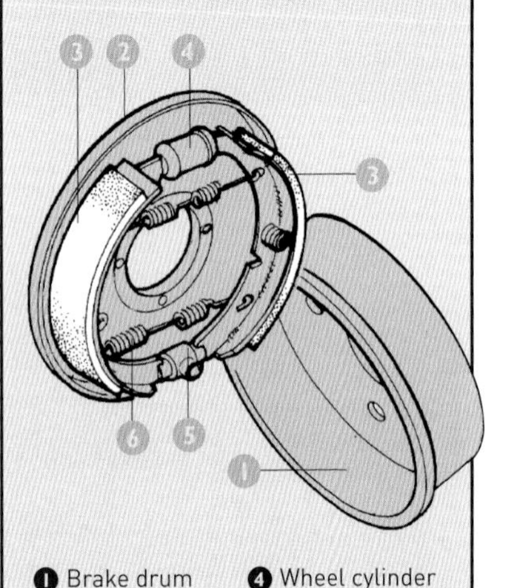

1. Brake drum
2. Back plate
3. Brake shoe
4. Wheel cylinder
5. Adjuster
6. Return string

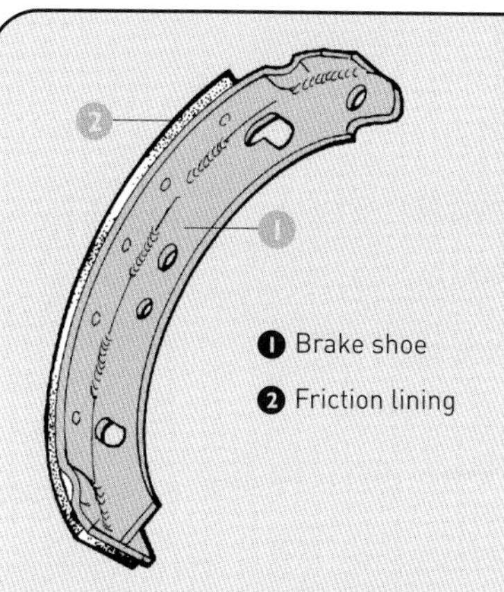

❶ Brake shoe

❷ Friction lining

The drum is mounted on the hub, which rotates with the wheels. The brake shoes are mounted on the backplate. They fit inside the drum, separated by one or two wheel cylinders containing pistons. When the brake pedal is depressed, the shoes are forced outwards by the pistons and press against the inside of the drum, braking the wheel through friction. When the brake pedal is released, springs return the shoes to their original position.

Drum brakes are enclosed (unlike disc brakes) and are prone to overheating, as air does not flow directly over the braking surfaces – heat has to pass through the drum before escaping.

Brake shoes last longer than the brake pads of disc brakes, as they have a larger friction area and because they only do around 30 per cent of the car's braking work. They usually need to be replaced around every 24–37,000 miles, but have them checked annually in case they wear more quickly.

All brake shoes must be renewed at the same time, otherwise braking could be uneven, causing the car to veer to one side when the brakes are applied. Drum brakes are normally self-adjusting, moving the brake shoes closer to the drum as the linings wear. A ratchet system operates the adjusting mechanism as the brake shoes wear.

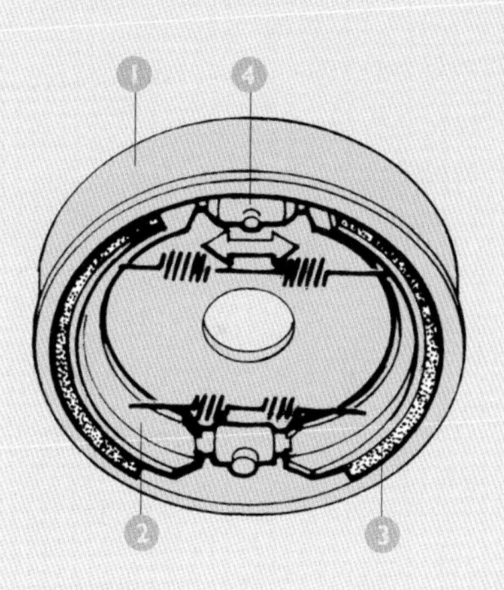

❶ Brake drum

❷ Brake shoe

❸ Friction lining

❹ Wheel cylinder

Brake fluid

The brake fluid is the 'life blood' of your car's braking system; if it becomes contaminated with air or water or, worse, begins to leak, the consequences could be disastrous.

Fluid reservoir

The level of brake fluid in its reservoir must be checked regularly (*see pages 130–31*). It is potentially very dangerous to allow the fluid to get too low, as braking efficiency could be reduced and air could enter the system, causing complete brake failure. In some cars, the clutch and the brakes share the same fluid reservoir.

Citroëns

If you have a Citroën, refer to your car handbook, as some models use a special kind of brake fluid. Never use the Citroën fluid in any other make or model of car.

WARNING

Brake fluid is composed of man-made materials, rather than natural mineral oils, which would cause the rubber seals and hoses in the hydraulic system to deteriorate. Brake fluid absorbs water from the atmosphere, which can cause a problem when the brakes are in frequent use. When the brakes become very hot through lengthy use or braking hard at speed, the heat can cause any water in the fluid to vaporize and create an air lock, resulting in a loss of braking efficiency (with the brake pedal feeling spongy when pressed rather than firm). It can also cause complete brake failure, the driver being able to press the brake pedal right to the floor without producing any braking effect at all, so it can be very dangerous. To help prevent an air lock, have the brake fluid changed at the recommended intervals to avoid the build-up of water in the fluid.

Brake fluid warning light

On some cars, if the fluid level becomes too low, a dashboard warning light comes on (*see page 145*). However, don't rely solely on the warning light to tell you when the level is low. It is powered by an electrical circuit, and if this is faulty, the light could fail to come on when the fluid level drops. Make regular checking of the brake fluid a part of your car maintenance routine.

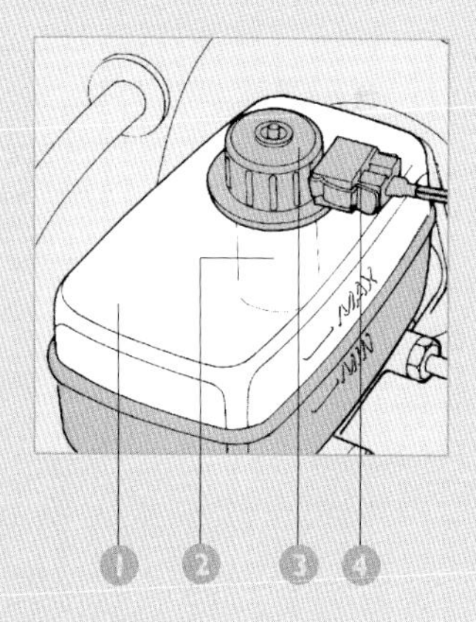

1. Hydraulic fluid reservoir
2. Level float
3. Filler cap
4. Electrical connection

WARNING

Brake fluid is toxic and corrosive. If you splash any on your skin or any fluid gets into your eyes, wash them with water and seek medical attention immediately. If any fluid is swallowed, again seek medical attention immediately. Some types of fluid are also flammable and could ignite if they come into contact with hot metal, or a spark or naked flame. Don't simply mop up any spills on paintwork or plastic: wash them off immediately with water and detergent, as brake fluid can strip paintwork.

Buying brake fluid

When topping up, it is best to use fresh fluid. Don't use brake fluid from a bottle that has been left open, as it becomes contaminated when exposed to air. Always keep the bottle sealed. Make sure that you use a good-quality fluid that meets the DOT 4 standard or higher – check for this on the label. If the fluid level drops again shortly after topping up, it means that there is a leak in the system, which is potentially very dangerous. Don't drive the car; contact a garage immediately.

Checking the brake fluid

Although the system is sealed, it is normal for the fluid level to drop over time, due to changes in atmospheric temperature and to compensate for wear in the brake pads and linings.

Routine check

- Check the level every week and before setting off on long journeys, and top it up when necessary.
- Never allow the fluid level to fall below the minimum mark on the reservoir. If you have to top it up repeatedly, such as once a week, there could be a leak in the system. Don't drive the car, and have the system checked immediately. A leak is potentially very dangerous and could result in a reduction in braking performance or even complete brake failure. To help keep the hydraulic system in good working order and to help prevent an air lock (*see page 128*), have the fluid replaced once a year at a garage, regardless of your annual mileage.

Checking fluid level

you will need

→ clean cloth
→ fresh brake fluid of the correct type
→ plastic funnel (possibly)

Brake fluid is toxic and corrosive; see the note on page 129.

❶ Park the car on level ground, set the handbrake and switch off the engine.

Refer to your handbook for the position of the brake fluid reservoir.

❷ If the reservoir is translucent, you may be able to check the level without opening it. It should be between the maximum and minimum marks.

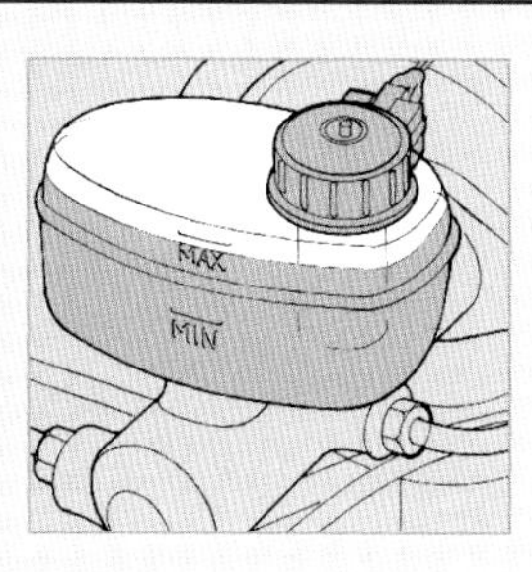

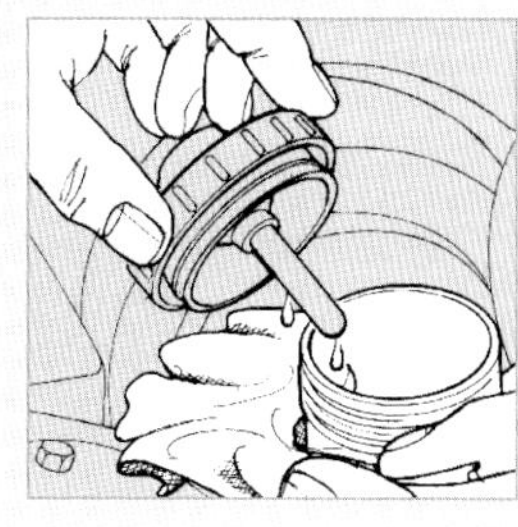

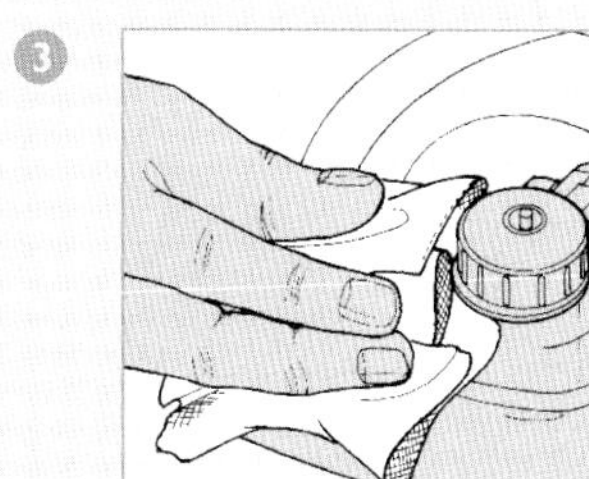

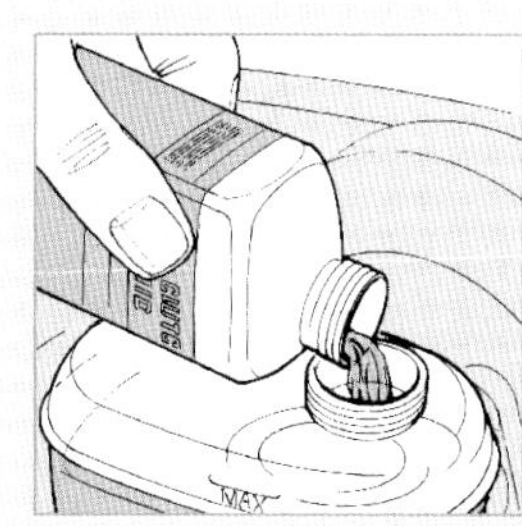

❸ If you cannot check the level from the outside, wipe the top of the reservoir clean and unscrew the cap. If dirt is allowed to enter the fluid, it could cause problems, so be careful not to allow any specks of dirt or anything else (such as water droplets) to enter the reservoir and contaminate the system. Don't leave the reservoir open for too long, to minimize the fluid's exposure to air.

❹ The inside of the cap may have a dipstick or projection that extends down into the fluid. If so, remove it carefully and have a clean cloth to hand to catch any drips. (Take care not to allow any threads or particles from the cloth to adhere to the dipstick.)

❺ Top up with fresh fluid to the maximum mark. Don't shake the bottle, as this could create air bubbles in the fluid, which could cause a reduction in braking performance or even total brake failure. Make sure that you do not overfill the reservoir.

❻ Check the condition of the fluid by rubbing a little between your fingers. If it feels gritty, take the car to a garage to have it changed. Wash your fingers immediately. If you can see any dirt or other form of contamination in the fluid, have it changed.

❼ Replace the cap, tightening it firmly.

Handbrake

On most cars, the handbrake (parking brake) operates on the rear wheels. It works independently of the foot brake for reasons of safety. If the hydraulic system operating the foot brake should fail, the handbrake can still be applied mechanically.

Two-cable

Each rear brake is controlled by a separate cable attachment to its own adjuster below the handbrake lever. This allows independent adjustment of the cables.

1. Handbrake lever
2. Cables
3. Guides
4. Adjusters

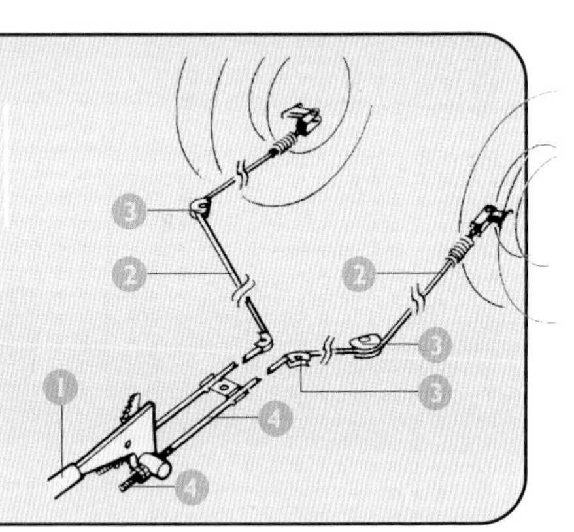

One-cable

Both rear brakes are linked by the same cable, which runs forward to pass over a yoke attached to a single adjuster below the handbrake lever.

1. Handbrake lever
2. Cable
3. Balance yoke
4. Adjuster

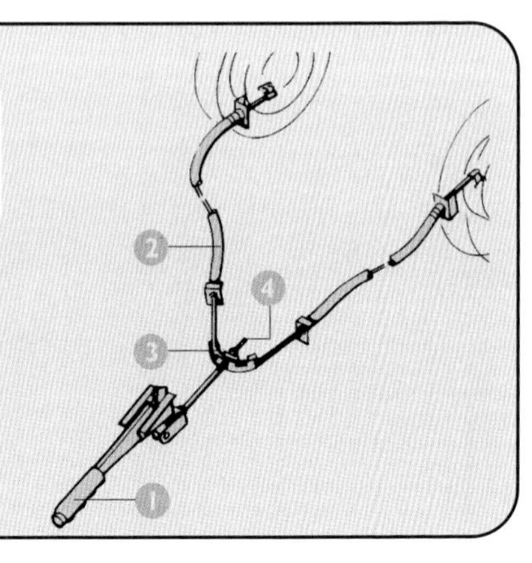

How it works

• The handbrake lever has a ratchet mechanism that locks into place when the lever is pulled up. The lever is linked to the rear brakes by a series of cables and metal rods.

• If the car has drum brakes fitted to the rear wheels, the handbrake operates the same brake shoes as those operated by the foot brake, but uses the cables and rods to apply the brakes instead of the hydraulic system. The handbrake on most cars has twin cables, one cable running to each rear wheel. The cables often stretch over time, but can be 'taken up' or adjusted at a garage.

• There are several different handbrake systems. On cars with disc brakes at the rear, the handbrake is often connected to small additional calipers and brake pads, or small drum brakes that are fitted to the centre of the rear brake discs.

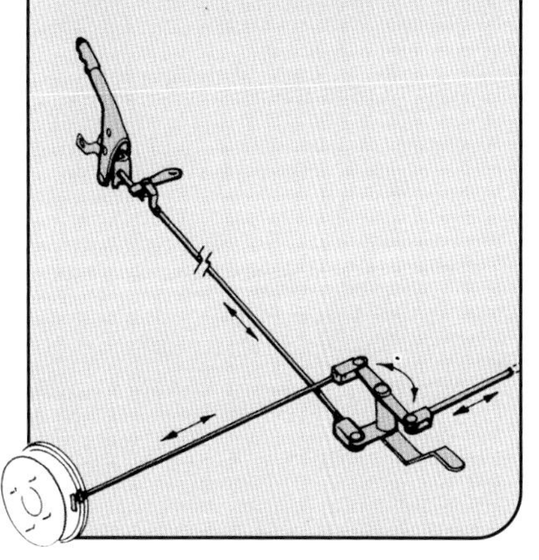

TIP

In very cold wintry conditions, park the car in gear to keep it from rolling, rather than use the handbrake. If ice forms inside the rear brakes or cables, it could become very difficult to release the handbrake cable. Only do this on level ground.

Check efficiency

Park the car on a steep hill, making sure there is nothing behind you. Apply the handbrake and release the foot brake. The rear part of the car should rise slightly, and the car should hold firm and not roll back. If the car does not hold its position, take it to a garage. The rear brakes may be incorrectly adjusted, or worn, or the handbrake cable may be frayed or have stretched and need adjusting.

Anti-lock brakes

ABS or anti-lock braking is fitted as standard to an increasing number of cars. It helps prevent the wheels from skidding when braking in wet or icy conditions by overriding the brakes' normal operation, applying them instead in short bursts or pulses.

The ABS system

An ABS system has an electronic control unit and wheel sensors that control the flow of brake fluid to the wheel cylinders, preventing the brakes from locking up.

1. Wheel speed sensors
2. ECU
3. Warning light
4. Modulator

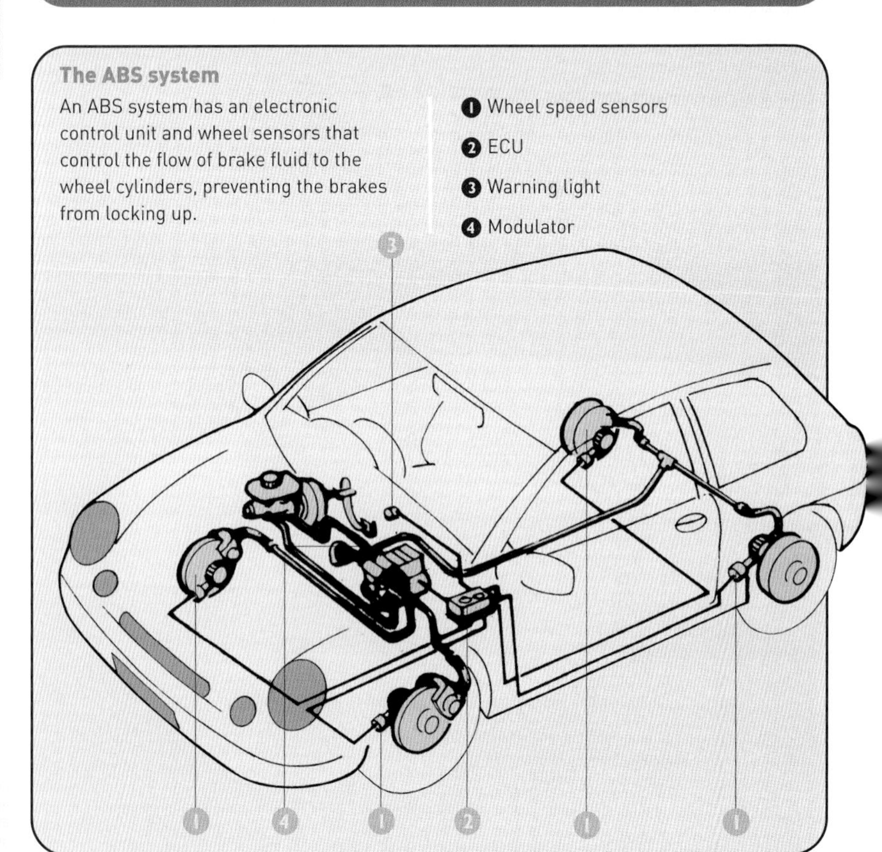

How it works

- An ABS system comprises wheel speed sensors, a pump (or modulator) and an ECU that controls the system. It operates on any or all four of the wheels, depending upon which are affected. The sensors monitor wheel speed and detect when a brake is about to lock, feeding this information to the system's ECU. This releases the brake by limiting the hydraulic pressure applied and the amount of hydraulic fluid being forced through to the wheel cylinders.

- When the wheel sensor detects that the brake is no longer locking, the ECU causes it to be reapplied, but if the sensor detects that the wheels are about to lock again, it releases them. This process of releasing and reapplying the brakes is repeated many times a second until the sensors detect that the wheels are no longer about to lock, or that the car has come to a halt.

- The driver can normally feel the ABS working through vibration in the brake pedal.

- If the ABS system becomes faulty or fails, it automatically shuts down and the dashboard ABS warning light comes on (*see page 145*), but this does not affect the main braking system, which continues to operate normally. If the ABS is faulty or fails, have it checked.

Brake lock

In an emergency, the instinctive reaction of many drivers is to slam their foot hard on the brake, but brakes can lock. When a car brakes, a great deal of its weight is thrown forward on to its front wheels, lightening the load on the back wheels, which may lock and skid.

Similarly, if the front disc brakes, which supply most of the braking power in most cars, are not working efficiently, the driver presses harder on the brake pedal to produce the required braking action. More hydraulic pressure than usual is applied to the brakes, which may also cause the rear brakes to lock.

It is possible for a driver to mimic the action of ABS by pumping the brake pedal repeatedly, a technique known as 'cadence' braking. The driver stamps on the brake pedal, but then releases it quickly and repeats this many times in quick succession. The wheels are brought to the point of maximum braking, just before they are about to lock.

This is a skilled technique, best practised on a skid pan under the expert eye of a tutor, but since ABS is now fitted as standard to many cars, drivers are less likely to be able to put it to use.

INTERIOR

Cleaning the interior

A little light housework carried out regularly inside the car will keep it clean and smelling fresh. There is a wide range of commercial cleaning products available for your car, but if you don't wish to buy these, you can simply use domestic cleaning products on the upholstery and carpet.

you will need

→ clean cloth/duster
→ soft nailbrush/sponge
→ soapy water
→ brush
→ commercial cleaner/ restorer (if required)
→ vacuum cleaner

TIP

If you run out of glass cleaner, you can clean the insides of the windscreen and windows by rubbing over them with a damp cloth or chamois leather, then finally polishing them clean with a folded sheet of newspaper. This works on the outside and the mirrors as well.

General

Empty and clean out ashtrays and storage compartments. Take up and shake floor mats, remove grit and surface dirt with a stiff brush, then vacuum both floor and mats. Brush loose dirt from the upholstery and vacuum the whole interior, getting into awkward areas with nozzles and special attachments – and don't forget the boot. Clean carpets with carpet shampoo.

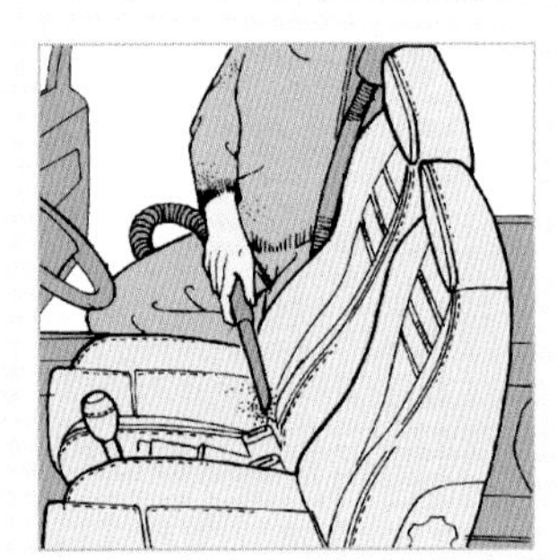

Upholstery

Check your car handbook for special recommendations on cleaning the upholstery. Rub marks on fabric upholstery with warm soapy water, using a clean cloth or soft nailbrush, but be careful not to soak it. Alternatively, use a commercial upholstery cleaner. If a fabric seat is badly stained, you may need to remove the whole seat cover (if possible) to clean it. Leather seats can be wiped with a damp cloth, and stubborn marks or stains removed with a commercial leather cleaner. PVC or vinyl upholstery can also be wiped with a damp cloth.

Trim

Dust and wipe the dashboard, fascia and trim with a damp cloth. Plastic fascia and trim are prone to fade in strong sunlight. Use a restorer (available from car accessory shops) to revitalize faded or marked trim.

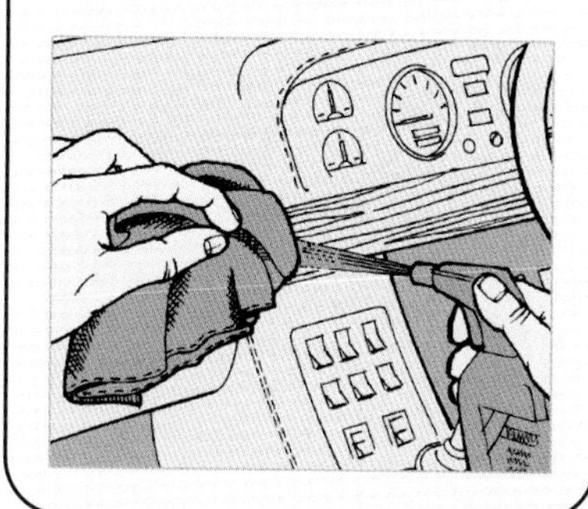

Windows

It is important to keep windows clean to ensure good visibility when driving and prevent them from fogging up too quickly. The inside of windows, particularly the windscreen and rear window, may acquire a thin film of grease and become smeary, a problem that is exacerbated if you smoke regularly in the car. A smeary windscreen hampers visibility at night. To guard against this, wash windows regularly with a commercial window cleaner, or use a simple solution of water and vinegar.

The dashboard

The gauges and lights on the dashboard allow you to monitor the function of certain parts of the engine at a glance, alerting you to faults. When you turn on the ignition, some lights come on, but go off once the engine is running. If any remain on, it could indicate a problem.

The basic dashboard

The layout of the dashboard varies from car to car, as do the number of lights and gauges and the form they take, but most cars have the gauges and lights shown in the drawing below.

The following pages contain a guide to their function and warning indications, but as these can vary slightly, check your car handbook and familiarize yourself with your own car's dashboard display.

Warning lights and gauges

It is important that warning lights function correctly. If a light stays on for no obvious reason, it could mean that the light is faulty or, if it fails to come on when it should, the bulb may need replacing. abnormal readings for no apparent reason. In both cases, consult a garage.

Typical features

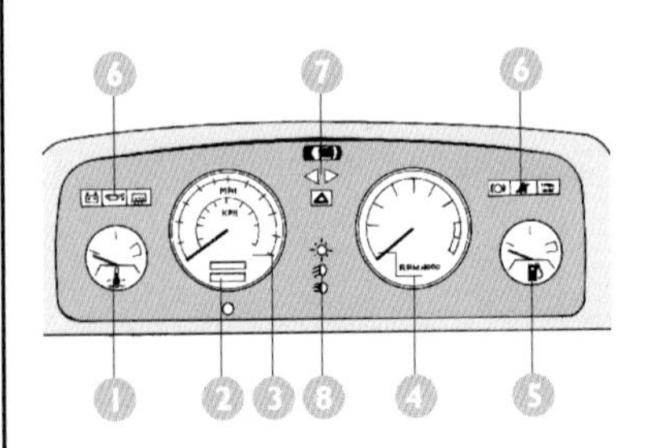

1. Water temperature gauge
2. Odometer
3. Speedometer
4. Tachometer
5. Fuel gauge
6. Various warning lights
7. Indicator turning lights
8. Main-beam warning light

Coolant temperature gauge

This indicates that the engine is running at the correct temperature.

When the engine is started, the gauge shows that it is cold, but as it runs and heats up, the needle rises to the 'normal' position (or green, or central dial position), indicating that the engine has reached the correct temperature. (If you are unsure of the correct gauge reading, check your car handbook.)

If the needle climbs beyond normal towards the red zone slowly, but does not reach it, the cooling system may not be functioning effectively. To check it, switch on the heater and allow it to run at its highest temperature. It should draw heat away from the engine, causing the temperature to fall and enabling you to continue on your way, but drive slowly and get to a garage as soon as possible.

If the needle is in or rises quickly into the red zone, the engine is overheating and there is a fault. Pull over and turn the engine off immediately. Do not attempt to drive any farther, or the engine could be seriously damaged. Not all cars have a temperature gauge, but all have a warning light (*see page 143*).

Fuel gauge

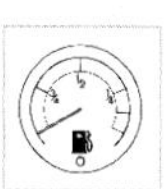

This indicates how much fuel is in the tank and usually incorporates a low-fuel warning light. The light comes on when there is only a limited amount of fuel left in the tank – your car handbook may tell you how much this is. If you keep a note of the mileage you do and the fuel you put in, you can work out the average number of miles your car does per gallon, which will give you a rough idea of how far you can drive when the light comes on.

TIP

Don't allow the fuel level to get very low, as sediment collects at the bottom of the tank and could enter, causing a blockage in the fuel line.

Fuel gauges are notoriously inaccurate and may show nearly empty when there is still quite a lot of fuel in the tank. Always fill up as soon as the warning light comes on, but preferably before.

Oil pressure warning light

- This comes on when the ignition is switched on and goes off when the engine is started. It lights if the pressure of the oil in the engine is too low.

- If it fails to go out or comes on while the engine is running, pull over and switch the engine off immediately, as serious damage will result if the car is driven while the oil pressure is low.

- If the light does go out once the oil has been topped up, check the level again in several days' time to make sure that it has not fallen again. If it has, look for leaks (*see page 251*) and have it checked at a garage.

- If the light goes off in the normal way, just after the engine is started, but then comes on again when the engine is idling, it could mean that the oil and oil filter need changing. Alternatively, it could mean that parts of the engine are worn, in which case replacing the oil and oil filter would not cure the problem. Take the car to a garage as soon as possible for an oil pressure test.

- If the light flickers on and off when cornering, it could indicate low oil pressure or a short circuit in the wiring. Again, take the car to a garage as soon as possible, as it may not be safe to continue running the car.

Oil level

Don't confuse oil pressure with oil level; this light does not indicate oil level (*see below*). But lack of oil can cause low oil pressure, so check the oil level with the dipstick, and if it is low, fill it up to the maximum mark (*see page 246*). Once you have filled up, check to see that the light goes out. If it does not, do not drive the car, but seek assistance immediately.

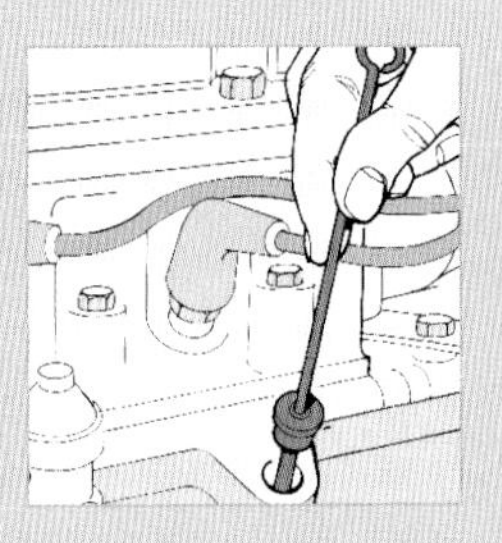

WARNING

Pull over and switch the engine off immediately if the oil pressure light comes on. If the engine runs for even less than a minute when the light is on, it could cause serious – and expensive – damage.

Oil level gauge

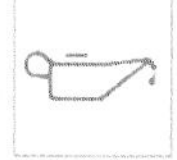

This is fitted to some cars and tells you how much oil is in the car without using the dipstick. It only gives an accurate reading when the car is parked on the level with the ignition switched on, but the engine off. The gauge will not work once the engine is running.

Air bag (SRS) warning light

This light comes on momentarily when the ignition is switched on and usually goes off after a few seconds.

If it remains on or comes on while you are driving, there is a fault in the system, and the air bags may not function correctly in an accident. The light might also flash or remain on if the airbag has been disarmed. The car can be driven, but have the system checked as soon as possible.

Coolant temperature warning light

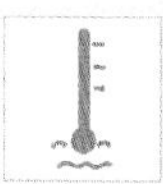

This light may come on when the ignition is switched on and go off a few seconds after the engine is started. If it remains on, there could be a fault in the cooling system, or the coolant level could be too low.

If it comes on while driving, this could indicate that the coolant level is too low or that the coolant temperature is too high and the engine is in danger of overheating. Pull over and switch off the engine as soon as possible. If you suspect the car is overheating, see page 297.

If you want to check the coolant level, see pages 178–79; allow the engine to cool down and top it up if necessary (*see page 181*). If the light comes on again shortly after you have topped up and restarted the car, stop and seek assistance. Don't drive the car any farther as the engine could be damaged from overheating.

In some cars, the light flashes red when the engine is overheating and blue when the engine is not getting hot quickly enough. Refer to your car handbook for details of the system in your make of car.

Battery charge warning light

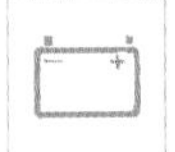

This comes on when the ignition is switched on, but goes out after the engine is started. If it remains on after the engine is started, or if it comes on while driving, this usually means that the battery is not being charged correctly (often due to a faulty alternator).

Pull over and stop the car as soon as possible. Open the bonnet and see if you can detect any strange smells or see any smoke. If you can, don't turn the ignition back on, as it could cause a fire; call for assistance immediately.

If you don't detect any of these signs, switch off all electrical accessories (radio, air conditioning, rear window heater, etc.) and take the car to a garage to be checked as soon as possible. You should be able to drive the car a short distance, but the battery could soon run flat, causing the engine to fail.

See also pages 194–95 for checking the battery's condition/reasons for a flat battery.

Electronic control unit light

This comes on when the ignition is switched on, but goes off when the engine is started.

If it remains on or comes on while you are driving, this indicates that the car's computer has detected a fault through its self-diagnostic system (*see page 164*). Quite a number of faults are possible, one of the most common being a defect in the emissions control system, in which case a reduction in engine performance may be noticeable.

If this light comes on, the car can usually be driven, but the fault needs to be identified and fixed at a garage as soon as possible.

Diesel pre-heat light

This comes on when the ignition is switched on, indicating that the heater plugs are operating. Wait for it to go out before starting the engine. In some cars, it does not come on if the engine is warm.

If the light remains on when the engine is started, the car can be driven, but seek assistance immediately.

Water in fuel filter light

(diesel engines only)
This light comes on when water needs to be drained from the fuel system filter (*see page 236*).

Brake warning light

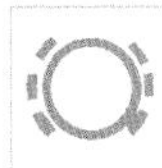

The brake warning light comes on when the ignition is switched on and the handbrake is applied. It goes out a few seconds after the engine is started and the handbrake has been released.

If it remains on once the engine is running and the handbrake has been released, first check that the handbrake has been fully released. If it has and the light is still on, it could indicate that the brake fluid level is low. Do not drive the car while the fluid level is low; the brakes could malfunction or fail. Check the fluid level and top it up if necessary (*see pages 130–31*).

If the light comes on while you are driving, pull over and check the brake fluid level and top it up if necessary. If this is OK, don't drive the car as it may not be safe to do so; seek assistance immediately.

TIP

If the brake warning light fails to come on when the ignition is switched on, it could be caused by a faulty bulb in the dashboard light itself. Have it checked at a garage as it is important that the warning light functions correctly.

Brake pad warning light

This light is fitted to some cars and indicates that the brake pads need to be renewed. The car can normally be driven, but ensure that the pads are replaced as soon as possible.

ABS warning light

The ABS light comes on momentarily when the engine is switched on and then goes off.

If it remains on once the engine has been started, or comes on while you are driving, there is a fault in the system. In this case, the ABS controller automatically disables the ABS system so that the brakes function in the normal way (but without ABS).

The car can be driven, but take it to a garage as soon as possible to have the system checked.

Safety

The ABS system is an important safety feature; don't be tempted to manage without it.

Other warning lights

Some cars have other warning lights fitted, such as a light to show when a seatbelt is not being worn, or to show that a door is open, or when the car needs to be serviced. Refer to your car handbook for the function of all these warning lights.

Speedometer

A speedometer is required to be fitted to every car by law to indicate the speed at which it is travelling, and takes the form of a dial or a digital display.

If the needle on the dial is wavering or stationary, it indicates a fault in the drive mechanism, which requires garage attention.

Heated rear window

In some cars, a light on the dashboard indicates that the rear window heater has been switched on, while in others, the button to switch it on lights up.

Rev-counter (tachometer)

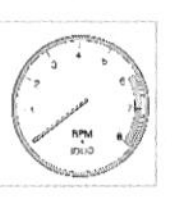

This indicates the speed at which the engine is turning (as opposed to the speed of the car itself) in thousands of revolutions per minute.

Trip meter

A trip meter indicates the distance travelled per journey. In some cars, the on-board computer also calculates average fuel consumption per mile.

Odometer

This records the total mileage travelled by the vehicle.

Cruise control light

This indicates that the cruise control system has been engaged.

Cruise control automatically maintains the car at a constant speed over long distances. If it fails or is not operating correctly, first check the fuse (*see page 208*). If the fuse is OK, do not use cruise control and have the system checked by a garage as soon as possible.

Turning indicator lights

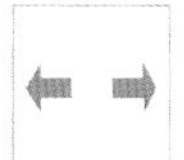

Flashing arrows on the dashboard show that the left or right front and rear indicators are working.

If the arrows do not flash or are not working normally, check that the front and rear indicator lights, and the side repeaters, are working correctly (*see page 75*). If they are, the dashboard light may be at fault, and you should have it checked at a garage.

Sidelights/headlights

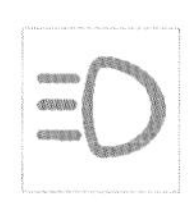

Warning lights are not normally used to indicate that side, rear and headlights are in use. However, dashboard illumination lights operate as soon as the sidelights are switched on.

A headlight main-beam warning light is fitted to remind the driver that the main beam has been selected.

Hazard warning lights

These alert other drivers to a possible hazard. They do not consist of separate lights, but make use of the right and left turning indicators, which are made to flash in unison.

Operated via a button or switch located on or near the dashboard, they normally show that they have been activated by means of a flashing light on the button itself.

Familiarize yourself with the button's location so that you can operate them quickly in an emergency. Hazard warning lights are used to warn others of a car's presence if it breaks down in an unexpected or dangerous place, if it is being driven well below the speed limit, or if it has to slow down quickly on a high-speed road.

Fog lamps

One or two lights appear on the dashboard, indicating that the front and/or rear fog lamps have been switched on.

THE ENGINE

Cleaning the engine

Working on a car engine can be hazardous, so when you venture under the bonnet, make sure you are aware of the potential dangers and follow the safety guidelines given here. Be particularly careful if the engine has been running; parts will be hot.

Opening the bonnet

Check your car handbook to locate the lever for releasing the bonnet. It is generally on the driver's side, beneath the dashboard. This releases the bonnet only partially – feel just under the front edge for a catch to release it fully.

All cars are fitted with struts that hold the bonnet open safely. Make sure the strut is located properly in its socket.

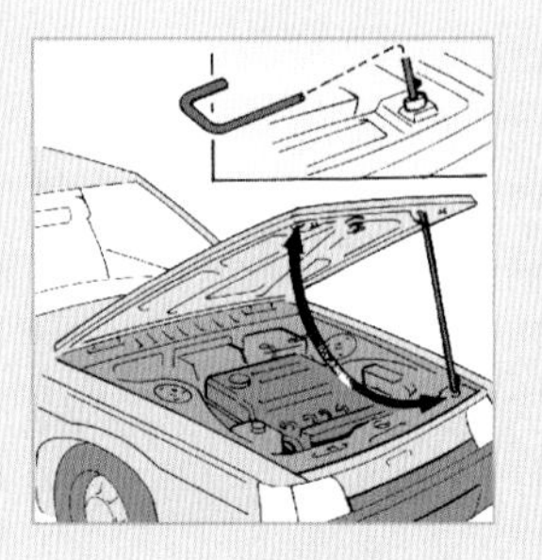

you will need

- → clean cloth or rag
- → plastic bags
- → pegs and elastic bands
- → commercial engine cleaner
- → hose and water

If you keep the engine clean, there is less chance of dirt falling into open fluid reservoirs, or into other parts of the engine, where it could cause extra wear or even damage. A clean engine also makes it easier to spot any leaks, or wear and tear on hoses and other components in good time. It also helps you to stay clean while working on the engine.

Cleaning the engine

Every car owner is familiar with the regular Sunday chore of cleaning the car, but the engine also benefits from being kept clean.

After a period of time on the road, the engine inevitably becomes caked in grime and grease. Keep it clean by wiping away dirt with a cloth, or use a commercial engine cleaner.

If the engine is really filthy, take it to a garage for steam cleaning.

Safety

Read the safety guidelines on pages 18–19 before carrying out any work on your car's engine.

Using a cleaner

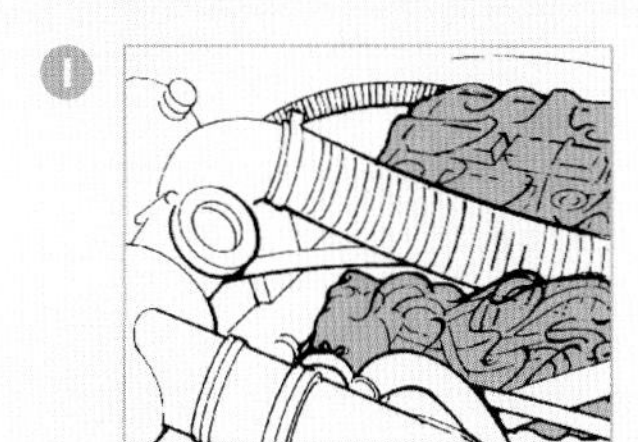

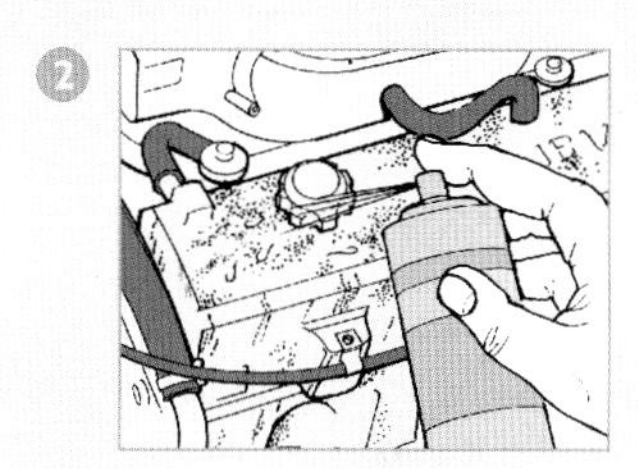

❶ If using an engine cleaner, protect the battery, distributor, spark plug leads, coil, pulleys and drive belts by covering them with plastic bags. Disconnect the plug leads from the plugs (*see page 216*), bundle them with the distributor cap and cover with a plastic bag. Secure the bags with elastic bands. Protect a diesel fuel injection pump.

❷ Spray the dirty parts of the engine with cleaner. Rinse off the cleaner with a hose, being careful not to spray too close to the plastic bags. Do not remove grease from any moving parts that need it.

❸ Wait for the engine to dry and remove the plastic bags. Since water and damp impede ignition, as a precaution, spray water dispersant on the spark plug leads, distributor, coil and battery (but not on the belts or pulleys).

Petrol engine

The heart of the vehicle is the engine, which contains the cylinders, pistons, valves, crankshaft, connecting rods and camshaft. This is the hard-working part where the power that drives the car is produced.

How it works

Most engines have four cylinders, although more powerful cars can have six or eight. The cylinders house the pistons, which move up and down producing the power that drives the vehicle. At top speed, they may be pumping up and down at 100 times a second.

The petrol engine burns a mixture of fuel and air, which is drawn into the combustion chamber at the top of the cylinder through a fuel-injection system (or, in older cars, a carburettor).

A spark from a spark plug ignites the fuel/air mixture, which burns and expands rapidly, forcing the piston down the cylinder.

Excess heat in the engine is dispersed by a cooling system (*see page 172*) and oil lubricates the constant action of the engine's moving parts (*see page 242*).

Inlet and exhaust valves at the top of the cylinder allow the fuel/air mixture into the cylinders and burnt gases out. They are operated by a camshaft.

A rod at the base of the piston connects it to the crankshaft, and the crankshaft is connected to the transmission system (gears). The downward motion of the piston turns the crankshaft, transmitting the motion to the transmission, from where it drives the wheels of the car.

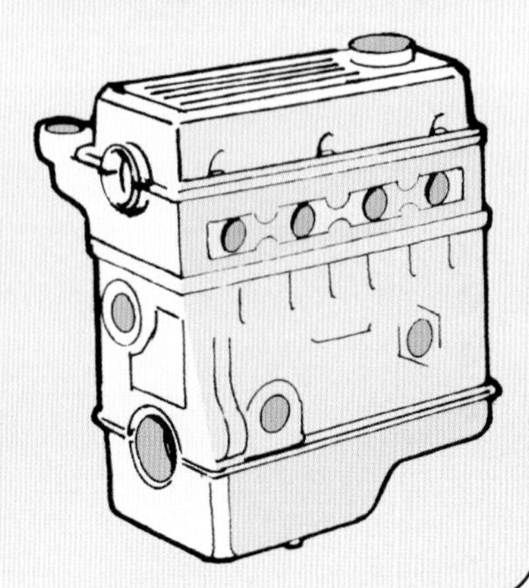

The interior of the engine

The engine comprises four major assemblies:

❶ The cylinder head containing the combustion chambers, valves (usually two per cylinder), and the inlet and exhaust ports. The cylinder head has a metal cover over the valve gear or camshaft.

❷ The cylinder block containing the cylinders and passages through which the coolant circulates. It may also contain the camshaft, although on many engines this is mounted above the cylinder head and is known as an overhead camshaft (OHC).

❸ The crankshaft assembly, which includes the pistons, connecting rods and the crankshaft itself, with a flywheel at one end.

❹ A metal sump at the base of the cylinder block acts as a reservoir for the oil that lubricates the engine.

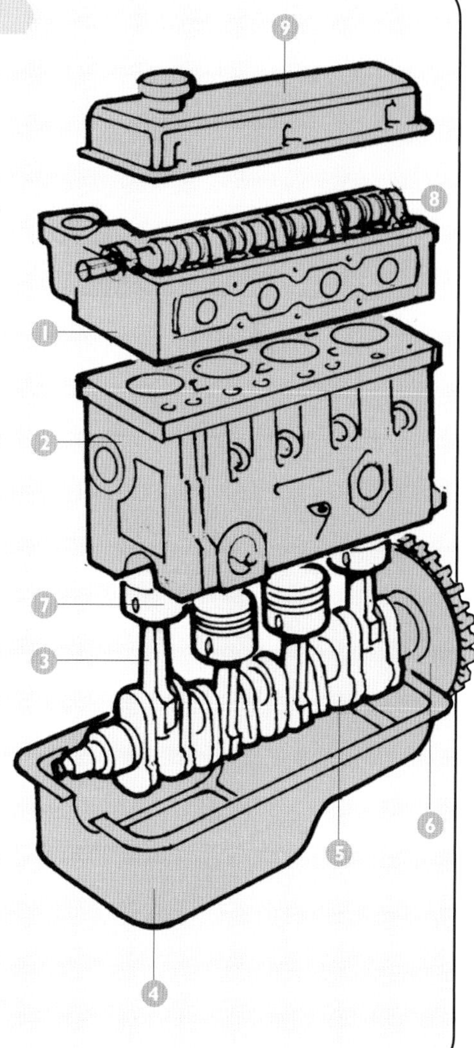

❺ Crankshaft

❻ Flywheel

❼ Pistons (fit in cylinders [tubes] cut into cylinder block)

❽ Camshaft

❾ Valve cover

The four-stroke cycle

The engine is the car's powerhouse, the place where the energy required to propel the car forward is produced. Most car engines operate on the 'four-stroke' cycle, whereby the piston travels up and down the cylinder four times to produce one power stroke.

Inlet stroke

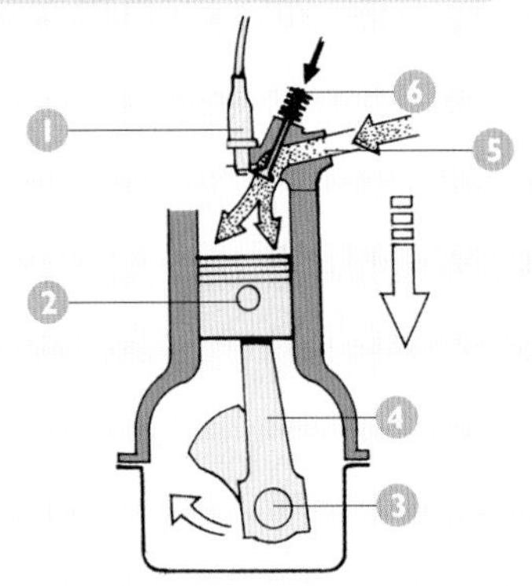

1. Spark plug
2. Piston descends, creating suction
3. Crankshaft rotating
4. Connecting rod
5. Inlet valve open, allowing air/fuel mix from inlet manifold
6. Inlet valve

With the inlet valve open and the crankshaft rotating, the piston is moving down. As it descends, it draws in a mixture of fuel and air through the inlet manifold and past the open inlet valve.

Compression stroke

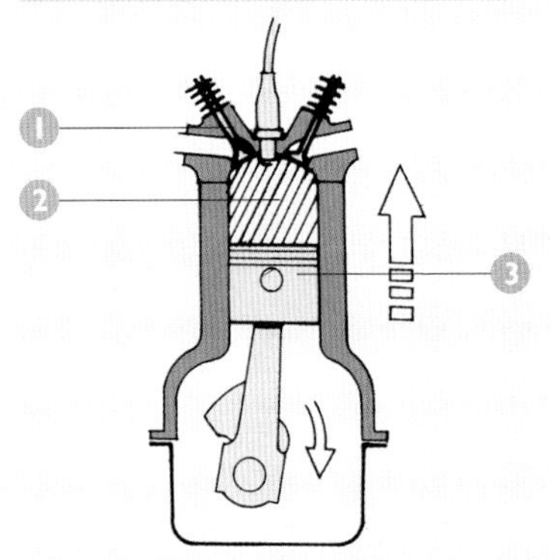

1. Inlet and exhaust valves shut
2. Piston compressing fuel/air mixture
3. Piston rises

With the inlet and exhaust valves shut, the rotating crankshaft pushes the piston upwards, compressing the fuel/air mixture into the combustion chamber.

Power stroke

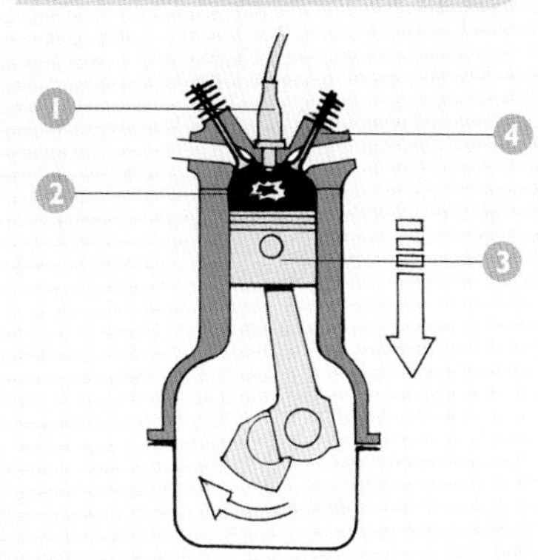

1. Spark plug emits spark
2. Fuel/air mixture ignites, burns and expands
3. Piston is forced down by expanding gases and turns crankshaft
4. Inlet and exhaust valves shut

With the valves still shut, the spark plug emits a spark and ignites the compressed fuel/air mixture. This burns rapidly and expands, forcing the piston down the cylinder and rotating the crankshaft.

Exhaust stroke

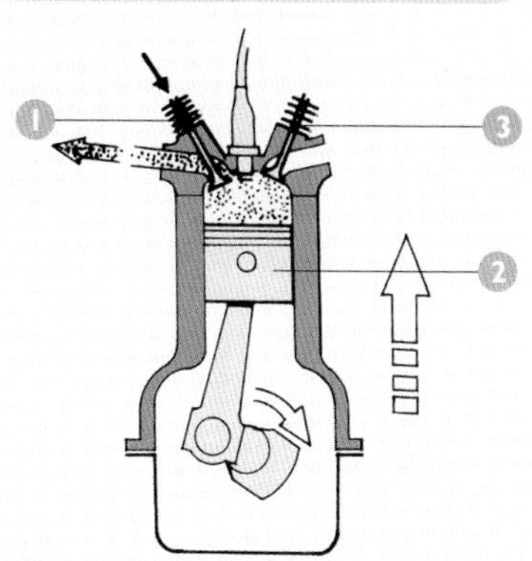

1. Exhaust valve opens, letting gases out
2. Piston rises, forcing gases out
3. Inlet valve shut

The rotating crankshaft pushes the piston back up the cylinder, forcing the burnt gases out past the open exhaust valve.

As the piston reaches the top of the cylinder, the exhaust valve closes, the inlet valve opens and the cycle begins again. The crankshaft rotates twice during the four strokes, and the camshaft once every four strokes, as it only needs to open the valves once during the cycle.

Forced induction

Some engines have an engine-driven pump (turbocharger or supercharger) that forces extra fuel/air mixture into the combustion chamber to produce even more power. A turbocharger is driven by exhaust gas, while a supercharger is driven by a belt or gears from the crankshaft.

The major engine components

The cylinders, pistons, camshaft, crankshaft and valves are concealed within the engine. Other components are located on the outside of the engine, but can be difficult to see if they are hidden beneath other engine parts. Their positions can vary from car to car.

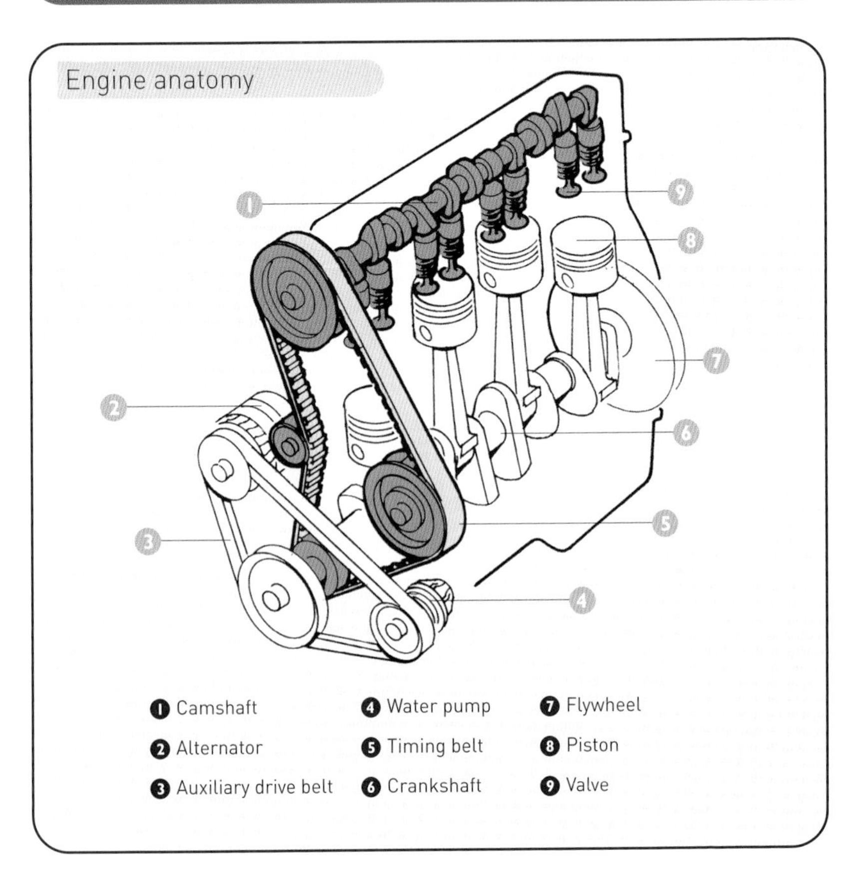

Camshaft

Driven from the crankshaft by a timing belt or chain, the camshaft controls the opening of the valves. Lobes (projections) on the camshaft open the valves by pressing on them as the camshaft rotates, while springs shut them again.

In most engines, the camshaft is positioned over the valves, known as an overhead camshaft or OHC. In older cars, the camshaft may be positioned beneath the valves, in which case it is known as an overhead valve engine, or OHV.

Twin cam

Cars with more than two valves per cylinder may have two camshafts to operate the increased number of valves efficiently. This type of engine is known as a double overhead camshaft (DOHC) or 'twin cam'. One camshaft operates the inlet valves, while the other controls the exhaust valves.

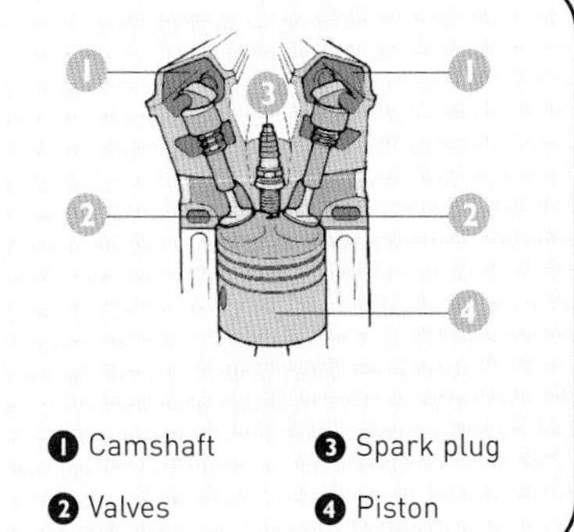

❶ Camshaft ❸ Spark plug
❷ Valves ❹ Piston

Crankshaft

The crankshaft is one of the most important parts of the engine. It converts the reciprocating (up-and-down) motion of the pistons in their cylinders into the rotary motion that is necessary to drive the car's wheels.

Using a system of pulleys and belts or chains, the crankshaft also drives the camshaft, water pump and alternator, as well as other engine components.

Flywheel

Located at the gearbox end of the crankshaft, the flywheel helps to balance out the up-and-down action of the pistons and ensure the smooth running of the engine.

The transmission system is connected to the engine at the flywheel (the transmission system is not shown in the diagram – *see page 252* for further details).

Valves

The valves control the flow of gases into and out of the cylinders. Operated by the camshaft, they regulate the intake of the fuel/air mixture via the inlet manifold, and the exit of burned gases via the exhaust manifold.

Most cars with four-stroke engines are fitted with two valves per cylinder, one inlet and one exhaust, but many high-performance cars have more valves per cylinder, and three, four or even five are possible. The greater the number of valves, the better the flow of gases (fuel/air mixture and exhaust), and the greater the efficiency of the engine.

The correct timing of the opening and closing of the valves is vital to the engine's performance.

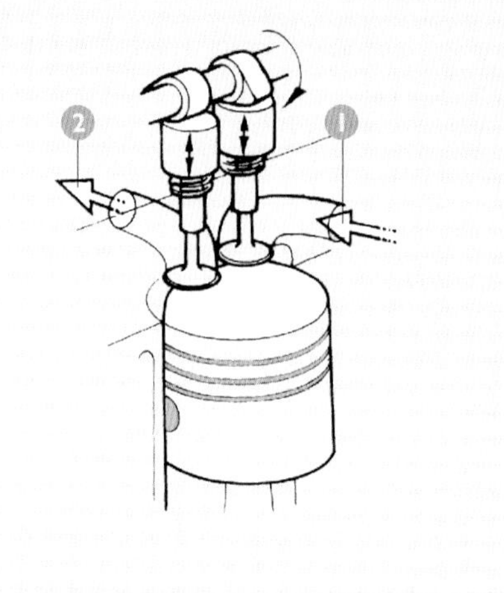

❶ Inlet valve

❷ Exhaust valve

Auxiliary drive belt

This is sometimes also known as the fan belt, as it used to drive the cooling fan, but in most cars the fan is now driven electrically. The auxiliary drive belt is turned by the engine and drives the alternator (*see page 189*) and water pump (*see page 177*).

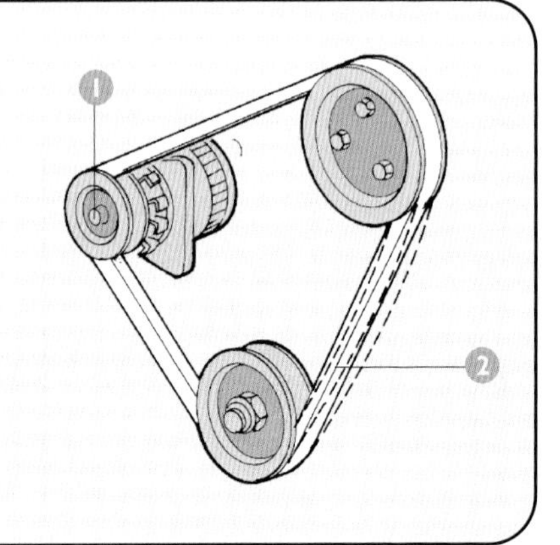

❶ Alternator

❷ Drive belt

The timing belt or chain

The timing or cam belt drives the camshaft and is generally made of reinforced rubber; in older cars, it can be a chain.

Renewal

Check your car handbook to see how often the timing belt needs to be renewed. It is vital that it is renewed at the correct intervals, as if it becomes slack, damaged or even breaks, it could cause severe damage to the engine.

Spark plugs

The timing of the spark is critical. It must happen at the right time for the engine to operate correctly. This is controlled by the ignition module (ECU) of the engine's computer management system.

For more information on spark plugs, see pages 214–19.

Starter motor

The starter motor is an electric motor that sets the engine in motion by rotating the crankshaft. It draws an electrical current from the battery. As the crankshaft rotates, it causes the pistons to move up and down as well as the ignition system to operate.

The downward action of the pistons sucks the fuel/air mixture into the cylinders and the four-stroke cycle takes over. The starter motor disengages as soon as the engine has started (*see also page 189*).

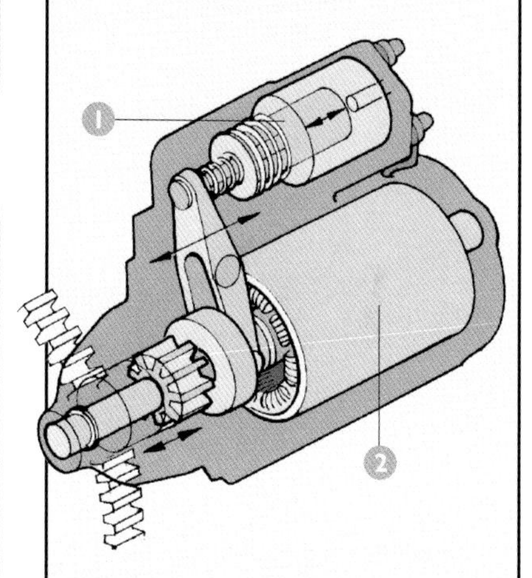

1 Solenoid

2 Starter motor

Engine capacity and layout

The more cylinders an engine has, the more powerful and smoother running it is; equally, the more cylinders an engine has, the more fuel it may use and the more expensive it may be to run. Engine capacity is measured in cubic centimetres (cc).

Number of cylinders

You can easily identify the number of cylinders an engine has by counting the number of spark plug leads. Most cars have four-cylinder engines.

Engine layouts

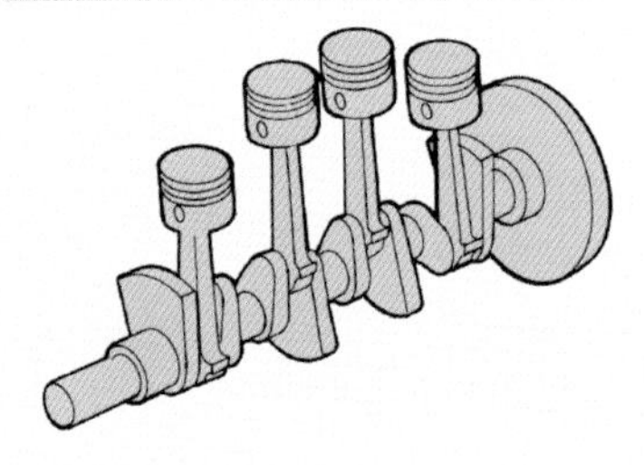

In the majority of cars, the cylinders are laid out 'in-line', which is a relatively simple and compact arrangement.

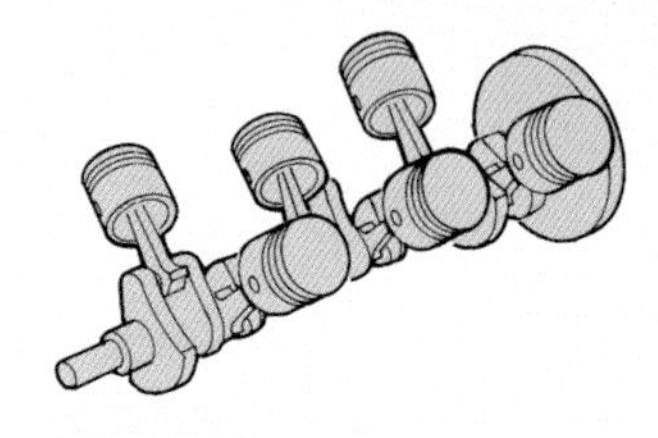

The V-engine arrangement is shorter than the in-line, so it can accommodate more than four cylinders. It is therefore suitable for high-performance engines.

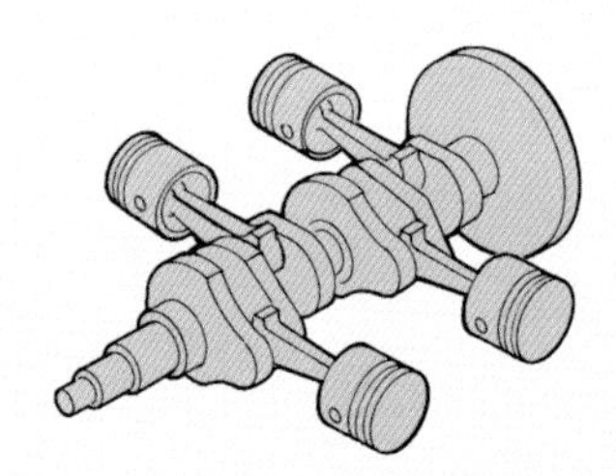

Horizontally-opposed engine layouts have two sets of cylinders opposite each other. This eliminates much of the vibration of other layouts, but takes up more space.

The diesel engine

- The petrol engine compresses a mixture of fuel and air, and ignites it with a spark, whereas the diesel engine compresses only air.
- In the diesel engine, air is taken into the cylinder and compressed at a much higher pressure (i.e. into a much smaller space) than in the petrol engine. As this occurs, it becomes so hot that it ignites the fuel as soon as this is injected into it. Therefore, the diesel engine does not need spark plugs to ignite the fuel.
- However, most diesel engines use heater plugs to warm the induction air when the engine is cold and ensure sufficient heat under compression to produce ignition. (See the description of the four-stroke diesel cycle on *pages 162–63*.)

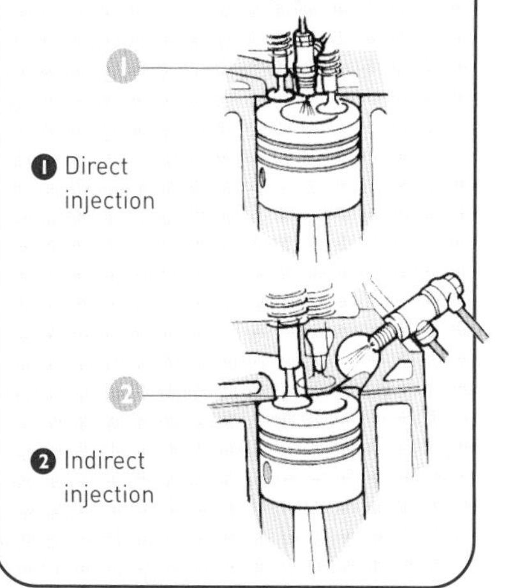

1 Direct injection

2 Indirect injection

Basic differences

Although the components and operation of the diesel engine are similar to the petrol engine (*see pages 152–59*), there are a few basic differences that mainly involve the ignition system – petrol engines have spark ignition, diesel engines have compression ignition.

Heater plugs

There is normally one heater plug per cylinder. They are switched on when the ignition is turned on. A light on the dashboard (*see page 144*) shows that they are operating and goes out after a few seconds, when they are hot enough to help start the engine.

Wait until the light has gone out before starting the engine. (If you don't wait, the engine may not start or it may create a lot of smoke.)

Diesel engines are not as susceptible to damp as petrol engines, as they have no electrical ignition system that needs waterproofing.

The four-stroke diesel cycle

As with a petrol engine, the diesel engine operates on a four-stroke cycle, the major differences being the fact that fuel is injected separately and that ignition is caused by heat generated during the compression stroke.

Direct/indirect injection

When fuel is injected directly into the compressed air in the cylinder of a diesel engine, it ignites quickly and with a lot of noise.

To make this process quieter, until relatively recently, diesel engines used indirect fuel injection – fuel was injected into a pre-combustion chamber connected to the cylinder by a small passageway. This slowed down the combustion and reduced the characteristic diesel 'knocking' noise.

However, in modern diesel engines, improved design controls combustion and has allowed a return to direct injection without the attendant noise.

A diesel engine is more fuel-efficient than a petrol engine, due to the different characteristics of its operation. However, a diesel engine is generally less powerful and is heavier than an equivalent-sized petrol engine.

Inlet stroke

With the inlet valve open and the exhaust valve shut, air from outside the engine is drawn into the combustion chamber as the piston descends in the cylinder.

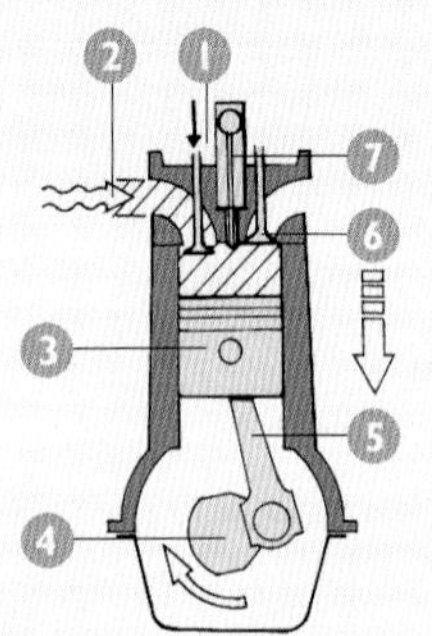

1. Inlet valve open
2. Air drawn into combustion chamber
3. Piston descends, creating suction
4. Crankshaft rotating
5. Connecting rod
6. Exhaust valve shut
7. Fuel injector

Compression stroke

The inlet valve shuts. The piston rises again and compresses the air greatly, making it very hot.

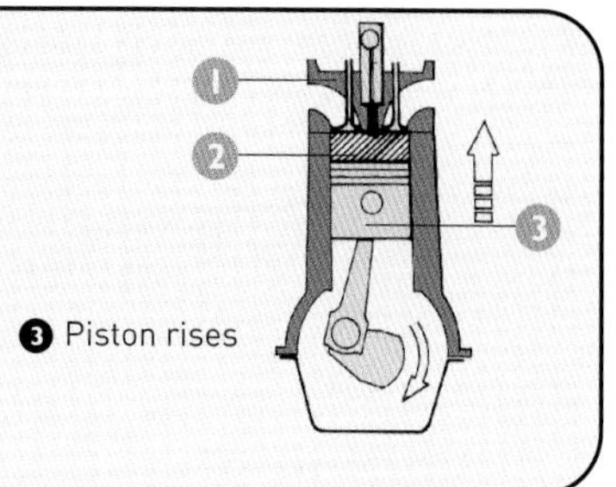

❶ Inlet and exhaust valves shut ❷ Air is compressed into top part of combustion chamber ❸ Piston rises

Injection/power stroke

Fuel is injected into the combustion chamber just before the piston reaches the top of its upward stroke. The fuel ignites immediately in the intense heat of the compressed air, expanding rapidly and forcing the piston back down the cylinder, where it turns the crankshaft via the connecting rod.

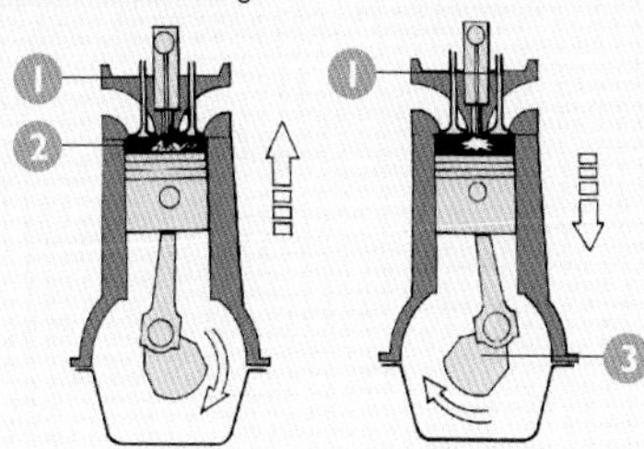

❶ Inlet and exhaust valves shut

❷ Fuel is injected into combustion chamber and ignites when piston nears the top of its stroke

❸ Air/fuel mix expands, forcing piston down to rotate crankshaft

Exhaust stroke

The exhaust valve opens and the piston rises again, pushing the burnt gases out of the combustion chamber. Then the cycle begins again.

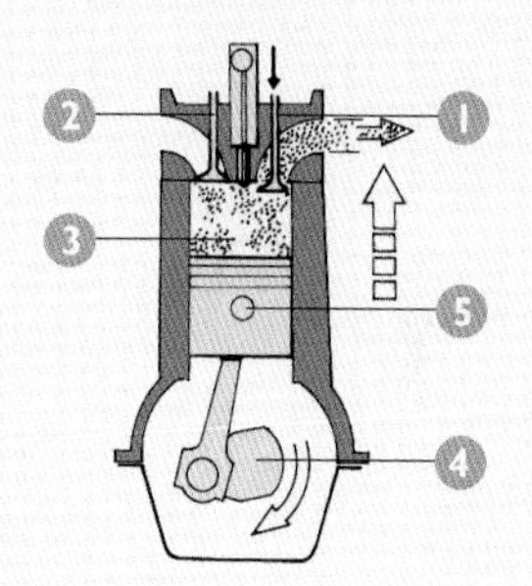

❶ Exhaust valve open, allowing burnt gases out

❷ Inlet valve shut

❸ Burnt gases

❹ Rotating crankshaft forces piston up again

❺ Piston rises, forcing gases out

Electronic control unit

The electronic control unit (ECU) or electronic control module (ECM) is the car's 'black box'. The majority of cars built after 1986 have this computer, which performs millions of calculations per second to monitor and control many of the car's systems.

One of the main reasons computers were introduced into cars was to comply with the emissions regulations introduced by governments worldwide. However, they also assist in fault finding and have simplified design by reducing wiring. The ECU makes it easier for a professional to service a car through its self-diagnostic system, but harder for the amateur, as more mechanical components are governed by the car's computer. Special equipment and expertise are needed to work on the ECU and use its self-diagnostic system.

Sensors

The engine management system is wired to sensors fitted to the engine's main components. These sensors constantly record and feed information back to the computer to indicate how the car is running (see below).

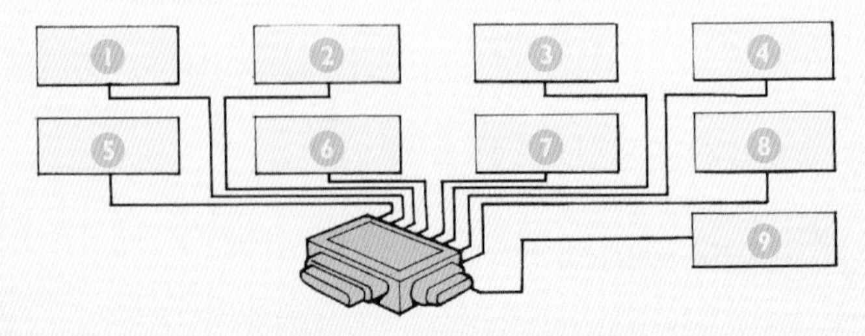

1. Crankshaft position
2. Engine speed
3. Inlet airflow
4. Engine temperature
5. Exhaust oxygen
6. Knock sensor
7. Induction air temperature
8. Throttle position
9. Cruise control

Automatic monitoring

A typical ECU monitors and controls the fuel/air mixture in the combustion chamber, the coolant temperature, ignition timing, idle speed, braking and traction, amount of oxygen in the exhaust system (emission control system), rate of acceleration and transmission. In some cars, additional components are monitored. The sensors produce electronic signals monitoring the components' performance. These are sent to the engine management system's microprocessor, which compares the data it receives with the data in its memory to check that the component is operating efficiently and whether it needs adjusting.

Vulnerability

As with home PCs, the car's on-board computer is not infallible and vibration, heat, grime and general wear and tear can all cause it to malfunction.

Furthermore, tampering with many of the car's electrical systems can cause problems with the ECU. In some cases, even disconnecting the battery can lead to difficulties. Consequently, it is best to entrust any work involving the electrical system to a garage.

Emission control

The ECU balances the requirements of power output, fuel economy and emission control. It regulates the air/fuel mixture (*see page 239*), assisting the catalytic converter to remove pollution from the exhaust.

Fault finding

The ECU has a self-diagnostic system fitted, which monitors and records faults and transmits them to a diagnostic tool. This can be read by a mechanic using a special fault code reader. Alternatively, faults may be indicated via a warning light on the dashboard, which shows you need to have the car checked.

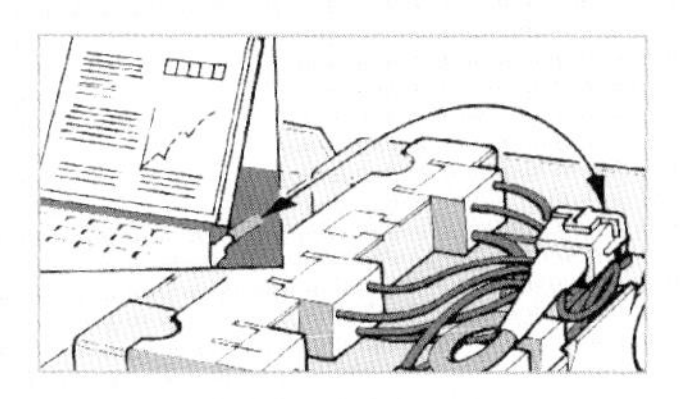

Less wiring

The more electrical features cars have, the more switches and wiring they require. To limit the mass of wiring needed, features located in the same area are grouped together into a module controlled by their own microprocessor. Cars can have as many as 50 microprocessors.

The exhaust system

This system is designed to carry the waste combustion gases from the engine to the atmosphere through a system of canisters and pipes beneath the car. At the same time, it is required to quieten the outgoing gases and to reduce the amount of pollutants they contain.

Design compromise

The most efficient type of exhaust system would be a simple assembly of pipes leading the exhaust gases out into the atmosphere, but since the noise would be appalling and emissions must be controlled, a silencer, expansion chamber and catalytic converter are positioned at intervals.

1. Exhaust manifold
2. Catalytic convertor
3. Expansion chamber
4. Silencer
5. Tail pipe

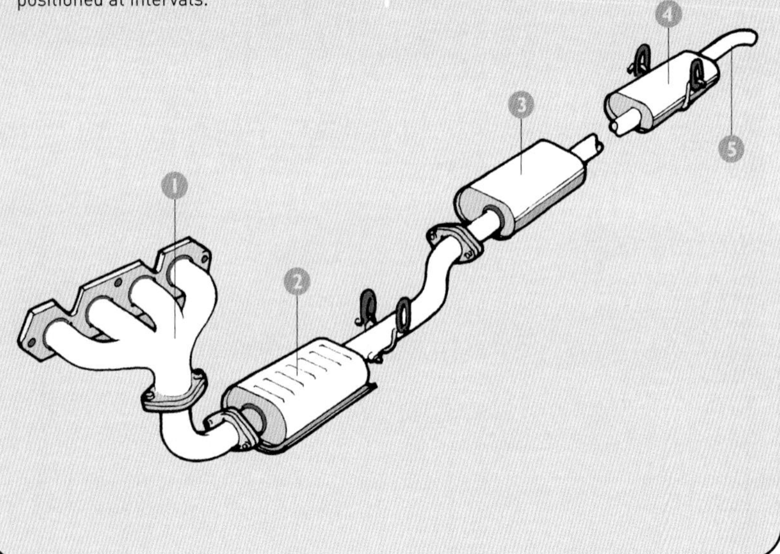

How it works

- The exhaust system typically consists of the exhaust manifold, front pipe, catalytic converter, expansion chamber, silencer and tail pipe.
- Each time an exhaust valve opens in the engine, a high-pressure blast of exhaust gas is discharged from the engine cylinder into the exhaust manifold. Without the exhaust system to quieten them, the discharge of these gases would be extremely noisy, like a small cannon firing repeatedly.
- The exhaust gases pass from the exhaust manifold, through the front pipe and into the catalytic converter, where the most toxic components – nitrous oxide, hydrocarbons and carbon monoxide – are converted into less harmful nitrogen, carbon dioxide and water.
- Then the gases pass through another pipe into the silencer, where they slow down and expand, losing much of their noise. Finally the gases pass through the tail pipe and into the atmosphere.

Variations

Cars manufactured before the early 1990s may not be equipped with a catalytic converter. Some luxury cars, where very quiet running is a requirement for passenger comfort, are fitted with an extra silencer called a resonator. This is designed to quieten the exhaust gases even further. As resonators tend to absorb more engine power, they are not normally fitted to conventional cars, but only to models that have power to spare.

Life expectancy

Exhaust systems made of mild steel eventually corrode and become unusable; the length of their life depends on the climate and conditions in which the car is driven. Stainless steel systems last longer but are expensive.

Materials

Most exhaust systems are made of mild steel, although some more expensive cars have stainless steel systems as standard. Mild steel systems last for around three years or so under normal conditions. Stainless steel systems can be fitted to most cars, at a price. Unless it is damaged, a catalytic converter should last the lifetime of the vehicle (which is good as they are very expensive to replace).

The exhaust manifold

This is usually regarded as part of the engine and doesn't need to be replaced with the rest of the system. It is normally made of cast iron, although some high-performance vehicles may have a manifold consisting of a series of steel pipes. The exhaust manifold is bolted to the side of the engine, near the top, and leads the exhaust gases from the engine cylinders to the front pipe.

The front pipe

This connects the exhaust manifold to the catalytic converter (if fitted).

The expansion chamber

Also called the front silencer, the expansion chamber allows the exhaust gases to expand and slow down in the exhaust system. This aids efficient use of the fuel by the engine, as well as reducing exhaust-gas noise to a degree.

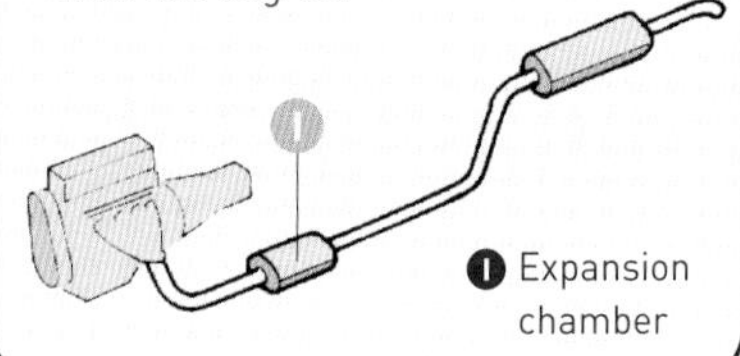

The catalytic converter

This is contained in a stainless steel casing. It consists of a ceramic honeycomb coated with special reactive materials that act as a catalyst. The exhaust gases from the engine contain polluting substances, such as nitrous oxide, hydrocarbon and carbon monoxide. When these substances pass through the catalyst, they react with the special coating and are converted into less harmful nitrogen, carbon dioxide and water. (*See also pages 165, 167, 239, 240.*)

1. Exhaust gases from engine
2. Ceramic honeycomb
3. Less harmful exhaust gases released

WARNING

The catalytic converter operates at very high temperature; it should never be touched when the engine is running or has recently been running. The whole exhaust system also gets very hot, including the tail pipe, and should not be touched when the vehicle is or has recently been running.

The silencer, or muffler

This is designed to quieten the outgoing exhaust gases to comply with noise regulations. Silencers allow the exhaust gases to expand and slow down, thus reducing their pressure and changing their sound frequency to produce less noise. Some silencers have a perforated pipe running through the centre, through which the exhaust gases pass, surrounded by sound-absorbent packing, usually a type of glassfibre wool, to reduce noise levels.

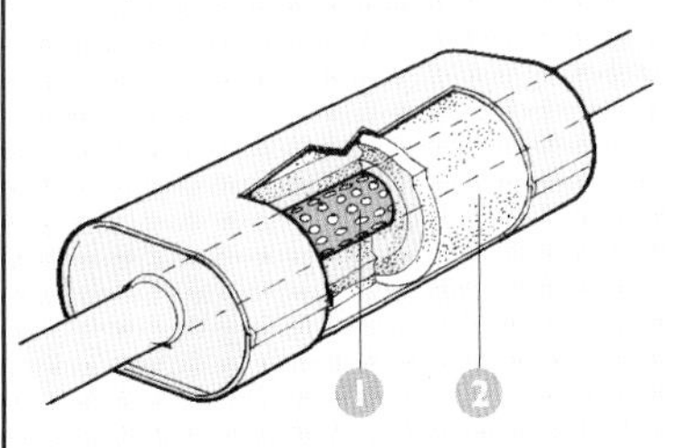

1. Perforated pipe
2. Sound-absorbent packing

The tail pipe

This directs the exhaust gases away from the vehicle so they will not be drawn into the passenger compartment.

WARNING

Exhaust gases are toxic and potentially fatal if allowed to build up in a confined space. Never run an engine in an unventilated area and allow it to fill with exhaust gases.

Modification

- Some car owners like to add big-bore tail pipes, or 'noisy' silencers, but these will do little to enhance fuel economy or the car's performance. All exhaust systems are designed to comply with legal requirements without unduly reducing engine performance and efficiency.
- Any modifications to the original system may adversely affect both the performance and economy of the engine – as well as possibly making the vehicle illegal.

Be safe and legal

It is a legal requirement that the exhaust system be kept in a safe and serviceable condition. Excess noise and leakage of gases are illegal, and the latter may also allow gases to be drawn into the passenger area, where they can cause drowsiness and could result in an accident.

Replacing the exhaust

If the exhaust system becomes excessively noisy or abnormally smelly, or if it knocks against the underside of the car, take the car to a garage or exhaust specialist to have the system replaced.

Noises

Noise can vary from an annoying whistle, through a small hole, to a loud roar if the exhaust breaks off in front of the silencer. Noise from exhaust leaks is worse during acceleration, while deceleration normally produces loud bangs as cold air is drawn into the hot exhaust gases and causes minor explosions.

If the exhaust starts to knock against the underside of the car, one of the rubber mountings may have broken. These can be replaced relatively easily at a garage, where the car can be put on a ramp to access them. A banging noise may also be caused by a broken exhaust pipe knocking against the car.

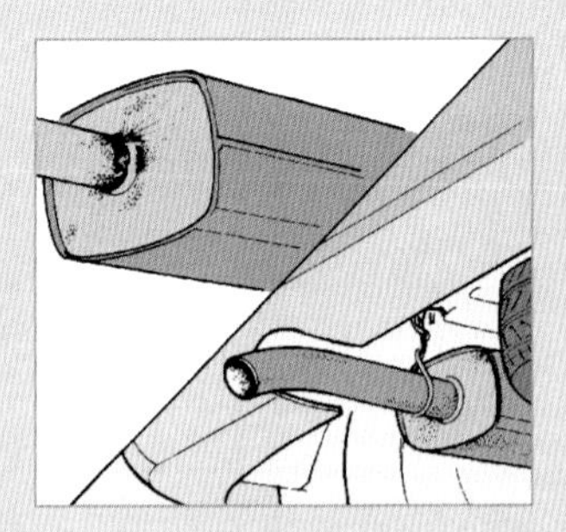

Smells

- Leaks from the exhaust can also produce smells.
- A pungent, smoky smell inside the car probably comes from a leaking exhaust pipe. It can also be detected outside the vehicle.
- Strangely, a smell of rotten eggs coming out from the exhaust tail pipe, which is actually sulphur dioxide, is the normal smell of a healthy catalytic converter!

Repair or replace?

It may be possible to have small holes repaired by welding or to use a diy repair kit, but this is not usually viable for large holes or broken pipes because the metal is very thin and there will be rust present.

It is usually sensible to replace the whole system (often with the exception of the catalytic converter, which is made of stainless steel) when a component fails. This is because most failures are due to rusting, and if one component has rusted through, the other parts will soon follow.

There is no need to protect the outside of the system against rusting, as this occurs from the inside due to the presence of water in the exhaust gases.

A variety of products is available, with which you can make your own repair to small holes or splits. These range from putty and gum to binding with a bandage. A bandage is ideal for repairing larger holes and splits while putty and gum will repair smaller holes. All should provide a gas-tight seal.

Have you got a leak?

A good way to tell if you have a leak is to switch on the engine and leave it idling, then place a wad of rag over the end of the tail pipe. (If the engine has already been running, the tail pipe will be very hot.) If the engine does not stop there must be a leak because if the system were sealed, pressure would build up and stall the engine.

DIY repairs

While it may be possible to make a temporary repair (for example, if the tail pipe is hanging down, it can be secured with wire or rope), this should only be regarded as a short-term fix. Take the car to a garage for attention to the problem as soon as you can.

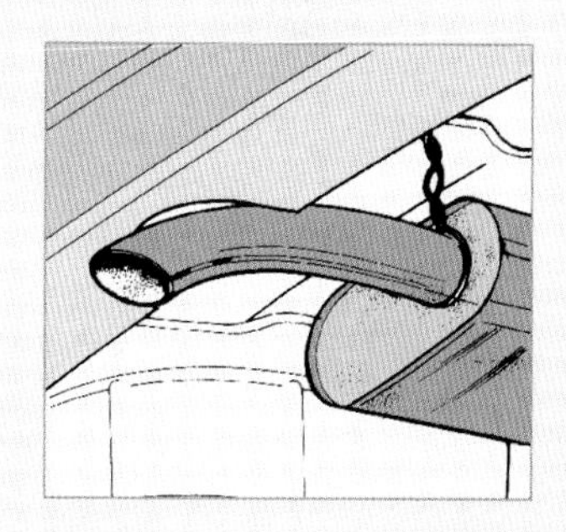

The cooling system

Together with the combustion process, the constant action of the valves and pistons in the cylinder block make this the hottest part of the engine. About half the heat generated is lost through the exhaust pipe, but if the rest were allowed to build up, the engine would seize up.

How it works

• To keep the temperature in check, the engine is provided with a cooling system, passages in the cylinder block and head being filled with a liquid coolant.

• The coolant (a mixture of antifreeze and water) circulates around the engine, through to the radiator, where it is cooled by air, and then back into the engine block in a continuous cycle.

• The coolant is forced through the system by a pump.

• A fan assists the cooling action of the radiator, and a thermostat ensures that the engine always operates at the correct temperature.

• Excess coolant is collected in an expansion tank.

• A separate circuit diverts coolant into a heater system, where it is used to control the temperature inside the car.

1. Expansion tank
2. Radiator
3. Thermostat
4. Water pump
5. Water jacket
6. Heater matrix
7. Cooling fan
8. Cooling fan thermo-switch

Coolant

In countries where the temperature can drop below freezing, antifreeze must be added to the cooling system during the winter months. Most car manufacturers stipulate that antifreeze should be left in the system all year round, as it helps protect the engine against corrosion.

The coolant mix is generally one part antifreeze to two parts water. This gives protection down to around –21°C, but for more extreme conditions, a half antifreeze/half water mix is recommended, giving protection down to around –36°C.

Check the car handbook for any recommendations concerning the type of coolant used and whether there are any restrictions on mixing with other types. Some car manufacturers recommend coolants that must not be mixed with others.

Automatics

Cars with automatic transmission may have a separate circuit built into the radiator to cool the transmission fluid. Alternatively, there may be a separate, small radiator for this purpose.

WARNING

Antifreeze and coolant are corrosive and toxic, so always store them out of the reach of children, keep containers firmly sealed, mop up spills with a cloth, and avoid contact with the skin. If coolant does come into contact with the skin, wash it off immediately with clean water.

Air-cooled engines

Some older cars have air-cooled engines. The cylinders and cylinder heads have fins that increase the surface area to disperse the heat.

When the engine is running, a fan surrounded by a metal cowling directs air over the fins to help the cooling process. A thermostatically controlled flap controls the flow of air. When the engine has just started, the flap is closed to enable the engine to reach its correct operating temperature quickly. Once the correct temperature is reached, the flap opens to enable more air to flow through the fins.

If a belt drives the fan, it is important to check this regularly and have it renewed as soon as there is any sign of wear.

The radiator

The radiator's role is to cool the coolant that is pumped through its network of tubes from the engine. It transfers the heat from the coolant (absorbed during the coolant's circulation through the passages in the engine) to the air that flows through the radiator.

How it works

The radiator consists of a network of thin horizontal or vertical metal tubes with metal fins attached. The fins increase the surface area of the tubes, enabling the coolant passing through them to cool more quickly.

The coolant flows from the engine through a hose into the top of the radiator. It then travels down through the network of tubes and back into the engine through another hose at the bottom.

When the car is driven, the forward motion forces air through the radiator, cooling the liquid inside.

1. Filler cap
2. Radiator matrix
3. Water inlet from engine
4. Water outlet to engine
5. Expansion pipe
6. Air flow

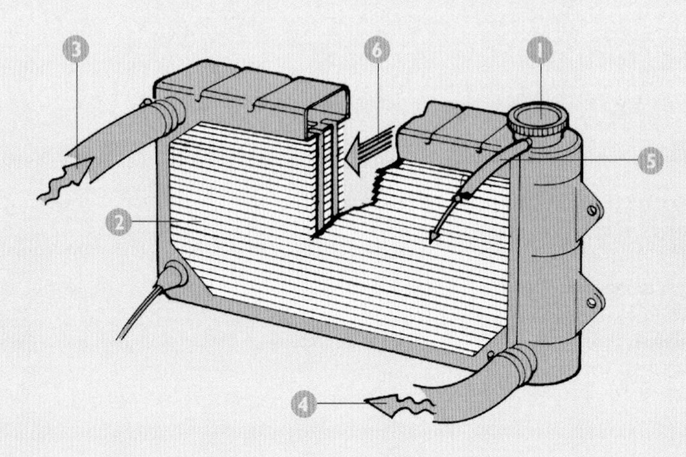

Checking and cleaning the radiator

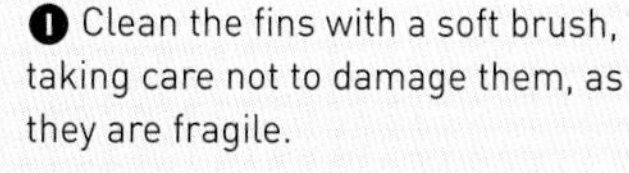

In most modern cars, the radiator's tubes and fins are made of aluminium. The tubes are arranged to run either vertically or horizontally across the radiator. It is important to keep the radiator free from dirt, which could impede air flow and reduce the cooling system's efficiency.

Radiators deteriorate with age, so check for rust and the build-up of deposits or discolouration that could indicate a leak. The fins of the radiator may become clogged with dead insects and dirt, preventing air from passing through it.

❶ Clean the fins with a soft brush, taking care not to damage them, as they are fragile.

❷ Alternatively, when the engine is cold, spray water through the radiator from back to front with a hosepipe, but ensure that the engine is cold first. Never spray cold water on to a hot radiator as it could crack and burst.

Protect any exposed electrical parts, such as the battery, coil, spark plug leads and distributor, with plastic bags, as this is a messy job.

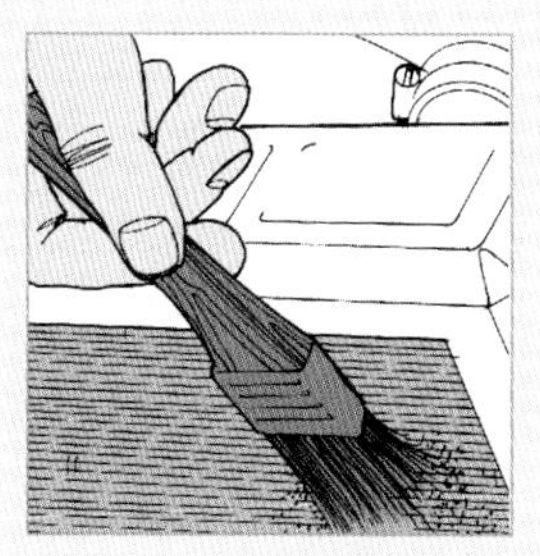

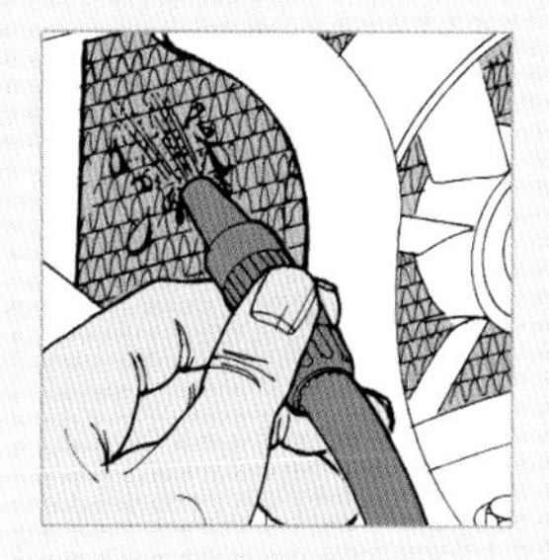

Clearing a blocked radiator

If the radiator is particularly dirty or is blocked internally (for example, if the tubes have become furred up with limescale), take the car to a garage where it can be removed to be cleaned or flushed out.

Repairing small leaks

Special sealing compounds are available for repairing leaks from very small holes. The pressure in the system forces the sealant into the hole, where it hardens. Only use these as a temporary measure.

The thermostat

The thermostat is a temperature-sensitive valve that controls the flow of coolant to the radiator. It is normally located in the cylinder head where the top radiator hose is connected. It helps the engine to warm up rapidly and to remain at its correct operating temperature.

How it works

- When a car starts, the engine is cold, so the coolant does not require the cooling action of the radiator. Therefore the thermostat remains shut, preventing coolant from entering the radiator.
- While the engine is warming up, the thermostat remains shut and coolant circulates through the engine only.
- As the temperature of the coolant increases, the thermostat gradually opens to allow coolant to pass through and enter the radiator.
- When the engine has reached the correct operating temperature, the thermostat will be fully open. Coolant now flows freely through the radiator.

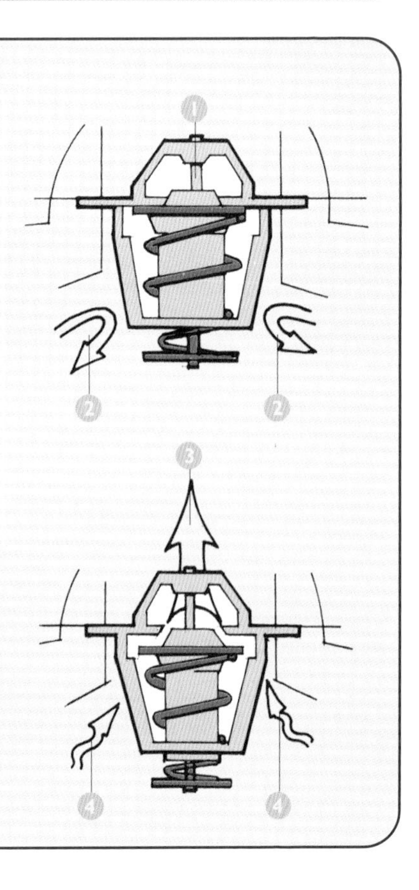

❶ Thermostat closed

❷ Water remains in engine

❸ Thermostat open

❹ Water flows to radiator

The cooling fan

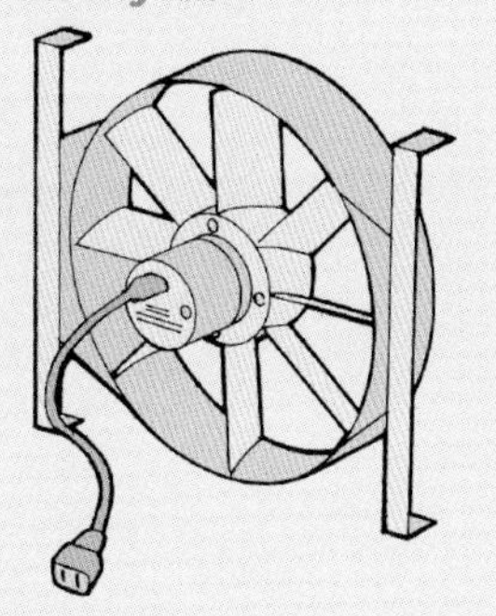

The fan assists the cooling process by forcing air through the radiator when the car is moving slowly or stationary.

In most cars, its operation is triggered by a thermostatic switch or the ECU.

In older cars, the fan may be driven by the auxiliary drive belt (*see page 158*).

Checking the cooling fan

❶ Check that the fan is working properly by running the engine with the car stationary. Keep an eye on the dashboard gauge.

❷ The needle should start to rise beyond the 'normal' reading and the fan should switch on to bring the temperature back down. If the fan does not switch on, have it checked by a garage.

Coolant temperature sensor

Located in the cylinder block or radiator, this monitors the coolant temperature and is connected to the temperature gauge on the dashboard. As the engine starts to warm up, the needle on the gauge will rise from cold to 'normal'.

Water pump

Driven by a belt connected to the engine, this pumps coolant from the base of the radiator into the engine and circulates it around the cooling system. If the pump is faulty, the engine will overheat quickly. Check the pump for signs of leakage.

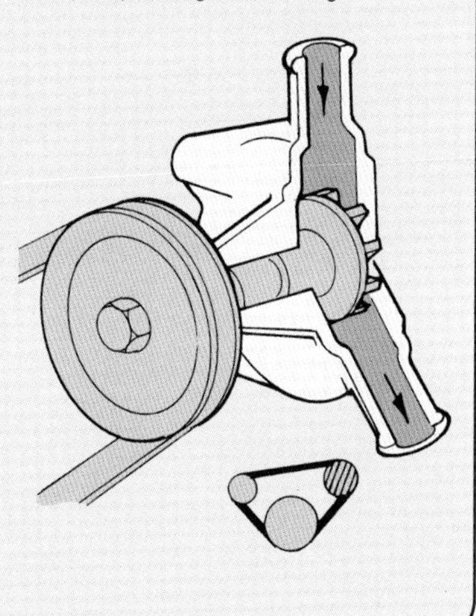

Coolant

The coolant circulates through passages in the engine, absorbing the heat generated by the combustion process. It is important to check the level of the coolant regularly, as if it is allowed to get too low, the engine could overheat, causing serious damage.

The expansion tank

1

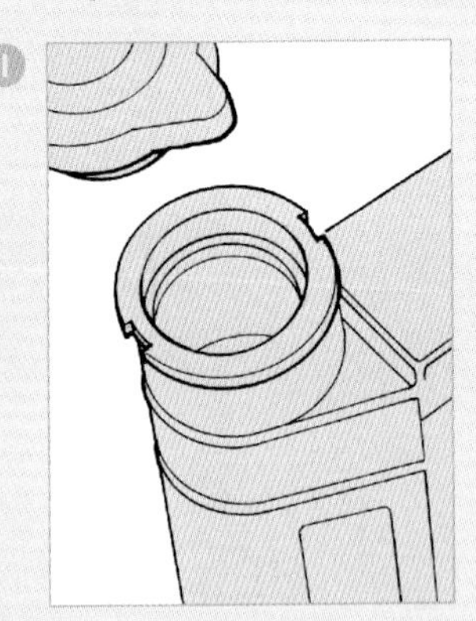

2

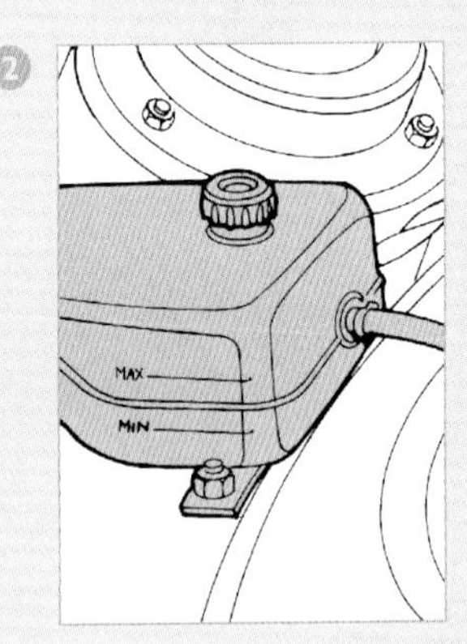

The coolant level is normally checked by inspecting an expansion tank or bottle. This is a plastic container that is either built on to the side of the radiator ❶ or is a separate container, positioned close to the radiator and connected to it by a hose ❷.

As the coolant circulates through the passages in the engine block, it absorbs the heat that is generated by the combustion process.

As the coolant heats up, it expands and the excess overflows into the expansion tank.

When the engine is switched off and begins to cool down, the coolant gradually contracts and is drawn back into the radiator, although some always remains in the expansion tank.

Checking the coolant level

The coolant level in the expansion tank varies according to the temperature of the engine. Check the level weekly when the engine is cold. It should be between the maximum and minimum marks on the side of the tank.

If the tank is transparent, you should be able to check the level without opening the pressure cap. If it is not, you may need to open the cap. (Important – first read 'Opening pressure caps' on page 180.) When the cap is open, look for the level indicator inside.

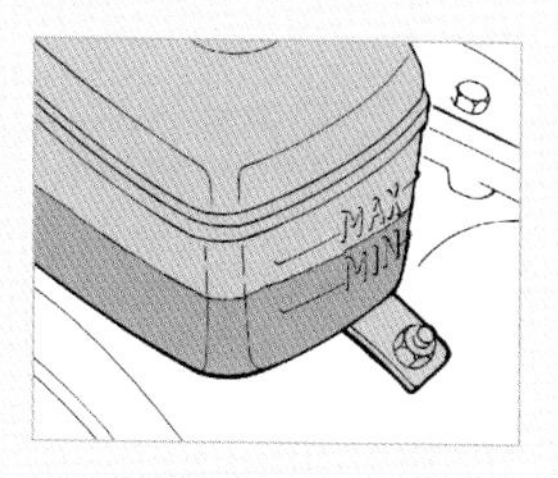

When the engine is cold, the level should generally be closer to the minimum mark than the maximum. If it is below the minimum mark, top it up (*see page 181*).

Radiator pressure cap

In some older cars, the coolant level is checked by removing the pressure cap from the radiator. (Important – before opening the pressure cap, read the instructions on *page 180.*)

Radiator pressure caps have a safety position – undoing the cap a half of a turn to its stop releases pressure and steam in the system.

Once the steam has escaped, the cap can be opened fully. Check the coolant level – it should be about 5cm (2in) below the top of the radiator. Top it up if necessary, following the instructions on page 181.

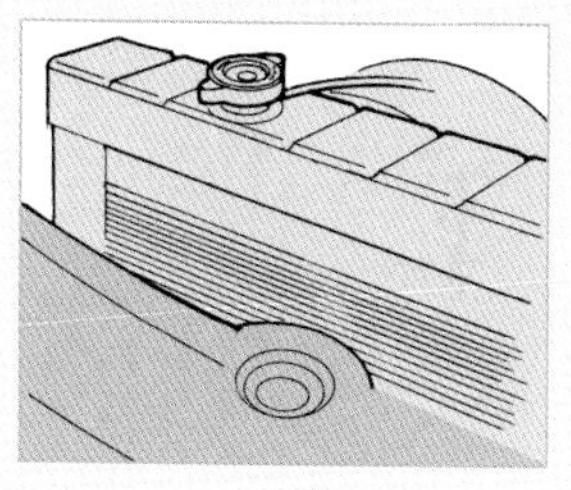

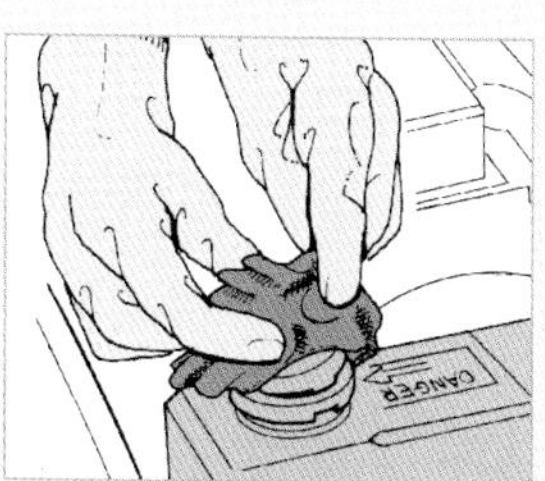

The pressurized system

The cooling system is pressurized and sealed with a cap fitted either to the top of the radiator or, more commonly, to an expansion tank. Pressurizing the system has the effect of raising the boiling point of the coolant so that it does not overheat in the system.

Opening pressure caps

If you have to remove the pressure cap while the engine is still warm, but not hot (although this is not recommended), wear a thick glove or cover the cap with a thick pad of cloth to protect against scalding.

Undo it slowly, pausing after the first half-turn to allow the pressure and steam to escape. Never lean over the cap while you are doing this in case coolant should burst out.

Remove the cap by pushing down and turning another half-turn.

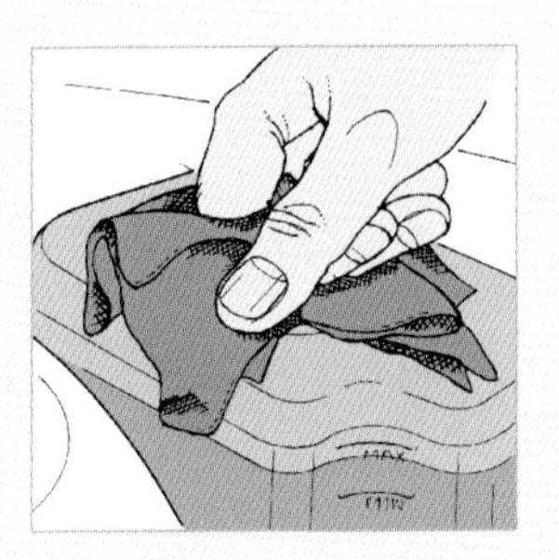

Replacing the coolant

- Check the car handbook to see how often the coolant should be replaced.
- The recommended interval is generally every two years, but it is a good idea to have it checked by your garage once a year before the onset of winter.
- When the coolant is replaced, the whole cooling system has to be drained and flushed out, an operation that needs to be carried out by a professional mechanic.
- The coolant in some cars is intended to last the lifetime of the car and never needs to be replaced. Check your car handbook.

WARNING

Never open the pressure cap while the engine is hot. It is extremely dangerous, as once the pressure is released, a scalding jet of coolant and steam could shoot out.

Topping up the coolant

It should not be necessary to top up the coolant regularly, as cooling systems in modern cars are sealed. If you do need to top it up, this could indicate that there is a leak in the system.

Never allow the coolant to fall below the minimum mark, as the engine could overheat and be damaged.

If the coolant, which can be green, blue or pink in colour from the antifreeze, looks rusty or dirty, it will need replacing (see opposite).

Check your car handbook for details on the kind of coolant you should use. It should have the same proportions of antifreeze and water as the coolant that is already in the system (*see page 173*).

you will need

- → plastic funnel (possibly)
- → protective gloves
- → clean cloth

WARNING

Never top up the coolant while the engine is hot, as it could crack the engine block. Wait at least 15–20 minutes or until you are sure the engine is cool.

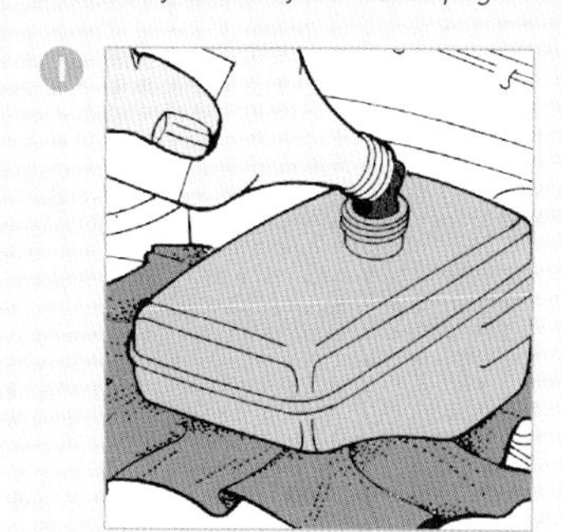

❶ If you have to top up with water alone, remember to add the correct amount of antifreeze at the first opportunity to prevent the antifreeze solution from becoming too weak.

❷ Don't overfill, and screw the pressure cap back on tightly. Mop up any spills, as the antifreeze solution is toxic and corrosive.

Looking for leaks

Inspect hoses, pipes and seals for signs of leaking, cracking and deterioration. Check that hose clips are tight.

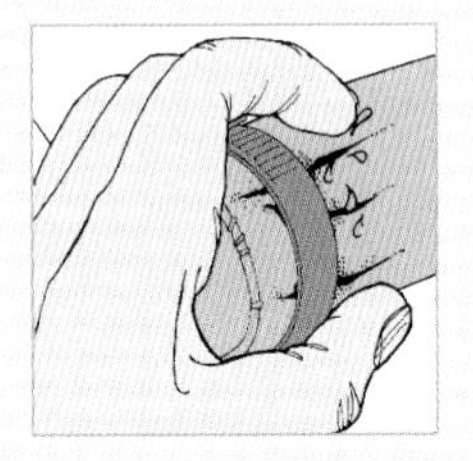

If you suspect a leak, but cannot see any obvious signs, start the engine and run it until the temperature gauge shows normal, then increase the engine speed for about ten seconds.

Make a visual check of the system for any small jets of steam or signs of leaking coolant. Take care not to touch any moving part or parts of the engine that are hot while doing so.

Checking belts

Inspect drive belts for cracks and frayed edges, and check the tension by pressing the middle of the longest run. It should give by about 12mm (½in).

If a belt is too loose or tight, have it adjusted at a garage, as it could cause the engine to malfunction or place excessive strain on the various components it drives.

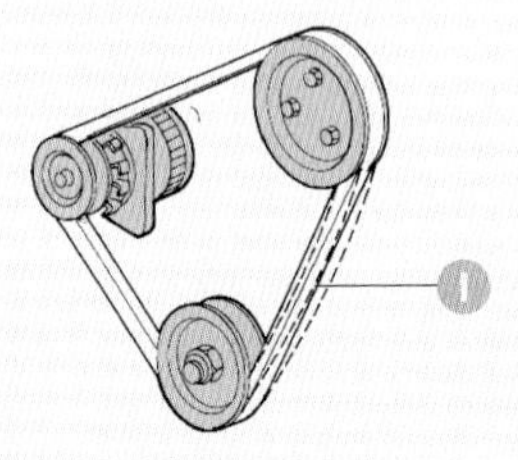

1 Free movement checked on longest run of belt

Signs of trouble

Warning signs that the thermostat is faulty include the passenger compartment failing to warm up properly and the engine being slow to warm up, both being caused by the thermostat not shutting completely. Alternatively, the engine may overheat rapidly while the radiator remains cool to the touch; this is caused by the thermostat not opening. If you suspect the thermostat needs replacing, take the car to the garage.

A leaking head gasket

The cylinder head gasket ensures that the joint between the cylinder head and the cylinder block is sealed tightly to prevent the escape of oil, combustion gases and coolant.

Signs of a leaking head gasket are bubbles in the coolant when the engine is running, a smell of petrol or exhaust fumes in the coolant, and oil in the coolant appearing as thick whitish deposits in the system's expansion tank.

Other signs are excessive water dripping from the exhaust pipe when the engine is hot, a loss of power, whistling noises from the engine, the engine overheating, and coolant in the engine oil appearing as whitish, mayonnaise-like deposits on the oil filler cap or dipstick. If you suspect that the head gasket is leaking, take the car to a garage as soon as possible.

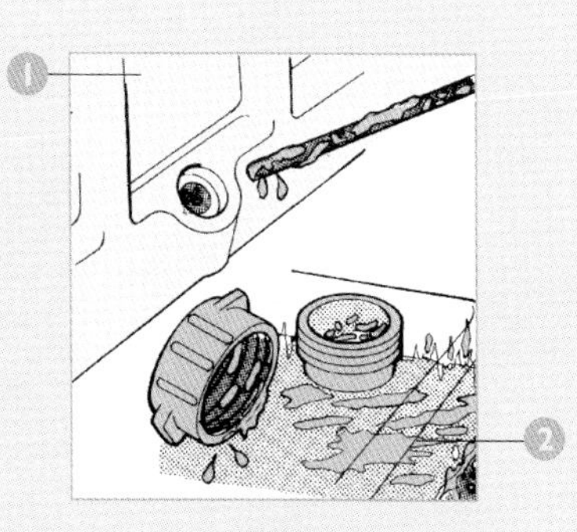

❶ Water/oil on dipstick

❷ Oil in expansion tank

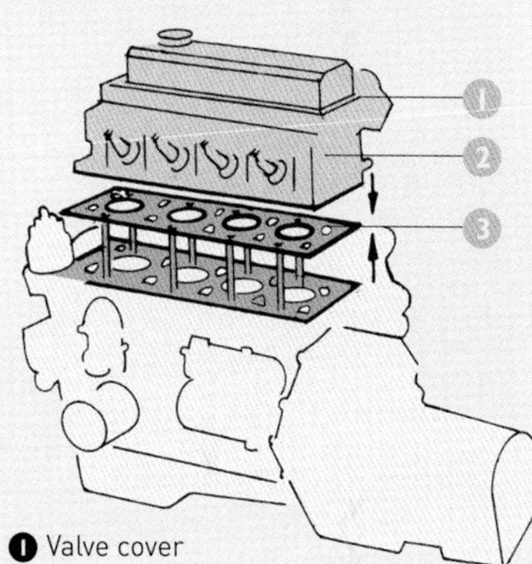

❶ Valve cover

❷ Cylinder head

❸ Head gasket

A faulty cooling fan

The cooling fan is normally operated electrically (*see page 177*). If it fails to come on when the engine is warm, but the car is stationary, the engine could overheat (when stuck in traffic with the engine idling, for example). If the needle of the temperature gauge on the dashboard begins to climb beyond 'normal' (*see page 143*), the engine is beginning to overheat. Make sure you have the fan checked at a garage.

Heating and ventilation

The heating and ventilating system is linked to the cooling system. It makes use of the heat generated by the engine to warm up the passenger compartment and also to demist windows. It also freshens the interior by introducing cool air from outside.

Hot or cold

Cooling: the fresh air from outside the car flows through ducts into the passenger compartment via various vents. The airflow can be boosted by an electric fan. Stale air is removed through ducts at the rear.

Heating: the air drawn in from outside the car passes over the heater matrix, which contains hot coolant from the engine. As it does so, it absorbs heat so that it is warm when it enters the passenger compartment. The mix of hot and cold air can be controlled to create the desired temperature.

Recirculation setting

This is used to shut off the supply of fresh air from outside the car, preventing fumes and bad odours from entering. However, as the air inside the car is constantly recirculating, it will soon become stale and could cause drowsiness due to the build-up of carbon dioxide, so don't leave the system on this setting for too long.

❶ Fresh air entering

❷ Stale air leaving

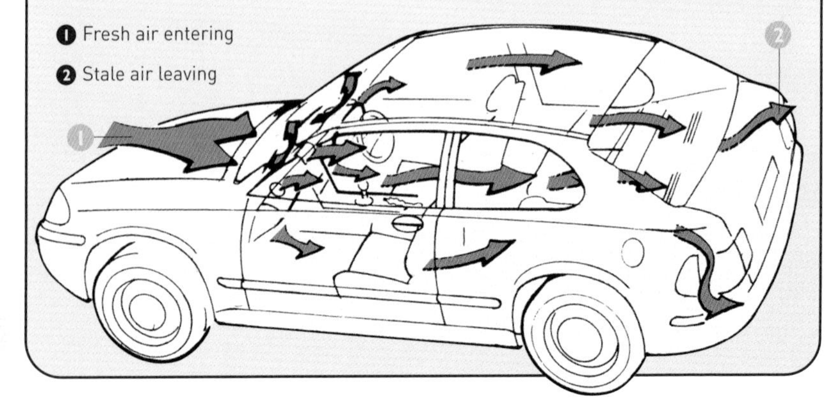

How it works

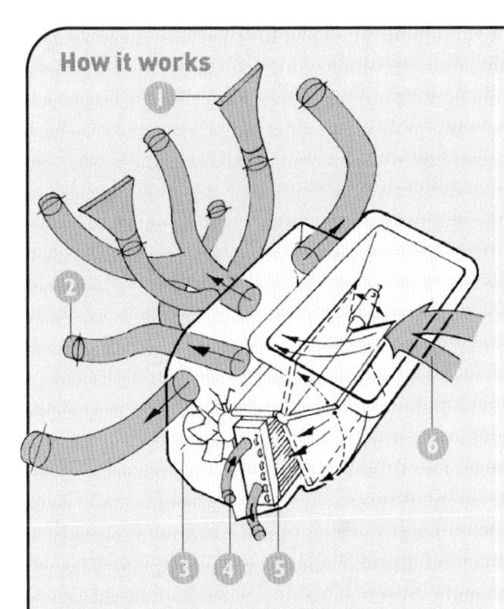

❶ Demister directed at windscreen

❷ Air flows through vents into passenger compartment

❸ Fan boosts airflow

❹ Coolant enters from engine

❺ Heater matrix warms air (if required)

❻ Air enters system from outside the car

The system consists of the heater matrix, an electric blower, air ducts, and flaps and vents operated by controls inside the passenger compartment, to direct the airflow as required.

The heater matrix is like a small radiator and is located in a duct leading to the car's interior. It contains coolant from the engine's cooling system (*see page 172*).

The electric blower drives a fan at varying speeds (controlled from inside the car), controlling the volume of airflow through the heating/demisting system.

Air is drawn in from outside the car through grilles, usually at the rear of the bonnet, just below the windscreen. It flows into the heater, where some of it passes through the heater matrix while the rest is directed to the ventilators.

Demisting

Windows fog up on the inside through condensation, caused by moist warm air coming into contact with cold glass. Use the 'air flow-through' setting to draw in fresh air from the outside. Keeping the interior of the windows clean will help reduce fogging slightly.

Heated rear window

In most cars, the heating elements of the heated rear windows (thin metal wires) are embedded in the glass. They are heated electrically and controlled by a switch on the dashboard. Some are timed to switch off automatically after around ten minutes. Use the rear window heater to demist the interior of the window or defrost the exterior, but if a layer of ice or snow has formed, this needs to be scraped off before the rear window heater can be effective. The heater is linked to a warning light on the dashboard that lights up when the heater is operating.

Air conditioning

The air conditioning system acts like a refrigerator, cooling and dehumidifying the air, and keeping it at the required temperature. However, air conditioning uses a lot of fuel. The engine is likely to use at least 10 per cent more fuel when the air conditioning is operating.

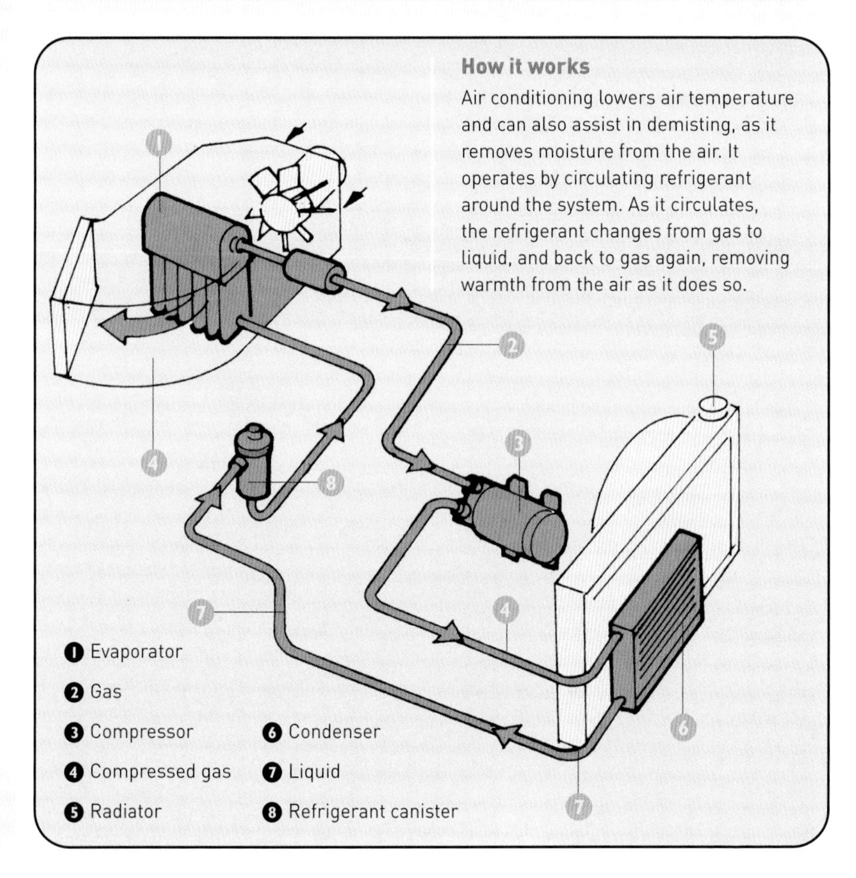

How it works

Air conditioning lowers air temperature and can also assist in demisting, as it removes moisture from the air. It operates by circulating refrigerant around the system. As it circulates, the refrigerant changes from gas to liquid, and back to gas again, removing warmth from the air as it does so.

❶ The compressor is mounted on the engine. It pumps refrigerant around the system and is normally driven by a belt from the engine crankshaft. It draws in refrigerant in the form of gas from the evaporator and compresses it, raising its temperature in the process.

❷ The compressed gas is pumped to the condenser. The condenser makes use of the air being forced through the radiator from outside due to the car's forward motion. This cools the compressed refrigerant and changes it from a gas into a liquid.

❸ The liquid flows to the evaporator, which is mounted in front of a fan. The fan blows the warm air to be cooled over the evaporator. As this occurs, the warmth from the air is absorbed by the cool refrigerant inside, cooling and dehumidifying the air before it is blown into the passenger compartment.

❹ As the warmth of the air is transferred to the liquid refrigerant, the refrigerant expands, heats up and evaporates, changing back to a gas.

Refrigerant

In some cars, the refrigerant canister can be inspected for humidity and to check the liquid inside. There should be a clear fluid flow visible a few minutes after the air conditioning is switched on. If the humidity is high, or if you suspect problems with the fluid, seek garage assistance. Do not try to do anything yourself, as the refrigerant is a potentially dangerous substance.

About 10 per cent of refrigerant is lost every year, which increases if the system is not used for long periods of time. To avoid this, operate the system for 5–10 minutes once or twice a month to keep it in good working order. The refrigerant needs to be recharged at intervals; check your handbook for details about this.

Signs that the air conditioning system needs checking are a bad smell, a greasy film on the inside of the windscreen and no cold air from the ventilating system. Don't use the system, as this could damage the compressor. Have it checked at a garage as soon as possible.

WARNING

Liquid refrigerant is dangerous, freezing anything with which it comes into contact. It becomes a toxic gas if exposed to a naked flame. If released into the atmosphere, it is harmful. Thus, repairs must always be carried out at a garage.

The electrical system

With an increasing number of electrical gadgets and systems, cars today consume much more electricity than in the past. You can't plug a car into the mains, so it needs to carry its own generator and storage system around with it.

How it works

The main components of the electrical system are the battery, alternator and starter motor.

When the ignition key is turned to 'start', a surge of electrical current is sent from the battery to the solenoid, which acts as a switch and allows the current through to turn the starter motor. Once the starter motor is running, it turns the engine crankshaft, which sets the engine in motion. The crankshaft drives the alternator by a belt, and once the engine is running, the alternator provides a continuous electrical charge to the battery so that it can power the car's electrical systems.

The following are electrically operated: Ignition system; ABS; fuel injection system; ECU (the car's computer) and microprocessors; cooling fan/ thermostat; lights; audio equipment; heater/air conditioning; rear window heater; electric windows/side mirrors; windscreen wipers/ screenwash; central locking/remote-control locking; sun roof; clock, temperature and other displays; alarm; engine immobilizer.

1. Alternator is driven by belt connected to crankshaft (not shown)
2. Pulley is connected to crankshaft
3. Solenoid
4. Starter motor
5. Battery supplies electricity to power light
6. Battery
7. Ignition switch

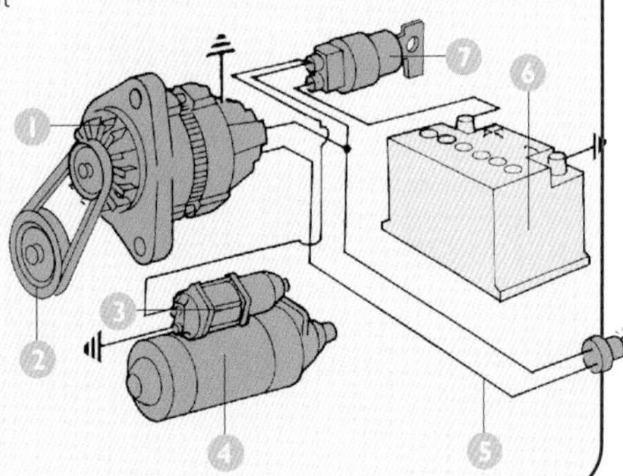

The battery

Almost all car batteries consist of six 2-volt cells, joined together to produce a 12-volt lead-acid battery. Each cell contains a series of lead and synthetic plates immersed in a solution of sulphuric acid and distilled water, called the electrolyte. This makes the plates react to one another and so create an electrical voltage.

There are two terminals (or posts) on top of the battery, one positive (+) and one negative (-). A lead (usually red) normally connects the positive terminal to the starter motor, while the negative terminal is connected by another lead (usually black) to the body of the car, which acts as 'earth'.

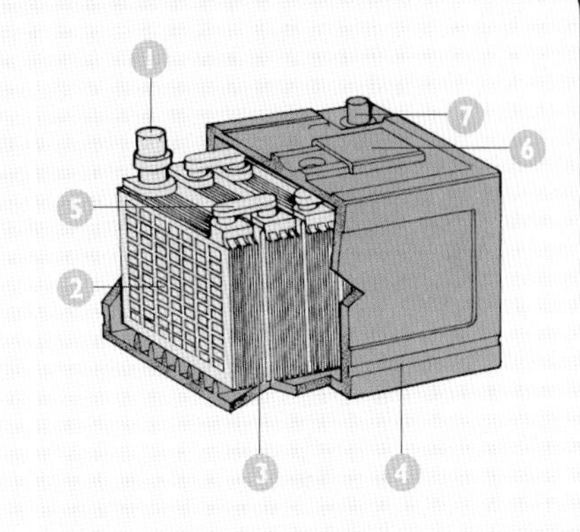

1 Positive terminal
2 Lead plates separated by insulating plates
3 Cell
4 Casing
5 Cell connector
6 Vent cover
7 Negative terminal

The alternator

The alternator generates electricity. While the engine is running, it provides a continuous electrical charge to the battery. It is driven by a belt from the crankshaft. Since the speed of the engine fluctuates constantly, the amount of electricity generated by the alternator also varies. To control this, a voltage regulator is mounted within the alternator casing.

The starter motor

This is situated on the side of the cylinder block. The starter contains a solenoid, which acts as a switch to allow current through from the battery. When the ignition switch is turned to the 'start' position, the starter motor turns the crankshaft and sets the engine in motion.

The battery

A battery's capacity must be sufficient to meet the electrical requirements of the car to which it is fitted. If its capacity is too small for the car, it will discharge too quickly, but if its capacity is too big, the car's alternator may not be able to charge the battery fully.

Types of battery

There are two types of battery, conventional (refillable) and maintenance-free.

Maintenance-free
Many modern batteries are maintenance-free and never need topping up. Sealed batteries usually have built-in indicators that change colour to show when they need to be charged or replaced. Check the manufacturer's label to see what the different colours indicate.

Conventional
The level of electrolyte needs to be checked regularly (*see page 196*).

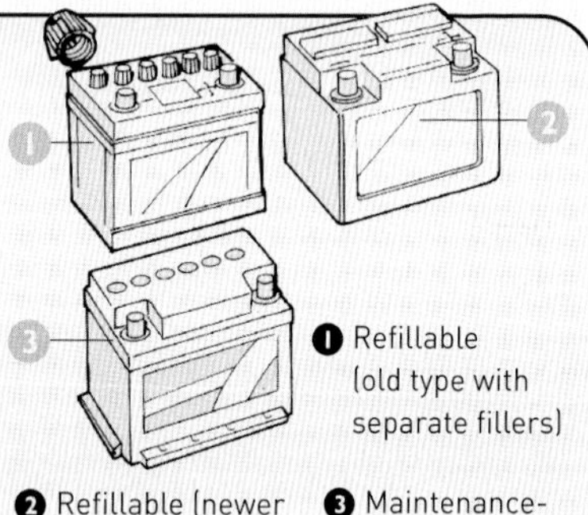

❶ Refillable (old type with separate fillers)

❷ Refillable (newer type with strip caps)

❸ Maintenance-free

Battery capacity reduces with age. New batteries are generally guaranteed to last around 2–4 years.

Capacity indicators

RC (reserve capacity) – indicates how many minutes the battery can supply sufficient current (25 amps) to power electrical equipment when the engine is switched off, before the voltage drops.

CCA (cold cranking amps) – indicates how much current the battery can deliver at freezing (–18°C) for 30 seconds before the voltage drops.

AH (ampere hours) – indicates how long the battery can supply a certain current before becoming discharged (e.g., 12 v at 40 AH indicates it can supply a current of 4 amps for ten hours).

What does the battery do?

The car battery is rechargeable. It does not generate electricity itself, but rather stores the electricity produced by the alternator (or more precisely, it stores the chemicals that produce electricity through chemical reaction with the lead plates in the cells).

Starting the engine: the battery's most important job. It supplies the electrical current needed to turn the starter motor, which starts the engine. The biggest demand placed on the battery is starting the car on a cold morning.

When the engine is running: the battery provides the electrical current needed to power the car's electrical equipment, lights, heater, etc. Problems can occur if the battery is disconnected when the engine is running.

When the engine is switched off: the alternator stops generating electricity. Any electricity required to power accessories such as the heater, alarm, etc. is therefore provided by the battery.

TIP

Batteries are affected by temperature and are less efficient in really cold conditions. Consequently, a battery that is already in poor condition simply may not have enough power to turn the starter motor on a freezing morning, when the engine oil will be thick and sluggish. To avoid problems, have your battery checked before each winter.

Buying a new battery

- Check your handbook for information on the correct type of battery for your car. If no such information is to hand, replace the battery with one of the same capacity. If the exact-capacity battery is not available, choose one with a higher rating, rather than lower.

- It is also preferable to replace the battery with one of the same type (conventional or maintenance-free), although this is not absolutely crucial.

- The physical size of a battery varies, so make sure you buy one that will fit your car and that has the positive terminal in the correct position. If in doubt, look it up in the manufacturers' charts normally on display at retailers.

- Bear in mind that batteries slowly lose their charge when not in use, so check that the battery you are buying is fresh and has not been lingering on a retailer's shelf for too long.

Battery safety

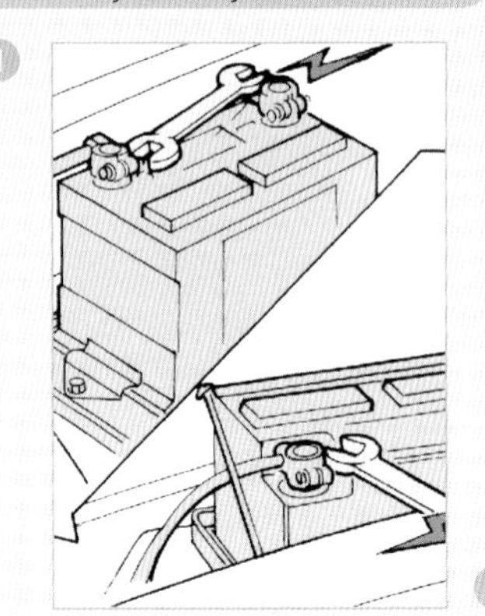

❶ Never allow anything metallic (or any liquid) to bridge both battery connections – this could cause the battery to explode.

❷ Never allow your spanner to touch a battery terminal and any other metallic part of the vehicle at the same time – this could cause the battery to explode.

❸ Always disconnect and connect the battery leads in the order specified in this book.

❹ Hydrogen gas is released when a battery is being charged, so don't smoke, and keep naked flames away in case an explosion is caused.

❺ Carry batteries carefully. If the battery is not sealed, wear protective clothing and be careful of electrolyte spillage. Car batteries are very heavy.

❻ Never disconnect a battery terminal while the engine is running.

❼ Dispose of old batteries safely (check with your garage or a local authority disposal site) because they contain acid.

Looking after the battery

Many modern batteries require very little attention. Nevertheless, the electrolyte level should be checked regularly (*see page 196*), although this is not necessary with maintenance-free batteries. It is also important to keep the battery terminals and connections clean and free from corrosion to ensure good electrical conductivity.

Cleaning the terminals

White deposits on the battery terminals are caused by corrosion from battery acid. This will impede the flow of electricity, as the leads will make poor contact with the terminals and, if left, the corrosion could eat into the metal.

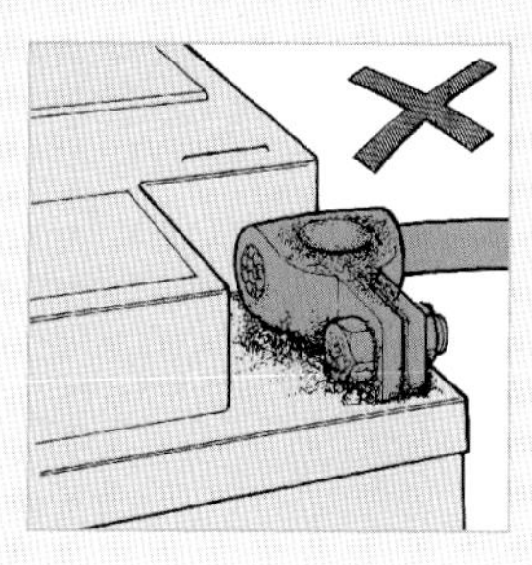

you will need

- → hot water
- → emery paper
- → spanner
- → petroleum jelly or battery grease
- → clean rag

Clearing acid corrosion

Pouring hot water over the terminals will clear acid corrosion, but care must be taken to ensure that the water does not link the terminals together (see opposite) and to avoid damage to other components. Also, ensure all the acid corrosion is washed away from the vehicle. Ensure the engine and ignition are switched off. Make sure you don't pour water on to any electrical components (distributor, spark plug leads, coil, alternator – cover them with plastic bags and dry battery thoroughly with a cloth). Once they are dry, the battery terminals can be smeared with petroleum jelly to slow down the formation of corrosion.

Checking the battery

❶ Check that the ignition and all electrical equipment (radio, lights, etc.) are switched off.

❷ Check that the battery leads are securely fastened to the terminals and that the end of the negative lead (connected to the car body) is also securely fastened. Make sure the connections are clean. Loose or dirty connections will impede the flow of electricity to and from the battery, so tighten and clean them if necessary (*see opposite*). Inspect the battery case and leads for cracking or other signs of wear.

❸ If you decide to disconnect the battery, note down the codes for reprogramming any electrical equipment (audio, etc.) and any other systems that would be affected by the loss of electricity caused by disconnecting the battery leads.

WARNING

Only disconnect the battery leads when they really need cleaning. Disconnecting the battery of a modern vehicle can disrupt electrical circuits and cause problems.

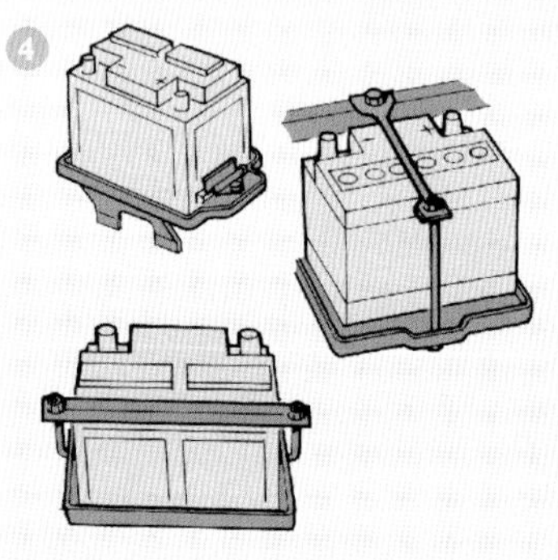

❹ Check that the battery is secure in its mounting. It should not be loose, as even a small vibration or jolt could cause battery acid to be spilled.

However, don't overtighten the clamp, as this could crack the battery case and cause electrolyte to leak.

WARNING

Always disconnect and connect battery leads in the order given opposite.

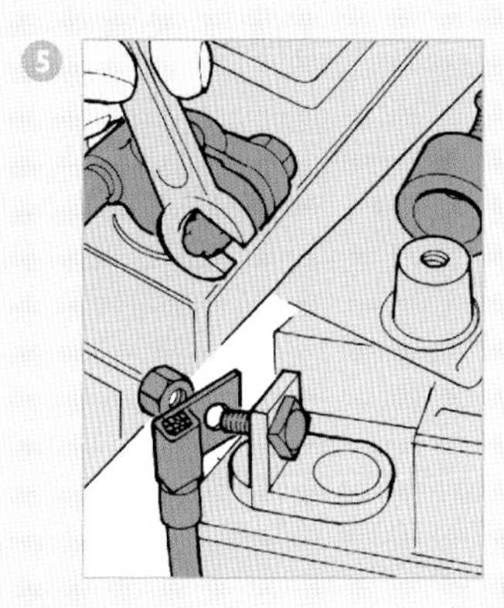

❺ To clean the terminals, loosen and unscrew the nut connecting the battery lead to the negative (-) terminal. (Always disconnect the negative terminal before the positive.) Disconnect the lead; you may need to wiggle it to get it off. Then disconnect the positive (+) terminal in the same way.

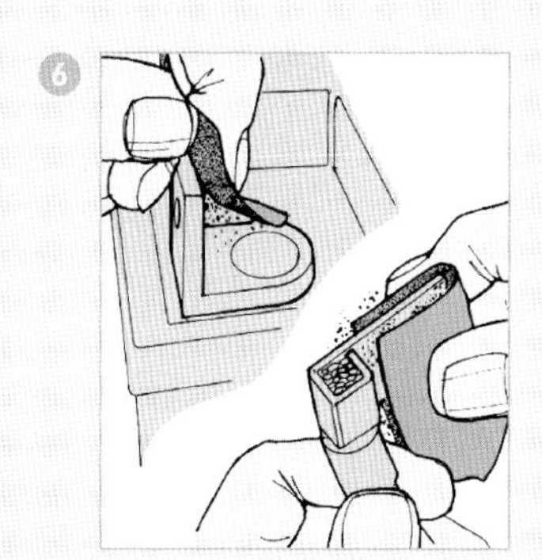

❻ Wipe the ends of the leads and terminals with a cloth to remove any dirt. Using the emery paper, clean both lead ends and terminals. Take care that no dust gets in your eyes.

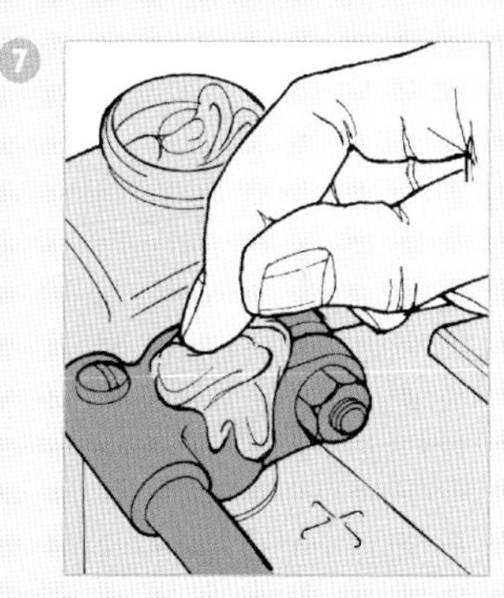

❼ Reconnect the leads to the terminals, connecting the positive (+) first, and then the negative (-). Ensure they are tight. Smear petroleum jelly or battery grease over the terminals to help prevent the formation of further corrosion.

❽ Check the negative lead where it attaches to the car body. If the connection is rusty or dirty, unbolt it and clean both the lead and its mounting with emery paper. Then

Checking the electrolyte

Most modern batteries are sealed, so it is unlikely that you will come into contact with the electrolyte inside them. If you do, however, remember that electrolyte is dangerous, as it contains sulphuric acid, which will burn skin and cause severe injury.

Checking the electrolyte

Distilled water can be lost from electrolyte over time, so check the level in a conventional battery every three months, and particularly before winter. If it is allowed to fall too low, the battery becomes less efficient.

Conventional batteries: if the level is low, top it up through the vents on top of the battery (see opposite).

Maintenance-free batteries: the electrolyte does not require checking, but colour indicators show when the battery should be recharged or replaced.

you will need

- → topping-up fluid, or distilled or de-ionized water
- → clean empty plastic bottle to hold distilled water
- → rubber gloves
- → screwdriver (flat-head)
- → clean cloth

Safety

If electrolyte:

- is swallowed, drinks lots of milk or water; seek immediate medical attention.
- contacts the skin, wash off with water immediately.
- gets in the eyes, flood with water; seek immediate medical attention.
- gets on clothes, remove clothing, as it could burn through.

❶ Park the car on the level with the ignition and all electrical equipment (radio, lights, etc.) switched off.

❷ If you have a battery with built-in indicators that change colour to show when it needs topping up, check the manufacturer's label to see what the colour indicates. If it requires topping up, follow the instructions from (5).

3

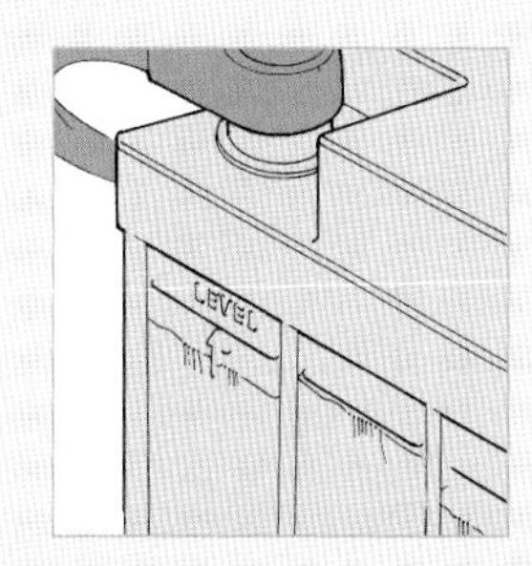

❸ If the battery casing is translucent, the required level should be shown on the outside, and you should be able to see the electrolyte level through the casing (see also your car handbook for guidance). Remember to check the level of each cell.

❹ If the casing is not translucent, prise off a vent cap with a screwdriver and check the level of electrolyte inside. It should just cover the tops of the metal plates. Remember to check each cell. You should not need to come into contact with the electrolyte inside, but as a precaution, wear rubber gloves.

4

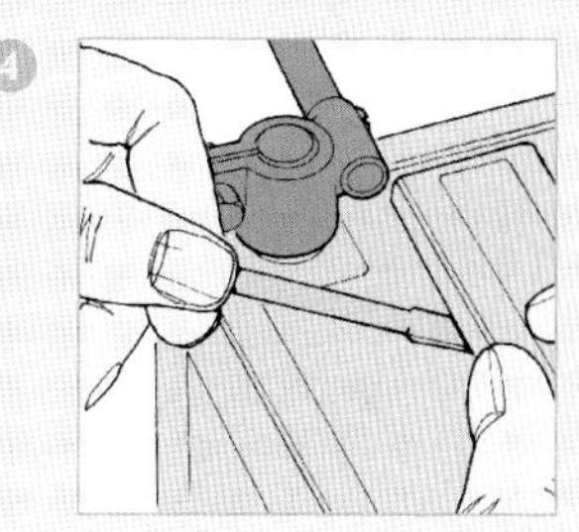

5

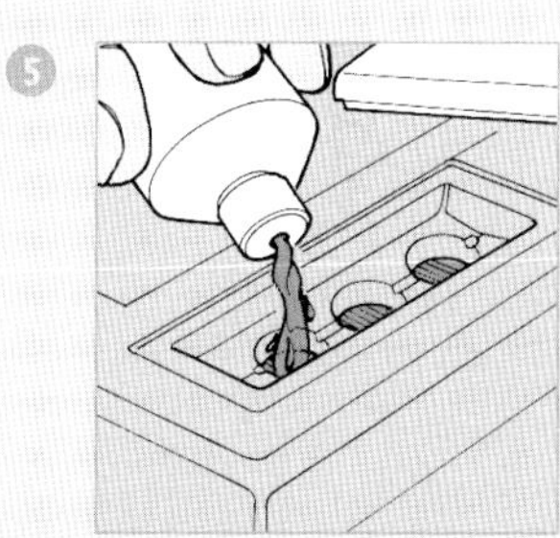

❺ If the level is too low, pour some topping-up fluid or distilled water through the vent hole until it just covers the tops of the plates. It may not be necessary to top up each cell. Be careful not to overfill, as excess electrolyte could squirt out of the battery during heavy charging.

❻ Replace the plugs or vent caps and wipe the top of the battery with a cloth to ensure it is completely dry. If a trail of moisture were to connect the terminals, it would short-circuit the battery, with disastrous results.

See the safety guidelines opposite.

Recharging a battery

If your car has not been driven for some time, or if the lights have been left on overnight, you will probably find that the battery is low or even flat. You can recharge it using an external charger.

Options

- If the battery is low, but you can start the car, you may just need to drive it for 15 minutes or so to recharge the battery.
- If the battery loses its charge regularly, the fault may not lie in the battery itself; have the electrical system checked at a garage. A battery in good condition should not normally need to be charged using an external charger unless it is flat (fully discharged) or has not been used for a long time.
- If the battery is completely flat, you may find that it will no longer hold a charge; your only option is to buy a new one.
- If a car is used mainly for short journeys, it is good practice to put the battery on charge occasionally, as it does not get fully charged on short journeys.
- Charge conventional and low-maintenance batteries at 3.5–4 amps for several hours or 1.5 amps overnight.

1. Mains plug
2. Battery charger
3. Charging rate indicator (ammeter)
4. Charger leads attached to terminals

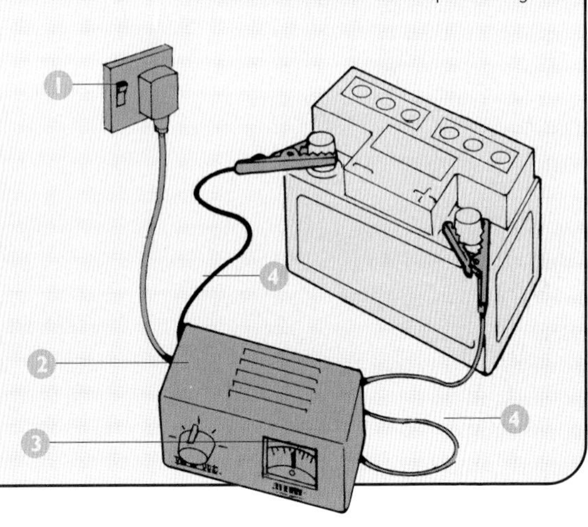

How to recharge a battery

you will need

→ battery charger
→ rubber gloves
→ protective clothing

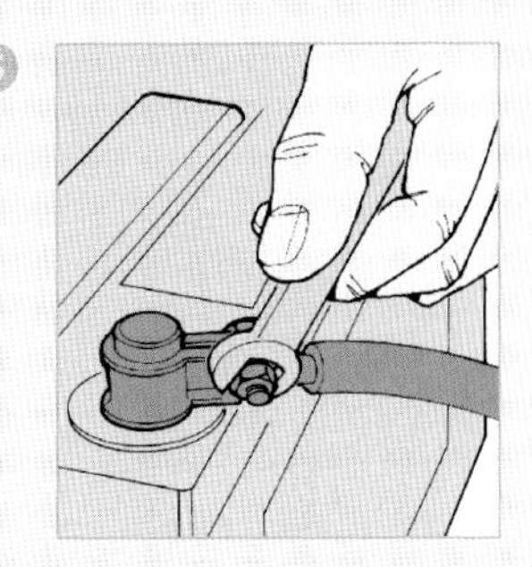

❶ In temperatures well below freezing, the electrolyte in the flat battery may freeze.

❷ Check by opening the vents (*see page 197*). Never attempt to charge a frozen battery.

❸ It is not necessary to disconnect the battery to charge it – it can be left in the car. However, if you wish to charge the battery outside the car, you will need to remove it. In this case, check that you have a note of the codes for reprogramming any electrical equipment (radio, etc.) or any other systems that would be affected by the loss of electricity caused when the terminals are disconnected.

❹ Ensure the ignition and all electrical equipment (radio, lights, etc.) are switched off before connecting the battery charger and plugging it into the mains. This will prevent any damage to the systems and equipment.

❺ If you are charging the battery outside the car, loosen and unscrew the nut connecting the battery lead to the negative (-) terminal. (Always disconnect the negative terminal before the positive.) Disconnect the lead; you may need to wiggle it to get it off. Then disconnect the positive (+) terminal in the same way.

WARNING

See the safety guidelines on page 196. Always disconnect and connect leads in the order given in the instructions that follow (*see also page 195*). This will reduce the likelihood of an accidental short-circuit, and resultant damage, occurring.

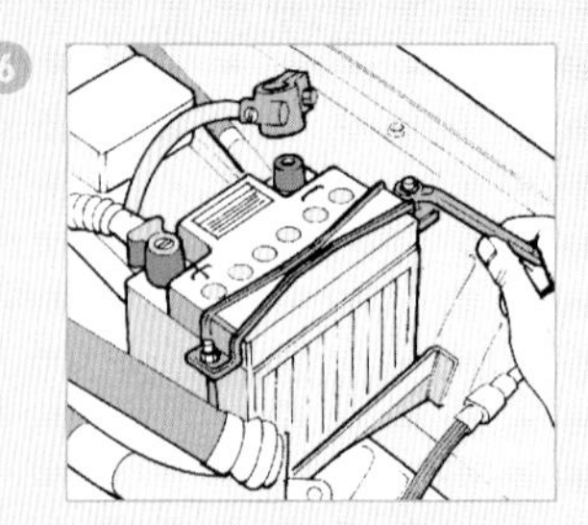

❻ Unscrew the clips that secure the battery to the mounting. If the battery is not a sealed type, protect yourself against electrolyte spillage with gloves and suitable clothing. Remove the battery, keeping it upright. It will be very heavy.

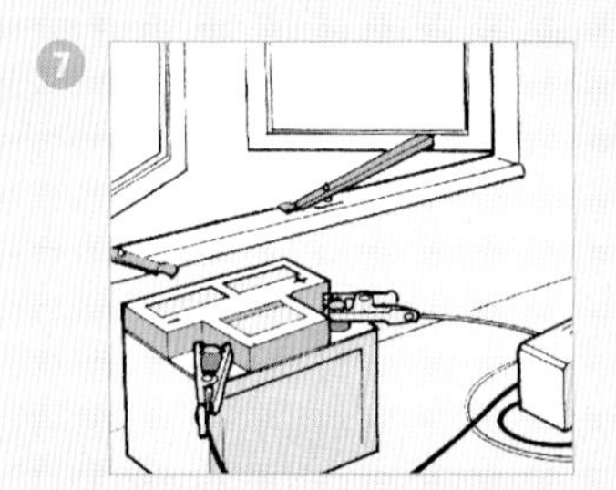

❼ Never charge the battery in a confined area or in a room without good ventilation. It gives off toxic fumes.

❽ Some vent caps contain small apertures that allow the hydrogen gases created during charging to escape. However, if there are no obvious vents in the caps, remove them before charging to make sure the gases can escape. Never smoke or allow a naked flame near a battery that is being charged, as this could cause an explosion.

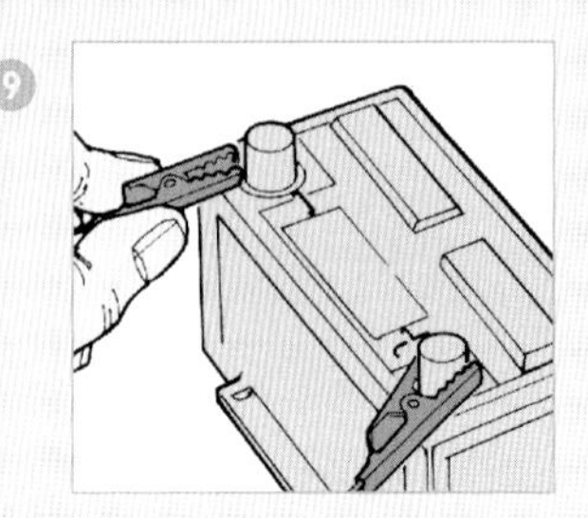

❾ Ensure that the battery charger is NOT yet switched on or plugged into the mains. Connect the positive charger lead (red) to the positive (+) battery terminal, then the negative charger lead (black) to the negative (-) battery terminal.

WARNING

Never charge a battery while the engine is running.

Recharge a flat battery as soon as you possibly can.

Never disconnect the battery while the engine is running.

If a battery being charged feels very hot to the touch, stop charging immediately.

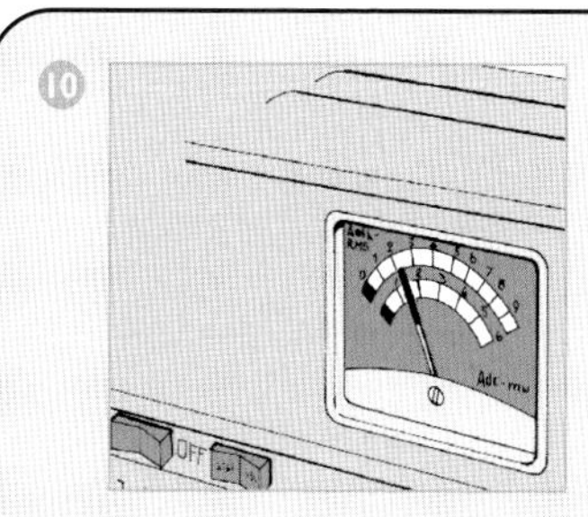

⑩ If the charger has adjustable charging rates, set it according to the operating instructions. Then plug it into the mains and switch on.

⑪ Instructions for how long to charge the battery should be supplied with the charger, but also check the battery casing, which may specify a recommended rate. Do not exceed any recommended rates. Maintenance-free sealed batteries should be charged at a slow rate. The length of charge needed depends on the strength of the battery charge. If no instructions are available, charge a 12-volt battery at 4–6 amps overnight. As the battery becomes charged, it will cause the charging rate to reduce.

Some maintenance-free batteries take a long time to charge and won't respond to some types of charger. If in doubt, seek professional advice.

Battery chargers

These have a charge rate that determines how quickly a battery can be charged.

Some chargers have a 'rapid charge' setting, but this cannot be used on all batteries.

Some have a boost setting to start an engine with a flat battery.

Some chargers automatically switch off when the battery is fully charged.

⑫ Periodically touch the casing of the battery. If it feels very hot, switch off the charger immediately and allow the battery to cool before beginning to charge it again at a lower charge rate.

⑬ When the charging is finished, switch off the charger and unplug it from the mains before disconnecting its leads from the battery.

⑭ If you disconnected the battery from its leads in the car, reconnect the battery leads to the terminals, this time connecting the positive (+) terminal first and then the negative (-) terminal.

Jump-starting

If your car won't start due to a flat battery, you can connect it to a fully charged battery in another car with jump leads. This enables you to start your car using current from the 'booster' battery.

Why is my battery flat?

Parasitic drain: if a car is not driven for a long period of time, electrical equipment that only requires a very low current to keep it running (such as an alarm or clock) can drain the battery.

Electrical equipment left on: if the lights, radio, etc. are left on for a time when the engine is not running (even for as little as a few hours), the battery can be drained of its charge.

Defective battery: a defective battery can be caused by low electrolyte levels, an electrolyte leak, or plates that are deteriorating. These cause it to lose its capacity to hold a charge.

Age: an old battery loses its capacity to hold a charge.

Loose, corroded or dirty battery terminal connections: these can impede the flow of electricity to and from the battery.

Charging problem: a faulty alternator or a loose alternator belt will interfere with the charging process and prevent the battery from receiving a full charge when the engine is running.

Extremes of temperature: modern batteries operate effectively over a wide temperature range, but extremely hot or cold weather can affect them adversely.

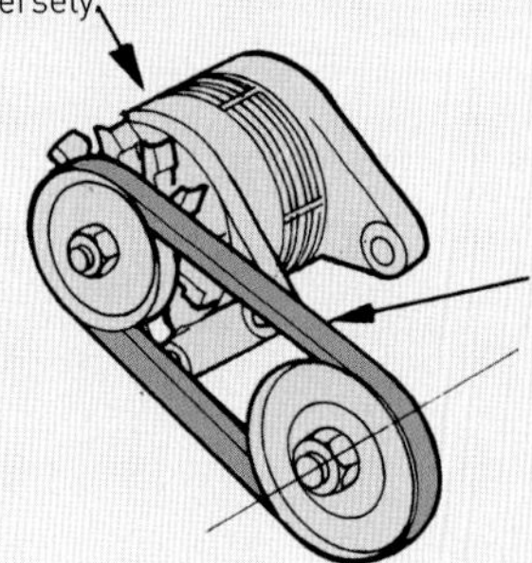

Using jump leads

❶ Check that both batteries have the same voltage (normally 12 volts). Do not jump-start a car if the batteries have different voltages.

you will need

→ jump leads
→ another car

❷

❸

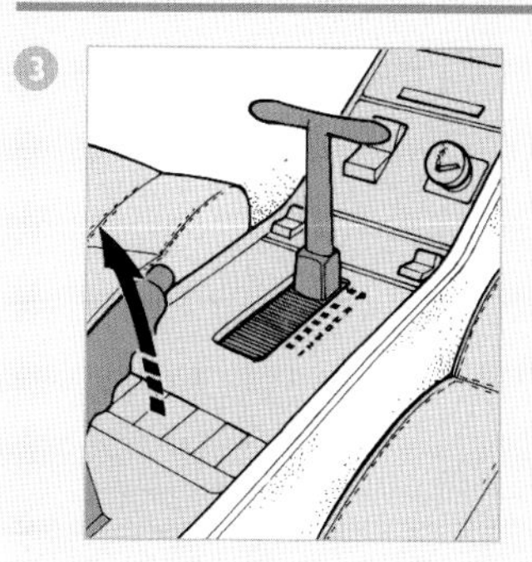

❷ Position the two cars so that they are not touching, but are close enough for the jump leads to reach across.

❸ Turn off the ignition and all electrical equipment (radio, lights, etc.) of both cars. Apply the handbrakes and put both cars into neutral (or 'park' for an automatic transmission).

❹ Don't let the jump leads touch each other, or let the clamps come into contact with any metal (other than the battery terminals) at any time while they are connected to any part of the cars.

SAFETY

Always disconnect and connect leads in the order given on the following pages.

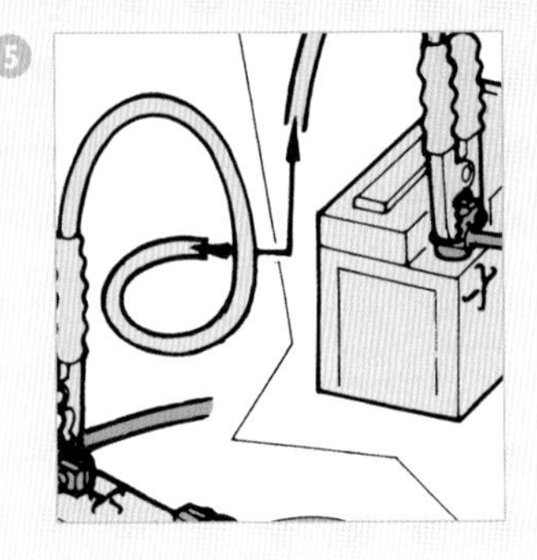

❺ Clamp one end of the positive (red) jump lead to the positive (+) terminal on the flat battery. Then clamp the other end of this lead to the positive (+) terminal on the booster battery.

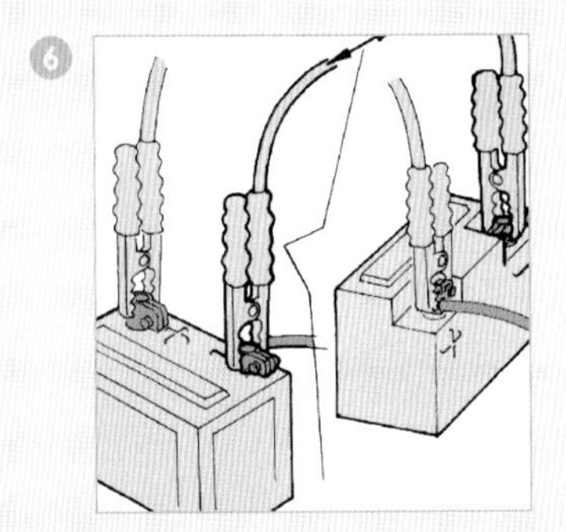

❻ Clamp one end of the negative (black) jump lead to the negative (-) terminal on the booster battery. Clamp the other end of this lead to the negative (-) terminal on the flat battery.

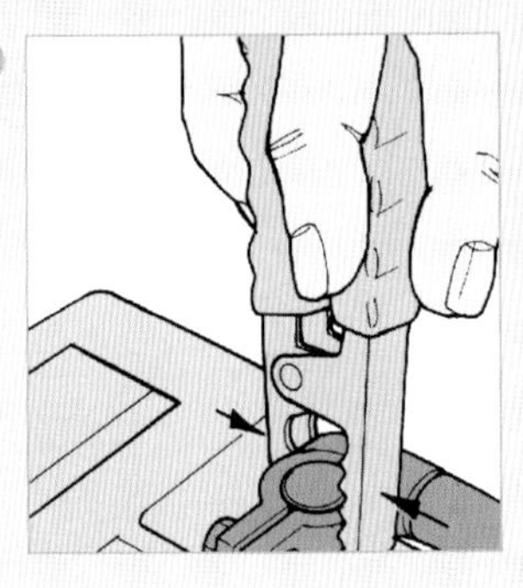

❼ Ensure both ends of both leads are making good electrical contact and that both leads are clear of the moving parts of both cars.

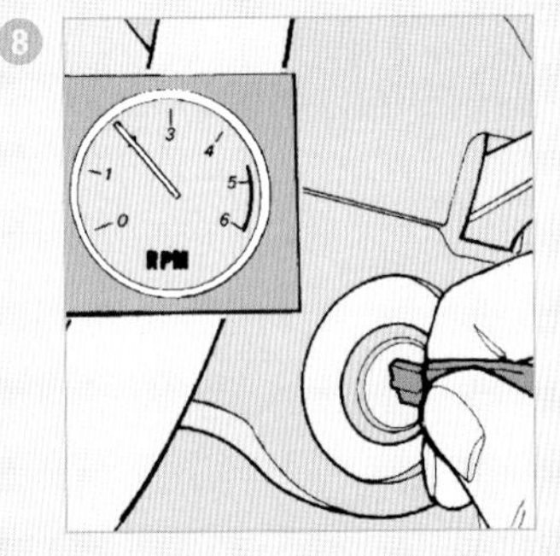

❽ Start the engine of the car with the booster battery and rev it to about 2,000 rpm. Hold it at this speed while trying to start the other car.

9 When the engine on the 'dead' vehicle is running, switch off the engine of the car with the booster battery.

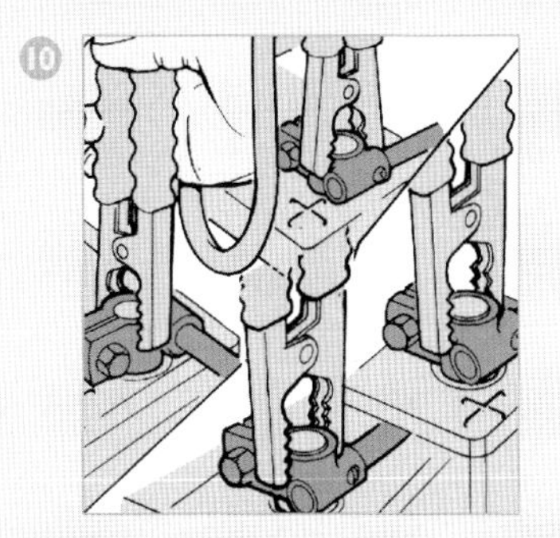

10 With the engine still running on the 'dead' car, disconnect the negative (black) jump lead from its battery. Then disconnect the other end of the negative jump lead from the booster battery.

11 Disconnect the positive (red) jump lead from the car with the booster battery, then disconnect it from the 'dead' car.

12 Leave the engine of the 'dead' car running at fast idle for at least 15–20 minutes, or drive the car for the same length of time to recharge the battery sufficiently to ensure restarting.

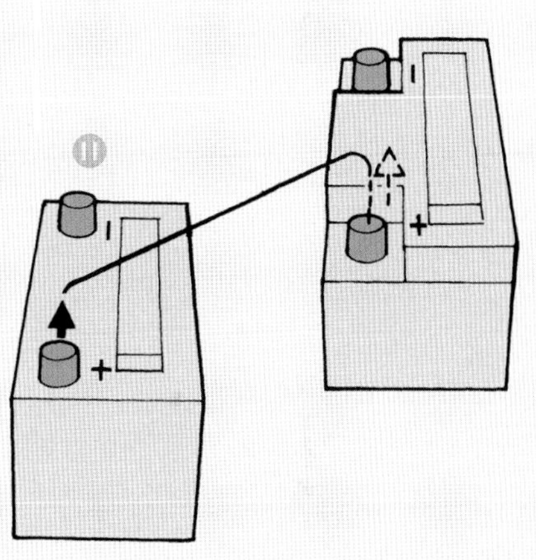

WARNING

You may find that some amateur mechanics recommend that you attach the negative jump lead to a metal part of the car, rather than attaching it to the negative terminal. However, you should ignore this advice, as making the connection in this way can fail to provide a good electrical connection and might result in overheating, sparking or even a fire.

Fuses

Many parts of the car, from the headlights and windscreen wipers to accessories such as air conditioning, are powered by electricity. Each of these devices has an electrical circuit protected by a fuse. If one of them fails, the first thing to check is the fuse.

Electrical circuits

In this simple electrical circuit, a battery supplies power to a bulb by means of two wires. One wire connects the positive terminal to the bulb – this is the live wire, which takes the current from the battery to the bulb. Another wire returns the current to the negative terminal – this is called the earth wire.

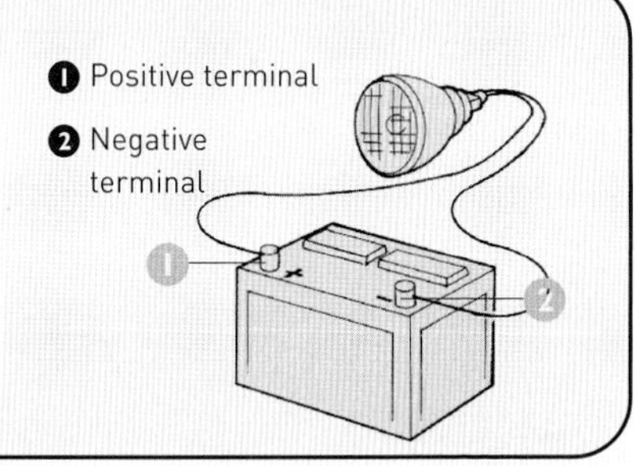

❶ Positive terminal

❷ Negative terminal

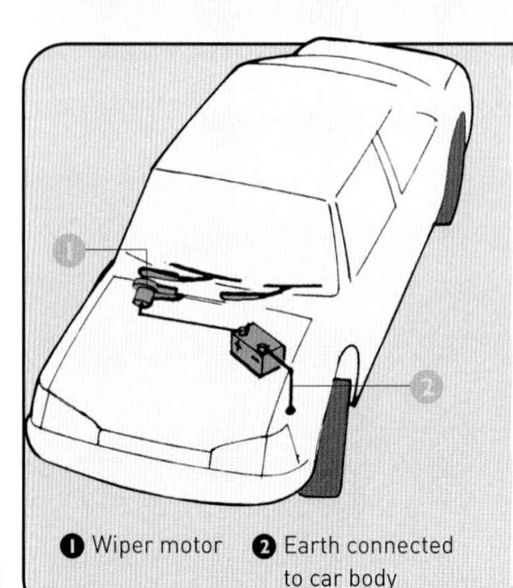

❶ Wiper motor ❷ Earth connected to car body

Earthing

As the body of the car is made of steel, which is a good conductor of electricity, it is used to form part of the electrical system. The negative terminal of the battery is connected to the body so that it can be used as the earth. Many of the car's electrical components have earth wires connected to the car body. The current flows through each component to the body and back to the negative terminal of the battery. In effect, the car body is functioning as a large piece of wire conducting electricity, although the voltage is too low to give you a shock if you touch it.

Switches

In the car, each electrical circuit comprises wiring, connections to the battery, a fuse, a switch and the component being powered. The switch makes and breaks the circuit. When the switch is off, the circuit is broken and electricity cannot flow through it; when it is on, the circuit is complete and electricity can flow through it, enabling the component to function. (Most electrical components in the car only work when the ignition key is 'on'.)

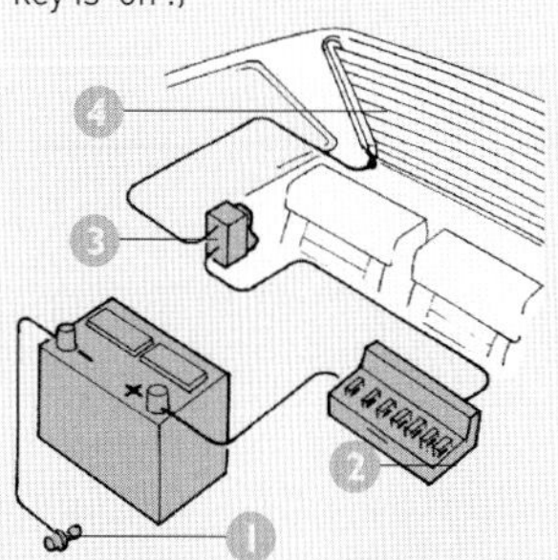

❶ Vehicle earth
❷ Fuse box
❸ Switch
❹ Heated rear window

Not every electrical device in the car is switched on and off by the driver. For example, the radiator cooling fan is operated by a thermostatic switch, which turns the fan on automatically when the coolant reaches a certain temperature.

Fuses

Fuses are safety devices that protect components and wiring. Consisting of a thin piece of conductor wire between two electrical contacts, a fuse is designed to 'blow' (melt and break) when the current passing through the circuit exceeds the amount needed to run the component. This excess flow is caused by a fault in the circuit, often a short-circuit. This occurs when wires accidentally touch each other (e.g., when insulating material becomes worn), shortening the route the current takes around the circuit. When the fuse blows, it breaks the circuit and the component fails to work. If the fuse did not blow, the wiring or component could be damaged by the high current, or a fire caused.

Replacement fuses

Replacement fuses can be bought at car accessory shops. They have standardized colour coding for easy identification. The most common type of fuse encases the thin wire in a plastic moulding – the wire may or may not be visible in this kind of fuse.

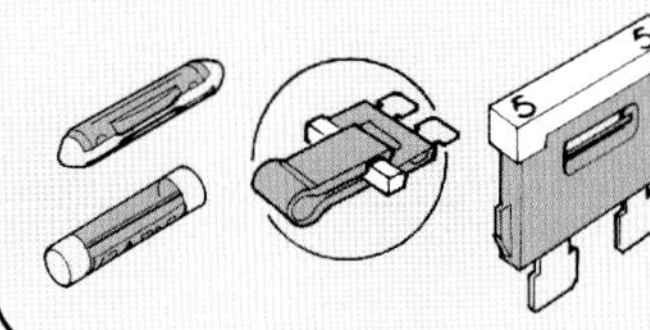

Blown fuses

• When a fuse blows, it is usually an indication that something is wrong with the component or its wiring. However, fuses do wear out, so if you replace a fuse, and the new one does not blow and the component works correctly, then the original fuse probably needed replacing because it was old.

• If a replacement fuse keeps blowing or blows again within a week or so, you should check that you have used a fuse of the correct rating. If you have used the correct replacement, have the system checked at a garage, as there must be a fault in the component or a problem with the circuit.

Changing a fuse

The fuses are kept together in a fuse box. If you are not sure of its location, refer to your car handbook. It is usually in the passenger compartment close to the dashboard, or under the bonnet.

In cars with two or more fuse boxes, one is usually in the passenger compartment near the dashboard and holds fuses that protect the electrical equipment operated from inside the car. The other is usually under the bonnet for electrically-powered engine components.

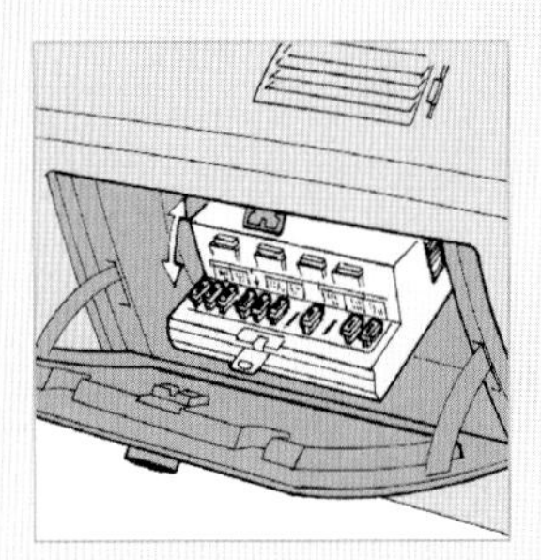

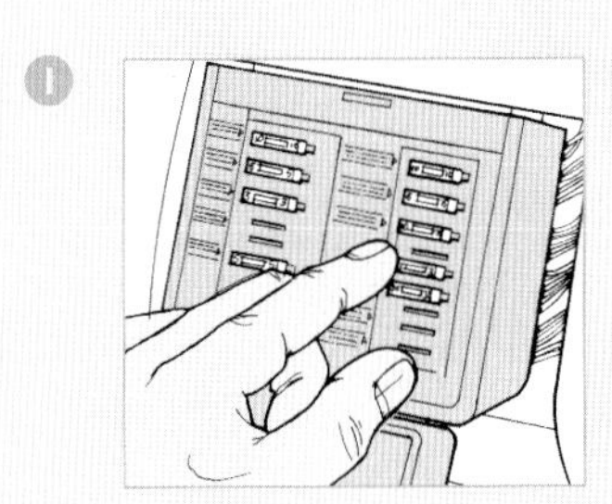

1 Switch the engine off, open the fuse box cover and refer to your car handbook to see which fuse corresponds to the failed component. Some components share a circuit and fuse.

WARNING

Don't try to replace a fuse with a piece of wire. This could cause a fire or damage the component.

❷ Make sure that the fuse is clipped firmly in place in the fuse box. Its metal ends or prongs need to make good contact for the electrical circuit to be complete and the component to function. With the component switched on, try pressing on the fuse. If the component works only when the fuse is pressed, it is not making a good contact.

❸ Remove the fuse to clean its contacts. You may be able to remove it by hand, or there may be a special tool (tweezers) provided in the fuse box for removing fuses.

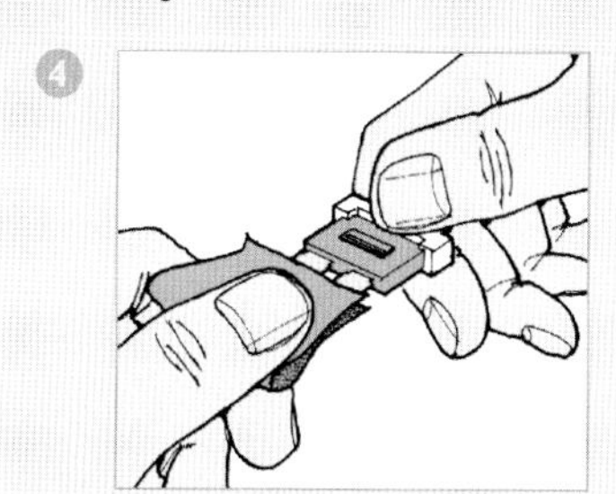

❹ Clean the metal ends or contacts of the fuse lightly with fine abrasive paper.

you will need

→ replacement fuse of the correct rating
→ fine abrasive paper

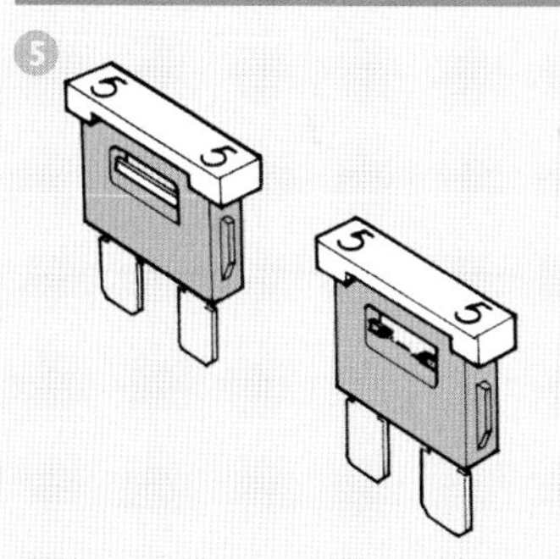

❺ If the component still does not work, remove the fuse and check if the central wire is broken. If it is, replace it with a new fuse of the correct rating (identified by the colour and number on the fuse). If you cannot see the wire, you will have to try replacing the fuse with a new one.

❻ Ensure the new fuse is clipped firmly into position and switch on the component. If the fuse blows again, there is a problem in the circuit or in the component itself. Have the car checked at a garage as soon as possible.

The ignition system (petrol)

Turning the key in the ignition switch sends electrical current down a wire to start the engine. The process used to be mechanical, involving a complicated system of contact-breaker points, but in modern cars, solid-state electronics have taken over.

System components

The ignition system of a modern car comprises the battery, ignition switch, coil, distributor, spark plugs and ECU.

1. ECU
2. Spark plug
3. Distributor
4. Ignition switch
5. Coil
6. Battery

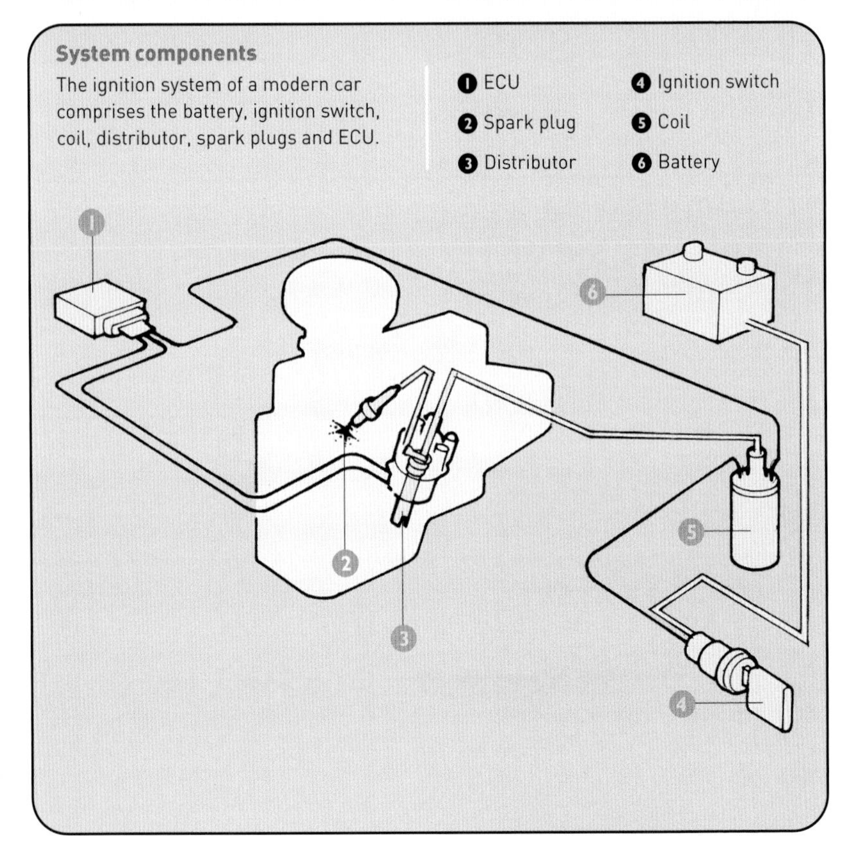

How it works

- Its job is to transmit a voltage strong enough to create a spark to ignite the fuel/air mixture and to control the timing of the spark. Some cars are now fitted with distributorless systems (*see page 212*).

- When the engine is switched on, the battery sends an electrical current to the coil. The coil amplifies the current and sends it to the distributor via a high-tension (HT) lead. Inside the distributor cap, a rotor arm is turned by the engine and distributes the current received from the coil in pulses via wires to each of the spark plugs, in the correct firing order.

- As the timing of the spark is computerized and electronic ignition systems have fewer components than the mechanical systems that used to be fitted, there is little the amateur can do to maintain the system. Diagnosing ignition faults is difficult without the right equipment and has to be left to the professionals.

Switching the engine on

There are several positions in the ignition switch through which the key has to turn before the engine is started. They vary according to each car, but here is a general guide:

Position 1 – the engine is not running and the steering wheel may be locked (you can normally only remove the key in this position). If the steering lock jams or the key is stuck and you can't remove it, rock the steering wheel gently while turning the key.

Position 2 – accessories such as the radio may be switched on, but the engine is not able to run.

Position 3 – the ignition system is on and various dashboard warning lights come on (*see pages 142–47*).

Position 4 – this operates the starter motor. The warning lights go out when the engine starts, except for the brake light if the handbrake is still on.

TIP

Don't leave the key in position 3 in the ignition if you do not intend to start the engine, as damage may occur to the components of the ignition system.

Ignition system components

Ignition system components are also part of the car's electrical system (*see page 188*). Most people are familiar with the battery and spark plugs, but the distributor and coil also play major roles in the ignition process, where the correct timing of the spark is vital.

The coil

This converts the 12 volts received from the battery to the higher voltage (14,000–18,000 volts) necessary to jump the gap in the spark plug and create an ignition spark.

The coil sends the high voltage to the distributor through a high-tension (HT) lead. Sensors relay information about the engine to the ECU to ensure its optimum performance at all speeds and loads. The ECU controls the switching of the voltage to the coil.

The coil is normally mounted under the bonnet, close to the battery.

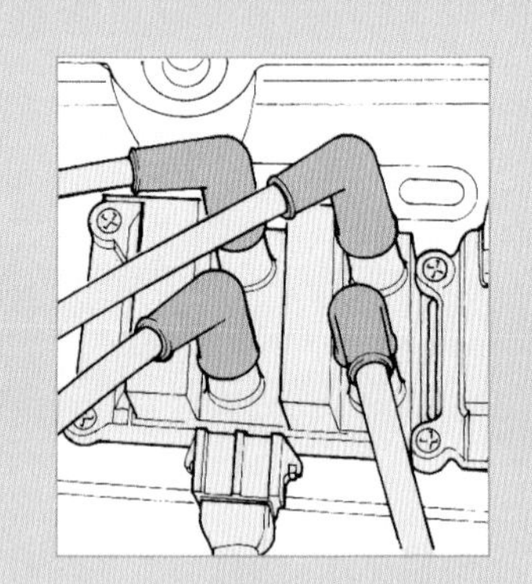

Distributorless ignition systems

Some cars have solid-state ignition systems that have no distributor. Instead of one central coil, some types of this system have one coil for each spark plug, situated directly on the plug itself. The spark plugs are located in the cylinder head. There are therefore no spark plug leads. The car's computer controls the timing of the spark. Without the distributor there is even less to maintain and fewer parts to wear out.

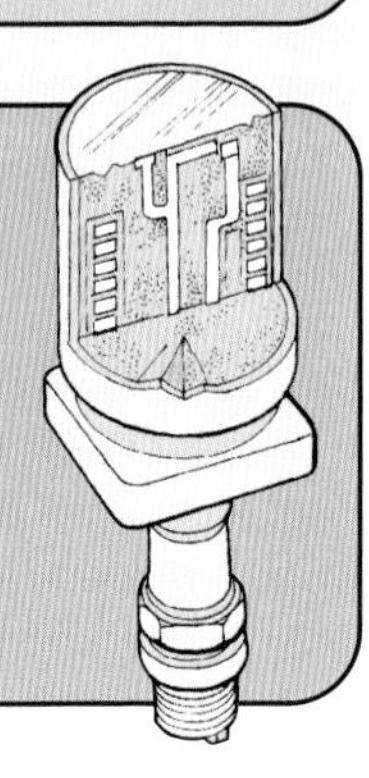

The distributor

It is the distributor's job to pass the high voltage it receives from the coil to each of the spark plugs in the correct firing order and at the correct time.

Inside the distributor cap is a rotor arm mounted on a distributor shaft that is usually driven by the engine camshaft. As it rotates it delivers a carefully timed high-voltage electrical impulse to each spark plug in turn.

The distributor is normally located at the end of the camshaft or on the side of the engine block.

Keep the distributor cap clean by wiping it with a cloth. Check it regularly for cracks, which could cause ignition problems.

1. High voltage
2. High voltage
3. Rotor arm
4. Spark plug

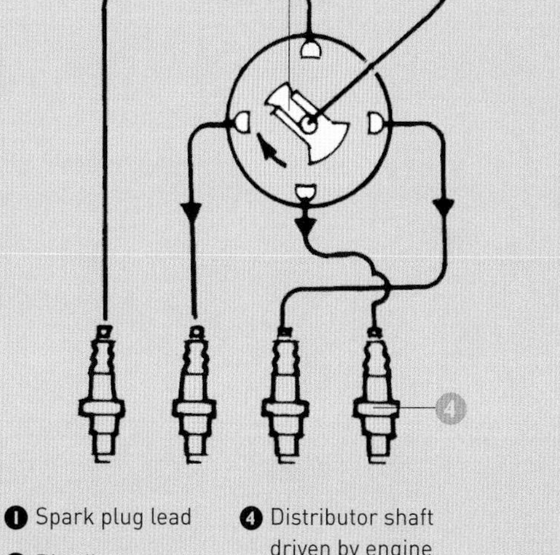

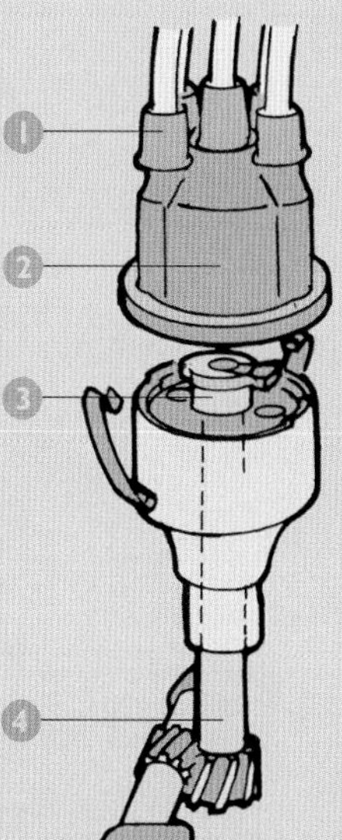

1. Spark plug lead
2. Distributor cap
3. Rotor arm
4. Distributor shaft driven by engine
5. Camshaft

Spark plugs

The spark plugs play a vital role in your car's ignition system, delivering the necessary high-voltage spark to the combustion chambers to ignite the fuel/air mixture, at the right moment, to make the engine run.

- Using the high-voltage impulses they receive from the distributor, the spark plugs deliver the spark that ignites the fuel/air mixture in the combustion chamber. They are screwed into the cylinder head at the top of the combustion chambers in the cylinder block and are connected by leads to the distributor cap.
- Spark plugs consist of a metal electrode (centre electrode) running through the centre of a ceramic insulator that protrudes slightly at one end. A thin metal arm (earth electrode) curves over the protruding end, leaving a small gap between the two. The high-voltage electrical impulse received from the distributor travels along the electrode and jumps across this gap like a tiny bolt of lightning. As it jumps across the gap it produces the spark that ignites the fuel/air mixture.
- Spark plugs should be replaced around every 12,000 miles.

1. Spark plug
2. Inlet and exhaust valves
3. Spark igniting air/fuel mixture in combustion chamber
4. Piston

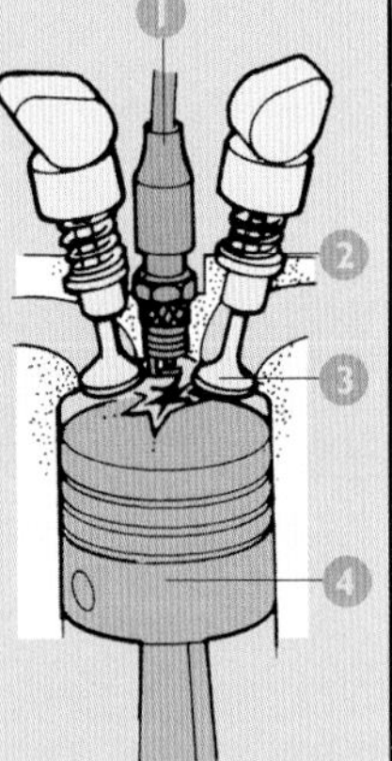

TIP

Keep spark plug high-tension leads clean and make sure they are pushed firmly on to the ends of the plugs, otherwise you may experience ignition problems.

Buying new spark plugs

It is very important to fit the correct type of spark plugs for the engine. If the wrong plugs are fitted, at best the engine could have problems starting and running efficiently, and at worst it could damage the engine. Check your car handbook or the manufacturers' charts that are displayed in retailers. The reach (length of the part that screws into the cylinder head) must be correct. Refer also to the letters and numbers on the spark plug, which indicate the plug's heat range.

Types of spark plug

Spark plugs are given a temperature range according to how quickly their centre electrodes can conduct away heat. For example, a 'cold' plug cools faster than a 'hot' plug because the heat has a shorter path to travel from the electrode to the plug body.

'Cold plugs' have shorter insulators and are normally fitted to high-performance engines that generate a lot of heat, while 'hot plugs' have longer insulators and are fitted to cars with less powerful engines.

Spark timing

The timing of the spark is critical. It is normally timed to occur just before the piston reaches the top of the cylinder on the compression stroke (*see page 154*). If it arrives too early, it results in a problem called 'pinking' (pinging noises – *see page 272*), which can lead to engine damage, and if too late it causes loss of power and overheating.

If you think the timing is wrong, have it checked at a garage.

As the timing of the spark is computerized, and electronic ignitions systems have fewer components than the mechanical systems that used to be fitted, there is little scope for amateur maintenance. Diagnosing faults is difficult and has to be left to the professionals.

1. Letters/numbers indicating spark plug's heat range
2. 'Reach' – part that screws into cylinder head

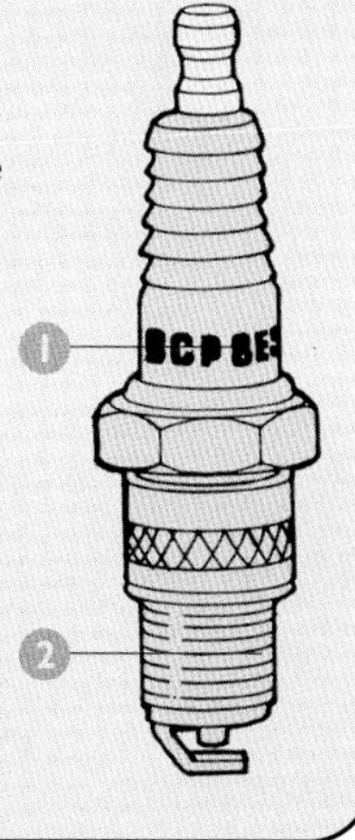

Replacing spark plugs

In many new cars, spark plugs are no longer easily accessible, being contained within the cylinder head casing, and you may need to leave the job of replacing them to a garage which has the special tools required. In most older cars, however, spark plugs can still be accessed.

Essential tools

1. Plug spanners
2. Feeler gauges
3. Gapping tool
4. Rubber tubing
5. Soft brush
6. Anti-seize compound

Replacing spark plugs

1. Ensure the ignition is switched off and the engine is cold.

2. The spark plugs are contained within the cylinder head casing but may not be easily accessible, being hidden by other components that have to be removed first. Check your handbook for instructions on how to access them.

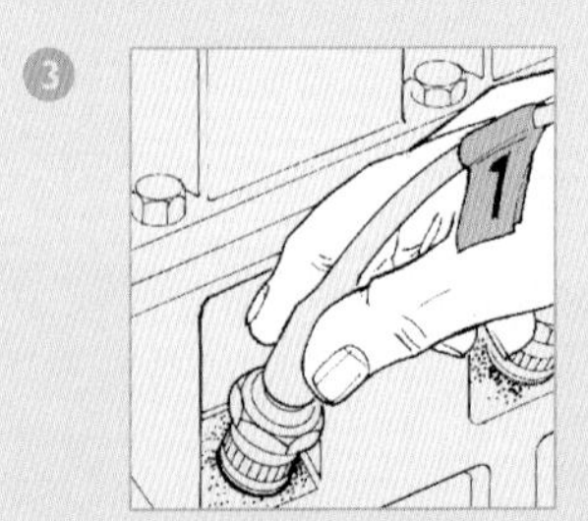

3. Remove and replace one spark plug at a time in order not to confuse the leads, or tape position numbers onto each lead before you remove them, so that you can reconnect them in the same order.

❹ Using the plug connector cap (not the lead itself), carefully pull the lead off the first spark plug.

❺ Unscrew the plug by several turns using the spark plug socket or spanner, but do not remove it. (Don't use too much force; if you cannot remove it, take the car to a garage where they have more specialized tools.)

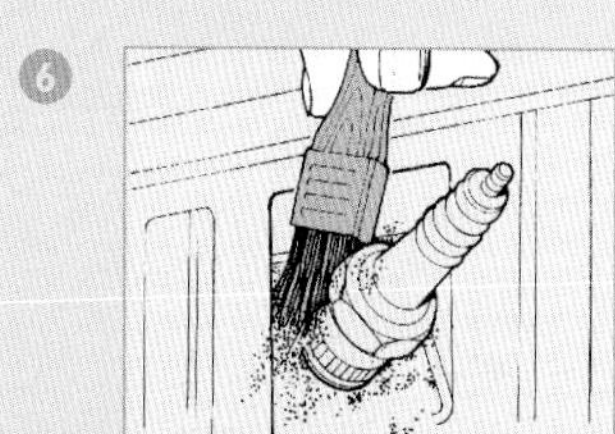

❻ Brush away any dirt from where the plug screws into the cylinder block. (Dirt falling into the cylinders could cause damage.) Carefully finish unscrewing the plug by hand and remove it.

❼ Although new plugs are being fitted, the gap between the electrodes still needs to be checked with a feeler gauge before fitting. Feeler gauges normally have their thickness marked on them. Refer to your car handbook for the correct spark plug gap for your engine and select the feeler gauge of the corresponding thickness. Slide it into and through the gap; it should be a tight sliding fit, i.e. you should feel a very slight drag from the electrodes, but otherwise the gauge should pass through freely.

you will need

→ a set of spark plugs suitable for your engine
→ spark plug spanner or socket*
→ feeler gauges
→ spark plug gapping tool**
→ tube of anti-seize compound
→ paintbrush
→ small length of rubber or plastic tubing (to fit over the end of the spark plugs to help screw them in)

*before buying a plug spanner, check your car handbook to see what size you need.
**a special tool that enables you to adjust the plug gap and may also contain a brush and feeler gauges.

❽ If the gap is incorrect, adjust it by bending the curved electrode. Do this by slipping the notch in the lever of the gapping tool over the electrode and gently applying pressure in the appropriate direction. Check the gap again with the feeler gauge.

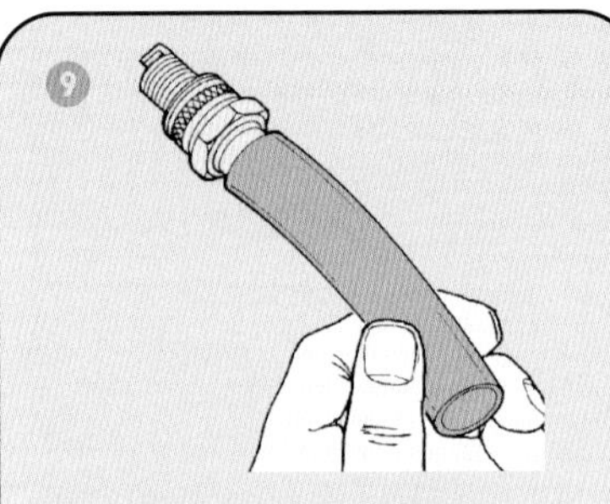

❾ Smear a little anti-seize compound onto the thread of the new plug to help it screw into the engine block. It is important to screw it in carefully as the threads can easily cross. Place one end of the tubing over the plug and using this, screw it in gently. The tubing will not allow you to use too much force and should slip rather than allow you to cross the threads.

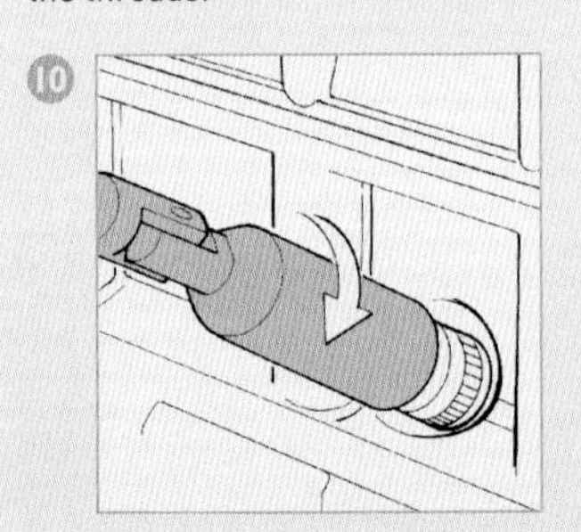

❿ When you have screwed the plug in as far as possible with the tubing, tighten it using the spark plug socket or spanner, but be careful not to overtighten. Replace the connector and lead.

A guide to performance

Check the spark plugs to make sure that they are in good condition as they affect the engine's performance, its fuel economy and the amount of emissions it produces. They also act as a guide to engine condition and performance and can help identify problems.

Potential problems

The fuel/air mixture will only ignite and burn efficiently if the proportions are correct.

When the engine is cold, a richer mixture is needed (more fuel), but once the engine is warmed up, the mixture becomes weaker (less fuel).

Examine spark plugs every 6,000 miles to check for carbon deposits and check that the spark gap is correct to ensure the engine is firing efficiently. If the engine stalls frequently or sounds erratic when idling, it may indicate that the plugs need replacing.

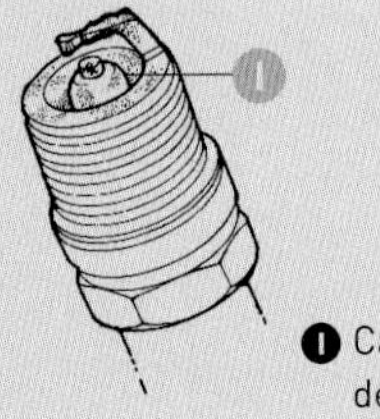

❶ Carbon deposits

Checking condition

Remove, check and replace each spark plug one at a time (to make sure you put them back in the correct position), following the steps on pages 216–217.

Examine the tip of each plug and check the gap between the electrodes (*see page 217*). Constant sparking gradually wears the electrodes until they become very rounded and the gap too wide. Always replace plugs with worn electrodes.

Even if only one or two spark plugs need replacing, a complete set of new plugs must be fitted as they all need to function at the same capacity to ensure the engine runs smoothly.

If any of the plugs have any of the abnormal deposits detailed as follows, the engine is not performing efficiently and needs professional attention. Replace the existing plugs and take the car to a garage where the problem can be identified and corrected. The garage will fit a new set.

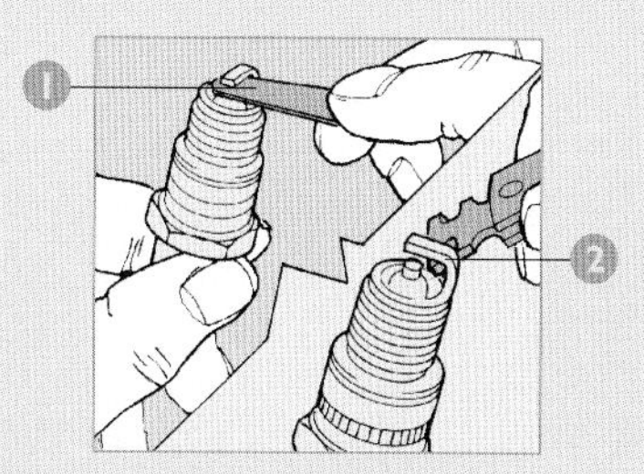

❶ Plug gap ❷ Adjust gap

Normal appearance indicating a well-tuned engine

Light grey/brown deposits, core nose lightly coated.

Abnormal appearance

Seek the help of a professional mechanic if you notice any abnormal deposits or appearance, including:

- **Very pale brown, almost white deposits:** the mixture is too weak and needs adjusting.
- **Black oily deposits:** a possible oil leak or a fault in the cylinder, which will cause poor starting and lack of power.
- **Black sooty powdery deposits:** these are carbon deposits; the mixture is too rich and will need to be adjusted.
- **Oily or black and oily, but with no deposits (i.e. smooth appearance):** the plug may be the wrong type for the engine (check the handbook) causing misfiring leading to erratic running and loss of power. Or, it may be old or damaged. Alternatively, you may only be making short journeys, so the car does not reach its correct operating temperature. Replace the plugs and take the car for a long run. Recheck the plugs to see if the oiliness has disappeared.

The ignition system (diesel)

One of the principal differences between petrol and diesel engines lies in the igniting of the fuel. In petrol engines it is ignited by a spark produced by the ignition system, but in diesel engines it is ignited by compression and there is no ignition system.

Diesel ignition

Diesel engines rely on the heat generated by compressing air to ignite the fuel. A heater plug is incorporated to warm the air first and aid cold starting.

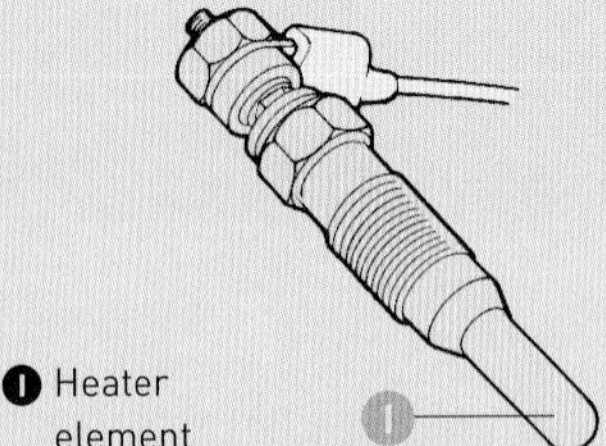

1 Heater element

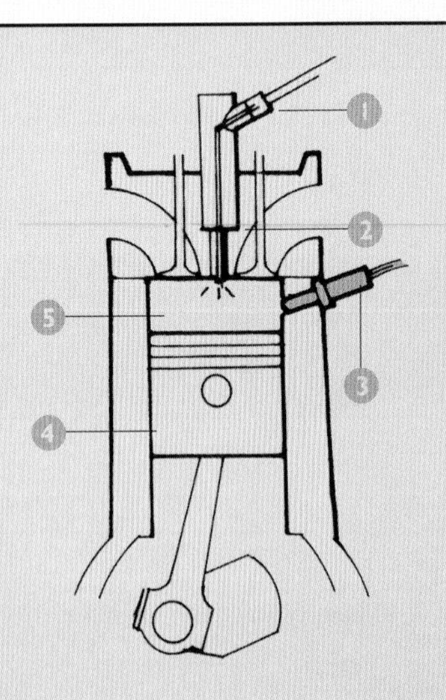

1 Fuel injector
2 Valve
3 Heater plug
4 Piston
5 Combustion chamber

TIP
HEATER PLUG LIFE

Heater plugs are long-lasting and don't need regular checking. They may only need to be replaced once in a car's lifetime, but if you have difficulty starting the engine, or if a lot of smoke is created when starting, have them checked by a mechanic.

How it works

• In diesel engines the fuel is normally injected directly into the cylinders, where it ignites on contact with the compressed air, which is very hot (*see page 163*). When the engine is cold, this process is assisted by heater plugs (also called glow plugs) containing electrically heated wires that help pre-heat the combustion chamber prior to the engine being started.

• There is usually one heater plug per cylinder, screwed into the top of the combustion chamber. Operated by an electronic control unit, they are activated when the ignition is switched on.

• A light on the dashboard comes on to show that pre-heating is taking place. The light goes out after a few seconds when the combustion chamber has reached the correct temperature and the engine can be started.

• If the engine is not started, a timer cuts off the current to the plugs to avoid draining the battery and overheating the plugs.

Post-heating

The plugs are normally switched off automatically once the engine is started. However, in some engines they remain on for a short period of time after the engine has been started. This is to assist ignition while the engine is still relatively cold. They cannot be cancelled for the first 15 seconds after starting, but after that they can be cancelled by pressing on the accelerator or if the coolant temperature rises to more than 60°C.

Ignition timing

Unlike petrol engines, diesel engines do not need an ignition module (ECU) to control the ignition system since there is no spark to be timed. However, diesel engines do have a fuel module controlling the timing and amount of fuel inserted (as do petrol engines).

Fuel

Petrol and diesel fuels are derived from crude oil, and are blamed for creating a lot of atmospheric pollution. There are more environmentally friendly alternatives available, such as LPG and electricity, but all cars pollute the atmosphere to some degree.

Petrol

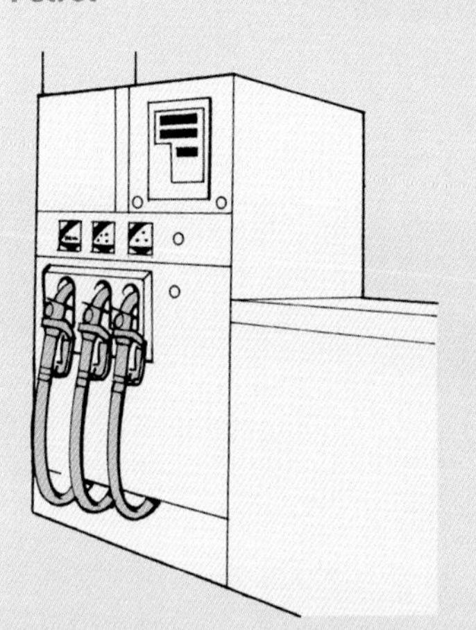

Petrol is graded according to its octane rating. Higher grades burn less quickly than lower ones. When too low a grade is used, it causes 'knock', a rattling sound due to the fuel/air in the cylinders igniting prematurely, which is harmful to the engine.

Diesel

Diesel thickens and becomes waxy in cold weather, restricting its flow. To combat this, most cars are fitted with a fuel heater to warm the fuel before it passes through the fuel filter and into the engine. Diesel can freeze in very cold temperatures, so try to park the car in a garage rather than leaving it outside. Anti-gel additives are available from accessory shops to help improve running and starting.

Petrol vs diesel

Neither diesel nor petrol can be said to be more environmentally friendly than the other. Diesel produces less of some harmful gases, although more of the particulates that cause respiratory problems. However, diesel engines are 20–25 per cent more fuel-efficient than those run on petrol, so diesel engines produce less carbon dioxide, simply because they use less fuel.

Octane grades

- Octane grades vary slightly from country to country, but the car's ECU is normally modified so that the car can be run on the grades of petrol habitually sold in a particular country.
- Check your car handbook to see which grade suits your engine best. Most cars are designed to run on the basic grade of petrol sold, and there are no appreciable benefits from running on a higher octane.
- Some cars with high-compression engines, such as sports cars, do require a high-octane petrol. High-octane petrol is no more environmentally friendly than a low-octane fuel.
- If you experience engine knocking, then it is essential to seek professional help, as it could cause serious engine damage if left unattended.

LRP (lead replacement petrol)

LRP was introduced to replace the leaded petrol required by many older cars. LRP is a high-octane unleaded petrol with additives to protect against valve seat recession (VSR) – wearing of the valve seats caused by using unleaded petrol in engines designed to run on leaded fuel.

If it is not possible to find LRP, ask the car manufacturer (or a garage or motoring organization) if your engine can be run on high-octane unleaded petrol with a VSR additive. This should be OK for most engines run under a normal load, although not for some high-performance engines. You can buy a VSR additive from accessory shops and petrol stations.

LPG (liquefied petroleum gas)

LPG is a gas that becomes liquid when it is stored under pressure. An engine run on LPG is around 20 per cent less fuel-efficient than one run on petrol. However, although it produces more carbon dioxide than diesel, provided the engine is well tuned, it produces fewer particulates and emissions than petrol and diesel overall. To run a car on LPG, the fuel system must be modified and a pressurized fuel tank fitted.

Cars that have been converted to LPG normally retain the original petrol system, making it possible to alternate between the two.

Filling the tank

Although filling the tank with fuel is something the motorist does regularly, it is also potentially very dangerous. When fuel is poured into the tank, an inflammable vapour is released, which becomes extremely volatile when it comes into contact with air. Therefore it is important to take precautions when filling up.

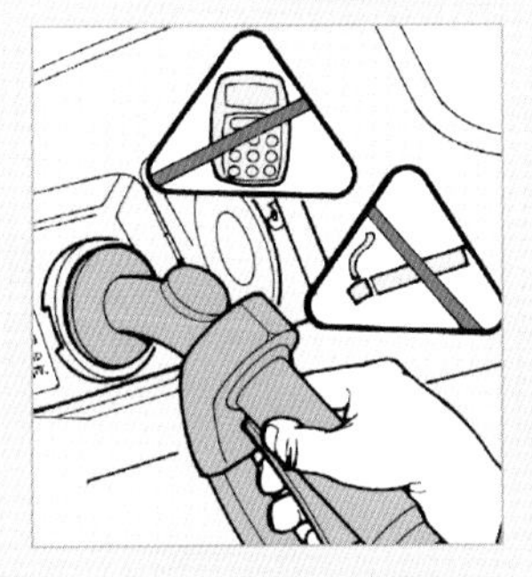

Ensure both the engine and the ignition are switched off. Don't smoke, and make sure there are no naked flames or sparks nearby that could ignite the vapour and cause an explosion. In addition, mop up any spillage and switch off mobile phones – their operation could generate a spark that could in turn ignite the petrol fumes.

Electricity

Cars run on electricity are powered by an electric motor driven by special batteries. Electrically powered cars are quiet and cause no exhaust pollution, unlike those powered by oil-based fuels (petrol, diesel, LPG). However, the production of electricity at generating plants produces carbon dioxide, which has a detrimental impact on the environment. Electrically powered cars have only a limited range, needing to be recharged every 50–100 miles, depending on the car. Full recharging normally takes around seven hours.

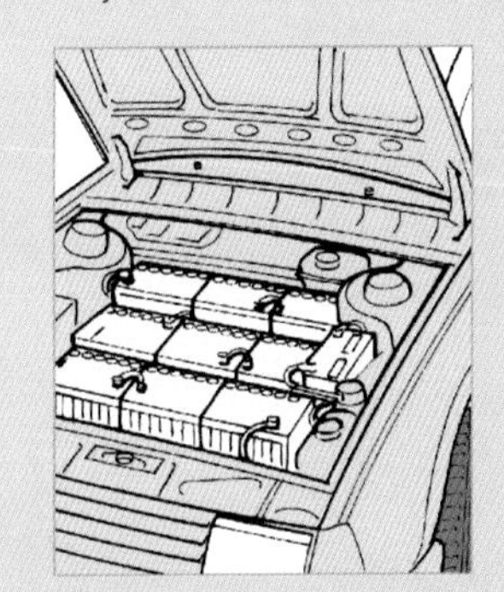

Fuel economy

Being more fuel-efficient is beneficial, both in financial and environmental terms – if less fuel is used, fewer emissions are produced. Once the size of the car and its engine capacity have been taken into consideration, fuel economy is very much about driving style.

• The larger the vehicle, the heavier it is and the more fuel is needed to drive it. The larger the engine, the more fuel it will use.

• Keep tyres inflated to the correct pressure. Under-inflated tyres increase fuel consumption by creating extra 'drag' on the road surface.

• Don't drive at high speeds. A car driven at 50 mph can use 25 per cent less petrol than at 70 mph. Check your car handbook for the optimum speed at which to drive your car for fuel economy.

• Don't over-rev the engine, particularly when starting, and drive smoothly, avoiding rapid acceleration.

• Switch off the engine when the car is stationary. The engine uses more fuel idling than it does starting.

• Use higher gears where traffic conditions permit; more fuel is used in the lower gears.

• The engine warms up faster when the car is being driven than when it is idling. Drive the car as soon as the engine is started, rather than leaving it to warm up by idling (provided visibility is not impaired by ice on the windscreen during cold weather).

• Air conditioning can increase fuel consumption by 10 per cent, so don't leave it on all the time.

• Avoid wind resistance caused by carrying loads on a roof rack. Carrying a heavy weight also increases fuel consumption; take heavy items that you don't need out of the boot.

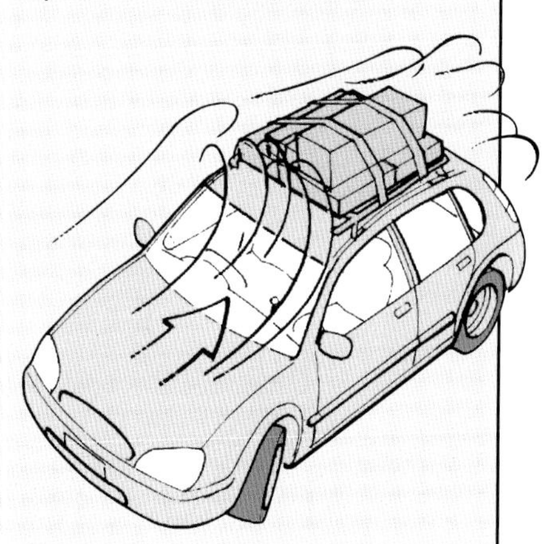

• Check the fuel cap to make sure the seal is tight; fuel can be lost through evaporation. Don't overfill the tank, to avoid loss through spillage.

• Have the engine serviced regularly. A well-tuned engine helps reduce emissions and keep fuel consumption to a minimum.

Fuel emergencies

You may think that you would never fill your car's tank with the wrong kind of fuel, but accidents do happen. If you are distracted while filling up, or have recently changed your car, you could absent-mindedly use the wrong pump.

WARNING

If you realize that you have put the wrong kind of fuel into your car's tank, see the following advice.

Petrol instead of diesel

If you have filled up with petrol, don't drive the car. (*See opposite.*) If you have only put in a few litres, stop and continue filling with diesel.

Diesel instead of petrol

Don't drive the car. (*See opposite.*)

Unleaded instead of LRP

If you filled the whole tank with unleaded, drive the car until about half the fuel has been used, then refill with LRP. Or, if you have only put in a small quantity of unleaded petrol, simply stop and continue filling with LRP.

LRP instead of unleaded

Don't drive the car, otherwise the catalytic converter (if one is fitted) will be damaged. (*See opposite.*)

WARNING

If the advice given on page 226 is 'don't drive the car' it is because once the engine is started, the incorrect fuel will be pumped through the fuel lines and filter to the injectors, and the whole system will have to be drained and cleaned. However, if the engine is not started, only the tank will need to be drained and cleaned. If you are at a petrol station, do not start the engine, but push the car away from the fuel pump and seek professional assistance.

Using reserve fuel

• If you carry reserve fuel for emergencies, it must be kept in a container that is approved for that purpose. It is illegal and dangerous to carry fuel in an unapproved container.

• Before pouring any of your reserve fuel into the tank, make sure the ignition and engine are switched off. Don't smoke and ensure that there are no naked flames close by, and switch off mobile phones. An inflammable vapour is released as the fuel is poured, so there is considerable risk of an explosion from a stray spark.

• If the engine does not start, there could be an air lock, or sediment from the bottom of the tank could be causing a blockage in the fuel line. Seek assistance. If there is a strong smell of fuel, or you suspect that a leak may have caused you to run out of fuel (i.e. the level has gone down more quickly than usual), don't drive the car until it has been checked, as a fuel leak is highly dangerous.

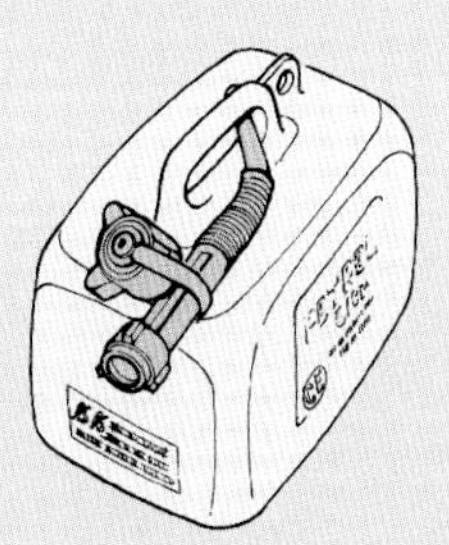

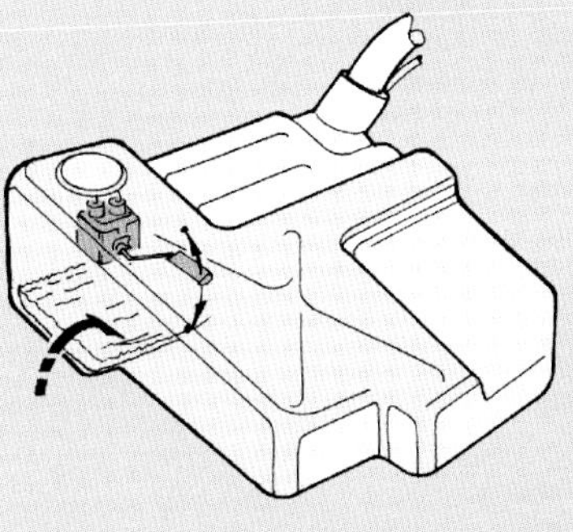

The fuel system

This feeds fuel from the tank to the combustion chambers in the engine. It ensures that the correct mixture of fuel and air is supplied to the engine at the correct time. Most modern engines have fuel injection systems, but older cars may have carburettors.

How it works (petrol engines)

In most modern cars, the system comprises a fuel tank, fuel pump, fuel lines (pipes), fuel filter, air filter, fuel injectors and emission control systems. Fuel is pumped from the tank through a fuel line via a filter (where any dirt is removed) to a metering unit. The fuel is then fed to the fuel rail and injectors. These spray the fuel in a fine mist into the stream of air that is drawn into the engine via the inlet valve. The fuel/air mixture is ignited in the combustion chamber (*see pages 154–55*). An ECU that is connected to various sensors adjusts the fuel/air mixture and volume of injection.

1. Tank
2. Pump
3. Excess fuel returns to tank
4. Pressure regulator
5. Filter
6. Fuel injector
7. Fuel rail
8. Air filter
9. Fuel pumped from tank

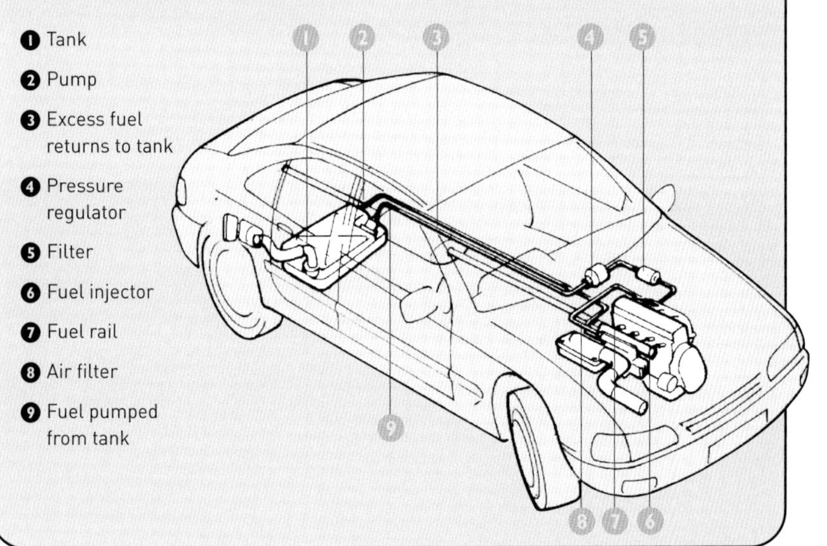

Carburettor systems

In some older cars, a carburettor supplies the correct fuel/air mixture to the engine. The system comprises a fuel tank, fuel lines, fuel pump, fuel filter, carburettor and air filter.

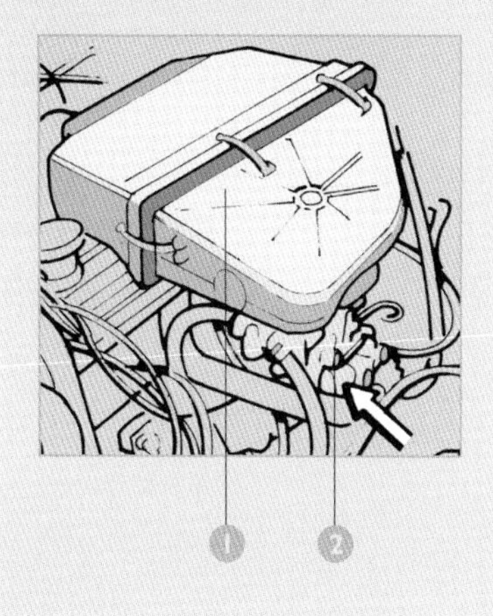

The fuel is pumped from the tank via a filter into the carburettor float chamber. Air is drawn into the carburettor via the air filter. As the air is drawn in, it creates a partial vacuum that sucks petrol from the float chamber into the air stream.

An inlet valve allows the fuel/air mixture into the cylinder, where it is burnt. A throttle valve connected to the accelerator controls the speed of the engine by regulating the fuel/air mixture that enters the cylinders.

Carburettors are complex and tend to require frequent adjustment.

1. Air filter
2. Carburettor

Diesel engines

The system normally comprises a fuel tank, fuel pump, fuel lines (pipes), fuel filter with integral water separator, air filter, injection pump, fuel injectors and emission control systems (*see pages 162–63*).

Leaks

If you suspect a leak or smell petrol, pull over, stop the engine immediately and seek assistance. Petrol is highly inflammable and there is serious risk of fire or an explosion if the fuel comes into contact with hot metal or a spark. Don't smoke or use your mobile phone near the engine, and don't drive the car until the leak has been identified and repaired.

Fuel system components

The fuel system's components are relatively uncomplicated in structure and function. Despite this, since a large amount of the system is inaccessible and because highly combustible fuel is involved, nearly all maintenance must be carried out by a professional.

The fuel pump

This is normally mounted inside or close to the fuel tank, and is driven electrically. It forces fuel from the tank through the fuel line to the injectors. On older cars with carburettors, the fuel pump may be mounted on the engine and is operated by the camshaft.

❶ Access plate (in boot floor) to fuel pump located in tank

❷ External fuel pump

The fuel filter

The filter removes dirt from the fuel, which could clog the system's small passages and jets. Dirty fuel causes the engine to run erratically and, in time, could cause engine damage. The filter is located in the fuel line, usually between the pump and injectors. Since replacing the fuel filter involves disconnecting the fuel line, this should be carried out at a garage. The filter should be replaced regularly – check your handbook for the interval.

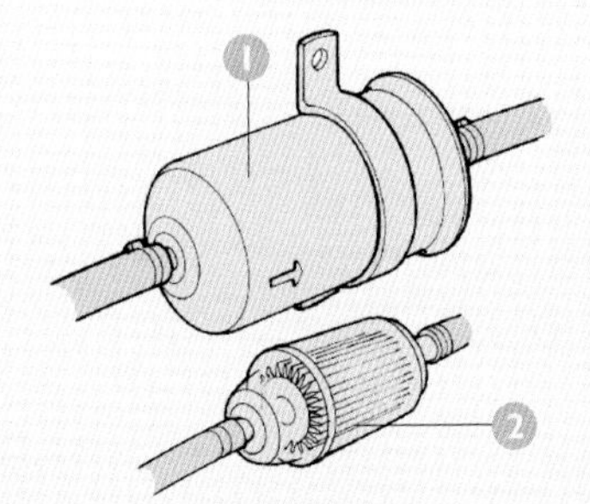

❶ Canister filter

❷ Plastic see-through filter

The air filter (air cleaner)

If dust finds its way into the engine, it causes wear and operating problems. The air filter is designed to remove dirt and dust from the air as it passes through on its way to the intake manifold to be mixed with the fuel. The filter is made of pleated paper and is usually circular or rectangular in shape. It sits in a metal casing on or near the top of the engine, connected via a large hose to the air intake duct. If it becomes clogged with dirt, exhaust emissions increase and the engine runs less efficiently.

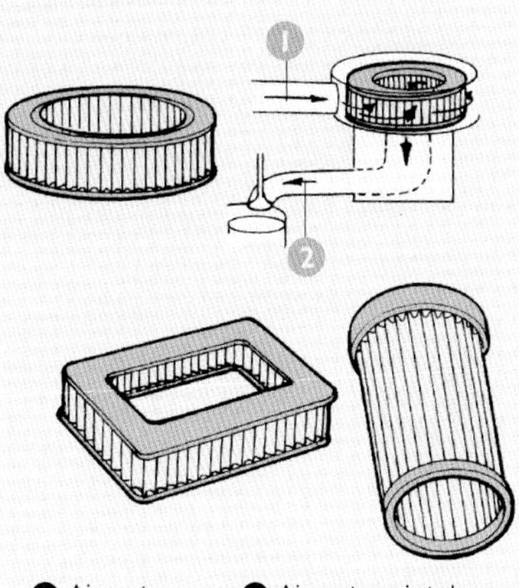

❶ Air enters via air intake ❷ Air enters intake manifold

See pages 234–35 for how to change the air filter.

The fuel tank

The tank is usually positioned some distance from the engine. Since most cars have front-mounted engines, it is normally at the rear of the car. A fuel line connects the tank to the fuel injectors. Its outlet is positioned slightly above the bottom of the tank so that the sediment that collects at the bottom is not drawn into the system. Petrol not used for combustion is sent back to the fuel tank through a second fuel line.

A dashboard light warns when the level of fuel in the tank is low (*see page 141*).

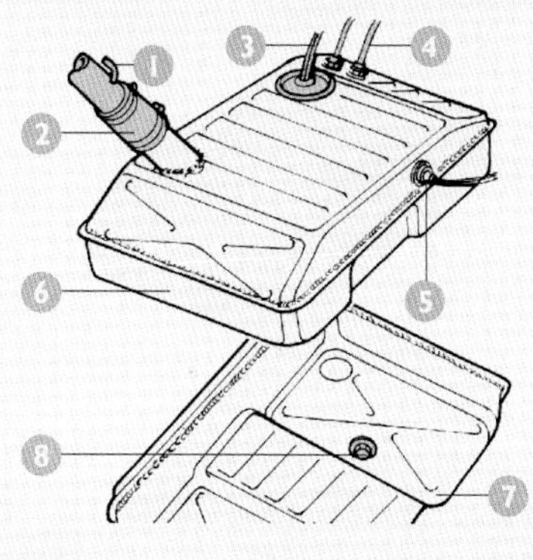

❶ Vent pipe
❷ Flexible hose
❸ Fuel pump
❹ Fuel lines
❺ Fuel-level sensor
❻ Fuel tank
❼ Bottom of tank
❽ Drain plug

Fuel injection

In older engines, the fuel and air required for combustion used to be mixed in a carburettor. However, this does not allow enough control over the mixture to comply with increasingly strict emissions regulations, so most modern cars have fuel injection.

How it works

The accelerator is connected to the throttle valve, which controls how much air enters the intake manifold. When the accelerator is pressed, it opens the throttle, allowing more air through via an airflow meter. Sensors (such as those monitoring the amount of air entering the engine, checking the position of the throttle and measuring how much oxygen is in the exhaust) feed information through to the ECU. The ECU then processes this data and uses it to calculate the correct amount of fuel to be injected and adjusts it accordingly.

1. Combustion chamber
2. Spark plug
3. Injector
4. Idle speed control motor
5. Throttle valve
6. Air filter
7. Air temperature sensor
8. Accelerator
9. Accelerator position switch
10. ECU
11. Fuel pump
12. Fuel tank
13. Oxygen sensor

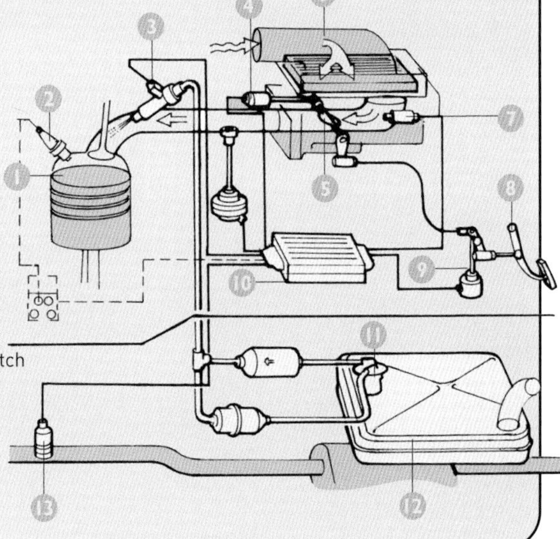

What is fuel injection?

Fuel injection is a method of regulating the amount of fuel delivered to the engine. It is more efficient than carburetion, as it enables the fuel/air mixture to be controlled more precisely.

Single vs multi-point

In a single-point system, a fuel injector sprays fuel into the top of the intake manifold, from where it is distributed to each cylinder. In a multi-point system, there is one injector per cylinder.

Fuel injectors

The fuel injectors are small valves that spray a mist of petrol directly into the air being sucked into the engine on the induction stroke. Fuel is supplied to the injectors by the fuel pump. The amount of fuel delivered by the injectors depends on the length of time they are open, which is controlled by the ECU. A fuel rail (pipe) supplies fuel to the injectors.

Over time, the injectors may become clogged with dirt, hindering fuel delivery or causing them to stick open and deliver too much petrol. Fuel system cleaners can be bought at accessory shops, or the system can be flushed out at a garage.

Fuel injection (diesel engines)

Diesel engines always use fuel injection. Unlike petrol engines, fuel is normally injected directly into the combustion chamber, although in some systems, it is sprayed into a pre-combustion chamber.

How it works

Fuel is drawn from the tank and is warmed by passing through a heater in the fuel line. It flows through a fuel filter, where impurities and water are removed; water collects at the bottom of the filter case. The fuel is then pumped to the fuel injectors. Air is drawn into the engine through the air duct and passes to the inlet manifold. The fuel pump is driven by the engine.

Direct vs indirect injection

Direct injection (*see also page 162*): air is drawn into the engine through the air duct and passes through the air filter into the inlet manifold. Each cylinder has a fuel injector, and fuel is pumped through to the injector for each cylinder. The injector sprays fuel directly into the combustion chambers in the cylinders.

Indirect injection (*see also page 162*): the fuel is pumped to an injector that sprays it into a pre-combustion chamber just above the combustion chamber, called a swirl chamber. There it is mixed with the incoming air, before being ignited.

Replacing the air filter

The air filter normally needs to be renewed around every 12,000 miles, or every year. If you are not sure which filter to buy, check your car handbook or ask the retailer (you will need to know the year, make, model and engine size of your car).

Air filter renewal

you will need

- → new filter (of the correct type)
- → screwdriver or spanner
- → clean cloth

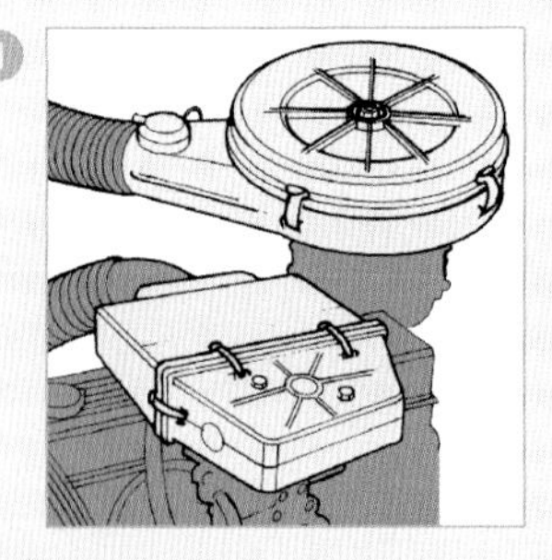

❶ Undo the screws, clips or bolts securing the filter cover and remove it. You may also need to disconnect a wiring plug and hose. The filter cover may be attached to a large hose, in which case simply move it out of the way.

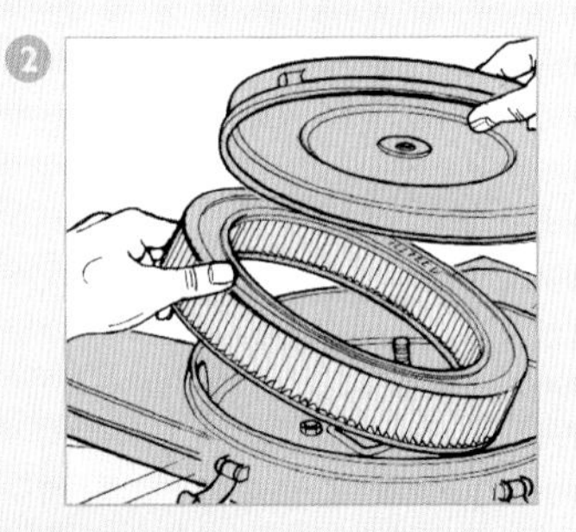

❷ Remove the filter, but before you do so, note how it fits into the filter housing, and which way up it is, so that you can fit the new one in the same way.

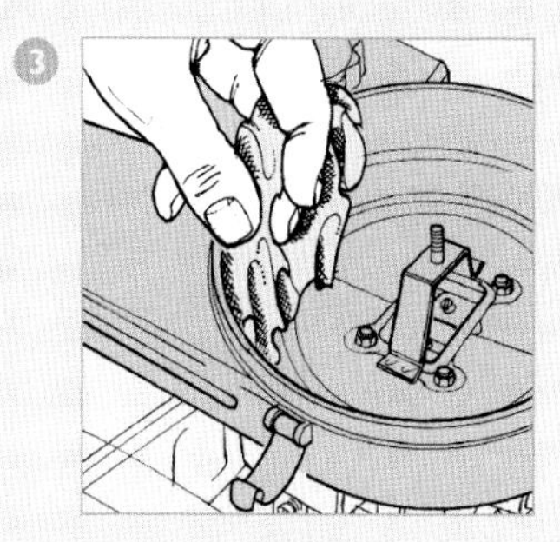

❸ Wipe the inside of the filter housing and cover to remove any dirt, being particularly careful not to allow dirt to fall into the air intake.

❹ If the filter appears coated with oil, the source of the problem needs to be identified. Take the car to a garage before you fit the new filter.

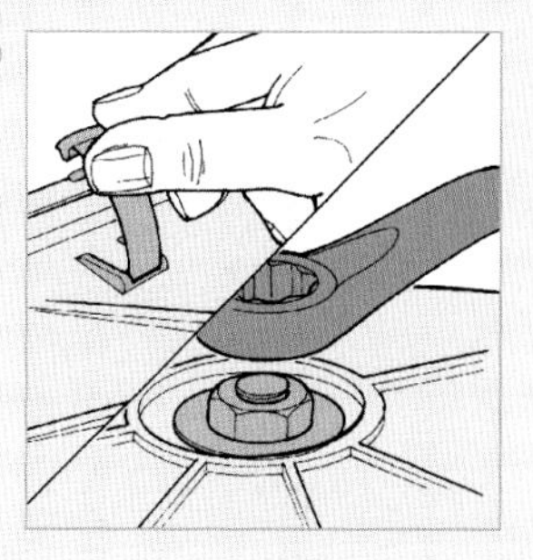

❺ Fit the new filter, replace the cover and fasten it securely with the screws, clips or bolts.

TIP

If only one portion of an old air filter appears clogged, you may be able to continue using it for a short while by turning the clogged portion away from the air intake duct. This should only be considered a temporary measure.

WARNING

Never be tempted to run your car's engine without an air filter. Not only could this allow dirt and dust into the engine, where it could cause damage, but also the mixture setting could be upset.

Draining the fuel filter (diesel)

Water becomes trapped in the diesel fuel system over time and needs to be drained regularly, normally every 6,000 miles, or six months, and always before the onset of winter in case the water should freeze and block the filter, preventing fuel flow.

Warning light

The water must also be drained if the 'water in fuel system' warning light on the dashboard comes on (not fitted to all cars). (*See page 144.*)

Renewing the filter

The filter should be renewed according to the manufacturer's recommendations, usually at around 12,000 miles. Since the method of replacing the filter varies from car to car, refer to your handbook. If it involves disconnecting fuel pipes, have it carried out at a garage.

Draining

1

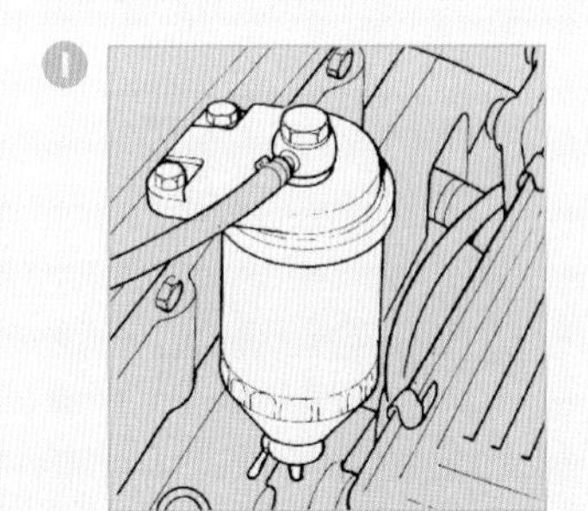

2

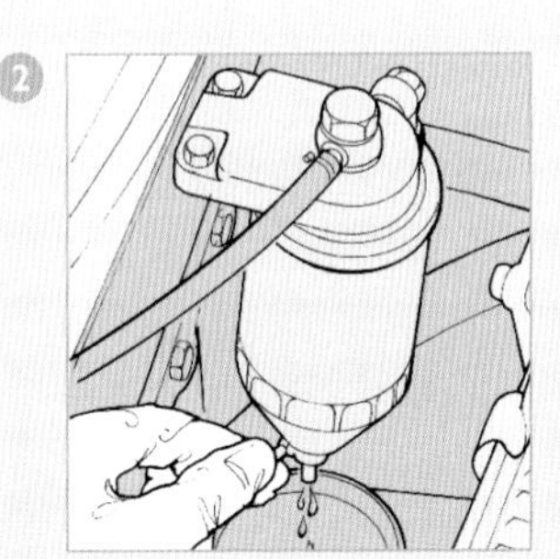

❶ Check in your handbook for the filter's location. (It may be at the top of the engine, close to the air filter.)

❷ A drain tap and tube are normally to be found at the bottom of the fuel filter housing.

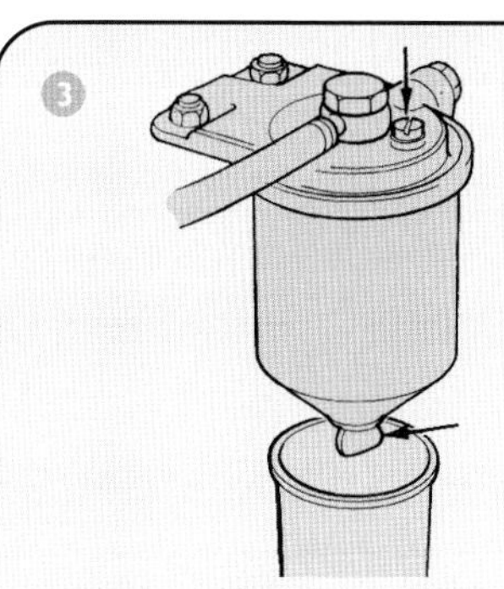

❸ Place a small container beneath the tap and open it.

❹ Allow the contents of the filter to drain into the container. At first, it will consist of water and fuel. Allow the contents to drain until only fuel runs out.

you will need

→ clean cloth
→ small container, e.g. a plastic cup

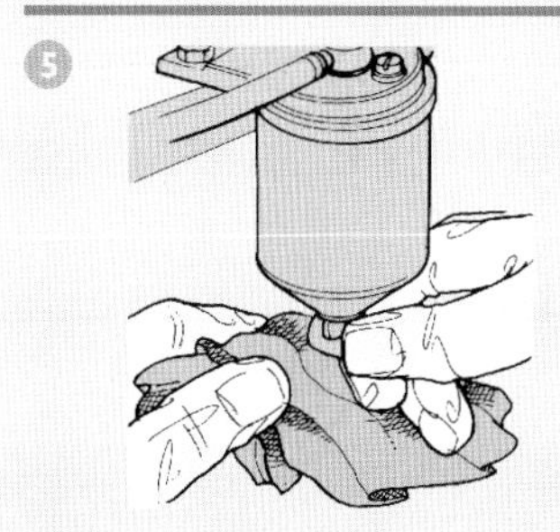

❺ Close the drain tap and tighten it firmly. Be careful not to spill any of the liquid, and wipe up any spillage immediately, as the fuel in it could ignite on contact with hot metal or a spark.

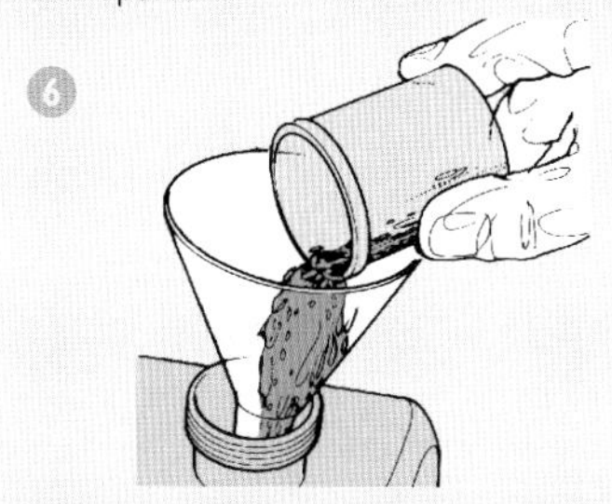

❻ Dispose of the drained liquid safely.

Emissions

When the exhaust gases produced by the combustion of oil-based fuel and air are released into the atmosphere, they are known as emissions. Checking your car's exhaust emissions forms part of the annual roadworthiness test in many countries.

Harmful effects

Exhaust emissions are blamed for many of the world's environmental problems – altering the climate, damaging the earth's upper atmosphere, creating a hole in the ozone layer. They can also cause health problems and the smog that affects some cities. Since nearly all cars run on the oil-based fuels (petrol, diesel, LPG) that create these harmful gases, most countries have drawn up strict emissions regulations. ECUs, fuel injection systems and exhaust systems now play an important role in the crackdown on emissions.

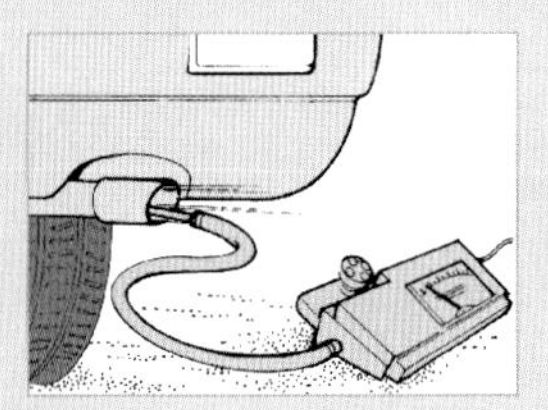

Exhaust emissions contain these harmful products:

- Carbon dioxide, which causes global warming and climate changes.
- Carbon monoxide and hydrocarbons, which are toxic.
- Nitrogen oxides, which cause smog.
- Particulates (such as soot), which cause respiratory problems.

Testing for emissions

Emissions testers are available from car accessory shops. They have a probe, which is placed in the end of the exhaust pipe, and the engine is run for a few minutes to obtain a reading. Alternatively, a garage can carry out an emissions test and will have more accurate equipment.

Emission control systems

Car manufacturers are constantly striving to improve the design of the emission control systems that help to reduce the amount of harmful emissions produced by car engines.

All cars have some forms of system fitted; the most common are outlined here and on pages 240–41.

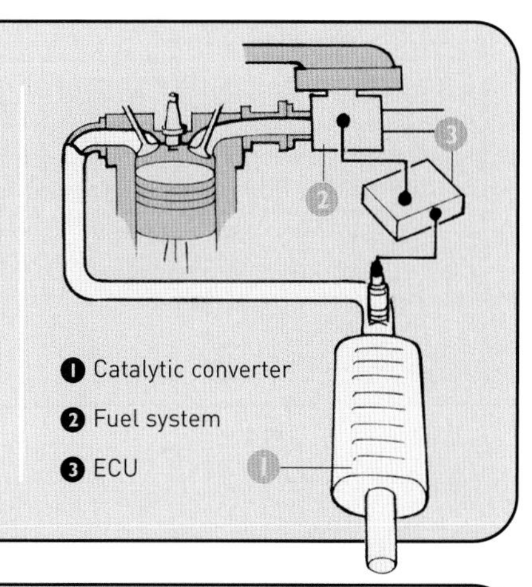

❶ Catalytic converter

❷ Fuel system

❸ ECU

Catalytic converter

• The catalytic converter is a stainless steel canister built into the exhaust system that greatly reduces the amount of harmful exhaust emissions produced.

• It contains a ceramic honeycomb structure coated with platinum, which acts as a catalyst on the gases flowing through it. The honeycomb format creates the largest possible surface area within the confines of the container to increase the efficiency of the catalytic converter. The catalyst induces a chemical reaction in the gases, changing them into less harmful forms and water vapour.

• The catalytic converter needs around 15 minutes to reach the high temperature at which it operates most efficiently, so when the engine is cold or only warming up, the converter is not very effective.

• A catalytic converter should last the lifetime of the vehicle, but this depends upon operating conditions.

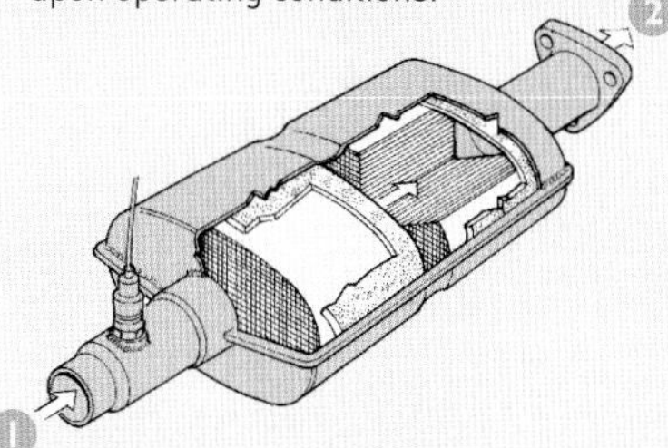

❶ Carbon monoxide, hydrocarbons, nitrogen oxides

❷ Carbon dioxide, water, nitrogen

Catalytic converter do's and don'ts

- Never push-start the car. It will damage the converter by soaking it with fuel and causing it to overheat.
- Don't use leaded or LRP fuel; the converter will be ruined.
- Due to its position underneath the car and the high temperature it reaches, care should be taken when parking in certain conditions, such as very dry grass or undergrowth that might be easily combustible. It is also very fragile, so care should be taken when driving over uneven ground.
- Keep the engine well tuned and maintained in order to avoid damaging the catalyst.
- Don't use fuel or engine oil additives, as they may contain substances that could damage the catalyst.
- Don't drive the car if the engine is burning oil (blue smoke from the exhaust), or if the engine develops a misfire. Seek advice at a garage.

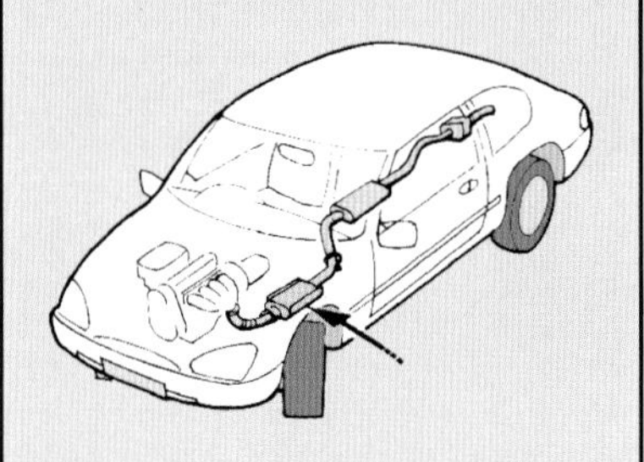

Exhaust gas recirculation

This system (EGR) is mounted on or near the cylinder block. It reduces nitrogen oxides by redirecting some of the exhaust gases through the intake manifold, back into the cylinders, where they are reburnt. A valve in the exhaust system, controlled by an ECU, regulates the flow of the recycled exhaust gases.

Evaporative emission

When the engine is switched off, the fuel in the fuel tank gives off vapours that are stored in a charcoal canister. The system (known as EVAP or EEC) prevents the vapours from being released into the atmosphere. When the engine is switched on, the vapours are drawn into the cylinders via the inlet manifold and are burnt during normal combustion. The flow of vapours into the inlet manifold is normally controlled by a valve. The EVAP is normally located at or near the front of the engine.

Positive crankcase ventilation

Nearly all cars are fitted with this system, which assists fuel economy as well as reducing emissions. When the engine is running, some of the gases in the combustion chamber leak into the crankcase, and from there into the atmosphere. Crankcase ventilation recirculates the gases back to the cylinder for reburning via a hose. The PCV valve controls the amount of gases that are recycled.

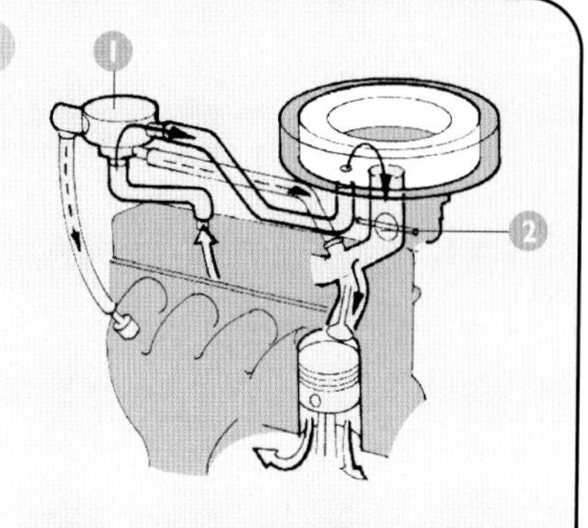

❶ PCV valve ❷ Engine air intake

Checking the PCV system

you will need

- → clean cloth
- → new PCV hose
- → new PCV valve

❶ Park the car outside or in a well-ventilated place. Leave the engine idling.

❷ Find the PCV valve. In fuel injection systems, it is on the intake manifold or inside the valve cover (top of cylinder head). Or look for the hose that goes from the valve to a point low on the engine block. Or consult the handbook.

❸ Detach the hose; note where it came from so that you can put it back.

❹ Clean the outside with a rag. Blow air through the hose. If it seems clogged, feels brittle or is cracked, replace it with a new hose.

❺ If it is OK, put it back.

❻ Connect one end of the hose to the engine block.

❼ Remove the PCV valve from its position on the valve cover or intake manifold.

❽ Attach the loose end of the hose to the PCV valve. Place a finger over the open end of the valve. If you can feel suction, the valve is OK. If you can't, replace it. Another test is to shake the valve – if it rattles, it is probably OK.

The lubrication system

Oil keeps the engine's components working smoothly in a wide range of temperatures. Its chief role is to reduce friction, but it also helps cool the engine and prevent corrosion and the build-up of deposits, as well as aiding fuel economy and acting as a sealant.

Variations

Most modern cars have front-wheel drive and two lubrication systems, one for the engine and another for the gearbox and final drive together. Rear-wheel-drive vehicles usually have three systems – for the engine, the gearbox and the final drive.

Warning light

If the pressure at which oil is pumped around the engine falls too low, some parts of the engine will not be lubricated sufficiently, causing excess wear and possible engine damage. An oil-pressure sensor in the engine is linked to a warning light on the dashboard. If it comes on, stop the car immediately (*see page 142*).

Benefits

Friction: without a film of oil between its moving parts, metal would grind against metal, and the engine would overheat and seize up.

Cooling: oil helps cool parts of the engine that become very hot, such as the pistons, by transferring excess heat to the sump. In most cars, the oil in the sump is cooled by air flowing over it. Some cars have oil-cooling radiators.

Sealant: engine oil acts as a gas-tight seal; during combustion, it prevents gases escaping from the cylinders.

Cleaning: oil helps clean the engine by removing deposits (tiny scraps of metal and carbon from combustion) from it, which are caught in the system's filters.

Fuel economy: oil helps improve fuel economy by reducing drag between the engine's moving parts, allowing them to work together smoothly. The more smoothly they work together, the less force, and therefore the less fuel, is needed to drive the engine.

How it works

The engine lubrication system comprises the sump, oil filter and oil pump.

Oil is drawn from the sump via a pick-up tube covered with a metal gauze filter (to help remove particles) and passed to the oil pump.

From the pump, it is forced under pressure to the crankshaft, through a disposable filter mounted on the engine block.

From the crankshaft, the oil is fed through passages drilled in the cylinder block to the camshaft and valve gear.

As the oil in the sump warms up, it gives off vapour, which rises through the engine, lubricating the pistons and cylinders in the process.

From the camshaft, the oil seeps back down into the sump. When the engine is not running, the oil collects in the sump.

A sensor near the oil pump monitors oil pressure and operates a warning light on the dashboard if it drops too low (*see page 142*).

1. Dipstick
2. Sump
3. Oil pick-up
4. Oil pump
5. Sump plug
6. Oil filter
7. Camshaft
8. Oil filler cap
9. Oil returns to sump

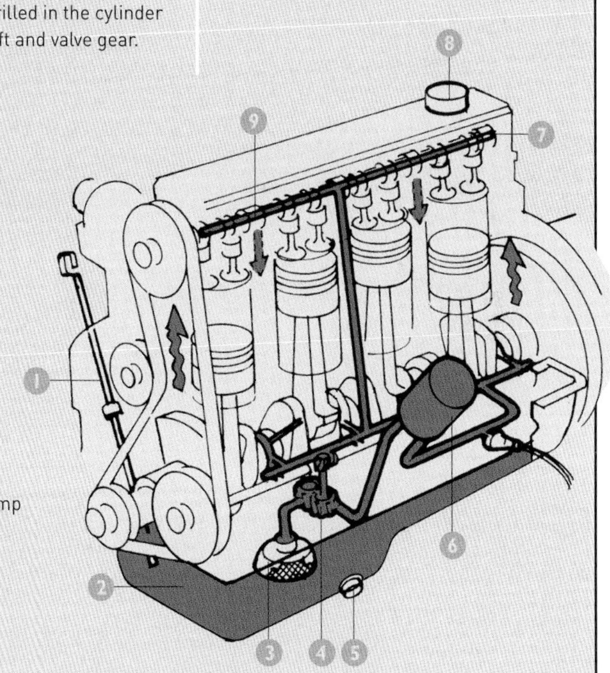

The sump

The sump is a metal casing beneath the crankshaft, at the bottom of the cylinder block, that acts as a reservoir for engine oil.

The oil pump

Located near or inside the sump, this pumps oil around the engine and is driven mechanically from the crankshaft or camshaft.

Oil seals and gaskets

A gasket is a piece of soft, oil-resistant material that acts as a seal between two metal surfaces. It is designed to prevent oil from seeping out of the engine block.

Gaskets can leak if they are damaged during fitting or have not been positioned correctly, if the bolts or screws holding them together have been overtightened, or just through general wear and tear.

Some joints are sealed with a thin layer of mastic (silicone) sealant.

The oil filter

In addition to the metal filter in the pick-up tube, a disposable oil filter fitted to the outside of the engine removes tiny pieces of metal, carbon deposits and dirt that collect in the oil. If allowed to build up, these could block small passages and eventually cause engine damage.

If the filter is not changed, it can become so clogged with dirt that the oil cannot pass through it easily. When this happens, a valve opens, allowing oil through to the engine, bypassing the filter, which results in unfiltered and potentially dirty oil circulating in the engine.

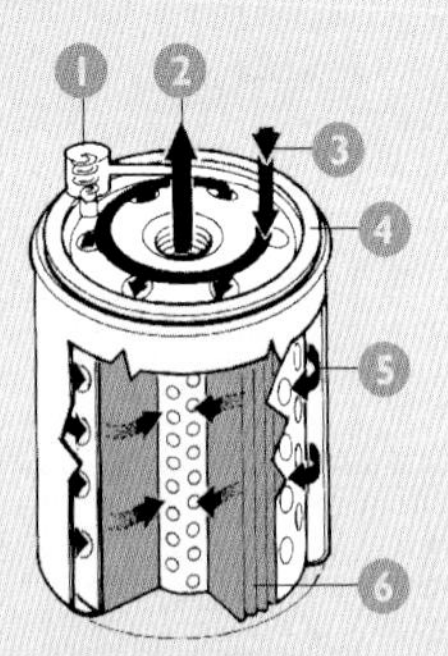

❶ Bypass valve ❷ Filtered oil leaving

❸ Oil enters filter from pump

❹ Rubber sealing ring

❺ Oil is pumped through filter from outer edge to inner

❻ Pleated paper filter element

Buying oil

It is important to buy the right oil for your car, to suit both its engine and the climate. Check your handbook for the oil recommended by the manufacturer. Always use the grade specified, for topping up as well as for a complete oil change. The engine performs best on the correct oil.

Diesel vs petrol

Most oils are suitable for either petrol or diesel engines (not both), so make sure you buy the right one. However, some modern synthetic oils are suitable for both.

SAE

Oil is graded according to its viscosity (its ability to flow). It becomes thinner when it is hot (flows well), and thicker when it is cold (flows less well).

Almost all oils sold for use in ordinary cars are multigrade. They contain additives that make their viscosity suitable for a wide range of temperatures. Look on the label for a set of figures prefixed by SAE, such as SAE 10W/40. The first, 10W, refers to its viscosity in winter – the lower the number, the thinner the oil and the better it is for cold conditions. The second, 40, indicates its ability to keep its viscosity and not become too thin in summer; the higher the number, the more suitable it is for warm conditions.

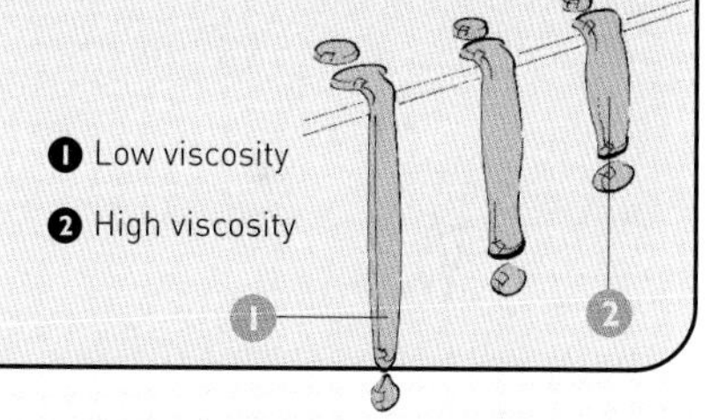

1 Low viscosity

2 High viscosity

API

The letters API (American Petroleum Institute) indicate that the oil meets certain minimum standards.

For petrol engines, the rating begins with 'S', followed by a letter denoting period of manufacture. For diesel engines, the rating begins with the letter 'C'.

Types of oil

Oil may be mineral-based, semi-synthetic or synthetic. Mineral-based oils are normally cheaper and are suitable for most car engines, whereas synthetic oils are more expensive and are used in high-performance engines.

Checking and topping up the oil

It is important to check the oil level regularly and keep it topped up. If the level is allowed to become too low, the engine may not be lubricated properly, resulting in extra wear of engine components and possibly severe damage.

Oil condition

Check the oil's appearance and feel by rubbing a little between your fingers. If it feels gritty or smells burnt, it should be changed.

Light brown or green: the oil is clean.
Black: the oil is dirty and must be changed (if this happens after a few hundred miles, check the feel, too).
Milky/water bubbles: coolant may be leaking into the sump; have the system checked.
Reddish: automatic transmission fluid is leaking into the sump; have the system checked.

Frequency

A new engine should not need topping up between oil changes, while an old and worn engine may need as much as a litre of oil every thousand miles. If you need to top up more than this, take the car to a garage.

Checking/topping up

you will need

→ plastic funnel
→ clean cloth
→ engine oil

❶ Always check the oil when the car is on the level, or the reading will not be accurate.

❷ Switch off the engine. If the car has been driven, leave it for at least five minutes before checking the oil, so that the oil has had a chance to settle into the sump.

❸ Remove the dipstick. It fits into a narrow tube that reaches down into the sump and normally is towards the front of the engine. It has a small handle. (Check your handbook if you cannot locate it.)

3

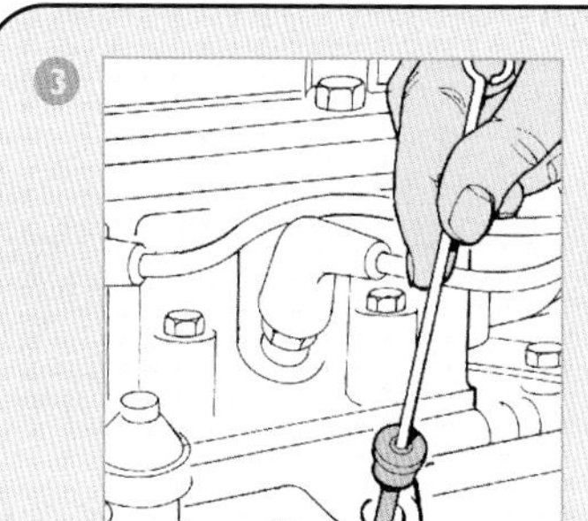

6

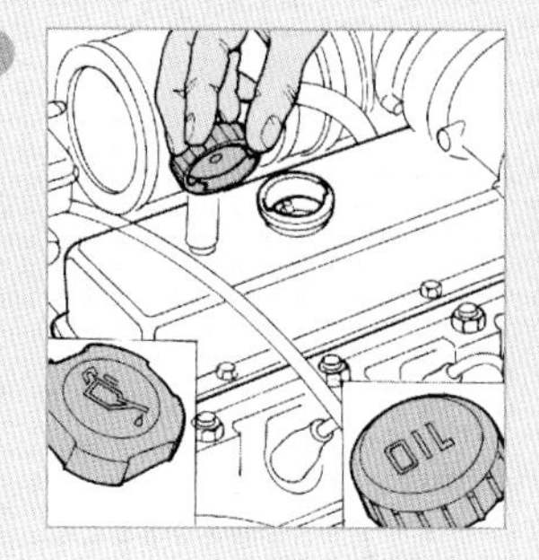

4

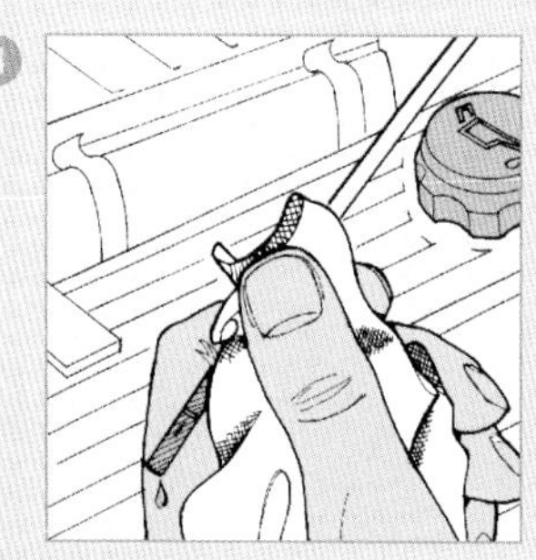

7

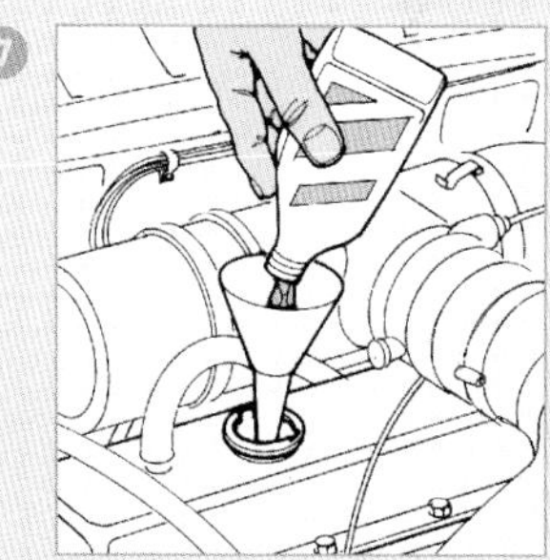

❹ Wipe the dipstick clean and replace it, making sure you push it right down as far as it will go into the tube.

❺ Remove the dipstick again and check the oil level; it should be on the maximum mark. If it is lower than this, top up the oil through the oil filler cap.

❻ Undo the oil filler cap – this is on the top of the engine and may be clearly marked 'Oil'. If you have any doubts, check in your handbook.

❼ It can be hard to judge how much oil to add, so pour it in gradually, using the funnel. (As a guide, if the level is on the minimum mark, it takes about 1 litre of oil to fill it to maximum.)

❽ Wait for a few minutes to allow the oil to filter down to the sump, then check the level again with the dipstick. Repeat the process, adding oil until it reaches the maximum mark on the dipstick.

❾ Don't overfill, as too much pressure could build up and blow a gasket or seal.

❿ Replace the oil cap, screwing it on firmly. Mop up any drips with the cloth.

Changing the oil and filter

Always change the oil at the recommended intervals. Changing it regularly makes a major contribution to prolonging the life of your engine. Oil deteriorates with age, becoming contaminated and losing its efficiency, which leads to premature wear.

Frequency

Check your car handbook for the recommended interval at which to change the oil. It is generally every 12,000 miles. However, if the car makes short journeys only, the oil never reaches its correct working temperature, resulting in the build-up of carbon deposits. In this case, it is recommended that you change the oil every 6,000 miles.

The filter

The filter must be renewed every time the oil is changed. When buying a new filter, refer to your car handbook to make sure you buy the correct one, or make a note of your car's year of manufacture and engine size, and ask the retailer. Unlike an air filter, which is fitted into a housing on the engine, the oil filter is a self-contained disposable unit.

Oil change

1. Park the car on the level and put the handbrake on.

2. Run the engine for a few minutes, as the oil will flow more easily when warm, and any sludge will drain away rather than collect in recesses inside the engine. Don't exceed five minutes, as the oil would be too hot and would burn you if it splashed on to your skin.

3. Switch the engine off and put the car in gear to prevent it from rolling while you are under it.

4. Unscrew the oil filler cap on the top of the engine (*see page 247*).

❺ Being careful not to touch any hot engine parts, such as the exhaust, crawl under the car and locate the oil drain plug in the sump. Place the shallow container beneath the plug.

6

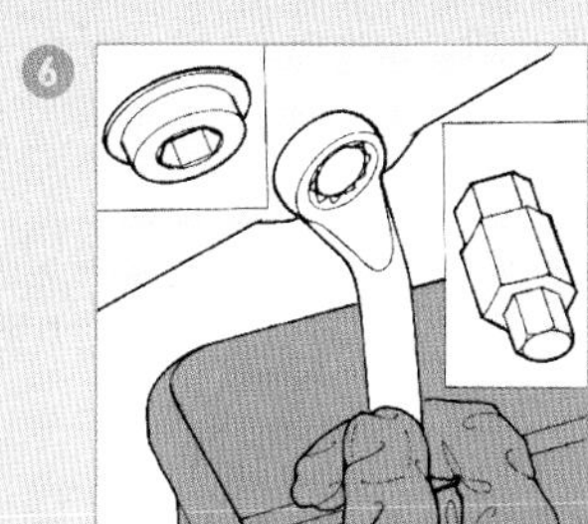

❻ Wearing gloves, loosen the drain plug slightly with the spanner or special tool. Finish unscrewing it by hand, taking the plug out quickly, as the oil will pour out.

7

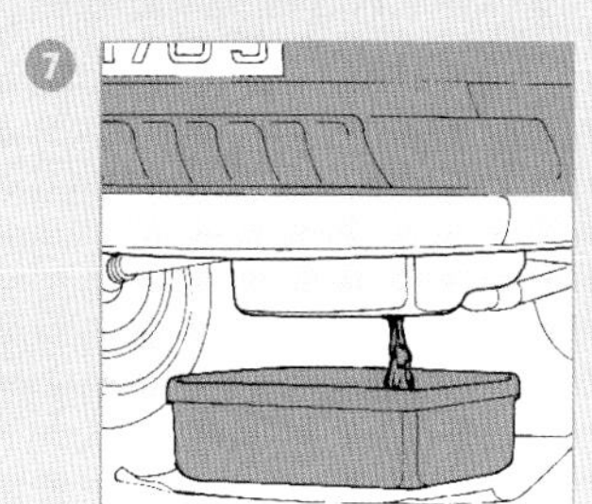

❼ Wait for about 15 minutes, or until the oil has finished draining, then wipe the area around the drain-plug opening.

you will need

→ shallow container to collect the old oil (usually around 5 litres)
→ spanner to release drain plug*
→ oil filter removal tool
→ new oil filter of the correct type
→ replacement oil drain plug sealing washer
→ new engine oil of the correct type
→ plastic funnel
→ cloth
→ plastic or latex gloves and old clothes

*a specially shaped spanner or tool may be necessary to open the drain plug; check your car handbook

TIP

You can buy specially designed oil drain containers from accessory shops. These make the job much easier, reducing the likelihood of accidental spillage.

❽ Wipe the drain plug clean and remove the old sealing washer. Replace it with the new one.

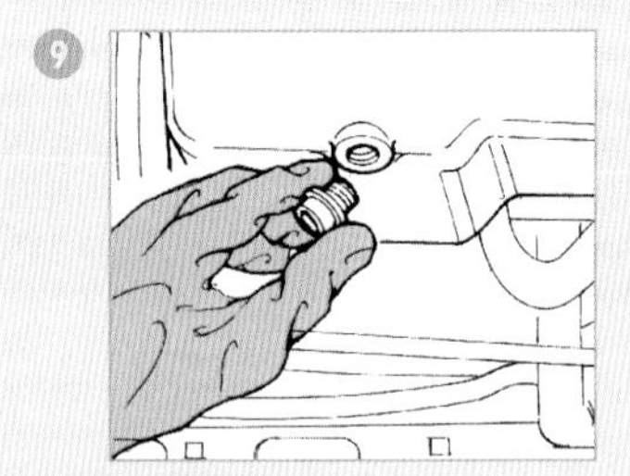

❾ Screw the plug back into the sump and tighten it. Don't overtighten it or cross the threads.

❿ Locate the oil filter. The cylindrical metal canister will be near the bottom of the engine. Refer to your handbook if necessary.

⓫ Although you have drained the oil, there will still be some left in the filter. Slide the draining container beneath the filter to catch any oil spilled from it.

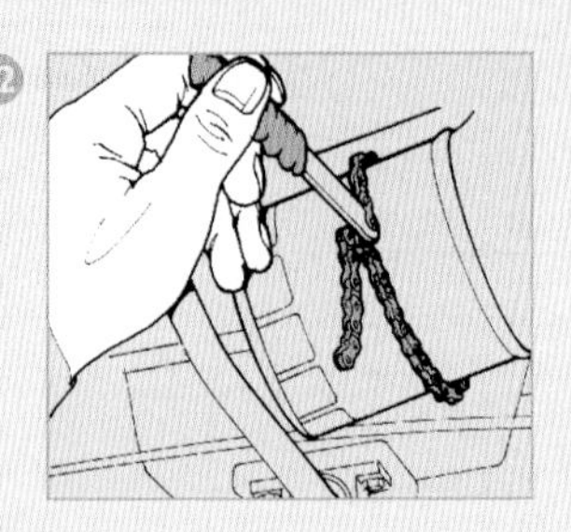

⓬ Loosen the filter with the oil filter removal tool and finish unscrewing it by hand. Wipe clean the filter sealing mounting on the engine.

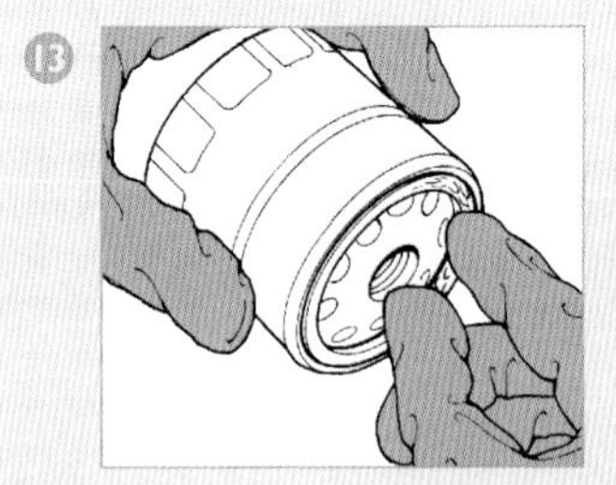

⓭ Lightly coat the rubber sealing ring of the new filter canister with a little clean engine oil and screw it on to the engine until the sealing ring makes firm contact with the engine mounting. Tighten it firmly by hand (do not use the filter removal tool).

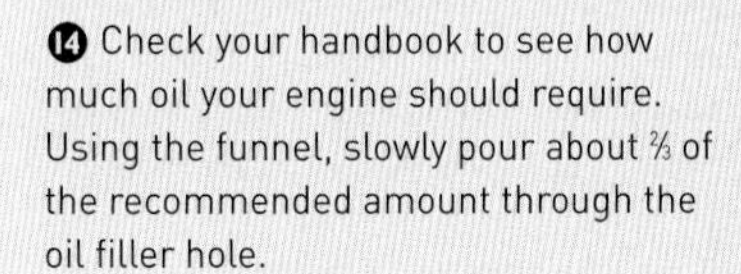

⓮ Check your handbook to see how much oil your engine should require. Using the funnel, slowly pour about ⅔ of the recommended amount through the oil filler hole.

⓯ Allow five minutes for the oil to drain down into the sump. Remove the dipstick and check the level.

⓰ If it is not up to the maximum mark, add a little more. Wait a few minutes and recheck the level. If necessary, repeat the process, but don't overfill.

⓱ Once the oil level is up to maximum, replace the filter cap and the dipstick.

⓲ Take the car out of gear and start the engine. The oil pressure warning light on the dashboard should come on, but go out after a few seconds, once the fresh oil has been pumped around the system. If it doesn't go out after several seconds, stop the engine and check for leaks around the filter and sump plug. If there are none, start the engine again. If the light still does not go out, switch off the engine and contact a garage.

⓳ If the light does go out, run the engine for a few minutes and check for leaks around the oil filter canister and drain plug on the sump. If you spot any, stop the engine and tighten them up, but don't overtighten.

⓴ If there are no leaks, stop the engine, wait for five minutes and check the oil level again. Top up the oil level if necessary.

㉑ Dispose of the old oil safely – in a waste tank at a garage, or at an authorized disposal site.

Checking for leaks

The most common problem is a leak. A sign is a black mark or drips on the ground where the car has been parked. If you suspect an oil leak, spread several sheets of newspaper under the engine, leave them for half an hour, then check for any drips. Also make a visual check of the engine, paying special attention to the oil filter, oil filler cap, sump drain plug (*see page 249*) and the seals on the engine (where metal surfaces are joined together). It can be hard to spot a leak, particularly if the engine is quite dirty, but look for shiny black seepages and drips. If you identify or suspect a leak, take the car to a garage. If you have to top up the oil more often than normal (*see page 246*), a leak could be responsible.

Keeping your engine clean will allow you to spot leaks as soon as they occur (*see page 150*).

The transmission system

The transmission is the name given to the group of components that passes the power of the engine to the wheels of the car. It adapts the speed of the engine to suit the conditions under which the car is being driven – its speed and load, the gradient of the road, and so on.

The transmission may deliver power to the front wheels, the rear wheels, or all four wheels simultaneously. Its layout varies according to the design of the car and position of the engine.

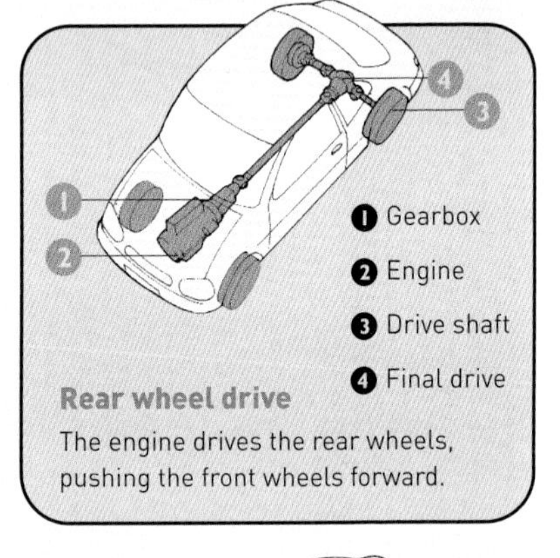

Rear wheel drive

The engine drives the rear wheels, pushing the front wheels forward.

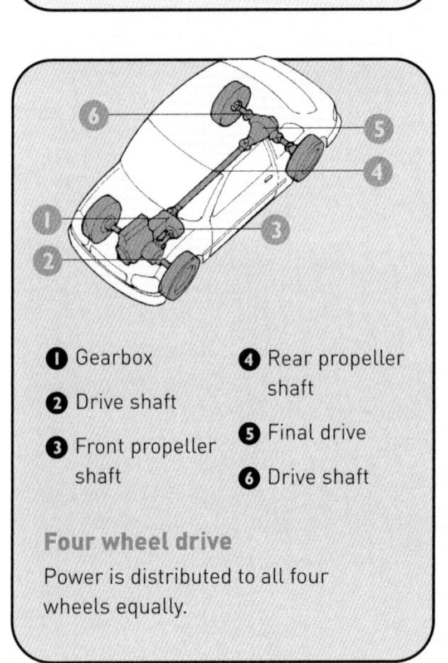

Four wheel drive

Power is distributed to all four wheels equally.

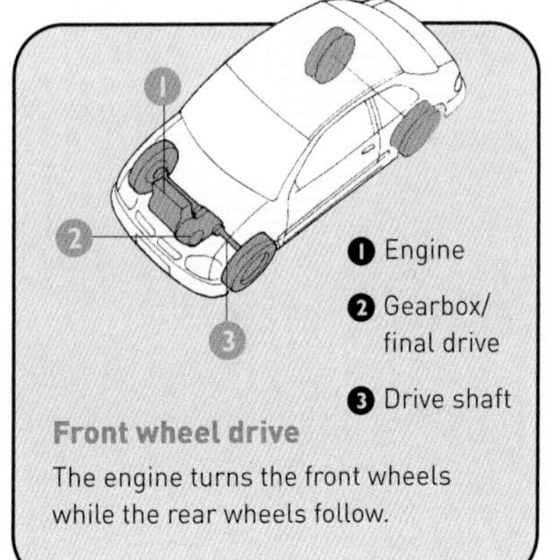

Front wheel drive

The engine turns the front wheels while the rear wheels follow.

The gears

• Gears are wheels of varying sizes with teeth that mesh. When two wheels are meshed and one is driven, it naturally drives the other one. If the wheel that is being driven is bigger than the one driving it, the big wheel will take longer to achieve a complete revolution than the small one (it will turn more slowly).

• In the car gearbox, gearwheels of different sizes are arranged in pairs along shafts. In this illustration, the small wheel on the input shaft is being driven by the engine and therefore is rotating at engine speed. It drives the large wheel (fixed to an output shaft), which turns more slowly because of its size. Since the large wheel is fixed to the output shaft, this shaft rotates at a slower speed than the input shaft. This is known as a reduction gear. When the gearwheel on the output shaft is smaller than that on the input shaft, the output shaft will turn more quickly than the input shaft.

The purpose of gears

Gears enable the engine to work at maximum efficiency under most conditions while ensuring that the car can be driven at a wide range of speeds. They enable the driver to make the best use of the power output of the engine to drive the car's wheels.

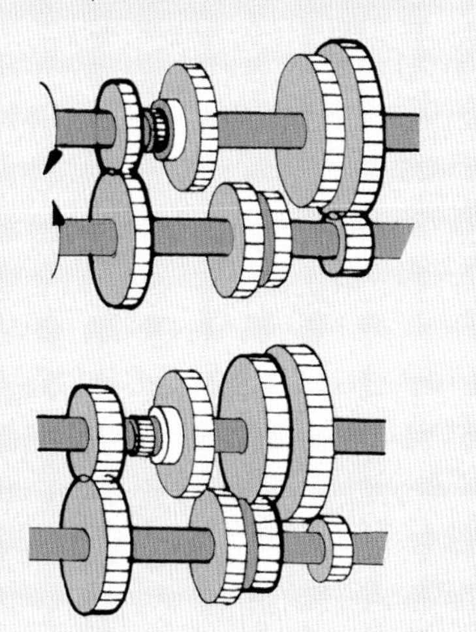

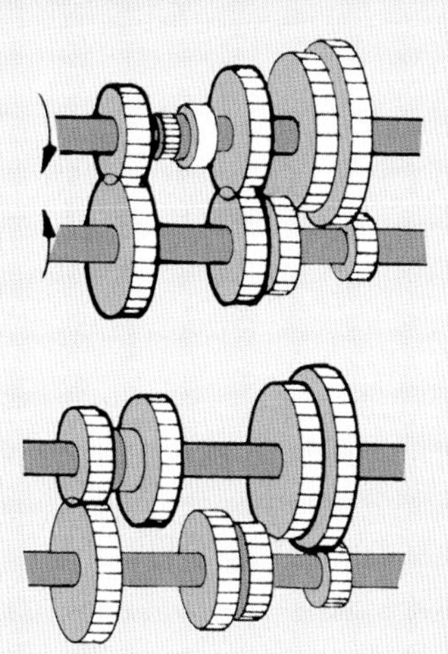

Engine speed

Engines are at their most efficient when running at a certain speed. This varies from car to car, but it is generally around 500–1,000 rpm below the maximum engine speed.

However, the driver needs to be able to drive the car at different speeds and to adjust the speed of the engine to suit different conditions (road surface, gradient, load) while ensuring the engine is working at optimum efficiency. The gearbox ensures that engine speed can be reduced or increased for a given road speed according to the conditions under which the car is being driven.

Torque

Torque is rotational force. In the car, it is the amount of force used to rotate the road wheels. The amount of torque produced by the engine depends on its running speed. The gears increase torque through 'leverage'. When starting the car from a standstill, or going up a steep hill, the driver needs plenty of torque, but less speed, so a low gear is selected. Once the car has built up speed, it no longer needs as much power to maintain that speed, so higher gears can be selected.

Slippery conditions

In dry conditions, there is plenty of traction – that is, the wheels are able to grip the ground well, so the amount of torque applied to the wheels can be high. In wet or icy conditions, too much torque makes the wheels slip, so the amount of torque has to be reduced.

Manual transmission

The driver uses a manual gear-change lever to select the correct gear for the conditions under which the car is being driven – speed, load (the combined weight of the car, passengers and goods), gradient, road surface, etc.

Rear wheel drive

Instead of being transmitted directly to the final drive (as in front wheel drive), power is passed by a propeller shaft to the rear-mounted differential.

Four wheel drive

Power is passed from the gearbox to a transfer box, which in turn sends it to the front and rear wheels. There is a differential at front and rear.

How a manual gearbox works

- In a conventional manual four-speed gearbox, there are four pairs of gearwheels arranged on parallel input, output and lay shafts. The input and output shafts are joined by a bearing, but can rotate at different speeds. The gears on the input and lay shafts are fixed and rotate together, while the gears on the output shaft can rotate freely. The teeth of the gears are permanently meshed. In five- and six-speed gearboxes, there are five and six pairs of gears.

- Power from the engine is transmitted to the gearbox by the clutch through the input shaft.

- Synchromesh hubs and collars are positioned on the output shaft between the gears and slide along the shaft. These ensure that each gear is spinning at the right speed before being engaged, producing a smooth gear change.

- When the driver selects a gear, a selector rod connected to a fork moves a synchro-hub along the output shaft towards the correct gear. The hub and its collar engage with the gear and lock it to the output shaft. As the input shaft rotates, it turns the output shaft via the lay shaft and the meshing gear. In this way, power from the engine is transferred from the input shaft to the output shaft (and from there to the final drive and differential).

Reverse: an extra gear wheel on a fourth (idler) shaft is used to reverse the rotation of the output shaft.

Neutral: no gear is engaged.

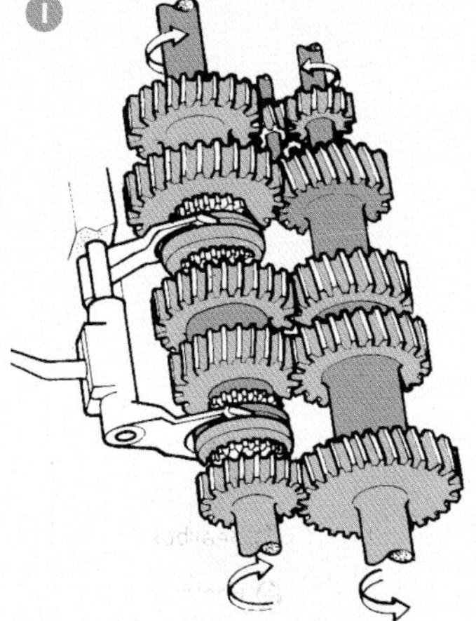

❶ Four-speed manual gearbox

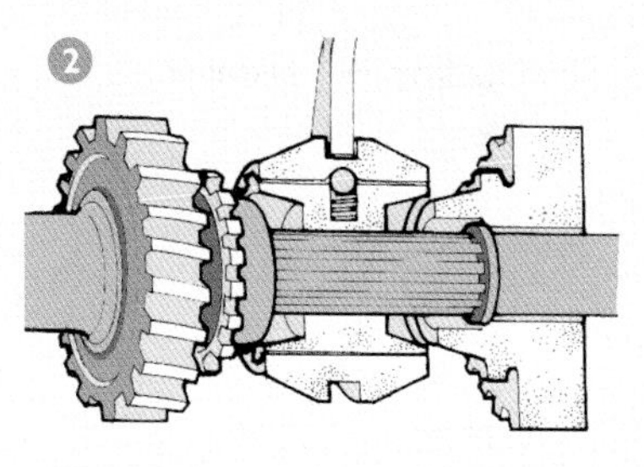

❷ Synchromesh hub

The clutch

The clutch connects the engine with the gearbox. When the clutch pedal is pressed, it disengages the engine from the gearbox (and driven wheels), enabling the driver to change gear and start or stop the car smoothly.

Components of the clutch

The clutch assembly is contained within a cover bolted to the flywheel, so the cover revolves with the flywheel.

The clutch plate (or friction plate) is mounted on, but free to slide along, the gearbox input shaft. It is lined on both sides with a layer of friction material. When the clutch is engaged, it revolves with the flywheel.

The pressure plate is a flat metal ring. It is attached to the clutch cover and revolves with the flywheel, whether or not the clutch is engaged.

A diaphragm spring controls the pressure plate. When engaged, it forces the pressure plate against the clutch plate and flywheel.

The release lever (operated by the clutch pedal) controls the release bearing, which releases the diaphragm spring.

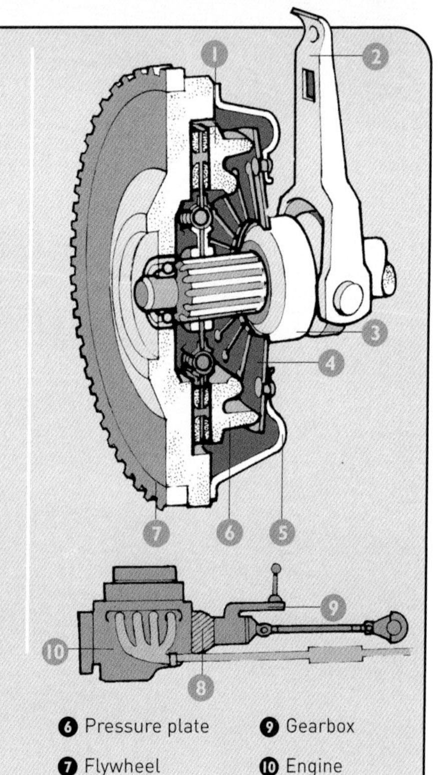

1. Clutch plate
2. Release lever
3. Release bearing
4. Diaphragm spring
5. Clutch cover
6. Pressure plate
7. Flywheel
8. Clutch
9. Gearbox
10. Engine

How the clutch works

- The clutch connects and disconnects the engine from the gearbox via the flywheel and clutch plate. When the engine is running, it spins a flywheel on the end of the crankshaft. The flywheel rotates at the same speed as the engine.
- The clutch plate's lining of friction material allows the plate to grip the flywheel when forced against it.
- As the clutch plate comes into contact with the flywheel, friction is caused by the two surfaces rubbing together.

At first, the friction is not enough to grip the flywheel completely and the clutch plate 'slips' against the flywheel. It starts rotating in the same direction as the flywheel, but not at the same speed. However, as the clutch plate is forced tightly against the flywheel, it begins to grip it more firmly, picking up speed until it is finally clamped hard against the flywheel and spinning at the same rate. Since the gearbox input shaft rotates with the clutch plate, it transmits the engine power to the gearbox.

The clutch disengaged

The driver presses down on the clutch pedal, releasing the clutch plate from the flywheel. The engine is no longer connected to the gearbox, so the driver can select another gear.

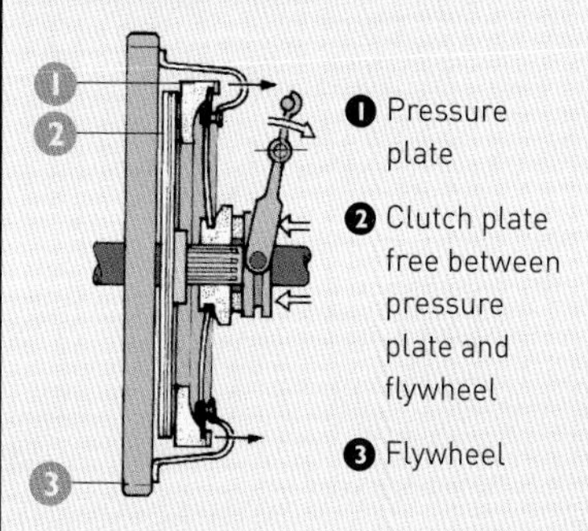

The clutch engaged

The engine is running and the driver's foot is off the clutch pedal. The clutch plate is clamped against the flywheel and is rotating with it, transmitting power to the gearbox and input shaft.

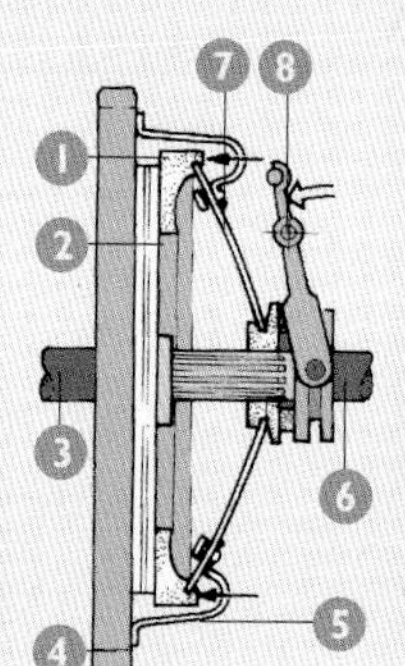

1. Pressure plate
2. Clutch plate
3. Crankshaft
4. Flywheel
5. Clutch cover
6. Gearbox input shaft
7. Diaphragm spring
8. Release lever

Operating the clutch

The clutch may be operated hydraulically or by a cable. Hydraulic systems (as below) can be identified by the clutch fluid reservoir behind the engine (see opposite). Cable-operated clutches tend to require more maintenance, as the cable can stretch and need adjusting or, though more rarely, snap or seize up.

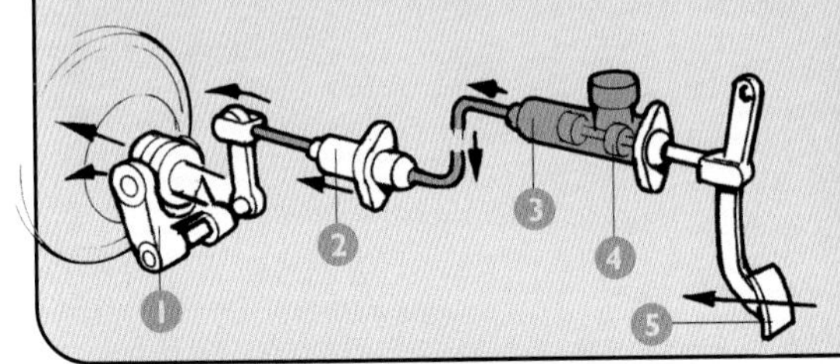

1. Clutch is disengaged
2. Slave cylinder
3. Clutch fluid
4. Master cylinder
5. Clutch pedal depressed

Clutch wear

In time, the friction material on the clutch plate can wear out. As it wears, the clutch plate may begin to slip against the flywheel rather than gripping it (see right). The more a clutch is used, the quicker it wears.

Driving style plays an important role in premature clutch wear:

- When stationary, don't keep the car in gear with the clutch pedal depressed; select neutral and release the pedal.
- Don't hold the car in gear on a hill by 'slipping' the clutch; apply the handbrake, select neutral and release the clutch pedal.
- Don't allow your foot to rest on the clutch pedal when the car is moving.

Signs of clutch problems

A slipping clutch: the car is less responsive when gears are changed and slower to pick up speed. The engine's revs rise without the speed of the car increasing noticeably, particularly when moving off from a standstill or climbing hills.

Clutch judder: the clutch judders and shakes when it is engaged or when the car accelerates.

The clutch may just be worn, or a component may be faulty. Alternatively, the clutch could have become contaminated with engine oil or hydraulic fluid, although this may still mean that the clutch plate has to be renewed. Have it checked at a garage.

Checking the clutch fluid

Cars with a hydraulically operated clutch may have a separate clutch fluid reservoir, or this may be combined with the brake fluid reservoir (*see pages 130–31*). Alternatively, the system may be sealed (check in your car handbook).

Check the clutch fluid at least once a month, and always before a long journey. If the fluid needs frequent topping up, there must be a leak in the system, which should be investigated by a garage. If the level gets too low, the clutch won't operate correctly.

Top up with brake fluid (the clutch and brakes use the same fluid), but make sure it meets the DOT 4 standard or higher, or as recommended in your handbook. Never use old fluid; when exposed to air, it absorbs moisture and won't perform efficiently.

WARNING

Brake fluid is toxic and harmful to skin. It is also flammable, so keep it well away from naked flames or anything likely to cause a spark. If splashed, wash it off skin with water immediately.

It will also damage painted surfaces, so wash off spills with clean water immediately.

1 Park the car on the level and switch the engine off.

2

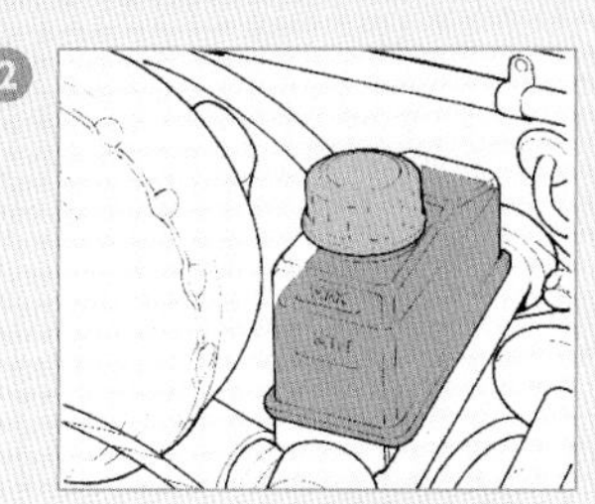

2 Provided the reservoir is translucent, you should be able to check the fluid level from the outside. It should be between the minimum and maximum marks on the side of the reservoir. If you cannot check the level in this way, wipe clean the top of the reservoir and unscrew the cap. The fluid level should be just below the top of the reservoir. Be careful not to allow any dirt to fall into the reservoir.

3

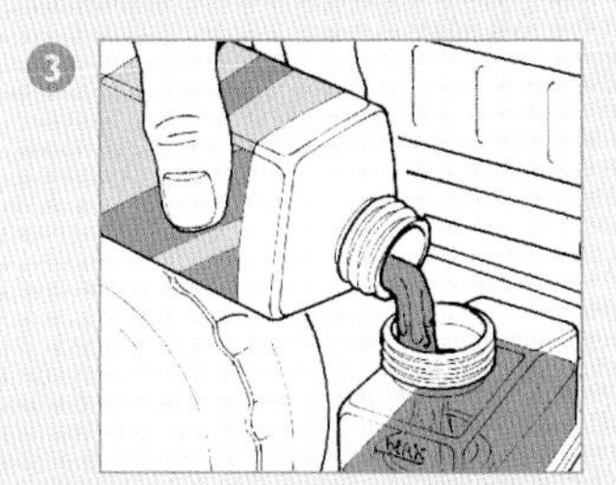

3 If the fluid needs topping up, unscrew and remove the cap. Using fresh brake fluid, top it up to the correct level and screw the top back on tightly.

Final drive and differential

The final major components in the train of parts that transfer the power of the car's engine to the driven wheels – whether they are at the front or the back of the car – are the final drive and differential, which contain gearwheel assemblies.

Propeller shaft

In a rear-wheel-drive car, this transmits the engine's power from the gearbox at the front of the car to the final drive and differential at the rear. To allow for the movement of the car's suspension over uneven ground, universal joints are fitted at each end of the shaft so that it can rise and fall with the suspension. On four-wheel-drive cars, there are sometimes two propeller shafts (to the front and rear axles), depending on the design of the vehicle.

1. Final drive and differential
2. Universal joints
3. Gearbox

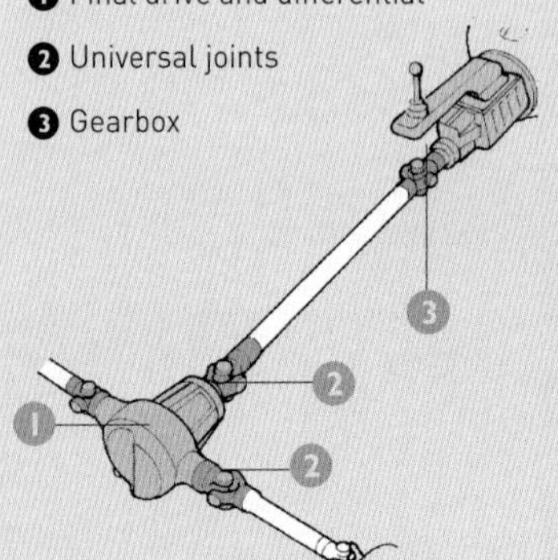

Universal joints/ constant-velocity joints

These joints are filled with grease and, in the case of constant-velocity joints, encased in rubber gaiters. The gaiters need to be checked regularly at a garage for damage, which could lead to the loss of lubrication and failure of the joint.

The drive shafts

These transmit the engine's power from the differential to the wheels. Depending on the car's design, they may incorporate universal joints or constant-velocity joints to accommodate movement from the suspension when travelling over uneven ground.

Final drive

This reduces the speed of the gearbox output shaft. The power output of the engine is directly related to its speed; an engine therefore has to run fast to produce sufficient power to drive the car. Due to the limited amount of space available in the engine area, the gearbox can only reduce engine speed by a certain amount. The final drive is the large reduction gear that brings engine speed down further to that necessary for driving the road wheels.

The differential

The differential is a gear assembly that transmits power from the final drive to the driven wheels. By allowing them to rotate at different speeds, it enables the car to turn left or right.

When a car turns a corner, the wheels on the outside of the turn have to travel farther than those on the inside, so need to turn faster. To achieve this, the wheels have separate drive shafts that meet at the differential, where a system of bevel gears allows them to turn at different speeds. A final drive and differential are mounted between each pair of driven wheels, the differential being inside the final drive.

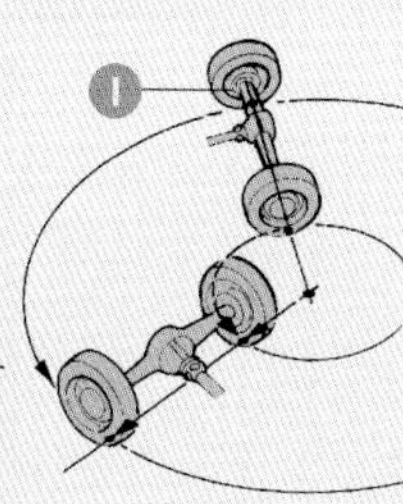

❶ The outer wheel travels farther than the inner, so the outer wheel must run at a faster speed.

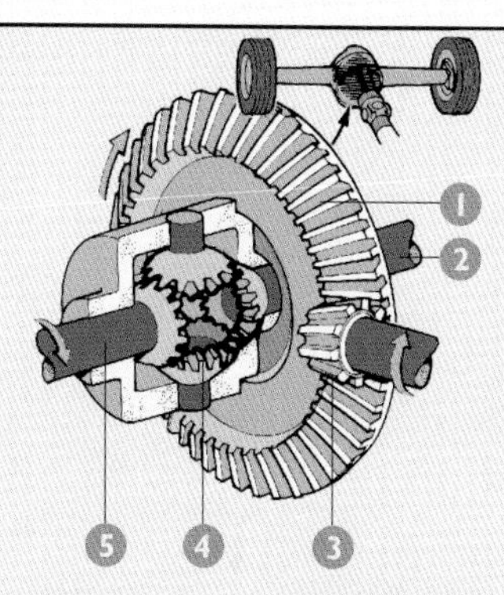

❶ Crown wheel
❷ Half-shaft
❸ Pinion gear
❹ Bevel gears
❺ Half-shaft

In a front-engined, front-wheel-drive car, the final drive and differential are often part of the gearbox assembly. In a rear-wheel-drive car, the final drive and differential are in the rear axle.

A four-wheel-drive car has front and rear drive/differential units; some vehicles have a third central differential, as the front wheels travel a different distance from the rear when turning.

Automatic transmission

The automatic transmission is fiendishly complicated. It comprises an automatic gearbox with a torque converter that performs the same function as the clutch in a manual transmission, and several sets of epicyclic (planetary) gears.

How it works

- Gear changes are carried out automatically as the system responds to changes in the car's speed. Some automatics have a manual lever for selecting the mode of operation (Drive, Park, etc.), while others have electric push buttons. The torque converter transmits power from the engine to the gearbox, which contains several sets of epicyclic gears. The gears are so called because some of them (planet gears) revolve around a central sun wheel.
- When one of the gears is held stationary, the speed of the others is altered by a system of hydraulic brake bands and clutches. The system works by fluid pressure, the fluid being drawn from a transmission sump by a pump and fed through a hydraulic system, transmission cooler and torque converter.
- A valve controlled by the accelerator pedal directs fluid through the system to carry out gear changes.

1. Output to propeller shaft
2. Clutch
3. Brake bands
4. Set of epicyclic gears
5. Input shaft connected to the engine

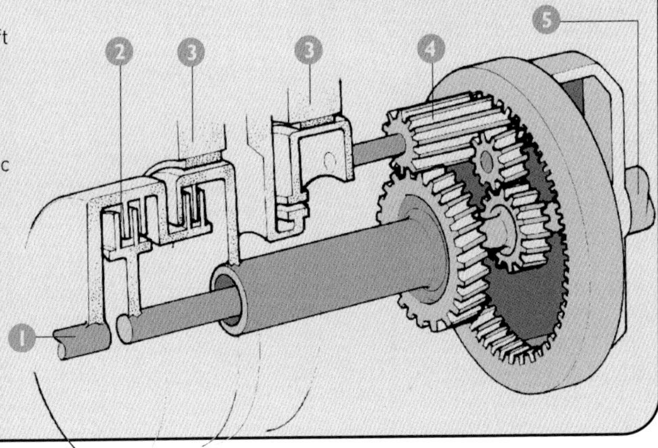

The torque converter

In automatic systems, a torque converter takes over the role of the clutch in a manual transmission. Like the clutch, it is bolted to the engine at the flywheel and disconnects the engine from the transmission so that the car can be started and stopped. It consists of a turbine immersed in transmission fluid and an impeller driven by the rotating flywheel. As the speed of the engine increases, the fluid is whirled around from the impeller to the turbine and back again, in a continuous cycle. The whirling fluid causes the turbine to rotate and turn the gearbox input shaft, transmitting power from the engine. An output shaft transmits the power to the differential or propeller shaft.

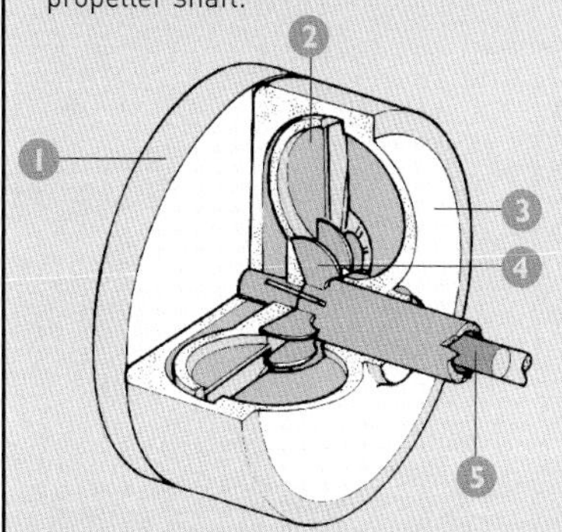

1. Flywheel linked to engine via crankshaft
2. Turbine
3. Impeller
4. Reactor
5. Output shaft to gearbox

Continuously variable transmission

This is a second type of automatic transmission system that contains no gearwheels, but instead has a heavy-duty chain belt running between two cone-shaped pulleys. One pulley is attached to the engine via an input shaft and the other to the output shaft. This system produces many more gear variations than other transmissions. Controlled by a hydraulic system, the chain belt runs on different parts of the pulleys.

Rest of the system

The other components of the automatic transmission (final drive, differential, propeller shaft, drive shafts) perform the same function as in manual transmission.

Cruise control

This is fitted to some cars with automatic transmission and enables the driver to maintain a set speed without touching the accelerator. Sensors on the drive shafts or wheel hubs monitor the car's speed and feed the information to an ECU, which controls engine speed in response.

TROUBLESHOOTING AND EMERGENCIES

Troubleshooting

If you look after your car well, even if it is old, you should enjoy many thousands of trouble-free miles. However, if problems do occur, you can use this guide to identify any faults.

Fault finding

Thankfully, modern cars are pretty reliable, but problems do occur, particularly when a car starts to age, or if it is not serviced regularly. It is impossible to cover all the causes for all the faults that may occur, since there are thousands of working parts in each car, but here is an A–Z of some of the most common problems. In many cases, professional help will be needed to sort them out, but possible causes are given to help you talk to the mechanic in a more informed manner.

See also 'Roadside emergencies', pages 288–303.

Air conditioning

Symptom	Possible cause	Action
Air conditioning not working (for air cooling/ventilation, see heater)		
Air conditioning not working effectively	Refrigerant needs recharging	Have it recharged
Unpleasant smell	Broken compressor drive belt	Have new belt fitted
	Airlock in system	Seek garage advice

Audio

Symptom	Possible cause	Action
Radio not working		
Radio not working	Blown fuse (*see page 208*)	Fit new fuse (*see page 208*)
	Bad connection	Check wiring connections
	Faulty radio	Seek garage advice
Poor reception on all stations received	Bad aerial connection	Check aerial connection
	Faulty aerial	Have new aerial fitted
Tape/CD unit faulty		
Tape/CD not working	Blown fuse (*see page 208*)	Check and replace fuse (*see page 208*)
	Bad connection	Check wiring connection
	Faulty unit	Seek garage advice

Battery charge

Symptom	Possible cause	Action
Battery charge dashboard warning light on (see also page 144)		
Light comes on while driving or won't go out when engine is started	Broken fan belt	Have new fan belt fitted
	Alternator not charging, or connector loose	Have new alternator fitted or have it removed and connector refitted

Brakes

Symptom	Possible cause	Action
Vehicle swerves when braking (see also page 125)		
Car pulls to one side when brakes applied	Brake shoes or pads grabbing or not operating	Seek garage advice. Do not drive the car
Brake pedal bouncing		
Brake pedal moves up and down when braking	Distorted brake discs or brake drums	Seek garage advice
Brakes squeaking		
Squeaking from brakes when braking	Hard spots on brake pads	Have new pads fitted
	Brake dust in brake drums	Have brake drums cleaned out
Brakes rattling		
Rattling from brakes when travelling at low speed	Anti-rattle springs on disc pads broken or weak	Have new anti-rattle springs fitted
Brake pedal stiff		
Brake pedal hard to push	Partially seized pedal pivot	Lubricate pedal pivot. Do not drive the car
	Brake servo not working or brake cylinders seized	Seek garage advice. Do not drive the car
Brake pedal squashy		
Brake pedal feels spongy when depressed	Air in hydraulic system	Have system bled
Brake pedal goes down too far		
Excessive pedal travel	Low brake fluid level	Check brake fluid level (*see page 130*)
	Air in hydraulic system	Have system bled
	Brakes need adjusting	Have brakes adjusted

Brakes continued

Symptom	Possible cause	Action
Need to press brake pedal harder than usual for normal braking		
Braking efficiency reduced	Brakes overheating during descent of hill	Allow brakes to cool and braking efficiency should be regained
	Worn brake pads or fault in servo unit	Seek garage assistance
Brake dashboard warning light stays on		
Warning light comes on while driving or stays on when engine is started and handbrake is released. Don't drive the car until you have established a cause	Low brake fluid level	Check brake fluid level (*see page 130*)
	Handbrake switch sticking	Have switch checked and lubricated as necessary
	Brake pads worn	Have new brake pads fitted
	ABS not working	Seek garage advice
Handbrake not working		
Handbrake does not hold car stationary	Cable needs adjusting	Have cable adjusted

Clutch

Symptom	Possible cause	Action
Clutch pedal hard to push down		
Clutch pedal movement very stiff	Partially seized cable	Have new cable fitted
	Partially seized hydraulic system piston	Seek garage advice
	Partially seized pedal pivot	Lubricate pedal pivot
	Partially seized clutch release lever	Seek garage advice

Clutch continued

Symptom	Possible cause	Action
Clutch pedal loose		
No tension on clutch pedal	Broken operating cable or fork, or leak in hydraulic operating system	Seek garage advice
Clutch screaming		
Clutch pedal screeches when pedal is depressed	Worn thrust bearing	Seek garage advice
Clutch jumping		
Drive not taken up smoothly (car jerks) as clutch pedal is released	Operating cable sticking	Have new cable fitted
	Oil on clutch plate	Seek garage advice
	Pressure plate distorted	Seek garage advice

Coolant light

Symptom	Possible cause	Action
Coolant temperature dashboard warning light on (see also page 143)		
Light comes on while driving or does not go out once engine is started	Coolant level low	Check level and top up (*see page 181*)

Engine

Symptom	Possible cause	Action
Engine will not keep running		
Engine starts, but stops when ignition key is turned back from start position	Faulty ballast resistor	Seek garage advice
Engine shaking		
Engine runs, but vibrates and shakes badly	Damp ignition leads	Wipe off ignition leads, ignition coil and distributor cap. Spray with aerosol water dispersant
	Faulty spark plug or plugs	Fit new spark plugs (*see page 216*)
	Faulty ignition leads	Have new ignition leads fitted by a garage
	Ignition timing wrongly set	Have timing adjusted
	Faulty ignition or fuel module, or fuel injectors, or loss of compression	Seek garage advice
Engine stops when idling		
Engine runs, but will not idle without stopping	Slow-running set too slow	Seek garage advice
	Faulty fuel or ignition module	Seek garage advice
Engine 'knocking'		
Heavy knocking sound from engine	Worn big-end bearing	Seek garage advice as soon as possible; there could be a serious problem
Tapping from engine	Camshaft and cam followers worn	Seek garage advice

Engine continued

Symptom	Possible cause	Action
Engine lacks power		
Engine sluggish on acceleration	Blockage in air intake	Have air intake cleaned out and new filter fitted
	Faulty fuel module or ignition module	Seek garage advice
Engine rattles		
Rattling or 'pinging' noise from engine when pulling hard uphill or accelerating (known as 'pinking')	Wrong grade of fuel	Change to correct grade (*see page 223*)
	Air/fuel ratio too weak	Have air/fuel mixture adjusted at garage
	Ignition timing wrong	Have ignition timing adjusted at garage
	Engine overheating	Check coolant level (*see page 179*)
Engine doesn't stop properly		
Engine runs on for a short time after ignition has been switched off	Engine overheating	Check coolant level (*see page 179*)
	Fuel shut-off valve not working, or hot spots developing in engine	Seek garage advice
Engine squeals or whines		
Squealing noise from engine, particularly when accelerating	Loose or worn auxiliary drive belt	Have belt adjusted or replaced at garage
Engine smells of fuel		
Smell of fuel from engine	Fuel leak	Check for fuel leaks. Seek garage advice, don't drive the car

Engine continued

Symptom	Possible cause	Action
Engine smells hot		
Excess heat from engine	Coolant level low	Top up coolant (*see page 181*). Also check for leaks (*see page 182*)
	Oil level low	Top up oil (*see page 246*). Also check for leaks (*see page 251*)

Exhaust

Symptom	Possible cause	Action
Exhaust noisy (see also page 170)		
Excess noise from exhaust system	Leak in system or broken tail pipe	Repair or replace parts as necessary (*see page 171*)
Exhaust knocking against vehicle structure	Broken support	Have broken support replaced at a garage
Rattles coming from exhaust system	Loose heat deflector	Seek garage advice
	Loose internal baffles	Have exhaust system replaced at a garage
Popping and banging from exhaust, particularly when engine is slowing	Air leaking into exhaust system somewhere	Have leak repaired or replace as necessary
Exhaust smoking		
Black smoke from exhaust pipe, particularly when accelerating	Blocked air filter	Fit air filter (*see page 234*)
	Air/fuel ratio wrongly set	Have air/fuel mixture adjusted at a garage
	Faulty fuel module	Seek garage advice

Exhaust continued

Symptom	Possible cause	Action
Exhaust smoking continued		
White smoke from exhaust pipe, particularly when accelerating	Faulty head gasket	Seek garage advice
Blue smoke from exhaust pipe when accelerator pedal released and gear changed down	Oil leaking into combustion chamber and being burnt	Seek garage advice
Excessive amount of water from exhaust tail pipe		
Water dripping from exhaust tail pipe	A slight amount is normal, but if excessive, head gasket may be blown	Seek garage advice
Smell of fumes inside passenger compartment		
Pungent, smoky smell inside car	Exhaust fumes leaking into car	Drive with windows open and seek garage advice as soon as possible

Fuel

Symptom	Possible cause	Action
Car using too much (see also pages 296 and 227)		
Car using too much fuel	Fuel leak	Check system for fuel leaks. Don't drive the car if you find one or if there is a smell of petrol. Seek garage advice
	Blocked air filter	Fit new air filter (*see page 234*)
	Faulty fuel injectors	Seek garage advice

Gears

Symptom	Possible cause	Action
Gears crunching		
Gears not engaging easily when the clutch pedal is fully depressed	Clutch operating clearance wrongly set	Have clutch operating clearance adjusted
	Low oil level in gearbox	Have gearbox oil topped up
	Synchromesh worn	Seek garage advice. Gearbox may need replacing with a new one
Gearbox noisy		
Whining noise from gearbox when driving	Low gearbox oil level	Have gearbox oil topped up
	Worn bearings	Seek garage advice
Gearbox noisy in one particular gear only	Worn gear or bearing	Seek garage advice
Rattling noise from gearbox in neutral	Worn bearings	Seek garage advice
Gear lever stiff		
Gears difficult to engage	Incorrectly adjusted gear linkage	Have gear linkage adjusted
Won't stay in gear		
Gearbox jumps out of gear	Worn selector mechanism	Seek garage advice
	Selector mechanism wrongly adjusted or synchromesh hub worn	Seek garage advice. Gearbox may need replacing with a new one

Gears continued

Symptom	Possible cause	Action
Automatic gear selector not working properly		
Selector pointing to the wrong gear	Selector cable incorrectly adjusted	Have cable adjusted
Engine starts in other than P and N positions	Selector cable incorrectly adjusted Faulty inhibitor switch	Have cable adjusted. Seek garage advice
Vehicle moves in P position	Selector cable incorrectly adjusted	Have cable adjusted
Automatic gears snatching		
Gears not changing up and down smoothly	Low transmission fluid level	Check transmission fluid level (*see page 108*)
	Control unit malfunction	Seek garage advice
Kickdown not operating properly		
Gearbox not down-shifting correctly on acceleration	Control unit malfunction	Seek garage advice

Heater

Symptom	Possible cause	Action
Heater/ventilator not working		
Fan blowing cold air only, not hot	Airlock in cooling system	Have system bled
Fan (blower) not working	Blown fuse	Check and replace fuse (*see page 208*)
	Bad electrical connection	Check wiring connections (*see page 209*)
	Faulty fan motor	Have new motor fitted

Leaks

Symptom	Possible cause	Action
Automatic transmission fluid leaking		
Light red/gold fluid leaking from pipes, transmission housing or oil cooler	Loose pipe connection, damaged oil cooler or leaking gasket	Tighten loose connection. Otherwise seek garage advice. If leak is not serious, monitor fluid level, but car can be driven in meantime
Brake fluid leaking		
Usually darkish fluid (unless newly replaced) leaking from brake master cylinder, brake pipes or around wheels – may leak on to road	Loose pipe connection or worn seal in master cylinder or wheel cylinder	Seek garage advice. Don't drive the car if you find or suspect a leak
Clutch fluid leaking		
Usually darkish fluid (unless newly replaced) leaking from pipes or seals	Loose pipe connection or worn seal in master cylinder or slave cylinder	Seek garage help. Clutch will not work if leak is serious, but if minor you can drive the car in the meantime, but monitor fluid level.
Coolant leaking		
Green/blue/pinkish liquid with noticeable sweet smell, especially if heater is on. Possible whitish deposits and leaks from radiator, hoses, gaskets	Loose hose connection or clip, cracked or worn hose, damaged gasket	Tighten connections or clips. It may be possible to repair cracks or holes in hoses temporarily with tape, or a radiator with a sealant (*see page 175*) but monitor coolant level carefully and seek garage help as soon as possible

Leaks continued

Symptom	Possible cause	Action
Fuel leaking		
Petrol – normally identifiable by strong smell; diesel by an oil smell; check under bonnet for signs of leakage	Loose pipe connection, split or damaged pipe, damaged seal	Seek garage assistance. Don't drive the car until the leak as been repaired: it could be dangerous
Manual transmission oil leaking		
Usually pinkish or light brown (or may be darker liquid leaking from gearbox housing). May have sweet smell	Worn seal	Seek garage assistance immediately. If leak is serious, severe damage could be caused if you continue to drive
Oil leaking		
Usually black (unless replaced recently), fluid leaking around the oil filter, oil filler cap, seals around engine block and from the sump. May leave marks on the road	Leaking gasket, or loose oil filter or oil drain plug on sump (*see page 249*)	Tighten filter (*see page 250*) or oil drain plug (*see page 250*). If this does not cure it, seek garage advice as soon as possible and monitor oil level in the meantime
Power steering fluid		
Amber/yellow or pink/red fluid leaking from pipes or steering rack	Loose pipe connection or worn seal in steering rack	Seek garage assistance as soon as possible. The car can be driven in the meantime if the leak is not serious, but monitor fluid level

Lights

Symptom	Possible cause	Action
Light(s) not working (see also page 74)		
Light(s) not working	Bulb blown	Fit new bulb (*see pages 76–77*)
	Fuse blown	Check and replace fuse (*see page 208*)
	Faulty switch	Have new switch fitted
Lights dimmer than usual		
Lights are dim	Bad electrical connection or low charge in the battery	Check wiring connections. Charge battery (*see page 198*)
Direction indicator lights flash too quickly		
Lights flashing too quickly	Bulb blown in one indicator light unit	Fit new bulb (*see page 77*)

Locking

Symptom	Possible cause	Action
Central locking malfunctioning (see also page 44)		
Central locking not responding to key	Faulty electric key	Seek garage advice
	Faulty solenoid(s)	Seek garage advice
Locking – remote control (see also page 44)		
Locking not responding to remote control	Battery in remote control needs changing	Replace battery
	Blown fuse	Check and replace fuse (*see page 208*)

Mirror

Symptom	Possible cause	Action
Heated mirror not clearing		
Heated mirror not working	Faulty heater element	Seek garage assistance
	Bad electrical connection	Check electrical wiring connections (*see page 209*)

Oil pressure light

Symptom	Possible cause	Action
Oil pressure dashboard warning light comes on (see also page 142)		
Light comes on while driving or does not go off when engine started. Don't drive the car until you have established the cause	Oil pressure is too low. Low oil level	Pull over as soon as you can do so safely and switch off the engine. Wait 5–10 minutes and check oil level (*see page 246*). Top up if it is low (*see pages 246–47*). If light is still on, don't drive the car; call for assistance. Engine damage could result
	Faulty oil pressure switch	Have new oil pressure switch fitted
	Fault in oil pump or pressure relief valve	Seek garage advice

Overheating

See page 297

Starting

Symptom	Possible cause	Action
Engine will not start (see also page 202)		
No warning lights on dashboard when ignition switched on and engine will not turn over	Flat battery	Charge battery (*see page 148*). If battery will not hold charge, have it checked at a garage
Dashboard warning lights come on when ignition is switched on, but go out when ignition key is turned to start position	Bad connections at battery terminals	Remove, clean and refit battery connections (*see pages 194–95*)
	Bad earth connection	Remove, clean and refit vehicle earth connections (*see page 195*)
	Flat battery	Charge battery (*see page 198*)
Dashboard warning lights come on when ignition is switched on, but there is only a click when key is turned to start position	Bad connection at starter motor	Have starter motor connection cleaned
Engine turns over, but will not start		
Engine turns over normally, but will not start	Damp ignition leads	Wipe ignition leads, ignition coil and distributor cap. Spray with water dispersant
	No spark at spark plugs	Check for loose connections at ignition coil
	Faulty ignition coil or ignition module	Seek garage advice
	No fuel	Refill with fuel
	Fuel system blockage or faulty fuel module	Seek garage advice
	Broken timing belt	Have new timing belt fitted

Starting continued

Symptom	Possible cause	Action
Engine difficult to start when hot		
Engine starts easily when cold, but difficult to start when hot	Air/fuel mixture too rich	Have air/fuel mixture adjusted at a garage
Engine difficult to start when cold		
Engine starts easily when hot, but difficult to start when cold	Cold-start device faulty	Seek garage advice

Steering

Symptom	Possible cause	Action
Steering pulling		
Vehicle pulls to one side when driving	Low tyre pressure	Check tyre pressure (*see pages 87, 89*)
	Brake dragging, or broken suspension spring	Seek garage advice
Heavy steering		
Steering requires more effort than usual	Low tyre pressures	Check tyre pressures (*see pages 87, 89*)
	Low power steering hydraulic fluid level	Check hydraulic fluid level (*see pages 108–109*)
	Fluid leak in power steering system	Seek garage advice
	Broken power steering drive belt	Have new belt fitted

Steering continued

Symptom	Possible cause	Action
Steering wheel shaking		
Steering wheel vibrates at certain speeds	Wheels out of balance	Have wheels balanced
Steering wheel vibrates all the time	Buckled wheels	Fit new wheels
Steering wheel vibrates when braking	Distorted brake discs or brake drums	Seek garage advice
Vehicle wandering		
Vehicle will not maintain a straight line	Low tyre pressures	Check tyre pressures (*see pages 87, 89*)
	Steering alignment wrongly set, or worn suspension or steering joints	Seek garage advice
Steering wheel loose		
Excessive free movement at steering wheel	Steering rack loose	Have steering rack mounting bolts checked
	Worn steering joints or rack	Seek garage advice
Steering rattling		
Rattling noise from steering at low speed or when cornering	Worn constant-velocity drive-shaft joints	Seek garage advice
Steering 'knocking'		
Knocking noise from steering when turning	Steering rack loose	Have steering rack mounting bolts checked
	Worn steering joints	Seek garage advice

Suspension

Symptom	Possible cause	Action
Vehicle bouncing		
Vehicle constantly bounces when driving, or wallows when cornering	Worn shock absorbers	Have new shock absorbers fitted at a garage
	Broken spring	Seek garage advice
Suspension knocks		
Knocking from suspension, particularly when cornering or braking	Broken spring, or worn suspension joints or bushes	Seek garage advice
Suspension hisses		
Hissing noise when driving over bumps	Worn shock absorbers	Have new shock absorbers fitted at a garage

Tyres

Symptom	Possible cause	Action
Tyres squealing		
Squealing noise from tyres when cornering	Low tyre pressures	Check tyre pressures (*see pages 87, 89*)
	Steering alignment incorrectly set	Seek garage advice

Tyres continued

Symptom	Possible cause	Action
Tyre tread wearing abnormally (see also page 92)		
Excessive tyre wear in centre of tread	Tyre pressures too high	Adjust tyre pressures (*see pages 87, 89*)
Excessive tyre wear around both edges	Tyre pressures too low	Adjust tyre pressures (*see pages 87, 89*)
Excessive wear on one edge of tyre only	Incorrect wheel alignment	Seek garage advice
Uneven tread wear	Wheels out of balance	Have wheels balanced

Vibration

Symptom	Possible cause	Action
Vehicle vibrates when accelerating		
Vibration from transmission when accelerating	Worn constant-velocity joint	Seek garage advice
Vehicle vibrates when driving		
Vibration at certain speeds	Wheels out of balance	Have wheels balanced
Vibration at all speeds	Low tyre pressures	Adjust tyre pressures (*see pages 87, 89*)
	Damaged tyre	Have new tyre fitted
	Buckled wheel	Fit new wheel
	Worn constant-velocity or universal joint, or steering alignment incorrect	Seek garage advice

Warning lights

Symptom	Possible cause	Action
Warning lights on dashboard (see pages 140–47)		
Warning light(s) come on or stay on	Engine lubrication, charging system, brake system, cooling system or fuel system fault, or faulty dashboard light	See relevant section in this book or seek garage advice

Wheels

Symptom	Possible cause	Action
Clicking noise from front wheel		
Clicking noise from front wheel at low speed, particularly when cornering	Worn constant-velocity joint	Seek garage advice

Windows

Symptom	Possible cause	Action
Heated rear window not working		
Heated rear window not clearing	Faulty heater element	Check heater element (*see page 63*) or seek garage advice
	Blown fuse	Check and replace fuse (*see page 208*)
	Bad electrical connection	Check wiring connections (*see page 209*)

Windows continued

Symptom	Possible cause	Action
Electric windows not working		
Electric windows not working – do not open or close	Faulty switch or motor	Seek garage advice
	Blown fuse	Check and replace fuse (*see page 208*)
Windscreen wipers not working		
Wipers do not work	Faulty motor or switch	Seek garage advice
	Bad electrical connection	Check wiring connections (*see page 209*)
	Blown fuse	Check and replace fuse (*see page 208*)
Wipers not working properly		
Wipers only operating at one speed	Faulty resistor pack	Have new motor fitted
Wipers do not 'park' correctly	Faulty park facility	Have new motor fitted

ACT QUICKLY

The troubleshooting checks given here are by no means exhaustive, but they do cover many of the common problems you may encounter with your car, their causes and the actions to take to put things right. If you do encounter a problem, even if it appears minor, don't ignore it and hope that it will go away – it won't. Often, if you catch a fault early, the cost of putting it right will be relatively low; leave it, though, and you could be faced with expensive repair bills, plus the inconvenience of being without your car for a long period of time while it is repaired.

Roadside emergencies

If you are lucky, you will never have to deal with a roadside emergency, but accidents do happen, and it is best to be prepared for them. Study the advice given on the following pages regularly so that you can commit it to memory.

Accidents

If you are involved in an accident, you must stop.

❶ Switch on your hazard warning lights and get out of the car.

❷ Be vigilant for your own safety and that of others. Remember that you are at risk from passing cars.

❸ Fire is also a hazard. Put out all cigarettes, etc.

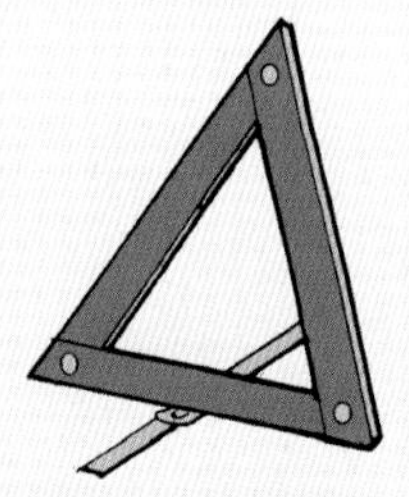

❹ Use whatever means you can to warn other drivers of the accident – use a red warning triangle if you have one. Get other drivers to switch on their hazard warning lights.

BE PREPARED

It might not be possible, of course, to read this book in the middle of an emergency. So, when you have a spare moment, read through this section. You may remember some of the tips it contains.

❺ If necessary call the emergency services, or ask someone to call them. Look out for useful landmarks to tell them where you are. On high-speed roads, look out for roadside markers.

❻ Move uninjured people away from the road to a place of safety.

❼ Help anyone who is injured, but do not move injured people unless they are in immediate danger.

❽ Don't remove a motorcyclist's helmet, unless it is essential.

❾ If there is spillage of any flammable liquids or gases, make sure no one is smoking and don't use mobile phones close by as there is a danger of explosion.

Details to record

❶ If you are directly involved, obtain the other driver's name, address, phone number, insurance details, and car make and registration number. You will need to give them your details.

❷ Note the details of any other vehicles involved (if more than one).

❸ Obtain the names and addresses of any witnesses.

❹ Record as much additional information as possible.

❺ If you have a camera to hand, take several photographs.

❻ Note any damage caused to vehicles or properties, or injuries caused to people or animals.

❼ Note the weather conditions and amount of light.

❽ If it is night, note whether the other car's lights are switched on.

❾ Make a careful note of what other people say happened.

❿ Make a note of the positions of the vehicles involved and particularly in relation to each other (make a sketch), and the positions of markings on the road, as well as traffic lights, bends in the road, etc.

⓫ Make a note of approximate distances from the kerb, centre of the road, etc.

⓬ Note the presence of any skid marks and debris on the road.

TIP

Make a note of the names and identification numbers of any police officers who attend. If the police ask you to make a statement, insist on having a copy and get it signed by the officer taking the statement.

When you get to your destination, write down as much additional information as you can remember.

Involving the police

The police should be called (or the accident should be reported to the police within 24 hours) if anybody or any animal is injured.

In a serious accident, if at all possible, don't move any of the vehicles until the police arrive. This will help them in investigating the incident. Ask any witnesses to wait for their arrival, too.

Breakdown on a normal road

Get the car off the road. You may have no choice, but if possible, stop the car in a village or town, not in an isolated spot where there are no facilities.

Make the car visible

If possible, get the car off the road and parked safely. If the car presents a possible hazard to other cars, put on the hazard warning lights (and sidelights if it is dark). If you carry a red warning triangle, erect it about 50m (155ft) behind the car. If you are just beyond a bend or on a hill, position the triangle so that drivers will see it well before they come upon the car, such as one bend farther back.

Phone for help

Call a breakdown or motoring organization, or a local garage using a mobile phone or pay phone. Once you have done so, stay with the car and await their arrival. If the car is parked safely, you can wait inside it, but as a precaution sit on the side away from the traffic. If the car is not parked safely, lock the doors and wait away from both the road and the car.

Animals

If you leave an animal in the car, remember to open a window slightly for ventilation, and to leave water in a container, especially if it is a hot day and you think you may be gone for some time.

If you are alone or are the only adult with children, see also page 292.

Going for help

if you have to walk to a pay phone, think about where the nearest one may be – perhaps behind you? Before you leave, take a good look around so that you can describe any useful landmarks. Wear appropriate clothing. If you don't have change for the phone or a phone card, remember you could phone a friend, reversing the charges, and ask them to call the breakdown services for you.

Breakdown on a high-speed road

High-speed roads are particularly hazardous if a breakdown occurs, because of the volume and speed of the traffic they carry. Great care is required.

Get the car off the road

Pull over to the hard shoulder or the side of the road, and on to a verge if possible. Get yourself and any passengers away from the car and the road. Broken-down vehicles are at great risk of collision from fast-moving cars. Turn your wheels away from the road so that if the car is hit from behind, it will not be forced on to the carriageway and into the path of oncoming traffic.

Make the car visible

Switch on the hazard warning lights (and leave the sidelights on if it is dark). Get out of the car on the side away from the traffic. Shut the windows and lock all the doors. If you carry a red warning triangle, position it at least 50m (155ft) behind your car. If you are just beyond a bend or on a hill, position the triangle so that drivers will see it before they come upon the car, such as one bend farther back.

Phone for help

Use an emergency roadside telephone if available – these should pinpoint your position automatically. If you use a mobile phone or pay phone, look for any landmarks or marker posts at the roadside that will help identify where you are.

Going for help

If you have to go for help on a high-speed road, it is particularly important to wear bright clothing and to walk where you are safe from traffic. Before you leave, take a good look around so that you can describe any useful landmarks. If you don't have change for the phone or a phone card, remember you could phone a friend, reversing the charges, and ask them to call the breakdown services for you.

If you are alone or are the only adult with children, see also page 292.

If you are alone or are alone with children

When you are alone, you are particularly vulnerable and should take extra precautions. If there are children with you, always consider their safety.

TIP

It is natural to feel vulnerable, but don't ask for help or accept any help from strangers. It is also important that you don't leave your car for any longer than you have to.

Phone for help

When you call for assistance, make it clear that you are alone, and you should be given priority. Make a note of any useful landmarks to help direct the breakdown services to you. Once you have called them, wait with the car for their arrival.

Waiting for help

If you are on a normal road

If the car is parked safely or is off the road, wait for the breakdown services in the car, on the side away from the road if possible. Lock all the doors and shut the windows. (If it is not parked safely, see the next paragraph.)

If you are on a high-speed road

Wait away from the car, but close enough so that you can get back in quickly if another car pulls up near you and you feel threatened. Lock all the doors except the front passenger door nearest to you and wait near this so that you can get in quickly if necessary. If you have children with you, leave both the front passenger door and rear door open so that you can all get in quickly.

Make sure the car is visible: see page 290.

Strangers

If someone stops to talk to you, get in the car, lock all the doors and talk to them through a closed window, or through a small gap at the top of the window. Don't worry about looking silly or offending someone. If they are genuine, they won't mind. Ask them for their identity, and tell them that the breakdown services and police have been called and are on their way. Once they have left and you feel the danger has passed, you can get out of the vehicle again.

Going for help

If you have to walk to a pay phone, think about where the nearest town or village may be – perhaps behind you? Before you leave, take a good look around so that you can describe any useful landmarks. Wear appropriate clothing and take valuables with you. If you don't have change for the phone or a phone card, remember you could phone a friend, reversing the charges, and ask them to call the breakdown services. Take children with you – don't leave them alone in the car. If you leave an animal in the car, open a window a little for ventilation (below) and leave some water in a container, especially in hot weather.

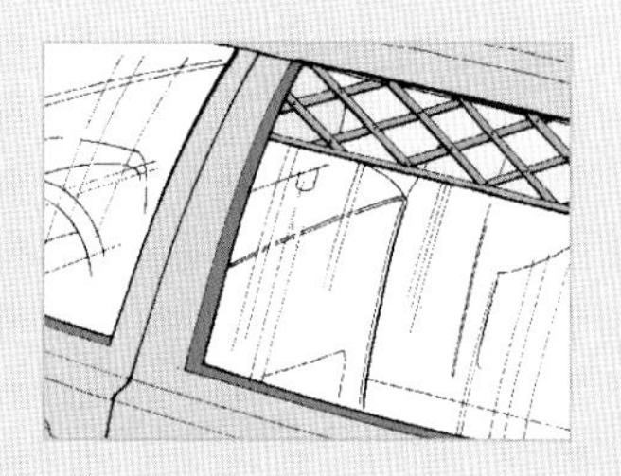

Breakdown service

If a mechanic arrives and you are in doubt about their identity, they should be able to show you an identity card. They should also have information about you (your name and details about your car and the breakdown). If you are still in doubt, ask for their identity number and phone the breakdown service to check that they are genuine (preferably not using a phone number that they give you – call directory enquiries).

TIP

During periods of extreme temperature, take appropriate precautions, such as keeping warm clothing and blankets in the car or carrying water with you.

Breakdown in a tunnel

❶ Switch on the hazard warning lights and switch off the engine.

❷ Get out of the car quickly.

❸ Call for help: there may be emergency telephones in the tunnel. Use the nearest one to call for help.

❹ If you have to use a mobile phone, move to the nearest emergency exit. Don't stand too close to the car and if there is a smell of fuel, stand well away from it. Flammable fuel vapour could be ignited by using a mobile phone.

❺ If the car is on fire, and you cannot drive it out of the tunnel, pull over to one side, switch off the engine and get out immediately.

❻ If the fire is small, there may be a fire extinguisher in the tunnel that you can use.

FIRE WARNING

If your engine is on fire, DO NOT open the bonnet. Operate the bonnet release catch, but still don't open the bonnet.

It may be possible to direct the fire extinguisher through the small gap that is created when the release catch is operated. It is extremely dangerous to open the bonnet – the fire could flare up immediately.

❼ If the fire is large, DO NOT attempt to tackle it. Move quickly to the nearest emergency exit – there is danger of explosion – and wait for the emergency services to arrive.

❽ If the car is on fire and you can drive it out of the tunnel, do so. Once out of the tunnel, pull over and stop the car as soon as you can safely. Switch off the engine and get out immediately. See points (6) and (7).

❾ If a car in front of you is on fire, stop at a safe distance behind it and switch on your hazard warning lights. If possible, help any people who are still in the car to get out. See points (3), (4), (6) and (7) .

Brake failure

Experiencing brake failure while driving is very frightening, but there are several things you can do to slow down and ultimately stop the car.

❶ Check there is nothing right behind you, take your foot off the accelerator and pump the brake pedal repeatedly – it may restore some braking power.

❷ Apply the handbrake in short bursts, change down through the gears, pull over and stop when it is safe to do so.

❸ Don't apply the handbrake continually, especially descending a hill – it could cause the rear brakes to overheat and fail. When the brakes fail, it is normally the hydraulic system that is at fault. Operated mechanically, the handbrake should still work, although it does not produce as much braking power as the hydraulic system.

❹ It is not safe to drive the car when the brakes have failed – you will need to seek assistance.

Fire

❶ If you think the engine is on fire, pull over and stop the car as soon as you can do so safely. Get yourself and all passengers out of the car immediately and move away from it.

❷ Call the emergency services.

❸ If the fire is small, and you have a fire extinguisher, you may be able to use it.

FIRE WARNING

If your engine is on fire DO NOT open the bonnet. Operate the bonnet release catch, but still don't open the bonnet.

It may be possible to direct the fire extinguisher through the small gap that is created when the release catch is operated. It is extremely dangerous to open the bonnet – the fire could flare up immediately.

❹ If the fire is large, do not attempt to tackle it. Stay well clear of the car – there is danger of explosion – and wait for emergency services to arrive.

Out of fuel

1. If you don't carry reserve fuel and you are a member of a motoring organization, they should bring fuel out to you if requested, although you may have to pay extra for this service.

2. Make sure the car is parked safely. If you cannot get it off the road and it could obstruct traffic, switch on the hazard warning lights (and sidelights if it is dark). If you carry a red warning triangle, erect it about 50m (155ft) behind the car; if you are on a hill or a bend, position the triangle so that drivers will see it before they come upon the car, such as one bend farther back.

3. If you have a container in which you can fetch some petrol, walk to the nearest garage.

4. Alternatively, phone a friend or family member and ask them to bring some fuel out to you. Or call a local garage – they may agree to bring a tow truck or fuel out to you, but this will probably be an expensive option.

5. If you have no container, but can get to a petrol station, they may sell empty petrol containers – if so, you could buy one and fill up on the spot.

6. Make sure the car is locked if you have to leave it.

7. If you are alone or with children, see also page 292.

Using reserve fuel

Make sure the ignition is switched off. Don't smoke, and ensure that there are no naked flames nearby. Switch off mobile phones. An inflammable vapour is released as the fuel is poured from the can into the tank, so there is great risk of an explosion from a stray spark.

Exhaust

If the exhaust pipe sheers off when you are driving, there is not much you can do. What remains of the exhaust will be very noisy, and you will need to get it repaired as soon as possible.

If the exhaust pipe is hanging off or dragging, you can tie it up temporarily with wire or strong string. If the car has just been driven, the pipe will be very hot to the touch. Wait for it to cool down.

Overheating

Overheating is normally caused by the cooling system not functioning correctly or when there is insufficient engine oil. When the engine has warmed up and reached its correct operating temperature, the arrow on the temperature gauge should be on 'normal'. If it rises beyond this and moves into the red zone, the engine is overheating. The coolant temperature warning light may light up on the dashboard (*see page 143*), or, in extreme circumstances, you may see steam coming out of the bonnet.

Serious overheating

If the needle of the temperature gauge swings into the red zone quickly, or if there is steam coming from under the bonnet, pull over and stop the car as soon as it is safe to do so. Don't drive the car while the engine is overheating. Serious engine damage could result.

❶ Don't open the bonnet fully immediately – you could burn yourself. Operate the bonnet release catch and wait for several minutes until any steam has escaped.

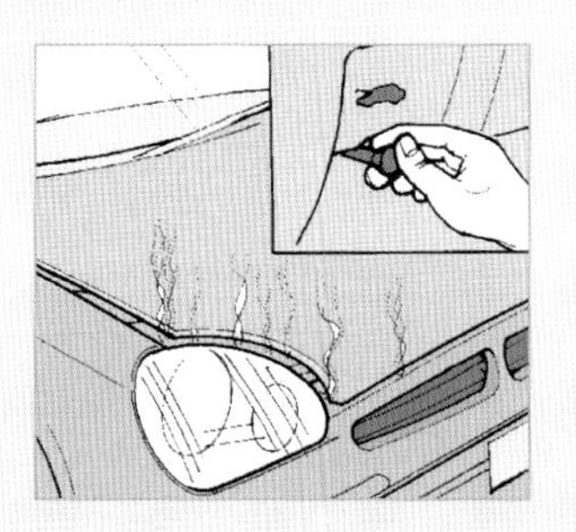

❷ Check the coolant level in the expansion tank. If you have to open the expansion tank pressure cap, see page 180 for safety precautions. NEVER open the cap when the engine is hot.

❸ If the tank is transparent, you should be able to see the level through the container. To obtain an accurate reading, the engine should be cold, as coolant expands when hot. You should wait at least half an hour for the engine to cool down. It will take longer than normal to cool down because it has become excessively hot. Don't check the level while the engine is still hot.

❹ If you check the level when the engine is still warm, it should be up to or above the maximum mark. If it is not, or if it is below minimum, then there is not enough coolant in the system. If the engine is cold, the level should be between the minimum and maximum marks, but generally closer to the minimum mark.

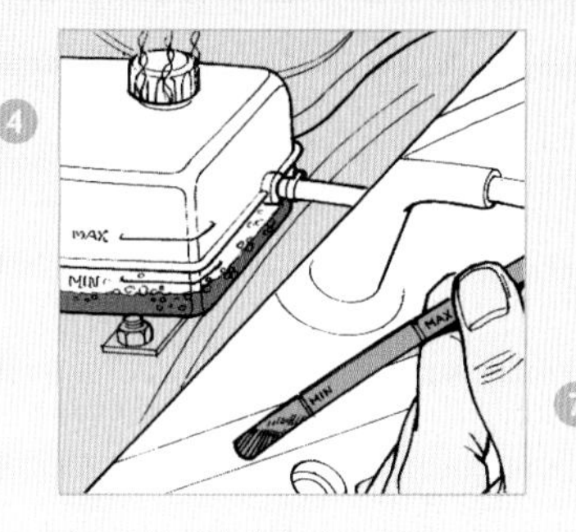

5 If you can see no coolant in the expansion tank, there may be a serious leak in the system. Topping up the coolant may not solve the problem, but it may be enough to get you home or to a garage.

6 If the coolant level is OK, see step (7). If the level is low, top it up (*see page 181*) but DO NOT top up while the engine is still hot. Wait at least half an hour from the time you switch the engine off before you top up. Pouring cold water into a hot engine could crack it. Plain water can be used to top up in an emergency, but add the correct amount of antifreeze when you are back home to prevent the coolant from becoming too weak.

7 If the coolant level is OK, leave the engine to cool down for 15 minutes or longer and check the oil level (*see pages 246–47*). If the level is low, top it up, following the instructions on page 247.

8 If the coolant and oil levels are OK, there could be a fault in the cooling system. You will need to seek assistance before you can drive the car.

Minor overheating

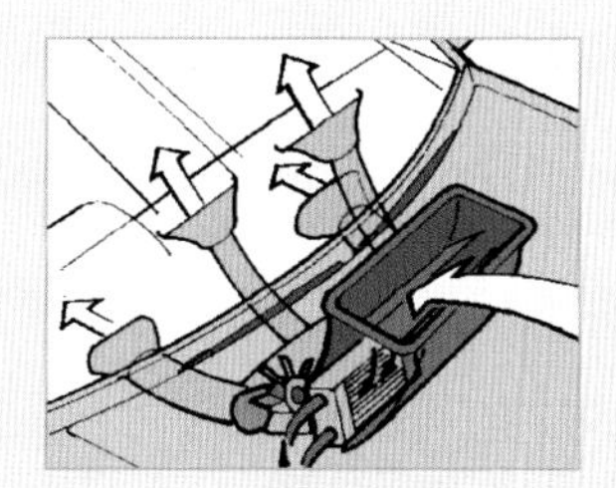

If the coolant temperature light comes on and/or the needle on the temperature gauge is climbing slowly into the red, turn off any air conditioning, open the windows and turn on the heater to its hottest setting, with the blower at full blast. It may be uncomfortable, but this directs heat away from the engine into the passenger compartment. The temperature should start to drop.

Puncture or blow-out

If the steering wheel suddenly jerks or you hear a loud bang and the car is difficult to control, it could be a puncture or blow-out.

❶ Keep calm and grip the steering wheel firmly. Check that there is nothing behind you, take your foot off the accelerator and start braking gently.

❷ Put on your hazard warning lights. Try to steer straight (don't over-correct) and get the car off the road as soon as it is safe to do so.

❸ If a puncture or blow-out occurs in heavy traffic, or where it is not safe to stop, put on your hazard warning lights and drive on very slowly. Look for a place to stop safely as soon as you can – driving on a flat tyre will damage the tyre and possibly the wheel rim, but you may have no other choice.

❹ If you cannot park the car safely or cannot get it off the road, leave on the hazard warning lights (and sidelights if it is dark). If you carry a red warning triangle, erect this about 50m (155ft) behind the car. If you are just beyond a bend or on a hill, position it so that drivers will have time to see it before they come upon the car, such as one bend farther to the rear.

❺ If you intend to change the wheel yourself, and you have no alternative other than to work on the traffic side of the car, remember that you are at risk from passing cars. Be very vigilant and wear bright clothing if possible. To change a wheel, see pages 98–101.

❻ If you don't want to change the wheel yourself, call a motoring organization or local garage for assistance, or use a tyre sealant – see below.

❼ If you are alone or alone with children, see also page 292.

Using a tyre sealant

Tyre sealant is a useful quick fix. It reinflates the tyre with pressurized foam, but the repair is not long-lasting, and you should have the tyre replaced or repaired as soon as possible. Some garages are reluctant to repair tyres that have been inflated with sealant due to the chemicals used and because it is a very messy operation. Follow the manufacturer's instructions printed on the canister.

To change a wheel, see pages 98–101.

The car won't start

Here are some possible causes; see also Troubleshooting, pages 281–82.

If you are alone or are alone with children, see also page 292.

Flat battery

Some electrical equipment may have been left on. If the central locking or remote control locking doesn't work (open the driver's door manually with the key) and no dashboard lights come on when the ignition is turned in the ignition switch, the battery is almost certainly flat. Ask for a jump start.

Bad electrical connection

If a battery terminal is getting hot, switch off the ignition and check for loose wiring connections. Waggle the wires and check that the connections are not loose. If they are, tighten them with a spanner or wrench. Check that the connections are clean, and if there is corrosion on the battery terminals, clean it off with fine abrasive paper (*see page 193*).

Starter motor

Faulty starter motor: if there is no sound from the starter motor, or if there is just a clicking noise, the starter motor could be faulty and you will need to seek assistance.

Damp components

If the weather is rainy or humid, the damp conditions could be the problem. Dry electrical components with a clean cloth and spray with water dispersant.

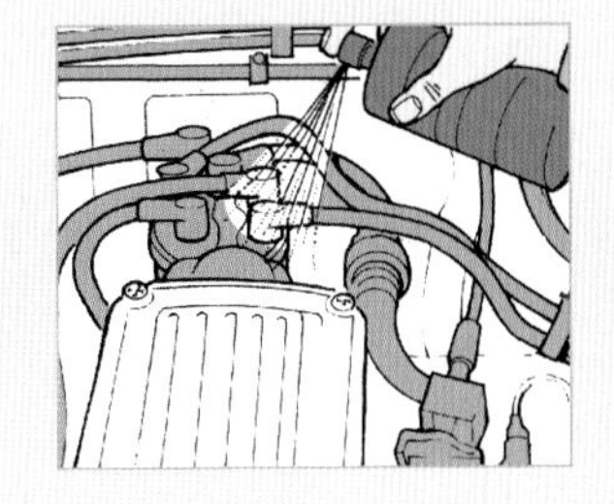

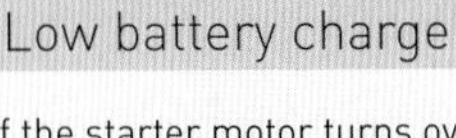

Low battery charge

If the starter motor turns over very slowly, or if the headlights are dim, there is probably not enough charge in the battery. Ask another motorist for a jump start (*see page 202*) – but if you are alone or with children, see also page 292.

Out of fuel

• Switch on the ignition and look at the fuel gauge. Is it reading low or empty? Is the fuel level warning light on? If it is, you may be out of fuel, although some fuel gauges give inaccurate readings (*see page 141*).

• If you have run out of fuel more quickly than you would expect, there could be a fuel leak. Can you smell fuel? If you can, don't drive the car; it could be highly dangerous and start a fire. Call out a motoring organization or a local garage.

• If your car is fitted with a switch that cuts off the fuel supply in the event of an accident, it could have been activated accidentally by driving over a bump in the road. See your handbook for information on how to reset it.

TIP

If the starter motor turns over, but the engine will not start, stop trying after a few seconds. Leave it for several minutes for the battery to recover and then try again for a few seconds. Do not try to start an apparently dead engine repeatedly – if there is no sign of life, the battery will soon become drained completely.

Push-start

You may be able to push-start a car with a flat battery.

• With the driver at the steering wheel, and a couple of people ready to push, switch on the ignition, release the handbrake, press in the clutch pedal and put the car in second gear.

• Keep the clutch pressed in and ask the people to push the car forward, building up to a fast walking pace, then release the clutch pedal.

• If the engine starts, the car will jerk forward. Press the clutch pedal down quickly to prevent the car from stalling.

• Keep the engine running, or preferably drive the car for around 20 minutes to recharge the battery.

• It is worth trying this a second time, if it doesn't work at the first attempt.

For reasons why the battery might be flat, see page 202.

Towing

If you have to tow another vehicle, follow these steps.

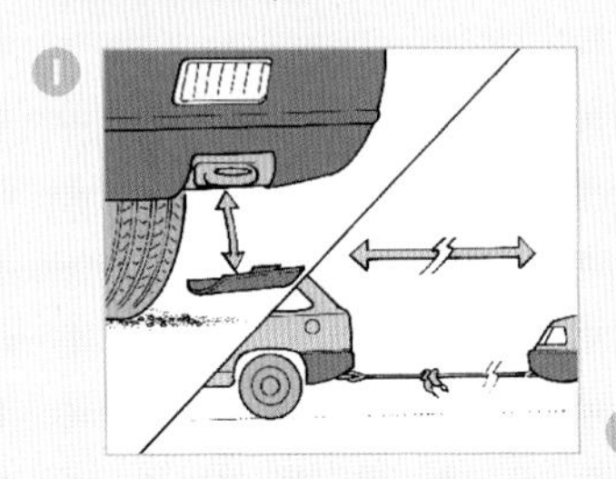

❶ Make sure that the tow rope is attached to both vehicles securely. Many cars have metal eyes (rings) for this purpose, sometimes behind flaps in the bodywork. If there are no eyes, don't attach the rope to the centre of a bumper; make sure you attach it to something firm and pad it with cloth if the rope lies across something sharp.

❷ Tie a piece of coloured cloth to the centre of the tow-rope to warn other road users of its presence.

❸ The ideal length for a tow rope is 4.5m (14ft 6in), but it should never exceed this.

❹ Switch on the hazard warning lights and the side and rear lights of the vehicle being towed, if it is dark.

❺ Make sure that both drivers know the route being taken.

❻ Before moving off, drive the towing car forwards slowly until the rope slack has been taken up.

❼ Keep your speed down (it should not exceed 40 mph/65 kph), and drive as smoothly as possible.

❽ Stopping distances are longer when towing, so start braking earlier than normal. Change down through the gears, braking gently.

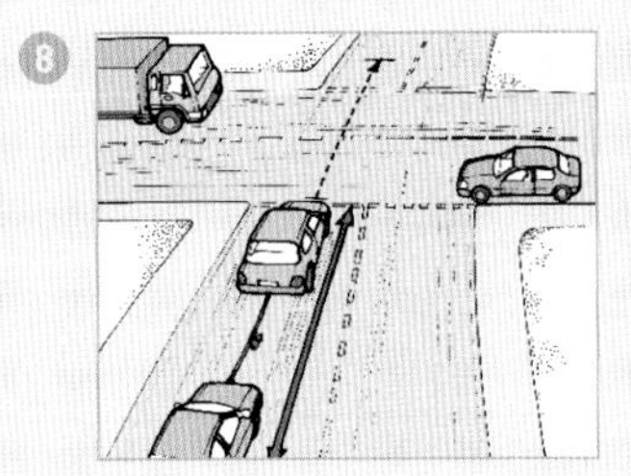

❾ Allow for the extra length when manoeuvring and turning corners.

❿ Don't tow a car that has been damaged in an accident – you don't know what systems could have been affected, and it could be dangerous.

If you are being towed

❶ You should display an 'On Tow' notice on the rear of the car and the number plate of the towing car.

❷ Switch the ignition key to the 'on' position to release the steering lock and select neutral gear.

❸ Switch on rear and sidelights, if it is dark.

❹ Try to keep the tow rope taut at all times and brake gently when the towing car brakes.

❺ If the engine can idle, leave it switched on so that the brake servo unit and any power steering can still work.

❻ Stopping distances are longer; brake gently and smoothly. If the engine is not idling, you will need to apply more pressure to the brake pedal than normal, as the brake servo unit will not be providing assistance.

❼ If you have power-assisted steering and the engine is not idling, the steering will feel heavier than usual, as the system will not be working.

❽ If your lights are not working, use hand signals to warn other road users.

Cars with automatic transmission must not be towed – it can damage the transmission.

Wheels stuck

If the wheels become stuck in mud or in snow, the engine revs when you put your foot on the accelerator and the wheels spin, but won't grip. Put a piece of old carpet or some other material that will provide traction in front of the wheels that are spinning. If you are not sure which are spinning, open the windows and rev the engine to see if you can hear where the noise is coming from.

Try letting a little air out of the tyres to flatten them slightly and increase the contact area with the ground – this may give a little more traction. Pump them up again as soon as possible. Only drive very slowly with low tyre pressures.

All-weather driving

Being prepared for extreme weather conditions, whether they occur in winter or summer, will reduce the likelihood of your being stranded with a 'dead' car.

Getting ready for winter

Whether the winters where you live are just rainy and foggy, or snow lies on the ground for months at a time, there are a number of things you can do to keep your car in good working order. Do these little jobs before the weather turns and it is just too cold and miserable to work on it.

Before the onset of winter

- Having tyres in good condition is important for safe driving in winter. Check their condition and make sure they have sufficient depth of tread (*see page 91*).

- Just before winter is a good time to have an annual service – make sure that the brakes, steering, coolant, suspension, wipers, tyres and lights are all checked, and ask for a service check sheet for reference.

- Renew wiper blades if they show any signs of deterioration (*see page 68*). They should be renewed once a year, so now is a good time to do so.

- Have the coolant replaced, and ensure that the proportion of antifreeze is adequate for the temperatures in which you will be driving (*see page 173*).

- Check the condition of the cooling system hoses (*see page 182*) and auxiliary drive belts (*see page 182*).

- Check the condition of all oils, fluids and filters if you have not done so recently (*see relevant pages*).

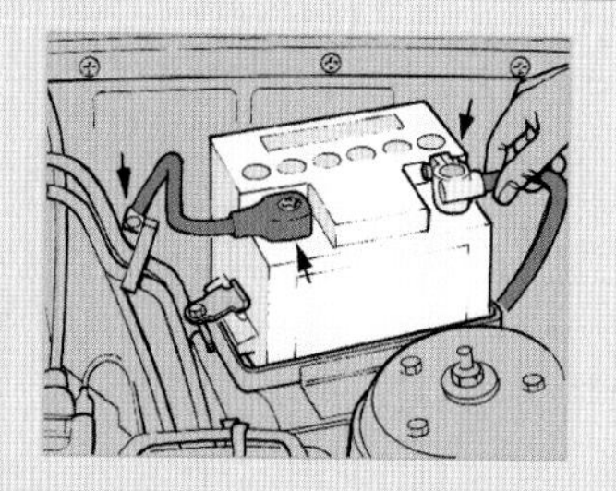

• Check the battery condition (*see page 194*). If you have to charge the battery frequently, replace it. Cold weather affects battery performance, and an old battery or one in poor condition may let you down.

• Spray a penetrating oil into all door locks – this will help prevent them from freezing up.

• Use a screenwash additive to prevent the screenwash from freezing.

• Keep the screenwash topped up, and make sure that the jets are clear (*see page 67*).

• Keep the windows clean, wiping them with a commercial glass cleaner. This will help prevent the inside of the glass misting up.

• Keep a clean dry cloth inside the car for wiping the windows.

• Check that the heater and demisters, the heated rear window and any heated mirrors are working.

• Check that all lights are working.

• Clean and polish the car to help protect the bodywork from road-salt damage.

• In climates where the temperature can drop below -15°C (5°F), a block heater can be placed under the bonnet, near the cylinder block. Switch it on several hours before you need the car, and it will warm the engine, allowing it to start and run more efficiently sooner. In order not to place too great a load on the battery, don't start the engine with any accessories on (lights, heater, etc.). Switch these on once the engine is started.

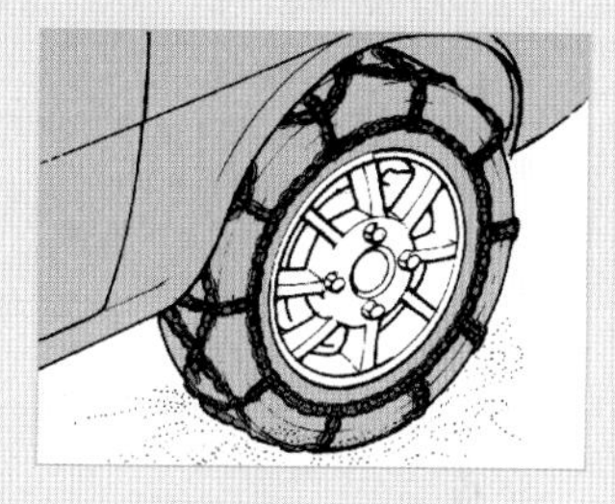

• If you are likely to encounter snow regularly, consider fitting 'mud and snow' tyres, which have a tread pattern designed to cope with these conditions. Or fit snow chains. These can be awkward to fit, so you might want to practise in advance. They must be removed as soon as they are no longer needed – don't use snow chains on metalled roads where there is no longer a reasonable covering of snow.

Extra equipment to keep in the car (*see also pages 12–16*)

1. A couple of pieces of old carpet or sacking to provide traction under the wheels if you become stuck in mud, snow or ice.
2. Snow chains

3. Small shovel

4. De-icing spray
5. Ice scraper
6. Lock de-icer
7. Spare set of car keys

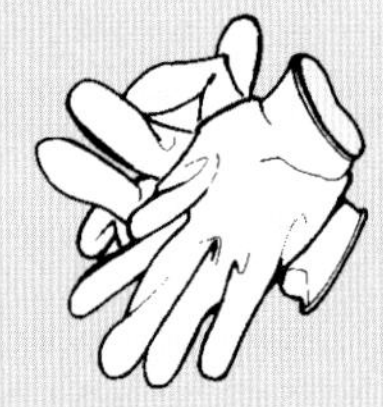

8. Gloves and appropriate clothing in case you have to work on the car outside
9. If you are likely to be making trips across country, fill up with fuel and take some reserve fuel with you in an approved container. Tell someone where you are going and when you are due to arrive. Consider if there is any further equipment you should pack (in addition to the list on pages 12–16 and the items here), such as:
10. Blanket(s) (emergency space blankets resembling a sheet of silver foil are very compact – available from outdoor pursuit shops)
11. Appropriate clothing
12. Water and food

13. Thermos with a hot drink or soup
14. Spare batteries for a torch
15. Matches or a lighter
16. Backpack (in case you are forced to leave the car)
17. Mobile phone, loose change for pay phone or phone card

Getting ready for Summer

Provided you are up to date with all the regular maintenance checks, and the car is in good working order, there is not so much to worry about in summer. However, there are still a number of sensible precautions that you can take to ensure safe and worry-free driving.

1. Is it time for a service? Check that the rigours of winter have not taken too much of a toll on brakes, steering, suspension, battery and tyres.
2. Make sure the coolant is topped up, and if necessary, keep some reserve topping-up fluid in the car.
3. Have the air conditioning serviced if necessary, and check that the ventilation system is working.
4. Check that the sun roof is working.
5. Keep a pair of sunglasses in the car.
6. Keep the screenwash topped up – to get rid of insects and dust. Check that the windscreen wiper blades are in good condition and the wipers are working.

7. Keep a good supply of drinking water in the car and, if your pet travels with you, take a container in which to give your pet a drink.
8. Keep a sun shield handy, to erect behind the windscreen when you leave the car. The passengers in the rear seats might benefit from sun shields being fitted to the side windows.
9. If you are planning a trip across country, fill up with fuel and take reserve fuel with you in an approved container. Tell someone where you are going and when you are due to arrive. Consider if there is any further equipment you should pack, such as:
10. Blanket(s) (emergency space blankets resembling a sheet of silver foil are very compact – available from outdoor pursuit shops)
11. Appropriate clothing
12. Water and food
13. Spare batteries for a torch
14. Matches or a lighter
15. Backpack (in case you are forced to leave the car in an emergency)
16. Mobile phone, loose change for pay phone, or phone card

Driving in bad weather

The golden rule for driving in bad weather is to proceed with caution. Kill your speed and be aware that if visibility is bad, other cars will have as much difficulty in seeing you, as you will in seeing them. Be super-vigilant.

Snow

Use dipped headlights if snow is falling, even in daylight. Keep your speed down. Avoid first gear and keep to second (even start in second). If you feel you are losing control, take your feet off the pedals and the car may regain traction.

When you want to brake, start slowing earlier than you would normally and apply the brakes gently. Don't make sudden steering movements or brake suddenly, as this is likely to cause the car to skid.

Cornering in ice and snow

You must take extra care and think ahead. If you brake while cornering, the car will slide and you could lose control. Change down through the gears and take corners slowly so that you don't need to use your brakes.

Descending in ice and snow

Keep the car in a low gear, which will help avoid the need to brake excessively. When you do have to brake, do so as gently as possible.

Climbing in ice and snow

Your speed must be kept down, but you need to keep up enough momentum in order not to stop on the slope – you may not be able to move off again due to wheelspin, or you could lose control. Use the highest gear you can for the gradient and keep to it. It is not easy to change gear on a slippery hill due to the likelihood of wheel spin and loss of speed. Keep up reasonable momentum, and leave a sizeable gap between you and the car in front in case it slows down or stops.

Driving in high winds

Remember that high-sided vehicles are vulnerable to cross-winds. Keep your speed down.

Ice

Icy conditions are treacherous. If the road surface looks shiny and wet, and it is very cold, it may be icy. If you see what look like puddles of water, they may be iced over. Black ice is invisible – it forms when rain falls on the road surface and freezes. Keep your speed down. Make all gear changes, braking and steering extremely gentle.

Fog

In daylight, when visibility is severely reduced by fog, use dipped headlights and/or front fog lights. Use high-intensity rear fog lights at night when visibility is down to 100m (330ft). Keep a safe distance behind the car in front and kill your speed. Remember that the road surface may be slippery and overtaking is far more dangerous than usual. Don't use the main headlight beams – fog reflects the light and you could dazzle other drivers. If you have to park on the road in fog, leave your sidelights on.

Surface water

Surface water increases the risk of skidding, as do mud, ice, snow, loose surfaces and wet leaves. Drive smoothly and keep your speed down. Don't brake suddenly, or make sudden steering movements. Don't accelerate suddenly while cornering.

If you skid

Quickly take your foot off the brake, depress the clutch pedal and release the accelerator. Steer in the direction of the skid. Try not to over-correct. If the front wheels are sliding too, try not to steer until some traction on the road surface returns.

Deep water

If water enters the exhaust pipe, it could cause the engine to stop; if it enters the engine air intake, it could do serious damage. Keep to the shallowest part (normally the centre of the road) and drive in first gear as slowly as possible. When clear of the water, check there is no one behind and test your brakes. Driving for a short way with them applied slightly will dry them out.

Useful information

UK

Child car seats

Advice on buying them and the legal requirements for their correct use.
www.childcarseats.org.uk

Driving abroad

Covers Europe, Australia, South Africa, USA/Canada.
www.drivingabroad.co.uk
Contains useful links and information on European speed limits, etc.
www.drive-alive.co.uk
Contains useful links and a UK/USA glossary of terms.
www.driveandstayalive.com

DVLA (Driver and Vehicle Licensing Agency)

Information concerning driver documentation, medical requirements for drivers, etc. www.dvla.gov.uk

MOT

Checklist of MOT requirements, advice on finding a test centre, etc.
www.ukmot.com

Motoring organizations

As well as providing breakdown cover, their websites also provide a wealth of information on many aspects of motoring, including driving in bad weather, towing a caravan, legal advice, etc.
AA: www.theaa.co.uk
Greenflag: www.greenflag.co.uk
National breakdown:
www.nationalbreakdown.co.uk
RAC: www.rac.co.uk

Road safety

Advice on all aspects of road safety.
www.thinkroadsafety.gov.uk

Republic of Ireland

Motoring organizations

AA: www.theaa.ie
RAC: www.rac.ie

National Safety Council, Ireland

Advice on road safety issues.
www.nsc.ie

Australia/New Zealand

General advice

Australian Transport Safety Bureau:
www.atsb.gov.abu
NRMA:
General motoring advice including maintenance, safety and security.
www.mynrma.com.au
Roads and Traffic Authority NSW:
Road safety, traffic information, documentation required, etc.
www.rta.nsw.gov.au

Motoring organizations

Australia Wide Assist Pty Ltd:
www.australiawideassist.com.au
Australian Automobile Association:
www.aaa.asn.au
New Zealand Automobile Association:
www.nzaa.co.nz
RAC of Western Australia:
www.rac.com.au

South Africa

South African Automobile Association:
www.aasa.co.za

Glossary

ABS (anti-lock braking system): a system that helps prevent skidding by applying the brakes automatically in very quick, short bursts.

Alternator: this generates electricity while the engine is running; it provides a continuous electrical charge to the battery so that the battery can power the car's electrical systems.

Auxiliary drive belts: sometimes known as the fan belt, these drive the alternator, water pump, power steering pump, air conditioning pump, etc.

Battery: this stores the electricity generated by the alternator; it provides the electric current necessary to turn the starter motor (to start the engine) and for the car's electrical systems.

Big-end: the large end of the connecting rod which is attached to the crankshaft.

Boot: see gaiter.

Brake disc: part of the disc brake system; a rotating metal disc attached to the hub of the road wheel. See disc brakes.

Brake fade: a loss of braking efficiency due to overheating of the brakes.

Brake pad: a metal plate lined on one side with a layer of friction material. See disc brakes.

Brake shoe: a curved metal plate lined with friction material on its outer surface.

Caliper (sliding, swinging or fixed): part of the braking system, it contains pistons that force the brake pads against the brake disc when the brake pedal is applied.

Cam belt: see timing belt.

Camshaft: a rotating metal shaft with lobes that control the opening of the inlet and exhaust valves; driven by the crankshaft.

Carburettor: a device in which fuel and air are mixed in the correct proportions for combustion before passing to the cylinders. Fuel injection systems have replaced carburettors on modern cars.

Catalytic converter: a device that converts noxious exhaust gases from the engine into less harmful gases before they pass into the atmosphere.

Clutch: a device that enables the engine to be disconnected from the gearbox (and therefore the driven wheels) so that the driver can start, stop and change gears smoothly.

Coil: an electrical device that converts the 12 volts received from the battery to the higher voltage needed during ignition (14,000–18,000 volts).

Combustion: the igniting and burning of the air/fuel mixture in the cylinders.

Combustion chamber: the area at the top of the cylinders in which combustion takes place.

Continuously variable transmission (CVT): a type of automatic transmission that contains no gearwheels, but operates via a hydraulically controlled system of belts (or chains) and expanding/contracting pulleys.

Coolant: a mixture of antifreeze and water that is pumped around the cylinder block to dissipate excessive heat and help maintain a constant engine temperature.

Cooling fan: propels air through the radiator to assist cooling; normally electrically driven.

Crankcase: the area of the cylinder block below the pistons, which houses the crankshaft.

Crankshaft: a metal shaft linked to a piston via a connecting rod. It transforms the up-and-down motion of the piston into a rotating motion.

Cylinder block: a metal block containing the cylinders, pistons, connecting rods and passages through which the coolant circulates.

Cylinder head: this is bolted to the top of the cylinder block; a metal casting housing the combustion chambers, valves, inlet and exhaust ports and, on OHC engines, also the camshaft.

Differential: a system of gears that transmit power from the final drive to a pair of wheels on either end of an axle; it allows them to rotate at different speeds, therefore taking corners without slipping or scuffing the tyres.

Direct injection: an engine in which fuel is sprayed directly into the combustion chamber from the fuel injector.

Disc brakes: generally fitted to the front wheels, consisting of a caliper holding two brake pads.

Distributor: a device that distributes the voltage received from the ignition coil to each of the spark plugs, in the correct firing order.

Distributor cap: mounted on the distributor; it holds one end of each spark plug HT lead and one end of the ignition coil HT lead; it operates with the rotor arm to distribute the high-voltage spark to the spark plugs.

DOHC (double overhead camshaft): an engine that has two camshafts, one operating the inlet valves and the other the exhaust valves. Enables greater engine efficiency and power output.

Drive belt: see auxiliary drive belts.

Driven wheels: the wheels that are connected to and are driven by the engine, e.g. the front wheels, on cars with front-wheel drive.

Driveshaft: a shaft that transmits drive from a differential to turn the road wheels.

Drum brakes: these are normally fitted to the rear wheels; they consist of a circular cast-iron drum, with brake shoes inside.

ECU (electronic control unit): a microprocessor that monitors and controls several of the car's systems and components electronically.

Electrolyte: a solution containing distilled water and sulphuric acid that conducts electrical current inside the battery; it can be in a gel form in modern batteries.

Emissions: gases or particulates (e.g. soot) from the car's exhaust system that are released into the atmosphere.

Engine management system: a system that uses ECUs to control the operation of the ignition and fuel injection systems.

Expansion tank: a container that holds coolant and collects excess coolant when it heats up and expands.

Exhaust manifold: a system of pipes through which the burnt gases from the engine pass into the exhaust system after combustion.

Fan-belt: see auxiliary drive belts.

Fault code: an electronic code that is generated by an ECU when the self-diagnostic system has detected a fault.

Final drive: a large gear assembly that reduces the engine speed still further (in addition to the gears in the gearbox), down to the speed necessary to drive the road wheels.

Flasher unit: a small unit that controls the flashing of the direction indicator lights. Normally located under the dashboard or in the fuse box.

Flywheel: a heavy metal disc attached to one end of the crankshaft; it helps to ensure smooth running by absorbing the vibrations produced by the up-and-down motion of the pistons.

Four-stroke cycle: describes the four operating strokes (inlet, compression, power, exhaust) of the piston in its cylinder. Most car engines are based on the four-stroke cycle.

Fuel injection: a computer-controlled method of regulating the amount of fuel that is mixed with the air prior to combustion.

Gaiter (boot): a flexible rubber casing over a joint; normally packed with grease, it is designed to protect against dirt getting into the joint, causing wear.

Gearbox: part of the transmission; a housing containing different-sized gearwheels arranged along two or more shafts that enable the driver to adapt the speed of the engine to suit the conditions in which the car is being driven.

Glow plug: see heater plug.

Handbrake: a mechanical brake, operated by cables or rods (as opposed to hydraulics) that acts independently of the footbrake to secure the car when parked.

Heater (glow) plug (diesel engines only): a device containing electrically heated wires that help pre-heat the combustion chamber or inlet manifold prior to starting the engine from cold.

HT (high tension): HT cable conducts high-voltage electricity.

Hydraulic: describes a system that operates by using fluid enclosed in pipes. When pressure is applied at one end via a piston, the fluid is forced along the pipe(s) to move a piston at the other end.

Idle speed: the speed at which an engine runs when the accelerator pedal is not being pressed; often referred to as 'tick-over, or 'slow-running'.

Ignition system: an electrical system that produces the sparks to ignite the air/fuel mixture.

Independent suspension: each road wheel can move up and down independently of the others.

Indirect injection (diesel engines only): fuel is sprayed into a pre-combustion chamber where it is mixed with air before entering the combustion chamber.

Inlet manifold: a series of pipes that allow air from the atmosphere to pass into the engine cylinders.

Jump leads: heavy-duty electrical cables with clamps attached at both ends to enable a car with a 'flat' battery to be connected to another with a healthy battery for starting.

Master cylinder: part of the hydraulic braking (and clutch) system, located below the brake (/clutch) fluid reservoir.

Mixture: the air/fuel mixture that is burnt in the cylinders during combustion; rich mixture = too much fuel; weak mixture = too little fuel.

Multi-point fuel injection (petrol engines only): there is one fuel injector per cylinder.

OHC (overhead camshaft): an engine layout where the camshaft is above the cylinder head; more common than OHV.

OHV (overhead valve): an engine layout where the camshaft is positioned in the side of the cylinder block.

Piston: aluminium 'plugs' that move up and down inside the cylinders bored into the cylinder block during the four-stroke cycle.

Power steering: a hydraulic system that supplies extra force to help the driver turn the steering; it only works when the engine is running.

Propeller shaft: in four-wheel-drive cars and cars with a front-mounted engine and rear-wheel drive, this transmits drive from the gearbox (at the front of the car) to the final drive and differential at the rear.

Rack and pinion: a commonly fitted steering system; a pinion gear moves the rack, which is connected to the road wheels to the right and left.

Radiator: part of the cooling system consisting of a network of thin metal tubes (with fins attached) through which hot coolant flows, allowing it to be cooled by air flowing through from outside the car.

Rotor arm: a small rotating device inside the distributor; it distributes the HT voltage to each of the spark plugs.

Self-diagnostic system: monitors and records many of the car's systems automatically; any fault detected can be read using a fault-code reader.

Servo unit: this assists the braking system; the more the brake pedal is depressed, the more additional pressure is exerted on the brakes; it only operates when the engine is running.

Shock absorber: part of the suspension system; a device fitted to each wheel, whose telescopic action enables it to absorb energy from the suspension springs to create a smoother ride.

Silencer (muffler): quietens the noise created by the exhaust gases on their way out of the car via the exhaust system.

Single-point fuel injection (petrol engines only): fuel is sprayed into the top of the intake manifold from where it is distributed to each cylinder.

Slave (wheel) cylinder: part of the braking system, with one or more in each drum brake; they contain hydraulic fluid and a piston that forces the brake shoes against the brake drums when the brake pedal is pressed.

Spark plug (petrol engines only): provides the spark required to ignite the air/fuel mixture in the combustion chamber.

Starter motor: this sets the engine in motion, but disengages once the engine has started.

Sump: a metal container at the base of the cylinder block that acts as a reservoir for engine oil.

Synchromesh: inside the gearbox, a system that ensures that the gear wheels and the output shaft are rotating at the same speed to produce a smooth gear change.

Suspension: a system of springs and shock absorbers that supports the vehicle on its road wheels; it cushions and controls the movement of the wheels when the car is driven over an uneven surface.

Thermostat: a temperature-sensitive valve that controls the flow of coolant to the radiator.

Timing belt: drives the camshaft in OHC engines; made of reinforced rubber.

Torque converter: a hydraulic device that connects the engine to the gearbox in cars with automatic transmission.

Transmission: the collective name for the group of components that transmit the power of the engine to the wheels of the car. It also adapts the speed of the engine to suit the conditions under which the car is being driven. Includes the clutch, gearbox, propeller shafts, drive shafts, final drive and differential.

Water pump: driven by a belt from the engine; it pumps coolant from the radiator into the cylinder block.

Wheel cylinder: see slave cylinder.

Index

Acknowledgements

I should like to thank Terry Temlett for his invaluable assistance and indisputable technical knowledge and expertise (thank you, Terry, and good luck with the Ferrari!), and of course my Dad, Jack, who is still in love with his old BMW and first taught me the value of looking after an engine properly.

Picture Acknowledgements

The publishers would like to thank the following for the use of pictures:

Corbis pp. 2, Tom Stewart; 10, Christoph Wilhelm; 50, Jim Vecchi; 80 and 148, Helen King; 264, Cameron

Getty Dennis Kitchen, cover image